FOREIGN FACTION

FOREIGN FACTION

A FORMER LEAD INVESTIGATOR BREAKS SIX YEARS OF SILENCE

Who Really Kidnapped JonBenét?

A. James Kolar

Ventus Publishing, llc
Telluride, CO
USA

FOREIGN FACTION
Who Really Kidnapped JonBenét?

SECOND EDITION: March 2013

1. Murder-Investigation-Case studies. 2. Murder-Psychology-Case studies. 3. Criminal Psychology-Case studies.

ISBN 978-0-9847632-0-7 Hardcover
ISBN 978-0-9847632-1-4 Paperback

Library of Congress Pre-assigned Control Number
LCCN 2012942683

Book Design: Karrie Ross www.KarrieRoss.com
Author Photo: Brenda Colwell Photography
Cover images: istockphoto.com (crown and person)

DEDICATION

This work is dedicated to the men and women of
the Boulder Police Department, past and present,
who never wavered in their pursuit of the truth....

In Remembrance of:

Deborah Lee, Kelly Lynn and Denny Converse Jr.
Forever a place in my heart...

PREFACE

*In the faces of our children we are granted
the opportunity to glimpse the future and the untimely
death of one irrevocably changes us all.*

*As criminal investigators, it is our chosen duty
to go willingly into the breach in defense of the weak
and the powerless: to stand tall in the face of adversity,
and to seek the truth no matter where
the course may lead.*

Justice deserves no lesser effort.

—Author: April 2006

ACKNOWLEDGMENTS

An author should always take a moment to recognize the people who have assisted, and encouraged them, as they moved forward in their endeavor to publish a manuscript of this magnitude. Friend, author, and fellow sailor, Robert Rubadeau, helped guide me through the writing process that he aptly describes as "navigating the hooptedoodle," and I am forever in his debt for his patience and sage advice.

Additionally, the technical aspects of producing a work of this caliber would not have been possible but for the assistance provided by legal counsel, Thomas B. Kelley, of the prestigious Denver law firm, Levine Sullivan Koch & Schulz, LLP; as well as the editorial, research, and design assistance provided by Regan R. Tuttle, Harry Stephens, Tricia Griffith, Tracey Woodrow, and Dan Pauley.

Moral support, and suggestions regarding media engagement, was provided by veterans of the news media, Carol McKinley, and Shelley Ross. Over the years I have come to admire, and respect these women for their constant display of professionalism, objectivity, and credibility in the world of international news reporting. I would like to think that I am fortunate to count them as friends, as we struggled to uncover the truth regarding the circumstances surrounding JonBenét's death.

More importantly, the men and women of the Boulder Police Department deserve special recognition for the heartache, pain, and ridicule, which they endured as they struggled to identify the people responsible for this horrendous crime. I owe a debt of gratitude to the many investigators who never hesitated to take the time to answer questions about their role in the murder investigation, explain the background about a particular course of action, or provide insight about the theories that had been considered over the course of the investigation.

To name but a few, I would like to thank the following people for their assistance, and contribution to my work in this investigation: Rick French, Tom Wickman, Steve Thomas, Tom Trujillo, Mark Beckner, Kurt Weiler, Ron Gosage, Greg Testa, and Shelley Hisey.

To many of those who provided support and encouragement behind the scenes: I say to you, Fair winds and Godspeed. May you always find a favorable wind at your stern, and a bright star to help guide your course.

PROLOGUE

The fifteenth anniversary of JonBenét Ramsey's death has recently passed, and authorities appear no closer to charging anyone in this murder than they were a year into the investigation. It is one of the reasons that I have decided to write in a candid and uncensored fashion about my experiences as a lead investigator in her death.

The destination in a journey is said to begin with the first step. What follows is the story of my journey and how I unexpectedly found myself involved in the middle of JonBenét's murder investigation. This book is a journal of my discoveries, some of which had been unearthed by the men and women who preceded my participation in this case and others that I stumbled upon on my own. In the final analysis, it comprises the cornerstone of my beliefs regarding a new investigative theory of the crime.

I have heard it expressed that the presumption of innocence does not attach until a defendant sits before the court at trial. Everything that goes before that event is an element of the investigative process, and I believe there are still active steps to be taken to achieve resolution and closure in this case. One has to be committed, however, to pursuing the truth, examining every lead of merit that presents itself, and be willing to explore the darker side of human behavior.

What follows is presented in four parts. Part One addresses the shape of the case as it developed before I became involved. Parts Two and Three provide a chronicle of what I learned and thought about the facts of the case and the development of my beliefs about the direction the investigation should take.

Part Four recounts some more recent developments and some of my further thoughts and beliefs about the case as it came to its likely final resting place. I should emphasize that my theories are nothing more than informed speculation, based only upon the matters stated as fact in Parts One, Two, and Three. In forming my beliefs, I relied on no information that has not been provided to you, the reader, in those parts of this work.

Thus, you, the reader, can take what is contained in Parts One, Two and Three and accept or reject my theories of the crime, or form your own.

I have undertaken this work not because I believe a prosecution of any perpetrator of this crime will likely result from it, but because I believe it will move public perceptions of this case closer to the truth. I believe that in turn it should provide valuable lessons for agencies involved in the criminal justice process, for families, and for anyone concerned about society's responses to unspeakable crimes such as the murder of JonBenét Ramsey.

≈ ⊕ ≈

T A B L E   O F   C O N T E N T S

PART ONE – Case History

PART TWO – Taking the Lead

Photo Array / Scanned Document Index

There are many autopsy photographs that depict the nature of the injuries sustained by JonBenét in this homicide, but the author has elected to present only a handful of such photographs in this work. They were chosen specifically to help the reader understand the description of the injuries that are analyzed in the manuscript.

Detective Lou Smit released many of the crime scene and autopsy photographs to the media in 2000 when he began to publically espouse his intruder theory. The majority of the photographs contained herein, and many others, are available for viewing via the Internet.

The one-to-one scaled Power-Point photographs of the stun gun and train track, spider web, and the glass shard sitting on the window-well frame, have not previously been viewed in a public forum.

1. Sketch – Pen and Ink Rendition of Ramsey Home & Train Room window well by Daniel C. Pauley
2. Photo 1 – Picture of front of Ramsey Home
3. Photo 2 – JBR Bedroom
4. Document – 3 Page Ransom Note
5. Photo 3 – Wine Cellar Hallway
6. Photo 4 - Wine Cellar Blanket
7. Photo 5 – Hi-Tec Boot Poon Print
8. Photo 6 – Paint Tray
9. Photo 7 – Maglite flashlight on kitchen counter
10. Photo 8 – Neck ligature
11. Photo 9 – Skull fracture
12. Photo 10 – Wrist Bindings
13. Photo 11 – Garrote / Hair
14. Photo 12 – Train Room / Suitcase
15. Photo 13 – JBR Abrasions
16. Photo 14 – Stun Gun / Pigs

PART ONE

Case History

The First Lead

Memorial Day 2009

A steady succession of thunderstorms and rain squalls had emerged from the southwest horizon for those past four days, all but consuming and saturating the holiday weekend. The dozen or so Aspen trees previously deposited at the roadside would have to wait for better weather before I could warm up the chainsaw and turn their length into properly sized pieces of firewood.

Lightening and a clap of distant thunder drew my attention to a menacing dark blue mass that promised more rain and sleet. The warmth emitted from the fireplace provided some solace for that late spring day, and I was again reminded that the date on the calendar doesn't necessarily equate to balmy spring weather when you are living at 9,000 feet above sea level.

Saturday evening brought a dusting of snow to the peaks surrounding my home and I expected to see more of that before

June had expired. The mountains of Colorado have their own idea of what comprises the seasons of spring and summer, and I guessed that I should be grateful that the leaves had finally emerged from the hold of winter.

That long holiday weekend seemed to have been one of procrastination, with a little bit of help from Mother Nature, whereby I was able to start and finish John Sander's most recently published book of 'Prey'. Interspersed with a little spring cleanup around the house, I finally found myself looking to the west on Monday afternoon, searching for the slightest glimpse of sunshine and the La Sal Mountain range.

The La Sal's are some 130 miles distant in Utah, and I cannot really see them from my living room window, but they are marvelous when viewed from the top of Lift 9 at the Telluride Ski Resort. The lift drops skiers at the ridgeline of "See Forever," a ski run that is aptly named due to its height of 12,000 feet and unparalleled 360 degree views of the San Juan Mountain Range.

It was from this perch above the world that I first became involved in the murder investigation of JonBenét Ramsey. I had been gone from the Boulder Police Department for over three years, having pulled the pin in 1993, after seventeen years of service to take the police chief's position in Telluride, Colorado. But there I was, conducting a surveillance operation at the behest of my former colleagues days after a 6-year-old "beauty queen" had allegedly been kidnapped and murdered in her home.

Boulder Police Department Detective Nate Vasquez called me on the previous evening of January 2, 1997, and asked if I was familiar with the homicide case they were working, advising that the parents of the murdered girl, John and Patsy Ramsey, had disappeared after departing Atlanta, Georgia on January 1st.

Boulder investigators were trying to get a handle on their location, and Vasquez indicated that they had determined that family friend "Pasta Jay" Elowski had rented a room in Telluride at the San Sophia Inn. Elowski was thought to be in town for the ski holiday and investigators were wondering if the Ramseys were hiding out with him in my jurisdiction.

We both agreed that it didn't seem likely that John and Patsy Ramsey would be in the mood for skiing after suffering the tragic loss of their daughter, but I indicated we would set up a surveillance on Elowski the following day to see what we could find out. I alerted my patrol sergeants, Harry Stephens and Norman Squier, to the operation, and we met early the next day to establish an observation point of the Inn and a vehicle registering to Elowski that was parked in the garden-level garage.

Not long after the breakfast hour, we observed a male matching Elowski's description retrieve some ski gear from the vehicle, and we subsequently followed him to the ski lifts. He was accompanied by a male and female couple who were determined not to be the Ramseys.

Through the course of the morning, Squier and I bird-dogged the trio as they made their way around the ski mountain. Stephens remained at the Inn to determine if he could spot the coming or going of John and Patsy, and monitored our radio traffic as we carried out the difficult task of spending a day of surveillance on the slopes.

I have to report that I am a moderately advanced intermediate skier, but the black diamond moguls tend to kick my tail, so it frequently fell to Squier to hang tight with the group when they charged down hills that were beyond my capabilities. Not that I didn't dive in for the sake of backing up and covering my fellow officer, but I didn't think a mutual-aid workman's compensation claim would sit well with Boulder authorities.

At one point however, Squier was close enough to hear Elowski talking mid-slope on his cell phone and thought he heard him expressing his sympathy to the party at the other end of the conversation and telling them to enjoy his house. It seemed that perhaps the Ramseys were staying in Elowski's Boulder home while he was partaking a ski vacation in Telluride.

It was at some juncture after 1:00 p.m. that my legs were screaming surrender and we had just off-loaded at the top of Lift 9. The sky was robin-egg-blue with not a cloud in sight, and I snapped several covert photographs of Elowski and his companions before slipping my Minox camera into my parka.

I drew a deep breath and took in the scenery around me. Mission accomplished. The Ramseys possibly had been located in Boulder, and I had survived a day of dodging moguls on the slopes. The snow-covered peaks of the La Sal Mountain Range were visible in the distance, and I took a moment to contemplate the serenity of the view. It seemed that I really could gaze into the distance forever.

I may have been able to see over 100 miles and beyond from the top of the world that day, but that spectacular view didn't reveal what the future was to hold for me or even hint at the fact that my involvement in the JonBenét Ramsey homicide investigation was far from over.

It never occurred to me that I had just handled my first lead in the case and that one day, in the distant future, I would become a lead investigator in what was to become one of the most bizarre murder investigations this country has ever witnessed.

Pen and Ink Sketch — a fictional rendition of the Ramsey Home as viewed through the basement Train Room window well, by Daniel C. Pauley

CHAPTER TWO

Foreign Faction

The following series of events are proposed as a new theory of the crime, based upon evidence that will be addressed in the latter parts of this work:

John Ramsey was a millionaire executive whose company conducted business overseas and had offices in Amsterdam and Mexico City. Boulder papers reported that sales had topped the billion dollar mark for his company not long before the Christmas Holidays of 1996. At some juncture one of John's business deals made someone very angry, and they decided to take their revenge by plotting to kidnap his daughter and hold her for ransom.

The Ramsey household had been busy in the days leading up to the holidays in December 1996. JonBenét had appeared in a Boulder parade, participated in a modeling event at a Denver shopping mall, and the family attended a handful of holiday parties while planning a second Christmas in Michigan, to be followed by a cruise on Disney's Big Red Boat to celebrate Patsy's birthday.

Patsy loved Christmas and had decorated extensively, opening her home to hundreds of people in previous years during the Holiday Parade of Homes. This was a special time of year, and the kidnappers sought to take advantage of the celebratory nature of the season. They intended that John Ramsey would pay for his transgressions.

The kidnappers had been loosely monitoring the patterns of the family in the days leading up to the holidays and set up an observation point of the Ramsey household not long after the fall of darkness on Christmas Eve. A non-descript van had been parked in the alley across the street behind the Barnhill residence, and the kidnappers would soon discover that the resident of this home was a family friend and neighbor who shared custody of the Ramsey's pet dog, Jacques.

Later that evening, long after the Ramsey children were presumed to be in bed, the overhead garage door of the Barnhill residence slowly rose, and the garage lights dimly illuminated the side of the panel van parked less than 50 feet away. The team of kidnappers in the van peered through the side window and observed an elderly gentleman pull a sheet from a bicycle leaning against a wall in the garage. As he rolled up the cloth, he gazed in the direction of the van and seemed to be looking directly through the window from which he was being observed.

A mouse of a dog pranced around the feet of the old man and then stepped slowly to the edge of the garage. It growled and chirped several barking sounds in the direction of the kidnapper's van. Turning in tight circles several times, it continued to chirp at the van.

A few moments later John Ramsey emerged from the darkness by the side of the house and greeted the elderly man. They exchanged a few muffled pleasantries, and the kidnappers took a sigh of relief as the attention of the elderly man was now diverted elsewhere. The watchdog lost interest in the van as well, and the kidnappers watched with interest as the two men bent and inspected the shiny new bicycle, reminiscing about their first experiences of riding a two-wheeler. Ramsey then departed, wheeling the bike by his side through the dark alley. He didn't give the van a second look as he headed back toward his home.

The garage door slowly closed, and the van was again cloaked in a blanket of darkness. The lights in the Barnhill residence immediately went out, and it was not long thereafter that the lights in the Ramsey home were extinguished.

John Ramsey's visit to the house located directly next to their observation post was unsettling, and the team of kidnappers debated moving to another location. But they had thoroughly scouted the entire neighborhood and come to the realization that, from this vantage point, they could watch the front of Ramsey home with ease and didn't have to risk the exposure of sitting right out on the street to do so. They ultimately decided to stay in place and settled in for a long night.

The lights in Burke's second floor bedroom were the first to burn early on Christmas morning, and it wasn't long before the kidnappers were able to observe movement in the living room of the home. Lights from the Christmas tree were plainly visible from the van, and gentle light cascaded from the living room windows to the darkened front lawn. Christmas was underway, and through a set of binoculars, the kidnappers felt as though they had a front row seat as they watched the kids begin to unwrap their presents.

The light of dawn slowly emerged, and several hours later JonBenét was out riding the new bike Santa had left for her that morning. They observed her movements over the course of the day and the comings and goings of other kids in the neighborhood.

A mobile team in a white compact vehicle drove through the neighborhood periodically, watching for the opportunity to snatch their target from the street with what was hoped to be a minimum of fuss. Another team circled the neighborhood blocks, primarily keeping an eye on the back alley entrance of the Ramsey home.

For some reason the kidnappers kept missing their chance as JonBenét was always in the company of another little girl when near the street in front of the house. Despite their desire to quickly seize the target of their objective, they considered it critical that there be no witnesses to this affair. ·

One of the teams, watching the alley at the rear of the residence, had seen John Ramsey drive away late that morning and a loose tail followed him to the Jefferson County Airport. He was observed to be packing some things into his plane, and it seemed apparent that the family was soon to be on the move. They radioed this information to the teams still at the house, but were told that there were too many witnesses about. The kidnappers had not seen an opportunity to seize JonBenét while alone.

Ramsey eventually led his surveillance teams back to the house, and the kidnappers pondered their next move. Should they storm the house and take JonBenét by force? Pretty risky in broad daylight they concluded. Perhaps they should wait until after dark and then try that tactic. It was clear that time was running out and that something had to be done before the Ramsey family flew away to an unknown destination.

Then an opportunity presented itself when the family packed up a few gifts and left in the family car. A loose tail followed them a short distance to the White residence where it was apparent that yet another holiday dinner party was underway. The Ramseys had left their home at approximately 5:00 p.m. on the evening of December 25, 1996, and this gave the kidnappers the opening they needed.

Darkness would soon fall, and the kidnappers moved up to the rear of the home under cover of the winter night. Entering the fenced backyard, they quickly moved to an interior corner of the house toward a ground-level window grate that was obscured from the view of neighbors. Quickly lifting the grate, the first team crawled into the basement of the house.

They had done their homework and used the same window that John Ramsey had broken earlier that summer when he was forced to break into his home after forgetting his keys. Now all they had to do was patiently await the return of the family.

The kidnappers began their exploration of the premises and became acquainted with the floor plans that had only been viewed as one-dimensional on an acquired set of blueprints up to that point in time.

One of the kidnappers, a female, rummaged through kitchen drawers and came upon Patsy's address book, removing a large black metal flashlight in the process. Setting the flashlight upon the counter she leafed through the book. Perfect!

She next found Patsy's notepad and pen in the kitchen and began to fashion an extensive ransom note, attempting to duplicate Patsy's style of handwriting from the address book at her side. The Ramseys had to know why JonBenét was being taken, and the note was used to explain a tale of vengeance and extortion.

The other intruder continued his exploration of the home, and at one point, sat on the floor of the hallway directly outside the doorway to JonBenét's bedroom. From there, he fantasized about the events that would take place that evening. He eventually settled into the living room, doodling on a newspaper and magazine as he tried to kill time, another "odd clue" left behind by the intruders according to statements later released by the Ramsey family.

The minutes passed interminably, and the two-way radio eventually crackled inside the dark home. The Ramseys were leaving the White residence. After a couple quick stops to deliver late Christmas gifts, the surveillance team confirmed it: The Ramsey family was headed back toward their home, and their patience had paid off. No outbound flights appeared to be scheduled for that evening.

The Ramseys later told police investigators that they arrived home a little before 10:00 p.m. All appeared to have been as it was when they left earlier in the day. Doors were locked, and there were no visible signs of a forced entry to the house, but John Ramsey had no reason to inspect the basement before retiring that night.

JonBenét was sound asleep in the backseat of the car after having endured a long day of presents, playing, and partying. John carried her directly upstairs and laid her on her bed. Switching on the bedside lamp, he left her in her clothing for Patsy to finish the task of getting her prepped for bed. He reported that he briefly played with Burke before taking a Melatonin tablet and turning in for the night. He was going to co-pilot the flight that was scheduled to leave Jefferson County Airport at 7:00 a.m. the next morning, and he needed some sleep.

Patsy stated that JonBenét went to bed in a red sweater and white sweat-pant type long johns. After tucking in her daughter, she went to the 3rd floor and stayed up to finish some last minute packing for the Disney cruise. She eventually climbed into bed next to a sleeping husband and set the alarm for 5:30 a.m.

Huddled in the dark labyrinth of the basement, the kidnappers listened intently as the house above them eventually became quiet. Perhaps 30 minutes had passed since the last human sound had been heard, and it was now time to execute their plan. A quickly whispered radio transmission was sent to their fellow conspirators outside. They needed another team to join the two kidnappers already concealed in the home. Two observers were to remain outside, one across the street in the van and another watching the rear alley of the home.

Not wanting to risk setting off a burglar alarm by using a ground floor door, the second team made their way carefully through the window grate and into the basement Train Room to join their partners. One of the men handed another a roll of polymer cord that was to be used in restraining JonBenét. They each checked their weapons and began to move toward the stairs.

Another whispered radio transmission to the spotter outside in the van: "We're moving. Let us know if you see any police cars on the street or if there are any transmissions on the scanner."

Moving up from the basement, one team moved to the forward grand staircase and slowly began their ascent. One of the men stopped at the second floor landing and moved slightly down the hall to view the doorway of Burke's bedroom. The door was partially closed and all was quiet at that level of the house. He peered down the dark hallway through the playroom that he knew led to JonBenét's bedroom.

A thumb's up signal sent the second man further up the grand staircase to the 3rd floor landing outside John and Patsy's bedroom. The floor was dark, and the sounds of the sleeping couple emitted lightly from the bedroom doorway. He stood motionless for a few moments to monitor any movement or signs of compromise. Hearing nothing, he stepped back to the head of the stairs and silently keyed his microphone.

The first team inside the house, comprised of a man and woman, heard the radio clicks signifying that the second and third floors of the house were secured. They then carefully ascended the narrow spiral staircase that accessed the back of the home by the kitchen. This led to the hallway outside JonBenét's second-floor bedroom and was at the opposite side of the home from the other occupied bedrooms.

The female, a stun gun in hand, gently pushed through the bedroom door and observed a small sleeping form on the bed. Followed by her male companion, they stepped closer in the dark and saw that JonBenét was on her stomach. Intending to take no chances of alerting the rest of the household to their activities, the female reached out to the right rear back of JonBenét and activated the stun gun. This electrical charge rendered her unconscious and incapable of fighting off her attackers. A piece of duct tape was quickly placed over her mouth to further aid in silencing their captive.

The male quickly applied a stretch of nylon cord to each of JonBenét's wrists. Strangely, the wrists were not bound tightly to one another, and the length of cord between her hands measured approximately sixteen (16") inches. Investigators would later wonder why the restraints had been applied in such an unusual fashion.

They quickly stripped a blanket from the bed, wrapped their little hostage into it and prepared to leave, but not before remaking the bed and turning down the covers. Thanks to the stun gun, there was no sign of a struggle in the bedroom. It looked like JonBenét had either flipped back her covers and climbed out of bed, or they had been in that condition awaiting her to turn in for the night.

Moving in the darkness with the child wrapped in the blanket was a challenge and especially so when it came time to navigate the tight circular stairway at the back of the house. The kidnappers couldn't risk traveling to the other stairway for fear of awakening the other people in the residence, so one of JonBenét's kidnappers was forced to carry her down the narrow confines of the metal stair way. One arm holding her close to his chest, the male kidnapper gripped the circular hand rail and slowly descended to the kitchen.

At some point during this process, JonBenét began to regain consciousness and began to protest. Frightened at being manhandled down the stairs, with a stranger's hand across her mouth, JonBenét reached up instinctively with her right hand and scratched her male abductor. According to her grandmother, JonBenét would likely have vigorously fought any attacker, and it may be surmised that she began to kick and scream when she realized what was happening.

The female kidnapper attempted to intervene at the bottom of the stairs, and JonBenét was able to graze her with her left hand in the struggle to free herself. As she continued to struggle, JonBenét scratched herself as well.

In an attempt to calm JonBenét, the female released her from the confines of the blanket. But this was only on the condition that she be quiet and stop struggling. Perhaps there was a threat to use the stun gun again. Secluded in the far end of the house in the kitchen, the female further coaxed JonBenét's cooperation with a bowl of freshly cut pineapple. Nodding her consent to cooperate, the female kidnapper then removed the piece of duct tape from JonBenét's mouth, and they moved to the dining room table.

Another of the men joined the team in the kitchen and crouched over the counter, reviewing the ransom note with the aid of Ramsey's flashlight. The 4th member in the house remained in the forward staircase, monitoring any movement of sleeping members.

The best laid plans sometimes go awry, and JonBenét was not to be fooled by these trespassers. She took one nibble of pineapple, swallowed, and then screamed at the top of her lungs. She slid from the chair and made a dash for the back hallway.

Successful in dodging the male-female team in the dining room, she sprinted through the kitchen. It was at that juncture that it can be presumed that events really began to unravel. In a bid to quickly silence JonBenét, one of the male kidnappers got a hand on her, and he too was scratched with her fingernails. Panicking as she was squirming loose of his grasp, the kidnapper struck out with the flashlight in his hand. The blow fractured the right side of her skull, and she immediately fell to the floor unconscious.

The injury to her brain was serious, and for all intents and purposes, she gave the appearance of being dead. But that eventually was determined not to be the case. Her heart continued to beat for what was estimated by pathologists to be another ninety (90) minutes, slowly filling her cranium with blood. Due to the lethality of the blow to her head, however, it is unlikely that she ever regained consciousness.

It may be presumed that the kidnappers argued and disagreed on their next course of action. They easily could have carried JonBenét from the house by exiting a rear ground floor doorway and escaped into the night. In that case, they would have retained possession of the object of their kidnapping and still had room to negotiate the delivery of their ransom. The family would have had no way of knowing that their daughter was seriously injured and nearly dead.

Yet for some reason, JonBenét was instead carried downstairs to the basement and subjected to the tortures of a pedophile. One of the male suspects was determined to carry through his team's vengeance, ransom money be damned, and remained in the home as his partners departed to resume their surveillance of the neighborhood from their outside posts. This was the act of the deranged "baby-killer" to whom Patsy would refer during her CNN interview on January 1, 1997.

"Keep your babies safe..." she admonished viewers, for there was a "killer on the loose in Boulder."

This monster's final act of cruelty was determined to be the ultimate causation of JonBenét's death. The pedophile tied a ligature around her neck and used it to strangle the last bit of life from her tiny body. Petechial hemorrhaging in her eyes indicated that she was still alive when strangled. As further insult, the perpetrator is believed to have inserted the broken end of the paintbrush, used as a handle in the garrote, into her vagina at or near the time of her death.

Death was ruled by the coroner to be a homicide by asphyxiation, and time of death was later estimated to have been at approximately 1:00 a.m. on the morning of December 26, 1996.

The target of his abduction, now deceased, was placed on the floor of the Wine Cellar. "Monster" stood over the unmoving form before him and tried to understand his feelings. Nothing. He felt nothing. Scanning the room, he observed a set of window screens along one wall and a couple of wrapped Christmas presents standing against another. Curious, the wrapping had been torn away at the top ends of each present.

Monster took one last look around and exited the room, carefully latching the door behind him. Unbeknownst to him, he had left behind an impression from the poon of his Hi-Tec boot in the mildew on the floor next to JonBenét's body, another clue left behind for investigators to contemplate.

Radio transmissions from his partners encouraged him to leave the residence, but Monster wanted to see and hear the reaction of the family when they discovered the disappearance of their daughter. This was no longer about money, but cruel and unusual vengeance.

The hours of the night slowly ticked by, and eventually Monster heard the tell-tale signs of an awakening family in the floors above him. He eventually heard Patsy scream out for John and listened as they discussed the ransom note and debated their calling of police. He listened to Patsy's near-hysterical telephone call to 911 and settled back into the shadows of the basement when he heard the voices of the first police officer arrive on scene.

It was not long thereafter that a uniformed sergeant swept through the basement, missing him in his darkened hiding space. The light of dawn was slowly beginning to creep its way through the basement windows, and Monster could make out the voices of additional police officers arriving at the scene.

Yet another police officer ventured into the basement and shining his flashlight here and there, passed by Monster in his hidey hole. He was flushed with excitement as the officer returned upstairs and then began to hear the voices of family friends who had been summoned to console Patsy.

And then some period of time later, a third person came through the basement calling out JonBenét's name as he looked around. This man was not a uniformed officer, but he spent some time inspecting the area around the Train Room window well, and Monster began to worry that his route of escape might have been discovered.

His heart nearly burst when the man unlatched the block of wood securing the Wine Cellar door and then stepped inside. Surely the girl's body would be discovered by this activity. But the man had apparently seen nothing, for he soon re-latched the door and reluctantly climbed the stairs back to the kitchen.

Monster felt that he had seen and heard enough. He had successfully eluded the observation of three people who had been through the basement that morning and the voices of those on the floor above him suggested that the house had been filling with a growing number of people. It was time to get out.

He moved to the window well and stood upon a Samsonite suitcase that had been used to help his partners leave the basement earlier that morning. Preparing to leave, he began to carefully leverage himself into the window well and then froze. Movement in the windows directly across from the grate caught his attention, and he observed John Ramsey standing in the den not more than fifteen feet from where he hid.

Craning his neck to get a better view, he saw John speaking to a female. It wasn't anyone Monster recognized, and it dawned on him that it must be a police detective. She held in her hand a small tape recorder and the handset of the telephone. "Damn", he thought. Ramsey would be stationed in the den to receive the ransom call, and he couldn't possibly escape in full view of all of the windows that faced the back yard from that room.

Monster climbed back down out of the window well and cursed as he accidentally scuffed the wall beneath the window with his foot. With a growing sense of panic, he began to consider his options.

After several minutes, he decided to venture up the stairwell to the first floor and nearing the top of the stairs, he again froze in place. A toilet had flushed. He listened intently as a water faucet was turned on and off, and then a door was shut. It was apparent that someone had been using the guest bathroom located near the top of the stairs.

Cursing himself for not doing a better job of memorizing the floor plan of the house, Monster remained in place listening for additional sounds that would alert him to the presence of another person. There is a butler door somewhere near the top of these stairs he thought: "All I have to do is make it to that door, and I'm home free."

Monster inched quietly toward the top of the stairs, knowing that at any instant another person could emerge from the doorway to enter the basement. His damp hand clutched a semiautomatic pistol in readiness.

His heart pounded in his chest as his ears searched for the tell-tale sign that anyone was nearby. Peering beneath the crack of the door, Monster decided to make his next move, and he lightly grasped and then turned the door knob. By millimeters the door slowly edged open, and the distant sound of voices opened up to him. They seemed to be coming from the far side of the house.

Stepping across the threshold of the door, Monster swore beneath his breath: "Which way is it? This place is a God-damned maze!"

Monster turned away from the voices and crept along a short hall. He was about to turn a corner when a police radio crackled so close he thought he was almost standing on top of it. He dared not peek around the corner, for the radio hung from the belt of a CSI processing the door for latent fingerprints.

The team in the compact vehicle had pulled back to Chautauqua Park located several blocks away on Baseline Road. Daylight was now in full bloom, and they were growing not only impatient, but alarmed. They had watched as a number of marked and unmarked police cars had visited the Ramsey home over the course of the morning. None had carried their companion away in handcuffs, so they presumed he still remained hidden somewhere in the home.

"What in the hell was he thinking?' protested the female.

Suddenly there was a break in radio silence, and Monster whispered his predicament to his partners on the outside. It was agreed that from their positions of surveillance, they would track as best they could the movement of the police officers and other people in the home and advise Monster when it might be possible for him to escape the home.

It was decided that no ransom call would be made and perhaps that would give cause for John Ramsey to leave the den and the police to retreat from the home.

The female started up the car and decided to make another pass by the house. It only took a minute before she pulled up to a Stop sign at the intersection of Cascade and 11th Street, a few blocks southwest of the Ramsey home. Another vehicle moving slowly in her direction caught her attention.

"Get down" she said urgently to her partner. He quickly slumped down into his seat and out of view of the passing vehicle. Her face darkened as she tracked the movement of the passing car. She made a quick right turn and drove away from the neighborhood.

"Okay, you can get up now."

The male passenger pulled himself out of the foot well and peered through the rear window. "What was it?"

"There was an unmarked police car. The passenger was videotaping all of the license plates of cars parked on the street."

Monster had moved back to the Train Room in anticipation of receiving the "all clear" signal to "go" from his partners on the outside of the home. He paced back and forth in the tiny space and then set a chair blocking the threshold of the doorway to the room. Anyone wishing to enter the room after him would have to move the chair and thereby alert him to their presence. It was risky, but it would give him a moment to be prepared to face any additional visitors who might come to the basement before his escape.

Time seemed to stand still until the radio transmission blurted into Monsters' earpiece:

"John Ramsey is in Burke's bedroom. He's scanning the street with a set of binoculars..."†

Monster knew this was his best opportunity for escape, and he quickly stepped onto the suitcase and climbed into the window well. As best he could, he peered into the windows of the den and at the rear entry door just feet from the grate. He could see no one, and he slid the grate forward and was rapidly out of the window well. Two seconds to replace the grate, and Monster sprinted for the back alley of the house.

There were no shouts of alarm or police officers yelling at him to "freeze." He continued his sprint to the north end of the alley and then slowed to a walk. Glancing in both directions and seeing no one, he crossed the street and continued up the next alley. Eventually, he circled around to the van and quickly climbed into the side door.

His partner greeted him with open arms.

"No police calls on the scanner...I think you got away clean."

Monster leaned back wearily and caught his breath. He glanced around the interior of the vehicle and grabbed a plastic bag. Pulling the remainder of the polymer cord from his pocket, he stuffed it, the stun gun, the roll of black duct tape, and the practice pages of the ransom note into the bag and cinched it closed.

Taking a quick look around before stepping out of the van, Monster moved to the trash can behind the Barnhill residence and deposited the "evidence" of the crime into the container.

Several moments later, the van moved off through the alley, and the trash can slowly receded from view as Monster turned the corner at the next block. Smiling, he turned to his partner:

"It never hurts to have a patsy ready to take the fall for you..."

⚏ ⊕ ⚏

The misleading clues left behind by the members of the foreign faction were confusing and puzzling, and ultimately sent some investigators flying away on the tails of wild geese.

"I didn't — I couldn't read the whole thing. I had just gotten up. We were on our, it was the day after Christmas, and we were going to go visiting, and it was quite early in the morning and I had got dressed and was on my way to the kitchen to make some coffee. And we have a back staircase

from the bedroom areas, and I always come down that stair-case, and I am usually the first one down.

And the note was lying across – three pages – across the run of one of the stair treads and it was kind of dimly lit. It was just very early in the morning and I started to read it, and it was addressed to John.

It said "'Mr. Ramsey.'" And it said, "'We have your daughter.'" And I, you know, it just, it just wasn't registering. And I, I may have gotten through another sentence. I can't. "'We have your daughter.'" And I don't know if I got any further than that.

And I immediately ran back upstairs and pushed open her door and she was not in her bed and I screamed for John."

—Patsy Ramsey's description of finding the ransom note during the CNN interview aired January 1, 1997.

Photo 1 - Ramsey Home 755 15th Street Boulder, Colorado/ Source: Boulder PD Case Files

≃ ⊕ ≃

CHAPTER THREE

Kidnapped

It was nearing shift change at the Boulder County
Regional Communications Center in the early
morning hours of December 26, 1996. Having worked most of the
holidays, dispatcher Kimberly Archuleta was looking forward to
spending the next few days off with her teenage son.

Dayshift relief dispatchers were coming into the center, receiving their briefing on the night's events when the light of a 911
phone console lit up at Archuleta's station at 0552 hours. She took
the call, and immediately sensed the urgency of the hysterical
voice of a female on the line.

A hush came over the center, and co-workers turned their
attention to Archuleta as she repeated the words of the 911 caller:
A six year old girl had been kidnapped.

Text of 911 Call

Patsy Ramsey: (Inaudible) police

Archuleta: (Inaudible)

Patsy Ramsey: Seven fifty-five Fifteenth Street.

Archuleta: What's going on there, Ma'am?

Patsy Ramsey: We have a kidnapping...Hurry, please.

Archuleta: Explain to me what's going on, Okay?

Patsy Ramsey: There we have...There's a note left and our daughter's gone.

Archuleta: A note was left and your daughter is gone?

Patsy Ramsey: Yes

Archuleta: How old is your daughter?

Patsy Ramsey: She's six years old...she's blond...six years old.

Archuleta: How long ago was this?

Patsy Ramsey: I don't know. I just found the note and my daughter/s (inaudible)

Archuleta: Does it say who took her?

Patsy Ramsey: What?

Archuleta: Does it say who took her?

Patsy Ramsey: No...I don't know it's there...there's a ransom note here.

Archuleta: It's a ransom note?

Patsy Ramsey: It says SBTC Victory...Please.

Archuleta: Okay, what's your name? Are you...

Patsy Ramsey: Patsy Ramsey. I'm the mother. Oh my God, please...

Archuleta: I'm...Okay, I'm sending an officer over, Okay?

Patsy Ramsey: Please.

Archuleta: Do you know how long she's been gone?

Patsy Ramsey: No, I don't. Please, we just got up and she's not here. Oh my God, please.

Archuleta:	Okay.
Patsy Ramsey:	Please send somebody.
Archuleta:	I am, honey.
Patsy Ramsey:	Please.
Archuleta:	Take a deep breath (inaudible)
Patsy Ramsey:	Hurry, hurry, hurry, (inaudible)
Archuleta:	Patsy? Patsy? Patsy? Patsy? Patsy?

Officer Rick French was the first to arrive on scene at 0556 hours and was greeted at the front door of the residence by Patsy Ramsey. John Ramsey was visible from the front door, standing in the kitchen at the end of a length of hallway that ran toward the rear of the house. French observed John Ramsey to be dressed in a long-sleeved blue and white pin-striped shirt and khaki pants. Patsy Ramsey's hair and make-up appeared to be neatly done, and she was dressed in a red sweater and black slacks.

Mrs. Ramsey immediately stated that their 6-year old daughter, JonBenét, was missing from her bedroom and that a ransom note had been found indicating that she had been kidnapped. John Ramsey directed French to 3 pages of paper spread out on the floor of a back kitchen hall. Mrs. Ramsey told French that she had stopped by JonBenét's bedroom at approximately 5:45 a.m. when headed downstairs that morning and found that her daughter was not in her room. She had come across the note as she proceeded down the back spiral staircase to the kitchen. She stated that she had originally found the 3-page note spread on the bottom treads of the stairs, but that her husband had moved it to its current location on the floor of the hallway, just outside of the kitchen.

French was told that Patsy Ramsey had immediately called 911 after showing the note to her husband, and he advised French that the house appeared to be locked as it had been left the previous evening. An alarm system for the home had not been used in some time, and they reported hearing nothing unusual during the night.

Ramsey told French that he had conducted a cursory search of JonBenét's room and that of his 9-year old son's while awaiting the arrival of officers. He reported that his 9-year old son, Burke, was still asleep in his upstairs bedroom. He had not been awakened by either of the parents to determine if he knew anything about JonBenét's disappearance.

French re-checked JonBenét's bedroom with John Ramsey and noted that the bedding had been pulled back as though one would be getting in to or out of bed. There was no sign of a struggle in the room and no sign of forced entry into JonBenét's locked second floor balcony door. It looked like the typical room of a 6-year old.

Sergeant Paul Reichenbach was the night shift patrol supervisor and finishing up the night's paperwork at his desk when he overheard French dispatched to the Ramsey home. He immediately headed for his car and was the second officer to arrive on scene at approximately 0610 hours.

French met Reichenbach at the front door and gave him a quick briefing, telling him there was a ransom note and he believed there may have been a kidnapping, but something didn't seem "right" to him. Many years of dealing with people under stress and at the peak of their emotions often give peace officers a "sixth sense," and something was beginning to tickle the edges of French's radar screen.

Reichenbach was shown the ransom note on the floor and, reading it, he began to formulate a response plan to the kidnapping. The note had specifically stated that the family was being watched. It seemed unlikely that a kidnapper would be parked outside the Ramsey home watching for police activity, but it wasn't unreasonable to think that they could be monitoring police radio frequencies, so Reichenbach ordered radio silence for the remainder of the call. Any further communication between officers working the case would be conducted by cell phone.

He called on the resources of the on-duty and off-duty Crime Scene Investigators- notified Sergeant Robert Whitson, the on-call detective supervisor, of the kidnapping and requested that Victim Advocates respond to the scene to assist in comforting the family. Reichenbach also took steps for the telephone company to set up a trap and trace on the Ramsey phone so that the source of any incoming phone calls for ransom could be traced.

While French remained with the parents, Reichenbach conducted an interior inspection of all three floors of the home, including the basement, and he did not notice any credible point of entry that drew his attention. He noted that at the far end of the basement was a white door secured at the top by a block of wood that pivoted on a screw. Reichenbach tried to open the door, but stopped when it was apparent that it would not have been either a point of entry or exit from the home.

During his inspection of the second floor, Reichenbach observed that the door to Burke's bedroom was open, and the lights were off. He moved quietly into the room, and Burke appeared to be asleep beneath the covers of his bed. Exiting, Reichenbach closed the door "nearly all the way" to prevent down-stairs noise from awakening the boy.

Following a walk-through of the home, Reichenbach then conducted a cursory search of the exterior and observed "frost on the grass and a little bit of snowfall" on exposed areas of the lawn. He noted that no one other than himself had walked through these areas.

Reichenbach noted that no snow had adhered to the rear patio and walkways. The driveway was wet but no foot prints / tracks were visible, and he observed no fresh signs of forced entry to exterior doors and windows.

After hanging up on the 911 dispatcher, Patsy Ramsey found the composure to make two additional phone calls. Family friends John and Barbara Fernie, as well as Fleet and Priscilla White were hurriedly summoned to the home. She told her friends that there was an emergency and that she needed them at her home. She had not told them that JonBenét had been kidnapped and that she needed their support.

It was close to 6:30 a.m. when the Fernies arrived and, from outside the rear kitchen / patio door, John Fernie was able to observe the ransom note still spread out on the floor of the hallway next to the kitchen.

Not long **thereafter**, Fleet and Priscilla White were the **next** family friends to arrive at the Ramsey home. Fleet White reported that within approximately 15 minutes of his arrival, he made a quick inspection of the basement of the home. He was purportedly the third person to visit the basement at that point of the morning.†

It should be noted that White's daughter, Daphne, had gone missing about a year earlier, and she was eventually found hiding in their home. Despite the existence of the ransom note in this instance, he took it upon himself to check the basement for JonBenét. He is the only person of record who called out her name as he searched the home that morning.

White observed a window to the Train Room to be closed and unlatched, and he was immediately drawn to the area. A particular upper left quadrant of the window was broken and it was large enough, about the size of a baseball that a person could reach through the space to unlock the window latch inside. Sections of fractured glass were missing from this part of the window, and he inspected the area closely for the remnants of these pieces.

He moved a hard-sided Samsonite suitcase that was standing beneath the window to look for broken glass. He didn't find any. The larger pieces of glass pane had already been removed, and it was subsequently determined that John Ramsey had broken the window and entered through that space when locked out of the house the previous summer. The glass from that breakage had been cleaned up, but the window had never been repaired.

White did find a small single kernel of glass on the floor, an apparent remnant from John Ramsey's earlier entry. He placed this on the ledge of the window frame and, leaving the window in its original condition, moved on to complete his survey of the basement.

White then moved from the Train Room to the white door of the Wine Cellar and, unlatching the wood block, partially opened the door to that room. Unable to locate a light switch for the windowless room, White failed to see a blanket on the floor that wrapped the body of JonBenét.

White returned upstairs and subsequently suggested that Burke be sequestered to the safety of his own home, in the company of his son, Fleet Junior, and visiting family.

Reports are in conflict as to whether or not White accompanied John Ramsey to awaken Burke. Ramsey reports that he alone awakened Burke and told him to get dressed and that his sister was missing. French made an attempt at an interview before Burke left the home, but was told that the boy had been asleep throughout the entire event and had no information to offer officers.

There is no dispute that White alone subsequently drove JonBenét's brother to his residence located in West Boulder. Before leaving home, Burke grabbed his Nintendo game, and he was gone by the time Detective Linda Arndt arrived at 0810 hours.

The exact timing of events is not clear, but French was purportedly the second person to inspect the basement after things had stabilized at the scene. He reported that he had briefly checked the garage and back doors of the residence not long after his arrival and had gone to the basement sometime before the arrival of civilians at the home.

Much has been made about his failure to discover the body of JonBenét in the Wine Cellar during this walkthrough, but like Reichenbach, one must understand what was going through his head at the time.

This was not a situation where a child was merely missing and possibly hiding in the home. The family was reporting a kidnapping of their child, and he had been shown a ransom note as proof. French was checking the interior of the home for a possible point of entry or exit that would have been used by a kidnapper(s). The door to the Wine Cellar was secured by a wooden block and it showed no sign of having been forcibly entered from the exterior. There simply was no reason at the time to go into that room.

CSI Karl Veitch arrived on the scene and handled the collection of the ransom note. It had been replaced and photographed on the stair treads as that had been the original location of discovery according to Patsy Ramsey. He then transported the note to the police department and photocopied it for investigators before securing it and going home sick.

Reverend Rol Haverstock, of the family's St. John's Episcopal Church, also responded to the home that morning and he, along with family friends, attempted to console a visibly distraught Patsy Ramsey. He was arriving at the home as Veitch was departing with the ransom note.

CSI's Barry Weiss and Sue Barcklow had arrived on the scene and began to look for a possible point of entry to the home. They examined doors and windows and began to dust for latent fingerprints. Weiss observed that the balcony door of JonBenét's bedroom was closed and locked. He noted that it had been a very cold night and observed a light coating of frost on the exterior bedroom balcony floor and railings. There were no marks of disturbance visible on the balcony prior to his testing of the surface. (Crime scene photos depicted before and after photos of the balcony floor with his footprints in the frost.) Anecdotally, another officer reported that the outside temperature had been observed to be 9 Degrees Fahrenheit one hour earlier at Tebo Plaza, approximately 5 miles distant from the Ramsey home.

Victim Advocates arrived on scene at approximately 6:45 a.m. as CSIs processed the scene for latent fingerprints. They reportedly followed the CSIs around cleaning up the messy fingerprint powder and were unwittingly destroying additional trace evidence that might have been discoverable.

Notification of the abduction had been made to Sergeant Robert Whitson, the on-call detective supervisor for the holiday.

He confirmed that the mechanics for installing a trap and trace on the Ramsey home phone had taken place. He called out detectives Linda Arndt and Fred Patterson and sent them to the home. Undercover narcotic unit detectives were called out and instructed to maintain surveillance for suspicious people and activities taking place in the neighborhood. He directed that a senior command staff page be initiated and alerted the D.A.'s office, the Boulder County Sheriff's Department, and the City's Public Information Officer of the investigation.

Whitson also contacted the Denver field offices of the Federal Bureau of Investigation, and they immediately began consulting with Boulder Police on the investigation.

Whitson subsequently responded to the home and spoke to John Ramsey. He briefed him on the investigative steps to be taken by the department and advised Ramsey of the FBI's involvement.

Photo 2 – JonBenét's bedroom viewed from doorway. Note lamp is turned on. Source: Boulder PD Case File / Internet

Ramsey reiterated his belief that the house had been locked the previous evening when the family had turned in for the night. Upon request, Ramsey provided Whitson with handwriting samples for both him and his wife. He grabbed a note-pad from the kitchen area that he apparently knew to contain samples of his wife's handwriting and wrote a sentence on another pad of paper as his own exemplar.

Whitson asked Ramsey about any suspects that came to mind, and he mentioned a former employee of his company, Jeff Merrick, who had left under difficult circumstances. Linda **Hoffmann-Pugh**, the family's current housekeeper, was also named, and this was due to her recent request for a monetary loan from his wife.

JonBenét's bedroom was secured with crime scene tape during Whitson's visit, and he subsequently returned to the Police Department with the handwriting exemplars. These were turned over to Detective Jeff Kithcart, the department's forensics fraud and handwriting examiner. Later that day, around the time of the discovery of JonBenét's body, Kithcart made an unsettling discovery. He observed handwriting on pages of Patsy Ramsey's note pad that started out in similar fashion to the opening words of the ransom note. The structure of the letters was similar to those of the ransom note, and pages had been torn out of the pad. It appeared to Kithcart that Patsy Ramsey's note pad may have been used to construct a practice ransom note.

Detective Linda Arndt brought recording equipment with her to the scene and not long after her arrival at 0810 hours, she determined that she would use the Den as her base of operations. She asked French to remain with Patsy Ramsey in the first floor Solarium as she briefed John Ramsey on what to say to the kidnapper(s) when they called. French continued to attempt to control the movement and activities of friends who now inhabited the home.

Arndt conducted a brief interview with Patsy Ramsey that morning and was told that she too thought the house was locked the previous evening. Mrs. Ramsey reported to Arndt that she had found the ransom note first before going to JonBenét's bedroom and this conflicted with what she had reported to French when he first spoke to her that morning.

She related possible suspicion of Linda **Hoffmann-Pugh** due to her recent request for a two- thousand dollar ($2,000.00) loan. Arndt was subsequently told by Father Rol that Patsy Ramsey also wanted her to know that **Hoffmann-Pugh** had previously men-tioned concerns about the kidnapping of JonBenét.

A copy of the ransom note was brought back to the house that morning by Detective Arndt, and the family and friends attempted to decipher its contents. Some thought the ransom demand, one-hundred-eighteen thousand dollars ($118,000.00), an odd amount for a ransom demand. They also thought the amount ridiculously low and knew that John Ramsey was well-capable of paying up to one million dollars ($1,000,000.00) in ransom for his daughter if necessary.

The length, content, and details provided by kidnappers in the note immediately raised questions for the investigators who were working the case that morning. The FBI, consulting in the case, had never seen a ransom note of its kind. In their experience, ransom notes were short and sweet and typically provided few details about the perpetrators behind a kidnapping.

Additionally, the note began by formally addressing John Ramsey. By its end, the kidnapper(s) spoke as though they were intimately familiar with John and the family.

Mr. Ramsey,

Listen carefully! We are a group of individuals that represent a small foreign faction. We ~~do~~ respect your bussiness but not the country that it serves. At this time we have your daughter in our posession. She is safe and unharmed and if you want her to see 1997, you must follow our instructions to the letter.

You will withdraw $118,000.00 from your account. $100,000 will be in $100 bills and the remaining $18,000 in $20 bills. Make sure that you bring an adequate size attaché to the bank. When you get home you will put the money in a brown paper bag. I will call you between 8 and 10 am tomorrow to instruct you on delivery. The delivery will be exhausting so I advise you to be rested. If we monitor you getting the money early, we might call you early to arrange an earlier delivery of the

money and hence a earlier
~~delivery~~ pick-up of your daughter.
Any deviation of my instructions
will result in the immediate
execution of your daughter. You
will also be denied her remains
for proper burial. The two
gentlemen watching over your daughter
do particularly like you so I
advise you not to provoke them.
Speaking to anyone about your
situation, such as Police, F.B.I., etc.,
will result in your daughter being
beheaded. IF we catch you talking
to a stray dog, she dies. If you
alert bank authorities, she dies.
If the money is in any way
marked or tampered with, she
dies. You will be scanned for
electronic devices and if any are
found, she dies. You can try to
deceive us but be warned that
we are familiar with Law enforcement
countermeasures and tactics. You
stand a 99% chance of killing
your daughter if you try to out
smart us. Follow our instructions

and you stand a 100% chance of getting her back. You and your family are under constant scrutiny as well as the authorities. Don't try to grow a brain John. You are not the only fat cat around so don't think that killing will be difficult. Don't underestimate us John. Use that good southern common sense of yours. It is up to you now John!

Victory!

S.B.T.C

None of the civilians on the scene that morning seemed to question or be concerned about the length of the note.

Arndt noted that John Ramsey seemed to be distracted throughout the course of the morning and was out of the den on at least 3 occasions during the time frame that they awaited the ransom call. He had to run to answer the phone when it rang.

The ransom note stated that kidnappers would call with instructions for the family between "8:00 and 10:00 am" and the passage of this time came and went, without any observed comment from Ramsey. It wasn't long after this that Arndt lost track of his movements. She reported that she first made note of his absence at around 1040 hours, and he didn't reappear until noon. Nearly 1 ½ years would pass before John Ramsey explained this absence.

CSIs had wrapped up their processing of the first floor of the home. Victim advocates Grace Morlock and Mary Lou Jedamus had followed them around, cleaning up the mess left by finger-print powder. Family friends were still in attendance, continuing their attempt to console Patsy Ramsey and had used the kitchen to prepare food and snacks for the group.

French had remained at the home throughout the morning and observed additional behavioral clues that tickled his sixth sense. For one, Patsy Ramsey had wanted him to remove his gun belt and uniform shirt as he stood by in the house. He thought it an odd request since he was there protecting the family against the members of a "foreign faction" who had entered her home and kidnapped her daughter.

Why was she so uncomfortable with a uniformed police officer being in her home?

There was another peculiar moment that captured French's attention. Patsy Ramsey had been crying throughout the morning and was being consoled by her friends. At one juncture, he observed that she had her hands up around her face, presumably to help cover her anguish. He was a little unnerved when he discovered that she was peering at him through her fingers. It was an odd moment that left him uncertain about what to think of the circumstances in which he found himself immersed.

Supervisors and detectives had convened at the Police Department following the passage of the ransom hour, and Arndt found herself to be the sole police officer remaining at the home. She had observed a marked difference in John Ramsey's mood when he re-surfaced at noon. He was anxiously pacing around the house shortly before 1300 hours, and in attempt to keep his mind occupied, Arndt suggested that he check the house from "top to bottom" for anything unusual.

Rather than follow the directions of the detective, Ramsey immediately led Fleet White to the basement.

White was interviewed on 3 different occasions by law enforcement authorities about the events that followed his visit to the basement with Ramsey. He told investigators that John Ramsey led him directly to the Train Room, and White told Ramsey about his visit to the room earlier that morning.

Ramsey related his break-in through the window from the previous summer, and they both checked around for more glass.† It was not clear from either of the men's later interviews whether they had opened the window as they looked for more glass, but Ramsey stated that both men got down on the floor to check for signs that the window hadn't been broken again. Preparing to leave the room, they moved a fireplace grate to check another closet, and Ramsey then moved out of the room and down the hallway toward the Wine Cellar. White was replacing the grate when he heard John Ramsey cry out "Oh my God!"

Photo 3 - Hallway leading to Wine Cellar. JonBenét's body was discovered behind this door, and the paint tray is on the floor to left edge of the doorway. Note the bag of golf clubs. Source: Boulder PD Case File / Internet

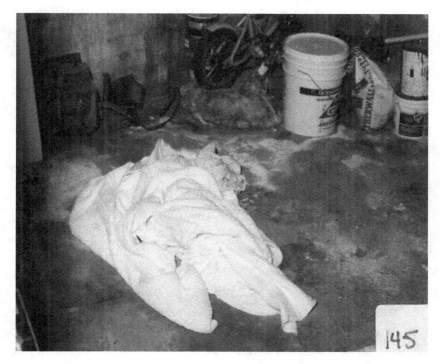

Photo 4 - The white blanket on the floor of the Wine Cellar that was wrapped around the body of JonBenét. Source: Boulder PD Case File / Internet

White stated that he rushed down the short hallway and joined Ramsey just as the latter flipped on the lights in the Wine Cellar. . He could now see the partially wrapped body of JonBenét. He leaned down to touch her bare ankles, which were visible outside the blanket, and later told investigators that they were cold to the touch.

White left Ramsey in the Wine Cellar and ran upstairs shouting for someone to call an ambulance.

Ramsey stated that he removed a piece of duct tape that covered JonBenét's mouth and also removed a cord that had been tied around her left wrist. He then carried her upstairs and was greeted at the top of the stairwell by Detective Arndt.

Arndt, alerted to events by White's shouting, saw Ramsey emerge from the basement carrying JonBenét upright and away from his body. JonBenét's arms projected above her head, stiff from rigor mortis. Arndt instructed Ramsey to place JonBenét on the floor, and she then checked for vital signs. JonBenét's lips were blue, and she was cold to the touch. Arndt could not find a pulse, and she noted an odor of decay. It was apparent that she had been dead for some period of time.

Arndt then picked up JonBenét's body and moved her to the living room, laying her on her back on a rug in front of the Christmas tree.

Barbara Fernie and Priscilla White had been with Patsy Ramsey in the Solarium when they heard Fleet's shouting for an ambulance and moved from the room. Patsy did not accompany them.†

Arndt and John Ramsey stood face-to-face over JonBenét's body, and he was told that she was gone. She then directed him to call 911, since she had no radio with her to contact her dispatch center, and to then go to his wife.

Ramsey left and returned approximately two minutes later, and before Arndt could stop him, he grabbed a blanket in the room and placed it over her body. Someone else placed a sweatshirt over JonBenét's bare feet. Not long thereafter Patsy Ramsey was led from the Solarium, supported in the arms of her friends, where she collapsed on her daughter's body.

Despite being instructed by Detective Arndt to stand guard at the top of the basement stairs, Fleet White returned briefly to the Wine Cellar during these events. He picked up the duct tape, touched the blanket that had been wrapped around JonBenét's body and handled a cigar box in the room.

Father Rol was leading the group in prayer when White returned upstairs. Patsy Ramsey was hysterical, wailing for Lazarus to raise her daughter from the dead.

Acting Detective Division Commander Sergeant Larry Mason arrived on the scene at 1320 hours and was accompanied by Denver FBI Supervisory Agent Ron Walker. They had learned of the discovery of JonBenét's body while meeting on the investigation at the Boulder Police Department.

Mason directed the evacuation of the home, now considered to be a crime scene in its entirety. Both he and Walker were reported to have inspected the Wine Cellar before leaving the home.

At approximately 1340 hours, Detective Bill Palmer overheard John Ramsey speaking on the phone and making arrangements to fly to Atlanta that afternoon or evening. Upon the conclusion of the phone call, Palmer told Ramsey that he couldn't leave town as he would need to stay to assist in the investigation of the murder of his daughter.†

The nature of this call was passed along to Mason, and he too spoke with Ramsey about leaving town. John Ramsey reportedly told Mason that he had to leave to attend a meeting "he couldn't miss." Sergeant Mason eventually convinced the father of the murdered child of the necessity of remaining in Boulder.

Fleet White and John Fernie had spoken to one another about where the Ramsey family could go, now that their home was being secured by police for a search warrant. It was agreed that the Fernies would make room for the Ramseys at their South Boulder home.

As the Ramsey family and friends were departing the home at approximately 1415 hours that afternoon, a taxi pulled up that contained John Ramsey's older son and daughter from a previous marriage, John Andrew and Melinda Ramsey. Melinda's fiancé, Stewart Long, was in attendance. Ramsey broke the sad news of JonBenét's death, and the family left for the Fernie residence.

The kidnap of JonBenét by a foreign faction had now become a homicide investigation.

"There is a killer on the loose...I don't know who it is. I don't know if it's a he or a she. But if I were a resident of Boulder, I would tell my friends to keep—keep your babies close to you, there's someone out there."

—Patsy Ramsey warning viewers during the CNN interview aired January 1, 1997.

Homicide

Boulder Police received a lot of criticism for having lost control of the initial crime scene, and they were soon playing catch-up to rectify the situation. What followed was one of the most thoroughly investigated homicides this country has ever witnessed.

The home had been sealed following Sergeant Mason's orders to evacuate the residence, and officers were posted to insure the integrity of the crime scene. Investigators gathered at the police department to strategize their next steps.

Detective Division Commander John Eller cut short his vacation and, leaving visiting family from Florida at his home, responded to the police department to direct the investigation.

FBI Supervisory Agent Ron Walker spoke to Eller briefly before leaving the department. Local authorities were responsible for investigating murder, and the FBI no longer had concurrent jurisdiction for a kidnapping.

"You need to look at the parents," he told Eller.

Statistically, only about 6 percent of child murders are committed by strangers. The percentages drop significantly when a child is found murdered in their own home. The veteran FBI agent reiterated that the parents had to be considered in the investigation of the death of this little girl.

Detectives and officers who had the opportunity to ask questions of John and Patsy Ramsey that morning before the discovery of her body had a general outline of what had occurred the previous evening of Christmas day. They had been told that the Ramseys had attended a dinner party at the White residence on Christmas evening and returned home before 10:00 p.m. John Ramsey reported that he read to both children before retiring for the night and that he had been the one to tuck JonBenét into bed.

It was related that both parents had thought the house to be locked before they went to bed that night, and John Ramsey had actually inspected the doors before retiring. No keys had been lost or stolen, and the only other people who had keys to the residence were Patsy's mother, John's oldest son (John Andrew), and the housekeeper, Linda **Hoffmann-Pugh**. Patsy's mother and John Andrew were both reported to be out of state for the holidays.

The family dog, Jacques, was in the custody of neighbor Joe Barnhill, who lived across the street from the Ramsey home. The family was headed to their vacation home in Charlevoix, Michigan early on the morning of December 26th, and the dog would remain at his "second home" in Boulder.

The officers were aware that Patsy Ramsey's version of finding the ransom note had changed. She initially told French that she had stopped by JonBenét's bedroom on her way downstairs that morning. JonBenét's bed was empty, and she proceeded downstairs to find the note at the bottom of the spiral staircase at the rear of the kitchen.

Patsy Ramsey had then told Detective Arndt that she had found the note first, and returned to the second floor bedroom of her daughter to discover her missing. There would be additional inconsistent statements to come in the following months.

Detective Kithcart had discovered what appeared to be a practice ransom note on a pad identified as belonging to Patsy. Written in black by a felt-tip pen were the following words:

"Mr. and Mrs. I"

The "I" appeared to Kithcart to be the down stroke of the pen that would start the capital letter "R." He felt that investigators needed to look for additional handwriting exemplars and pens that may have been used to author the note.

Commander Eller appointed CSI Mike Everett as the lead technician responsible for directing the collection of physical evidence from the scene. Another investigator was assigned the task of writing search warrant affidavits for the home, and consideration was given to obtaining warrants for the home of Linda **Hoffmann-Pugh**, the housekeeper, and John Ramsey's office.

After several re-writes of the affidavit as directed by the D.A.'s office, investigators finally returned to the Ramsey home to continue their processing of the scene. The seal on the front door was broken at 2036 hours on the evening of December 26, 1996.

CSIs carefully worked their way through the residence, videotaping the premises before any additional processing took place. 35 mm still photographs were taken that evening as well.

JonBenét's body had remained in place where Detective Arndt had placed it in the living room earlier that day, and Boulder County Medical Examiner John Meyer accompanied investigators to the scene that evening to personally oversee the removal of her body. An autopsy to determine the cause of her death would be undertaken the following morning.

It had been a long and emotionally draining day. Investigators concluded their work for the night and resealed the home at approximately 0021 hours.

Boulder residents would learn of the crime the following morning.

Missing Girl Found Dead

A 6-year-old Boulder girl reported kidnapped early Thursday was found dead in her parent's home later that afternoon. It is Boulder's first official homicide of 1996.

Police detectives and crime scene investigators began searching the home late Thursday after securing a search warrant. No details of what they found were disclosed.

Although the official cause of death was not yet known, Police Chief Tom Koby said the case is considered a homicide. The child had not been shot or stabbed, said Detective Sgt. Larry Mason.

No arrest had been made as of press time, and police had no suspects, Mason said.

The Boulder County coroner's office refused to discuss details of the case, though an autopsy will be performed today, according to city spokeswoman Leslie Aaholm.

*The child was 1995 Little Miss Colorado and a student at Martin Park Elementary School, according to a family friend. Patsy Ramsey traveled around the country with JonBenét to attend her daughter's beauty contests. "They were so serious about this beauty queen stuff, but they never put any pressure on her. She was Little Miss Colorado in 1995." **said** Dee Dee Nelson-Schneider, a family friend.*

"She had her own float in the Colorado Parade of Lights in December 1995, and Patsy walked along the side of the float the whole parade to make sure (JonBenét) was safe. That's how protective Patsy was."

—Elliot Zaret and Alli Krupski *Boulder Daily Camera,*
    December 27, 1996

CSI Everett and other investigators would return to the home on the morning of Friday, December 27th at 0925 hours and resume their search for evidence. During his exploration of the premises, Everett observed spider webs, approximately ten inches (10") in length, on the southwest edge of the window grate that covered the Train Room window well. These were attached to bricks, rocks and foliage near the grate. He noted that the foliage near the grate didn't appear to have been trampled or disturbed.

CSIs would continue to photo-document their exterior search of the residence though unfortunately, the spider webs described above were not photographed in detail.

Also, a triangular-shaped cobweb attached to the lower-left window frame of the Train Room window well was photographed by 35 mm film and video.

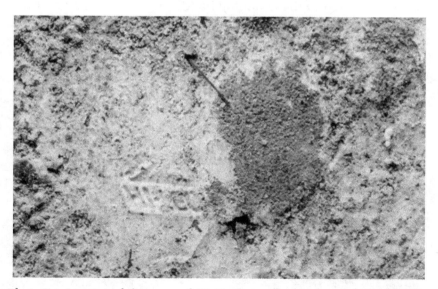

Photo 5 - Imprint of the poon of Hi-Tec boot print on floor of Wine Cellar. Source: Boulder PD Case File / Internet

During their initial processing of the home, the Wine Cellar was examined in detail, and investigators noted the imprint of the poon of a boot in some mildew on the floor next to where

JonBenét's body had been concealed. It was from a "Hi-Tec" brand hiking style boot, and there appeared to be another partial boot or shoeprint impression nearby.

The poon of the boot was insufficiently distinguishable for comparison purposes, however. More specifically, there was nothing in the label of the boot impression that would help match it to another boot because of a wear pattern or other irregularity. Its presence in the cellar could only illustrate that at some point in time, perhaps days or months prior to the discovery of JonBenét's body, someone wearing a Hi-Tec boot had stood in that room.

CSIs would make another important discovery during their search of the home.

Broken shards of wood from a "Korea" paintbrush handle would be found on the floor outside the entrance door of the Wine Cellar. A portion of the matching handle was found in a paint tray near the door, and this would eventually be matched to the broken wood handle used in the garrote that had killed JonBenét.

Photo 6 - This paint tray contained remnants of the Korea paint brush used in the garrote to murder JonBenét. Source: Boulder PD Case File / Internet

It appeared that the garrote had been constructed at the entrance to the doorway of the Wine Cellar, and investigators believed that JonBenét's murder had taken place in that very location.

One additional odd piece of physical evidence would be discovered sitting in plain view on the top of a kitchen counter. Standing upright amidst food articles, a black Maglite brand flashlight, similar to the type used by police officers, had been observed by the CSI's processing the crime scene. There were no identifying marks on the flashlight, and no officer who had been present at the scene claimed ownership. CSI's collected the flashlight as possible evidence.

Photo 7 - Maglite flashlight left on kitchen counter. Source: Boulder PD Case File / Internet

It was processed for latent fingerprints, inside and out, but nothing could be lifted from its surfaces.

The Ramseys would later indicate that they may have owned a similar style of flashlight, and stated that it had been kept in a kitchen drawer. It had been given to them by John Andrew, but the fingerprint powder depicted in the photograph of the flashlight altered its appearance in such a way that it apparently threw off their identification of the gift.

John Fernie and housekeeper Linda **Hoffmann-Pugh** would subsequently identify the flashlight as belonging to the Ramsey family, both having seen it in the home before the kidnapping.

The presence of the flashlight on the kitchen counter was never fully explained, however. It would later be identified as a possible weapon used in the blow to JonBenét's head.

Investigators and CSIs worked through the day, collecting and tagging numerous items of potential evidence. They would return again the following morning and continued to process the home for evidence for 10 straight days, having sought two additional search warrants over this period of time.

While CSIs carefully worked their way through the Ramsey home, Eller had detailed a team of police officers to round-the-clock security at the Fernie residence, and they were on-site not long after the Ramsey family took refuge in the home of their steadfast friends.

Heeding the FBI's advice, he wanted to know what the family was saying and doing in the aftermath of the discovery of JonBenét's body.

In the interim, following the autopsy of JonBenét, Sergeant Mason was tasked with attempting to arrange an interview with family members. There were a number of questions that investigators had not been able to ask of John and Patsy Ramsey during their wait for the ransom call. He and Detective Arndt visited the Fernie home, temporary quarters for the Ramsey family, on the evening of Friday, December 27th in an effort to schedule more detailed interviews.

Family friend Mike Bynum, a former Boulder County prosecutor, was present and apparently providing legal advice to John Ramsey. JonBenét's pediatrician, Dr. Francesco Beuf, was also present. He refused to let Patsy be interviewed. She was under the influence of medication and described as being too distraught to even consider responding to the police department to answer questions about the murder of her daughter.

Mason and Arndt left the Fernie home that night empty handed, unable to secure a firm date and time for a follow up interview.

The following morning, Saturday, December 28th, 1996, investigators were notified by Boulder County Assistant District Attorney Pete Hoffstrom that the Ramsey family was now being represented by attorneys.† Any questions of the family regarding the circumstances surrounding the death of their daughter would have to be put to writing and presented by Hoffstrom to their legal counsel.

No face-to-face interview between Boulder Police investigators and Ramsey family members would be scheduled for months.

CHAPTER FIVE

Cause and Manner of Death

Detectives Tom Trujillo and Linda Arndt were tasked with attending JonBenét's autopsy which began early on Friday morning, December 27, 1996. A handful of people stared down at the small body bag on the examining table that contained the remains of the 6-year-old girl. Present within the cramped spaces of the morgue's autopsy theater were representatives from the Boulder Police Department and the Boulder County Coroner's and District Attorney's offices.

Each of the men and women present attempted to mentally prepare themselves for what was about to come. The cold act of dissecting the lifeless body of a child was something you never become accustomed to, and child homicides in Boulder were a rarity. It is difficult to put aside the thoughts that the child lying on that examination table could be one of your own.

The stench of death never seems to leave these particular environs, invading every pore of your body and having been there before, you sadly realize that it may take days for the distinctive odor of the morgue to fade away from memory. The visual aspects of this type of work, however, rarely leave your consciousness.

Eventually the coroner's office began the process and removed the custody seal that had secured the body bag the previous evening.

The small bag containing JonBenét was unzipped, pulled away, and she was gently placed on the examining table. She was observed to be wearing several pieces of clothing that included a white, long-sleeved knit shirt bearing a star of sequins on the chest, a pair of size 12 Bloomies brand underwear, and a pair of long underwear type pants.

They all watched as Dr. Meyer removed the loosely tied piece of white nylon cord that remained attached to JonBenét's right wrist. Her father had already removed the loop that had encircled the left wrist when he had discovered her body. Dr. Meyer noted that the loop was loose enough that he could place his fingers between the cord and JonBenét's wrist.

The length of the cord between the loops that had been placed around her wrists was determined to be approximately fifteen and a half (15 ½") inches and both ends of this cord were frayed. The loops of the cord had been tied so loosely around JonBenét's wrists that they left no telltale marks or abrasions on her skin.

Another piece of similar looking cord was embedded in JonBenét's neck. The loop around her head was determined to be configured with a slip knot, with the trailing end leading from the midline of the back of her neck and wrapped around a splintered stick. The stick measured approximately four and a half (4 ½") inches in length, and both ends were splintered. The word "Korea" was printed on the stick.

The trailing end of the cord extended approximately four (4") inches beyond the slip knot, and the end of the cord was frayed. The length of cord departing the portion of the slip knot encircling JonBenét's neck to the stick measured approximately seventeen

(17") inches. The end of the cord that had been wrapped around the stick was observed to be burned / melted.

The cord around her neck was situated in a horizontal fashion with a slight vertical cant as it reached the back of her jaw line. This position indicated that the cord had been applied manually and was not consistent with a death caused by a vertical hanging.

Hair from JonBenét's head was entangled in the slip knot, and it appeared that force had been applied by pulling on the end of the cord with the wrapped stick, embedding the cord in the flesh of her neck. Dr. Meyer had to clip some of JonBenét's hair in order free the ligature from her neck.

The stick was later determined to be a portion of a broken paintbrush handle found in an art tray near the entrance to the Wine Cellar. The slip knot was situated at the rear of her head, so it was presumed that JonBenét had been facing away from the perpetrator as they had tightened the noose around her neck.

Dr. Meyer carefully cut, marked, and removed the garrote from JonBenét's neck. The remaining furrow was dark red in color and revealed how deeply embedded the cord had been buried into the flesh of her neck.

An examination of her eyelids and the conjunctiva of her eyes revealed the presence of petechial hemorrhages, pinpoint blood vessels that had burst when JonBenét had been strangled. These hemorrhages indicated that JonBenét had been alive when the garrote had been applied and tightened around her throat.

A triangular shaped bruise was observed on the front of JonBenét's throat and below the line of the embedded cord. It was approximately the size of a quarter and located left of the midline of her throat.

Dried mucous from her nose had been smeared down the right lip and cheek. Marks from the straight edge of the duct tape that had once been placed over her mouth appeared visible, suggesting that the mucous was already in place before the duct tape had been applied.

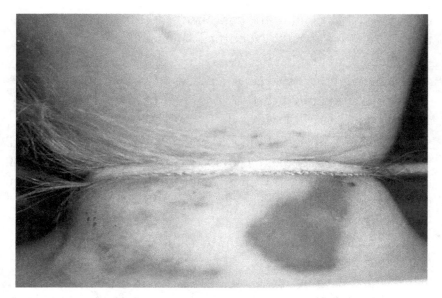

Photo 8 - Neck abrasions and garrote. The triangular shaped bruise was thought to have been caused by the twisting of JonBenét's shirt while tightened around her neck. Note the other lower abrasions, and suspected fingernail marks above the cord. Source: Boulder PD Case File / Internet

There was an orange-red colored circular shaped mark on JonBenét's right cheek, between her ear and jaw line of undetermined origin.

Paper bags had been secured over JonBenét's hands before she had been removed from the living room of her home the previous evening. These were removed and the fingernails of each hand were carefully clipped into envelopes with the hopes that DNA, epithelial cells, or trace blood evidence would be there to help identify her attacker(s).

A heart drawn in red ink was observed in the palm of her left hand.

JonBenét's clothing was removed and bagged for the collection of other trace fibers and evidence that might be present. Obvious items of trace evidence, fibers, hair, were collected from the clothing before they were removed from her body and bagged.

Upon their removal, the underwear and long-johns were observed to contain dried, yellowish colored urine stains and the underwear contained two small circular stains of blood in the crotch. The location of the urine stains were to the front of the clothing, and it was thought that JonBenét had been lying on her stomach when her bladder let go at the time of her death.

The examination of the outer skin of her body revealed some other minor scrapes, abrasions, and marks. Located upon the top of her left shoulder were signs of scrape marks. Her lower left leg had another abrasion that was thought to be a scratch mark.

On the lower left quadrant of her back were two distinct red marks that, upon closer inspection, Dr. Meyer identified as abrasions. They appeared similar in size and round in shape, measuring 3.5 mm in distance from one another.

At some point during the process, investigators decided to stop their examination of JonBenét and considered the possibility of fingerprinting her skin. Several telephone calls were made to other agencies in an attempt to determine if there was a successful method for retrieving latent fingerprints from the skin of a deceased person.

They weren't able to determine if there was any tried and true technique that would be successful, but they did try a technique that involved the use of Magna powder, a specific type of fingerprint powder that utilized a magnetic brush to move and collect the powder over the surface believed to hold latent fingerprints. Investigators were not successful in lifting any latent fingerprints from JonBenét in this fashion.

Dr. Meyer conducted an external examination of JonBenét's genitalia. He had observed spots of blood in the crotch of the underwear she had been wearing when her clothing had been removed, and this alerted him to the possibility that there was a cause for this evidence to be present.

He observed that there was fresh trauma located at the 7:00 o'clock position at the hymeneal opening. The area was inflamed and had been bleeding, and it appeared to Dr. Meyer that a foreign object had been inserted into JonBenét's genitalia at or near the time of her death.

The site of the damaged tissue was excised and prepared for a pathology slide. Later examination would reveal the presence of 'cellulose material' in the membrane of the hymeneal opening that was consistent with the wood of the paintbrush used as a handle in the cord of the garrote.

He noted that he didn't consider this injury the result of a particularly vicious assault with a foreign object. A very small splinter of material was discovered during microscopic examination, and more trauma to the site would have been expected if the perpetrator had been intent on physically torturing the child.

Dr. Meyer also observed signs of chronic inflammation around the vaginal orifice and believed that these injuries had been inflicted in the days or weeks *before* the acute injury that was responsible for causing the bleeding at the time of her death. This irritation appeared consistent with prior sexual contact.

An alternate light source (ALS) was used to scan JonBenét's body in search of other trace evidence and fluids. The area around her upper thighs illuminated traces of fluid and indications that she may have been wiped clean with some type of cloth. Investigators thought perhaps that the fluid source reacting to the ALS was semen, but swabs of the area would later **reveal it** to be a smear of blood.

Per autopsy protocols, Dr. Meyer collected tissue samples from of a variety of internal organs, and this included the contents of JonBenét's stomach. He found no traces of food present in her stomach but did collect the remnants of what appeared to him to be raw pineapple from the upper duodenum of her digestive tract. Scientific examination would later confirm his preliminary opinion: JonBenét had consumed raw pineapple not long before her death.†

There had initially been no outward appearance of an injury to JonBenét's head. No trace of blood had been observed in her hair, and the scalp did not reveal signs of any type of injury. So as Dr. Meyer began his internal examination, investigators were surprised to learn that she had suffered a severe blow to the upper right side of her skull. A linear fracture covered the entire length of the upper right side of her head, from the parietal to occipital bones of her skull.

The injury was rectangular in shape measuring approximately eight and one half inches (8 ½") in length by one and three quarters (1 ¾") to one and one- half inches (1 ½") in width, and fractured bone from the skull had caused extensive damage to the brain below. Fresh subdural hematoma was apparent as well as subarachnoid hemorrhaging. There was cerebral edema (brain swelling) observed.

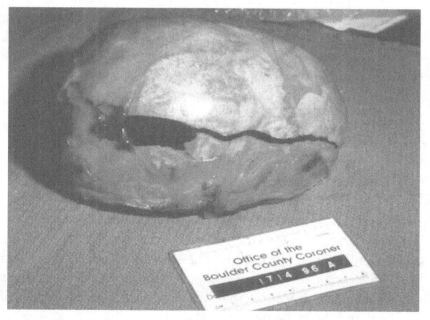

Photo 9 - Rectangular shaped skull fracture that traverses the right side of the head. Source: Boulder PD Case File / Internet

Dr. Meyer told the investigators that it would have taken some time for the brain swelling to develop, and there likely had been a period of JonBenét's survival from the time she received the blow to her head and when she was eventually strangled. He reported that this would have been a lethal blow, and that he did not think it likely that she regained consciousness.

The bulk of the autopsy had been completed by mid-afternoon, but Dr. Meyer wanted another opinion about the injuries that had been inflicted upon the genitalia. Over the course of the investigation, a number of forensic pathologists would study JonBenét's injuries and offer their professional insight into what had happened to this little girl.

Dr. Meyer called together the Boulder County Child Fatality Advisory Review Team that afternoon, a protocol established by the coroner's office that called for the review of all child fatalities that took place in the county. Members who served on the team were comprised of people from the Boulder Police Department, Boulder County Coroner's Office, the Boulder County Sheriff's Department, the Boulder District Attorney's Office, and the Boulder County Department of Social Services.

The team was provided with a briefing on what had taken place at the Ramsey home following the report of the kidnapping, and Dr. Meyer gave an overview of the autopsy findings. A number of things were discussed during the meeting, and the group determined that there were a number of questions that needed to be researched.

They were interested in the family history and wanted to know if there had been any signs of previous sexual abuse with members of the family. There was an interest in determining if there had been any recent behavioral changes with the children at their schools. It was suggested that the teachers and classmates of JonBenét and Burke be interviewed.

They were interested in determining if Patsy had ever been abused as a child and what kind of behavioral changes had taken place after her bout with cancer.

They also wanted to know how the parents were interacting with their son, and felt it necessary that an interview be conducted with him by investigators.

The first meeting of the Child Fatality Review Team completed, Boulder Police investigators now had another set of investigative priorities established for them in the early stages of this investigation.

Following the meeting, Dr. Meyer returned to the morgue with Dr. Andy Sirontak, Chief of Denver Children's Hospital Child Protection Team, so that a second opinion could be rendered on the injuries observed to the vaginal area of JonBenét. He would observe the same injuries that Dr. Meyer had noted during the autopsy protocol and concurred that a foreign object had been inserted into the opening of JonBenét's vaginal orifice and was responsible for the acute injury witnessed at the 7:00 o'clock position.

Further inspection revealed that the hymen was shriveled and retracted, a sign that JonBenét had been subjected to some type of sexual contact prior to the date of her death.

Dr. Sirontak could not provide an opinion as to how old those injuries were or how many times JonBenét may have been assaulted and would defer to the expert opinions of other medical examiners.

Dr. Meyer would prepare a brief press release at the end of the day, announcing that the cause of JonBenét's death had been "asphyxiation by strangulation." Estimating the time of death would take a little longer to establish and was not mentioned in the announcement regarding her murder.

The manner of death was ruled to be a Homicide.

Interpreting the Injuries

D r. Meyer was concerned about JonBenét's vaginal injuries, and he, along with Boulder investigators, sought the opinions of a variety of other physicians in the days following her autopsy. Dr. Sirontak, a pediatrician with Denver Children's Hospital, had recognized signs of prior sexual trauma but neither he nor Dr. Meyer were able to say with any degree of certainty what period of time may have been involved in the abuse.

Experts in their field, physicians and forensic pathologists were consulted from St. Louis, Missouri; Dade County, Florida; Wayne County, Michigan, and Philadelphia, Pennsylvania to name just a few. They examined the series of photographs that depicted the injuries and came to the opinion that JonBenet had been subjected to sexual intrusion prior to the insertion of the foreign object that had created the injury at the time of her death.

It was their opinion that the type of injury present with the hymen suggested that several different contacts had been made in the past and that digital penetration was consistent with this type of injury. The physicians were unable to date the previous injury or specifically quantify the number of times JonBenét had been assaulted, but were confident in their opinions that she had been subjected to sexual contact prior to the day of her murder.

This particular information suggested that someone close to JonBenét had been responsible for abusing her in the weeks or months preceding her murder. As is often the case involving this type of childhood abuse, investigators had to consider the possibility that a family member, relative, or someone close to the inner circle of the family was responsible for the prior acts and possibly the murder of JonBenét. Someone had to have had access to JonBenét on repeated occasions to have perpetrated these injuries.

Dr. Lucy Rorke, a neuro-pathologist with the Philadelphia Children's Hospital, helped explain the timing of some of the injuries sustained by JonBenét. She told investigators that the blow to the skull had immediately begun to hemorrhage, and it was not likely that she would have regained consciousness after receiving this injury. The blow to the head, if left untreated, would have been fatal.

The presence of cerebral edema, swelling of the brain, suggested that JonBenét had survived for some period of time after receiving the blow to her head. Blood from the injury slowly began to fill the cavity of the skull and began to build up pressure on her brain. As pressure increased, swelling was causing the medulla of the brain to push through the foramen magnum, the narrow opening at the base of the skull.

Dr. Rorke estimated that it would have taken an hour or so for the cerebral edema to develop, but that this swelling had not yet caused JonBenét's death. "Necrosis," neurological changes to the brain cells, indicated a period of survival after the blow that could have ranged from between forty-five (45) minutes and two (2) hours.

As pressure in her skull increased, JonBenét was beginning to experience the effects of "brain death." Her neurological and biological systems were beginning to shut down, and she may have been exhibiting signs of cheyne-stokes breathing. These are short, gasping breaths that may be present as the body struggles to satisfy its need for oxygen in the final stages of death.

The medical experts were in agreement: the blow to JonBenét's skull had taken place some period of time prior to her death by strangulation. The bruising beneath the garrote and the petechial hemorrhaging in her face and eyes were conclusive evidence that she was still alive when the tightening of the ligature ended her life.

The medical consultants considered the timing of the tracking of the pineapple that had moved through JonBenét's digestive track. It was generally agreed that the timing of the ingestion of this fruit could have coincided with the time frame regarding her head injury. It was estimated that it would have taken between two to five hours for the pineapple to move through her system. It appeared to investigators that she had eaten the pineapple not long before receiving the blow to her head.

Dr. Werner Spitz, forensic medical examiner for Wayne County, Michigan, had conducted extensive studies on the wounds caused by the application of force and was considered a leading expert on the topic.

He offered an opinion on the sequencing of injuries that had been inflicted upon JonBenét during her murder:

1. This first injury sustained by JonBenét was believed to have been the constriction marks on the sides and front of her throat. He believed that her assailant had grabbed her shirt from the front and twisted the collar in their fist. The cloth from the edge of the collar had created the discolored, striated bruising and abrasions on the sides of her neck, and the knuckles of the perpetrator had caused the triangular shaped bruise located on the front side of her throat.

2. JonBenét reached up to her neck with her hands to attempt to pull away the collar causing some nail gouges / abrasions with her fingernails on the side of her throat.

3. Released from the grasp of the perpetrator, JonBenét turned and was struck in the upper right side of her head with a blunt object. Dr. Spitz would subsequently offer the opinion that the barrel of the Maglite brand flashlight found on the kitchen counter of the Ramsey home was consistent with the rectangular shape of the skull fracture. JonBenét's head injury continued to bleed internally until her strangulation.

4. The blow would have rendered JonBenét unconscious and accounted for the absence of any additional defensive wounds on her body. (Dr. Meyer had noted during autopsy no further signs of struggle, i.e. broken fingernails, bruising on her hands or fingernail scrapes on her face near the duct tape.)

5. Inflicted perimortem with her death, was the insertion of the paintbrush handle into JonBenét's vaginal orifice. The presence of inflammation and blood in the vaginal vault indicated that she was still alive when this assault took place, but it was believed that this took place at or very near the actual time of her death.

6. The last injury sustained was the tightening of the garrote around JonBenét's throat that resulted in her death by strangulation / asphyxiation.

Investigators would also enlist the aid of a knot expert, John Van Tassel of the Royal Canadian Mounted Police. He would eventually determine that the slip knots used in the wrist and neck ligatures were of standard fare. The end of the cord wrapped around the remains of the paintbrush were observed to be concentric loops and ended in a simple hitch that secured the knot in place. Again, there was nothing particularly fancy about the knots suggesting that a skilled perpetrator had been responsible for tying them.

Investigators took note of the fact that the end of the cord wrapped around the broken paintbrush handle was burned – melted. The manufacturer of these types of nylon cords will burn or melt the ends during production so that the ends will not fray and disassemble. In this instance, it appeared that the cord tied around the handle of the garrote was the first piece used from a new roll of cord and that the pieces of the other ends, all frayed, had been cut with a sharp instrument.

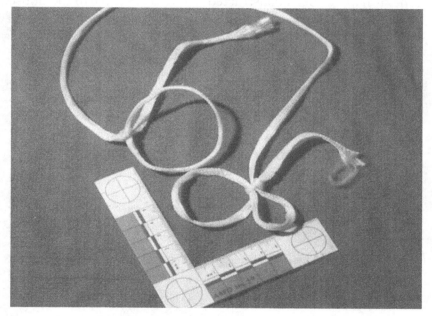

Photo 10 - Wrist bindings used to tie JonBenét. The length of cord between the wrist loops was 15 ½ inches Source. Boulder PD Case File / Internet

If the pieces of cord had been used in sequence to their cutting and assembly, it appeared to investigators that the garrote could have been the first of the pieces applied in JonBenét's death. The piece of cord used to bind her wrists, an important element in the *control* of a kidnap victim, might not have been applied until after the noose had been wrapped around JonBenét's neck.

This fact, coupled with the odd length of cord that separated the loose bindings used on her wrists suggested that some form of "staging" might be taking place.[1] It was a matter of speculation to be certain, but only the killer would know for sure the sequence in which the cord had been applied to JonBenét.

Moreover, given the fact that JonBenét's hair was entangled in the slip knot at the back of her neck, investigators concluded that the perpetrator had fashioned this ligature spontaneously at the scene. It had not been constructed before their entry to the house.

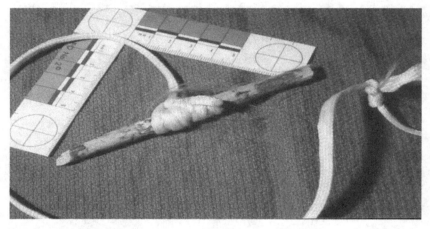

Photo 11 - JonBenét's hair intertwined in knot at stick and loop of garrote. This instrument was constructed at the scene at the time of her death. Source: Boulder PD Case File / Internet

As noted previously, John Ramsey had removed the piece of tape covering his daughter's mouth upon discovering her body. Investigators would closely examine the markings on JonBenét's face to determine the location of its placement. Mucous emitting from her nose suggested to them that the tape had been placed over her mouth after some period of time and not necessarily at the outset of her abduction.

Additionally, there was the impression of a perfect set of imprints of JonBenét's lips on the sticky side of the tape.

Investigators thought that if she had been alive and struggling at the time of its placement, the imprint would have been irregular and smeared.

Mucous beneath the tape and the perfect imprint of lips led investigators to believe that this might have been another element of staging that had taken place after JonBenét's death.

Investigators would subsequently obtain records of JonBenét's medical treatment from the office of her Pediatrician, Dr. Francesco Beuf. They would learn that JonBenét had visited the doctor's office on thirty-three (33) occasions over the previous three (3) years and that Patsy Ramsey had called his offices three (3) times on the evening of December 17th. The reason for those calls was never determined.

It should be noted that JonBenét's pediatrician contradicted the opinions of the experts who believed prior sexual contact had taken place before JonBenét's murder. Having seen and treated JonBenét for various ailments on thirty-three occasions over the course of a 3 year period of time, he would state that he never witnessed signs of vaginal abuse being present during her visits.

And though it was reported that a number of these visits were for vaginitis thought to be related to JonBenét's bedwetting problems, it is not clear if it were his practice to conduct full vaginal exams on 6-year-old girls at the time that he provided this statement.

As helpful as all of this information was in painting a picture of what happened to JonBenét, it did not specifically identify the person responsible for her murder.

Rowan and Blewitt Incorporated
Memorandum
To: The News Media
From: Pat Korten

John and Patsy Ramsey have cooperated extensively with police and other law enforcement authorities since the very beginning of their investigation, and this cooperation will continue. Written answers to all the written questions submitted by the Boulder Police Department have been delivered to them this afternoon.

——Press release provided by Ramsey publicist Pat Korten in
    January, 1997

Media Wars

On Saturday, December 28th, 1996, Assistant District Attorney Pete Hoffstrom informed detectives that the family had retained legal counsel and were not willing to meet with police investigators. He suggested that any questions they had be reduced to writing, and he would forward these to Ramsey defense counsel.

A list of 16 early questions was presented to Hoffstrom, but it took weeks before the answers to these basic questions were returned to authorities. Clarifying questions posed were like the following:

- What was JonBenét wearing when she went to bed that night?
- What did JonBenét have to eat that night?

These were basic things that police had not been able to record during the hectic events of the morning.

Rick French at one point characterized his efforts at obtaining information as a series of twenty hectic and scattered discussions taking place, during which time some things were never pinned down.

The circumstances surrounding these early events were puzzling to investigators. It was understandable that the family needed the time to make arrangements to bury their child, but why wouldn't the family want to meet with the people responsible for investigating the death of their daughter?

The Ramseys had not yet returned to Boulder after the services in Georgia and were already taking steps to engage the media. At some juncture during their stay in Atlanta, a family friend with connections was able to arrange an interview with CNN.

This course of action, and the fact that attorneys had been hired to represent the Ramsey family, reportedly upset Fleet White, who had accompanied the family to Georgia for the services. White could not understand why the family was delaying their return to Colorado to begin their interviews with authorities.

At one point, White became agitated during a telephone conversation with John Ramsey's brother, Jeff, and headed to the family home to continue the discussion. The brother was frightened by the conversation, and Don Paugh, Patsy Ramsey's father, reportedly hid a handgun beneath the cushions of his living room couch in anticipation of trouble. John Ramsey calmed everyone down before White arrived, and nothing further came of the incident.

Rod Westmoreland was said to have been responsible for setting up the CNN interview for John and Patsy, but the Ramseys would later state that it was Fleet White who had encouraged them to go on national television.[2] This representation was entirely contrary to White's expressed feelings for the matter, and he was having a difficult time with decisions being made by the family during this time. He subsequently booked a commercial flight home rather than fly on the private jet that transported the family and other friends.

John Ramsey stated during the January 1, 1997, CNN interview that the family was now ready to return to Boulder and work with authorities, but that didn't come to fruition. They instead took refuge in the home of "Pasta Jay" Elowski and appeared to continue to fortify their team of attorneys. John Ramsey went so far as to hire attorneys to represent members of the Paugh family, and even his ex-wife, Lucinda Johnson.

A Denver-based private investigative firm, Ellis Armistead, joined the team of attorneys being assembled to work the Ramsey's side of the inquiry.

The Washington, D.C. public relations firm of Rowan and Blewitt was retained, and soon Pat Korten was handling the media and releasing public statements for the family.

Police continued to attempt to set up one-on-one interviews with each of the parents, but no one could agree to a time and place or the duration of said interview. The days stretched into weeks, and the weeks lapsed into months. At one juncture, police had agreed to meet with the family at an off-site location from their headquarters, but subsequently cancelled just days before the meeting, after the FBI counseled them that the interviews should be taking place on their home turf.

Ramsey attorneys had a field day with the media. They claimed cooperation on the part of the family, but that the police were being obstinate.

The father of Polly Klass, a 12-year-old child kidnapped and murdered by a pedophile in California in 1993, publically criticized the Ramsey family in early January 1997 for their behavior in the matter:

"I think the parents made some terrible mistakes thus far by hiring lawyers and a publicist and refusing to talk to police."[3]

From his personal perspective, Marc Klaas believed that the parents of a murdered child ought to be working side-by-side with police investigators and not hiding behind the legal pads of high-priced attorneys.

In the meantime, Ramsey's PR firm began to get busy and helped publicize the formation of a foundation named in memory of JonBenét. A non-profit 501 (c)(3) corporation was established with John and Patsy Ramsey listed as the board members, and appropriate paperwork was filed with the State of Colorado and the IRS on March 31, 1997. Subsequent tax documents reported that the "JonBenét Ramsey Children's Foundation" intended to do the following:

1. Provide opportunities to children to develop their talents
2. Build a strong spiritual foundation in children
3. Promote the safety of children
4. Promote education on effective parenting and nurturing
5. Affirm and recognize children who demonstrate compassion for and service to others.
6. Recognize responsible journalism that affects children and families and promotes good in the world for children

The foundation listed its intention to fund organizations or programs that met the objectives listed above. It did not intend to conduct any fundraising efforts, but indicated that it would rely upon donations from family members, friends, corporations and unsolicited donations to fund its charitable causes.

The foundation also publically offered a reward of $100,000 for information leading to the arrest and conviction of the person(s) believed responsible for the kidnap and murder of JonBenét. A reward poster depicting a photograph of JonBenét was printed for distribution along with a private telephone tip line, with no association to the police department or Crime Stoppers listed on the document.

Press releases prepared by the PR firm appeared with some regularity in the Denver area print media throughout the spring and summer of 1997.

A website, www.ramseyfamily.com, was established in the spring of 1997, and the reward information was posted there, along with a chronological history of the press releases that had been prepared in the Ramsey's private search for the perpetrators of the crime.

The Ramseys had also hired retired FBI profiler John Douglas to assist them in the case. His involvement is covered a little more in depth in a later chapter, but Douglas flew to Denver and met with their attorneys on January 8, 1997.

By this time, rumors of prior sexual abuse had been flowing through the media reports, and people were jumping to the conclusion that John Ramsey had been responsible for the molestation of his daughter. Regrettably, some of JonBenét's reward posters would show up around town with the father's name plastered all over them.

Douglas reports that one of the primary reasons he had been retained by attorneys was to evaluate the possible involvement of John Ramsey in the death of his daughter. Though they did not specifically say it, he was under the impression that his attorneys wanted to know if their client was guilty.[4]

Douglas met with John Ramsey for a couple hours on the morning of January 9, 1997, and proceeded to go over the events of the kidnapping. Ramsey became very emotional as he described finding the body of his daughter. To the relief of attorneys, Douglas advised that he didn't believe their client had been responsible for the murder of JonBenét.

Douglas then met jointly with John and Patsy in the presence of their attorney. Both parents spoke of their experiences and recollections of the day that JonBenét had been kidnapped and murdered and stated that they wanted to cooperate with authorities in their investigation. Based upon their behavior, Douglas formed the opinion that neither of the parents had killed JonBenét.

Though he had not specifically been hired by Ramsey attorneys to establish a criminal profile of the perpetrator(s) believed responsible for this crime, Douglas offered an early theory during his meeting with the family. He thought that perhaps a "personal cause offender" may have been involved, primarily because of the revenge aspects noted in the ransom note.

Attorneys had to have breathed a sigh of relief. A nationally recognized expert in the field of criminal profiling had voiced the opinion that neither of the parents was believed responsible for murdering their daughter.

In spite of not having had the opportunity to review the full complement of police reports, Douglas would eventually work up a behavioral profile for a possible offender that would subsequently be included in advertisements prepared by Ramsey's PR firm.

Douglas would be interviewed by network media regarding his participation in the investigation, and he eventually devoted an entire chapter to this effort in one of the many books he authored on the subject of "criminal profiling."[5]

Police, prosecutors, and Ramsey attorneys continued to do battle in the media as they tried to find common ground for a follow-up interview with the parents. Both sides eventually reached consensus. John and Patsy would be interviewed individually by police investigators on April 30, 1997, for a time period not to exceed eight (8) hours. Breaks and lunch would take place over the course of the day of questioning.

What a coup. Over four (4) months had passed since the discovery of JonBenét's body, and now Boulder Police had finally been able to convince the parents of this murdered child to sit down with them to answer some basic questions about the death of their daughter.

The Ramseys would continue to broadcast their message to the media following that interview. In July 1997, they issued another press release that seemed to decry the Boulder Police Department's focus on them as suspects in the murder of their daughter.

The release, really an advertisement, listed behavioral clues that the public should be alerted to, and requested that anyone with information contact their private team of investigators who were "taking a new approach to their search."

They announced that the perpetrator(s) might have exhibited the following type of behavior around the time of the kidnapping:

- Conflict with a female
- Conflict with family
- Financial stress
- Marital problems
- Legal problems
- Employment problems
- Did that person then suffer a traumatic event, such as the break-up of an important relationship, loss of a job, or some other disruption in his life that could have triggered violent behavior? Did that person express hostility and anger at either of us or our family? Was he depressed, perhaps using drugs or alcohol?

In August, they issued an advertisement in which they asked the public if they recognized some aspects of the handwriting depicted in the ransom note and included certain letter combinations found in the wording of the note.

In another release, the public was asked to recall details about a male who purportedly had been approaching little girls around the 1996 Christmas holidays. This was the first Boulder Police investigators had heard about such a tip, and the details on how this lead was developed are scant.

The press releases and advertisements would continue unabated for a number of years as the Ramseys financed their own search for the person(s) believed responsible for the murder of their daughter.

The first six months of the investigation were a rocky time, however, as the Ramseys proclaimed that there was a killer on the loose in Boulder.

City authorities contradicted that opinion, continuing to maintain that Boulder was a safe community and that its citizens shouldn't be concerned that a child murderer was running amuck. These statements suggested that police were not hunting for a kidnapper / intruder who would have been responsible for the crime. If not an intruder, then who *was* responsible for the murder of this six-year-old girl?

The politics of the media wars made for good entertainment, and it seemed that at every opportunity the Ramsey publicists were chastising Boulder Police for focusing all of their investigative efforts on the family and not on other potential suspects.

The media exchanges would go on for years.[6]

The First Forty-Eight

L aw enforcement officials will often tell you that the initial steps taken in the first twenty-four to forty-eight hours in any felony investigation, and especially in a homicide inquiry, are crucial to the success of resolving a case.

Witnesses need to be located and interviewed; search warrants for potential pieces of evidence need to be prepared and executed before they are hidden or destroyed; suspects need to be developed, identified and interrogated; alibis need to be checked out and other timelines regarding events need to be mapped out.

The first hours can be a very hectic time, and due to the many tasks that are required of a significant investigative effort, many resources are poured into the first days of a criminal investigation.

In this particular instance, however, the *primary witnesses* to this abduction and murder had driven away from the crime scene shortly after the discovery of the body of the victim. Instead of immediately gathering the family at the station for more detailed interviews, Boulder Police were rallying their resources to properly handle the processing of the crime scene, and to track down several of the suspects who had initially been named by them.

It never occurred to them that the parents would not be ready and willing to sit down with them after they had taken care of some of these critical tasks, one of which included having a clear understanding of how JonBenét had died. The forty minutes spent with John Ramsey on the evening of December 27th, following the completion of the autopsy of his daughter, failed to establish a firm date and time for a follow-up interview, and it left detectives wondering what was going on.

That did not deter investigators, however, from moving forward in their attempts to interview other witnesses, or potential suspects in the case.

Ramsey housekeeper, Linda **Hoffmann-Pugh** and husband Mervin Pugh, lived in Ft. Lupton, about a forty-five minute drive from Boulder. Because she had been named as a possible suspect by the parents, BPD Detectives Fred Patterson and Greg Idler paid her home a visit on the afternoon – evening of December 26th, not long after the discovery of JonBenét's body.

Word of the kidnapping and murder had not yet reached the **Hoffmann-Pugh** household, and the detectives obtained some preliminary information before explaining the nature of their visit. Patterson advised that Boulder Police had received a call that morning reporting the kidnapping of JonBenét.

The first words out of Hoffman-Pugh's mouth were, "Oh my God! Oh my God!"

Patterson told her that there was a kidnap note. **Hoffmann-Pugh** was beginning to exhibit signs of distress, and he told her to settle down and to listen to what he was trying to say. He again explained that there was a note and that JonBenét was missing, and that they were talking to a number of people who knew and worked for the family.

Hoffmann-Pugh again exclaimed, "Oh my God," and stated that she "would never do anything like that."

She told the investigators that several months earlier she had talked to Patsy about JonBenét and Burke walking to school alone, and JonBenét playing outside on her skates. She had wondered if Patsy was ever fearful of JonBenét being kidnapped under those circumstances. Hoffmann-Pugh reported that she had talked to no one other than Patsy about those concerns.

Hoffmann-Pugh seemed to be unclear as to what was happen-ing, and asked the investigators if JonBenét was gone, if she was still missing at that moment.

The detective paused momentarily, and then told her that JonBenét had been murdered.

Hoffmann-Pugh screamed, and broke down so completely that the investigators were unable to complete as thorough an interview as they had desired. The remainder of their questions would have to wait until the following day.

Investigators would eventually learn that Hoffmann-Pugh had requested a loan of two-thousand dollars ($2,000.00) from Patsy to help pay the rent, purchase some car parts, and to complete some dental work her husband needed. He too had done some odd-jobs around the house over the years for the Ramsey family, and this included decorating the home for the Christmas holidays and family parties. The Christmas trees and decorations had been stored in the Wine Cellar and basement of the home.

Like many others who would be interviewed by BPD investigators, Linda Hoffmann-Pugh described the home as a warren of doors and oddly placed rooms. Finding the specific door that led to the basement was no easy task, and she felt that whoever had perpetrated this crime had to have had some level of familiarity with the layout of the home.

During her follow-up interview, Hoffmann-Pugh indicated that there were not a lot of extra sheets for JonBenét's bed, and she reported that JonBenét had been wearing pull-up diapers during her first six months of employment with the family. She had been wetting the bed nearly every night of the week.

Hoffmann-Pugh indicated that the bed-wetting eventually subsided, but that it had begun again in the month or so preceding the 1996 Christmas holidays. It went on nightly for about a week, and then she thought it to be occurring every other night. **Hoffmann-Pugh** indicated that she worked every other day. When she arrived at the home, the sheets to JonBenét's bed were already stripped and in the washing machine located in the hallway outside her room. She indicated that this activity was taking place right up until about a week before JonBenét's murder.

Hoffmann-Pugh also told investigators that the bed-wetting problem extended to the soiling of her sheets. She reported once finding fecal material the size of a grapefruit in JonBenét's bed.†

JonBenét's problem with bed-wetting was of interest to investigators, and it figured as one early component in their theory that Patsy Ramsey may have lost her cool with her daughter over this behavior.

Investigators queried **Hoffmann-Pugh** about the type of duct tape and cord she had seen around the house during her employ-ment with the family. Nothing that she could recall seeing matched the description of the implements used in JonBenét's murder.

Investigators wondered, given their examination of the cord used in the garrote, if one or both of these items had been recently purchased items. Their requests for a search warrant seeking credit card charges, like similar requests for telephone records, were shot down by the D.A.'s office, and it would be months later in November, 1997, that a white, Stansport brand nylon cord would be identified as the make of cord used to bind and garrote JonBenét.

In May, 1997, investigators had purchased examples of this type of nylon cord from the Boulder Army Store and McGuckin's Hardware. They would eventually determine that Patsy Ramsey had purchased an item from the sporting goods section of McGuckin's on December 2, 1996, for $2.29, the same price as that of the nylon cord purchased by the detectives during their investigation.

The McGuckin receipts did not specifically detail the *identity* of the items purchased, but investigators thought it too coincidental that the cord had come from the same part of the store, and had the same retail price as Patsy Ramsey's receipt. By the time this information came into their hands, however, the video surveillance tapes at the store had already been recorded over.

Investigators were surprised to learn that Ramsey attorneys and their investigators had already interviewed Fleet White on the afternoon of December 27th. In fact, they had called him on the afternoon of the previous day, not long after the discovery of JonBenét's body.

White's interview with BPD detectives took place late in the day on December 27th, and ultimately, he would be interviewed on three separate occasions regarding his activities at the Ramsey home.

White told investigators that Patsy had called his home early Thursday morning, December 26th, indicating that something had happened, and she needed them to come over immediately. He, and his wife, Priscilla, drove to the home and observed uniformed police officers on the scene. They soon learned that JonBenét had been kidnapped and that a ransom note had been left.

Something apparently didn't ring true to White, and despite the presence of a kidnap note that demanded ransom, he decided to take a tour of the basement to look for JonBenét. He indicated that this was within approximately 15 minutes of his arrival at the home.

White's daughter, 6-year-old Daphne, was a playmate of JonBenét, and she had gone missing about a year previously. She was eventually found asleep in the family home, so White was intimately familiar with the feelings of panic that were generated under such circumstances.

Ransom note notwithstanding, White called JonBenét's name as he moved through the rooms of the basement. He found himself looking at a broken window pane in a series of three windows that opened to a subterranean window well. The window was closed, but not latched, and he observed a hard-sided Samsonite suitcase standing flush against the wall directly beneath the window. He spent some time inspecting the area for signs of freshly broken glass and moved the suitcase to get a better look at the floor.

White told investigators that he only found a "small kernel" of glass on the floor and placed it on the windowsill before leaving the room. He left the window in its closed, unlatched condition.[7]

He then moved out of the Train Room, and down a short, dead-end hallway to a storage room that would later be identified as the Wine Cellar. A block of wood rotated on a screw to secure the door to this room, and he reportedly "unlocked" the door and peered inside. It was pitch black inside the windowless room, and unable to find a light switch, he closed the door and secured it with the wood block.

White returned upstairs and didn't mention his tour of the basement to anyone at the time.

The house began to fill with people that morning, as additional police officers, CSIs, and victim advocates arrived to take care of business. Father Rol Holverstock had been summoned to help console Patsy. It wasn't long before family friends were inquiring about the status of Burke. Was he okay? Was he still asleep?

Patsy was a veritable wreck, and they thought it probably wasn't a good idea for Burke to see his mother in her condition. Fleet White volunteered to take Burke to his house, where visiting family were caring for his children. The Fernies decided to send their children there as well.

White indicated that Burke was retrieved from his bedroom by his father, and according to the latter, was told that his sister was missing. He was going to spend some time at his friend's house,

Fleet White Jr., so he quickly dressed and grabbed his new Nintendo computer game before heading out of the house.

White left the Ramsey home with Burke before the first detectives arrived on the scene, which was at approximately 0800 hours. He later told investigators there had been very little conversation between the two of them in the car, and that Burke asked him no questions about his sister's disappearance, or about the presence of uniformed police officers in his home that morning.

White returned to the home after depositing Burke with his relatives and would ultimately accompany John Ramsey to the basement when Detective Arndt suggested that the house be checked "from top to bottom" for anything unusual early that afternoon.

White reported that he had followed Ramsey to the Train Room where they spent some time talking about the broken window. Ramsey told him that he had broken into the house through that window earlier that summer, and that he had failed to have the glass repaired. He had said nothing about the placement of the suitcase beneath the broken window.

They looked around for signs of more broken glass, and finding none, Ramsey then moved from the room.

Concurrent with this activity, White had stopped to move a fireplace grate that was blocking a closet in the Train Room. Quickly checking the interior, he had moved the grate back into place and was headed out into the hallway when he heard John Ramsey scream. He indicated that he was right behind Ramsey and saw him kneeling down next to JonBenét's body in the Wine Cellar.

An overhead light had been turned on in the room, and he saw that JonBenét was wrapped in a blanket on the floor. Her feet were sticking out at the bottom, and he bent over to touch them: they were cold to the touch.

White stated that he then immediately ran upstairs, shouting for someone to call an ambulance. Ramsey was close on his heels, carrying the body of his daughter outstretched before him. Detective Arndt directed Ramsey to put her down at the top of the basement stairs, and she then subsequently moved the body to the floor of the living room.

Detective Arndt had directed White to stand guard at the top of the basement stairs before moving into the living room with JonBenét. For unknown reasons, he again went to the basement and took a quick look around the Wine Cellar. He told investigators that he handled a piece of black duct-type tape from the floor and had also handled a cigar box in the room. Leaving these items behind, he then returned upstairs and awaited the cavalry.

Investigators learned that Ramsey attorneys had been quick to contact the Fernie family as well. It seemed that the family had been dedicating resources to the search for the killer(s) as quickly as law enforcement authorities.

John Fernie reiterated a tale similar to that of Fleet White: the early morning phone call of some emergency taking place at the Ramsey home and the request that they come immediately. Fernie had arrived by way of the back alley and had approached the rear kitchen door to see the ransom note spread out upon the floor inside the home. It was upside down from his perspective, but he was able to read the salutation, "Mr. Ramsey," and the sentence of the first page before heading around to the front of the house.

Fernie joined the company of two uniformed officers and the Whites at the street-side entrance to the home. He was directed to the solarium, and later that morning, was able to read a photocopy of the full three pages of the ransom note that had been brought back to the home. He thought the note was very personal, and written in a "condescending" manner towards John Ramsey. He noted at one point during his interview with detectives that the note didn't make sense to him, and that it seemed to contain "some kind of fakey stuff." Things just weren't adding up to him.

Fernie seemed to recall that someone, John Ramsey he thought, had said that the doors to the home had been checked the previous evening and that all had been dead-bolted and securely locked. Ramsey had checked the doors again that morning to be certain that JonBenét had not gotten out of the house. At one point that morning, the time uncertain, but as police were processing the scene, Fernie reported that a draft was coming through the house, and he located the source: the door on the north side of the house by the Butler Pantry was standing open, and he shut it.

Over the course of interview, conducted on January 1, 1997, Barb Fernie shared a concern that had raised a question for her. As things were developing in the house on the morning of December 26th, she had begun to ask if Burke had awakened yet. She was aware that like her son, Burke was an early riser and typically got up in the morning around 5:30 a.m. She and her husband had been at the house for a while, and like others, were beginning to wonder if Burke was sitting up in his bedroom, awake and alone, while all of the commotion was going on downstairs.

She pointed out a discrepancy that created some additional concern for her. She told the investigators that Patsy Ramsey had told her on the morning of December 26th that she had just "given the ransom note to John," after finding it on the spiral staircase.

More importantly, however, Mrs. Fernie stated that she didn't know Patsy had screamed out for her husband that morning. She apparently was under the impression, based on her conversation with Patsy on the morning of the kidnapping, that she had somehow just handed off the note to her husband. Several days later, it didn't make sense to her that Burke would not have been awakened when Patsy screamed John's name.

Mrs. Fernie had been pondering the question: If John Ramsey had been able to hear Patsy scream from his bathroom on the 3rd floor of the house, why not Burke? *His* bedroom was just down the hall.

The Fernies offered their home as temporary shelter to the Ramsey family after police secured *their* home for search warrants. Barb Fernie would be interviewed again by BPD detectives not long after returning from the Georgia funeral services, and details of some of her observations are covered in a later chapter.

Father Rol Holverstock, pastor at the St. Johns Episcopalian Church, had been called to the Ramsey home on the morning of December 26th by John Fernie. The Fernies had earlier recruited the Ramseys to the church, and the pastor was well known to Patsy.

Interviewed by detectives on December 30th, Father Holverstock indicated that he had been summoned to the home to help calm Patsy, and estimated that he had arrived between 6:30 and 7:00 a.m. He described his observations of the activities taking place at the time of the discovery of JonBenét's body.

Father Holverstock advised he had been heating a glass of water in the kitchen microwave when things began to happen. Fleet White had a look on his face that he'd "never seen before," and racing past him through the kitchen, exclaimed that JonBenét had been found.

The next thing he knew, he was standing in the foyer area near the top of the basement stairs, and John Ramsey had his daughter in his hands. It was Holverstock's recollection that Ramsey blurted out, "I don't think he meant to kill her, because she was wrapped in a blanket," or that "she was warm, she was wrapped in a blanket."

Ramsey told Father Holverstock that he had taken "the tape off her mouth," and mentioned something about removing something from JonBenét's wrists or hands.

The scene was described as being "frantic" and "out of control" once JonBenét's body had been found. He did his best to lead the group in prayer after JonBenét had been moved to the floor of the living room. Father Holverstock described JonBenét's body as being cold and stiff, and that he had tried to conceal the ugly bruise on her neck by moving a blanket over her torso. He shared with the detectives that he was having a difficult time letting go of that image.

In their effort to continue to gather possible leads, Boulder investigators interviewed a number of other people. Some were family friends, employees of Ramsey's business and those involved in the beauty pageant circuit. One interview took place with family friend Barb Kostanick.

She reported that JonBenét had told her about a "secret Santa Claus," who was going to make a special visit to her after Christmas. This bit of information seemed to suggest that someone who had access to JonBenét may have been responsible for setting up this "secret" arrangement.

Investigators had to consider the possibility that JonBenét had gone willingly with her abductor because he was known, and familiar to her. Some began to point the finger at Santa Claus himself, Bill McReynolds.

"Santa Bill" was an elderly man who had played Santa Claus at several of the Ramsey holiday parties in previous years. He was not in the best of health in December 1996, but had somehow convinced Patsy to hold another Christmas party where he again was able to play the starring role for the children in attendance.

Boulder Police detectives would subsequently clear Santa of any involvement in the crime, but that didn't mean that other intruder theorists didn't resurrect his name from time to time.

A neighborhood canvas was also conducted to determine if anyone, or anything suspicious had been seen on the night of the kidnapping.

The Colby family, who lived in the alley behind the Ramsey home, had a 10-year-old son who sometimes played with Burke. They also had two dogs that reportedly barked every time they heard someone in the alley. Mrs. Colby indicated that her dogs did not bark at all Christmas night.

The Brumfit family, who lived directly south of the Ramsey home, reported that a southeast corner, ground-floor room light typically left on during the night had been observed to be out around 0230 – 0300 hours on the night of the murder.

The neighbor on the immediate north, Scott Gibbons, told detectives that he had been in his south-facing kitchen around midnight on Christmas night. He observed that the upper lights in the Ramsey kitchen were on, but dimmed low.

Gibbons didn't observe anyone inside the residence at the time, and noted that it was not unusual for lights to be on in the home at night. The following morning, around 0800 hours, he had seen the north kitchen door standing open. Investigators noted that this would have been during the time that CSIs were photographing and processing the home for latent fingerprints.

Investigators were initially told by Melody Stanton, who lived across the street and southeast of the Ramsey home, that she didn't want to become involved in the investigation and reported that she had heard nothing unusual that night.

During a follow-up canvass, Stanton appeared to be more willing to cooperate. She told detectives that she had gone to bed around 2200 hours on Christmas night. Her open bedroom window faced in the direction of the Ramsey home, and she thought she had heard a child scream sometime between the hours of midnight and 2:00 a.m.

The scream of a child at that time of night was of definite interest to the investigators, and they would subsequently return to the Ramsey home to conduct simulated tests on the possibility that Stanton was correct in her observations. For unknown reasons, however, she would later recant her statement, and it was a clue that only seemed to add to the confusion of the investigation.

A number of neighborhood doors were knocked upon during Boulder PD's canvass of the area. Unfortunately, no one came forward with any probative information that could help identify the person(s) responsible for JonBenét's kidnap and murder.

CHAPTER NINE

Ransom Note and 911 Audio Tapes

The ransom note is undeniably one of the most important pieces of physical evidence that was left at the scene by the person responsible for either murdering JonBenét, or having had a hand in the circumstances surrounding her death. No other explanation has been produced that would otherwise account for its presence in the home.

Given the manner in which events unfolded in this crime, the question arises as to what real purpose was intended in the crafting of this document. As explained in later chapters, the motive for a kidnapping typically involves an exchange of a victim for something of value. In this instance it appears as though no true effort was made to remove the kidnapped victim from the home so that an exchange could eventually be made for the one-hundred eighteen thousand dollars ($118,000.00) demanded in the note.

Since the motive may have been something other than monetary gain, it was theorized that a pedophile may have been responsible for authoring the note and had done so to throw investigators off the true path of motive.

In spite of a demand for ransom, some investigators theorized that the perpetrator of this crime was a disturbed child molester who had developed a raging obsession with this beautiful little girl.

It had also been theorized that it was someone who was intimately familiar with the family and extremely angry over some perceived wrong committed by John Ramsey. Had this individual set out to destroy Ramsey's life by torturing and murdering his daughter?

Or, was there another motive? Had someone in the immediate family crafted the note to draw suspicion away from a family member's involvement in the death of JonBenét? If this was the case, was JonBenét's death an accident or one of premeditation?

Those were the perplexing questions facing investigators as they attempted to piece together the puzzling aspects of this child's murder.

Patsy Ramsey described the circumstances under which she first found the note but she was not clear as to whether she had carried it upstairs to John when she rushed to JonBenét's bedroom, or if he alone had been responsible for removing it from the spiral stairs tread. Under these circumstances, one or both sets of their fingerprints should have been found on the note.

One thing is certain, however. The only latent fingerprints found on the note belonged to Colorado Bureau of Investigation forensic handwriting examiner Chet Ubowski. No other latent fingerprints were located, either for Patsy or John Ramsey, or for the "kidnapper" who had left the note behind to clarify their alleged motive for the commission of the crime.

The origin of the note was called into question within the first few hours of the kidnap investigation. When Sgt. Bob Whitson asked John Ramsey for samples of handwriting for him and his wife, Ramsey grabbed a pad of paper and wrote out the following: "Now is the time for all good men."

He also produced another pad of paper from the kitchen that he described as belonging to Patsy. Sgt. Whitson subsequently transported these handwriting exemplars to the police department and gave them over to Detective Jeff Kithcart, the department's fraud and handwriting examiner. Kithcart was charged with conducting a preliminary analysis of comparing known handwriting samples to the ransom note for elimination purposes.

During his examination of Patsy Ramsey's note pad, Kithcart made a startling discovery. As he thumbed through the pad, looking at the handwriting, he noted what appeared to be the start of another ransom note. The words started out at the top of the page, as the addressing of a name would be written, "Mr. and Mrs. l".

The "l" looked like the down stroke of the capital letter "R" that could signify that the writer was preparing to address the note to "Mr. and Mrs. Ramsey." It was an important discovery because it appeared to him that the note pad identified as belonging to Pasty may have been used by the kidnapper(s) to write the original ransom note. Moreover, it suggested that the ransom note may have been composed from materials within the home and not prepared before the kidnapper(s) had entered the residence.

Kithcart headed to the briefing room where police investigators and FBI agents were discussing the investigation to share his discovery, but ended up walking into a chaotic scene. The group had just received word that JonBenét's body had been found in the basement of the Ramsey home. It would be several hours before he would be able to share this information with people in charge of the investigation.

The entire notepad would eventually be examined by agents of the Colorado Bureau of Investigation, and they determined that the ransom note had indeed been written on Patsy Ramsey's pad of paper.

Chet Ubowski determined that the first 12 pages of the notepad were missing. Police never found these pages, and it was presumed that they had been discarded as a matter of routine and not necessarily germane to the criminal investigation at hand.

The next four pages, 13 through 16, were intact and contained miscellaneous writings, doodling and some lists.

The next sequence of pages, 17 through 25, were missing and had been torn from the pad and were never found by police. The "practice note," discovered by Kithcart, was located on page 26. Ubowski observed on page 26 signs of ink bleed-through from the missing 25th page.

The perforated tabs at the top of the sheets of paper on which the ransom note had been written were matched to the torn tabs remaining on the notepad. Comparison of the torn segments of the 3-page ransom note matched the missing pages 27, 28, and 29.

To investigators, it appeared that at least one, and perhaps two attempts had been made at starting a ransom note on pages 25 and 26 before the final product was completed on pages 27 through 29.

Ubowski further advised investigators that, based upon his examination of handwriting on the ransom note, and known samples collected from Patsy Ramsey, he believed 24 out of the 26 letters of the alphabet matched her handwriting style.

Seven (7) latent fingerprints were able to be developed on the notepad, and CBI technicians identified one print as belonging to BPD Sergeant Robert Whitson, the person who had collected the pad from John Ramsey on the morning of the kidnapping. A print belonging to CBI Technician Chet Ubowski was identified, and the remaining five (5) latent prints were identified as belonging to Patsy Ramsey.

Boulder investigators called upon the expertise of the United States Secret Service for an examination of the felt tip pens collected from the Ramsey residence during the execution of their search warrants. Three felt tip pens had been seized from a cup holder located on the kitchen counter beneath the telephone that Patsy Ramsey had used to call 911.

The Secret Service, responsible for investigating counterfeit currency and forgery cases maintains the largest database of ink exemplars in the world. They examined the ink from each of the writing instruments submitted by Boulder authorities and eventually identified a pre-November 1992 water-based Sharpie felt tip pen as the instrument that had been used to write both the practice and ransom notes.

The ink on the ransom note exclusively matched the ink from one of the Sharpie pens found in the kitchen of the Ramsey home and was not far from where John Ramsey had produced the note pad belonging to his wife.

The combination of the CBI and Secret Service forensic findings were significant. It meant that the author of the note had used instruments found within the home to craft their ransom demands. To investigators, this information meant that the perpetrator(s) had not been very well prepared. Who goes to the trouble of planning an elaborate kidnapping and forgets to bring a ransom note to the scene?

It was apparent that it had taken some time to write the note and given the possible existence of a practice note and additional missing pages from the pad, investigators wondered why an intruder would take such an extraordinary risk of being discovered by taking the time to write the note while in the home. The author either was a sociopath who had no fear of confrontation with the family or they had to feel very much at ease in their surroundings.

The "hard" forensic examinations completed, Boulder authorities now turned their attention to the "softer" science of handwriting mechanics and linguistics. They were sometimes criticized for their efforts of "shopping" for a handwriting expert, for over the course of the investigation no fewer than 5 nationally recognized handwriting experts would compare known handwriting samples of potential suspects to the writing of the ransom note.

One by one, experts eliminated the handwriting exemplars of one potential suspect after another. This included the early exclusion of JonBenét's father and her siblings.

And while opinions varied as to their certainty, no one could eliminate Patsy Ramsey as the possible author of the ransom note. There continued to be indications that she was altering her handwriting exemplars, and she eventually would provide 5 different sets of handwriting samples over time.

CBI agent Chet Ubowski would tell investigators privately that he believed Patsy Ramsey was responsible for authoring the note, but seemed unwilling to testify to that opinion in an open court of law.

Vassar Professor Donald Foster was brought into the case by D.A. Alex Hunter mid-year in 1997. Foster, unlike the other handwriting experts utilized up to that point in time, focused his examination of written materials on the "textual analysis" of the content of the document. This involved more than studying and comparing the mechanics of how a letter of the alphabet was *written,* but what he described as the "distinctive linguistic fingerprint" that each individual forms over the course of their lifetime.

Foster's hypothesis is that we are unable to falsify who we are when we compose our written words. Our sentence structure, use of punctuation and spacing, word usage and a combination of other identifying features create a signature unique to each individual. He has been quoted as saying that, "No two people have the same vocabulary or writing style....a writer's use of language is as distinctive, as inimitable, as unique as one's DNA."

Professor Foster first made a name for himself as a graduate student at the University of California in 1984 where he was studying Renaissance literature. He found an anonymous poem eulogizing a murdered actor and after some period of extended research proved it to be a lost 1612 work of William Shakespeare.

Years later, after having further refined his techniques, he discovered the identity of the author who anonymously wrote the highly publicized book, *Primary Colors*. Foster utilized a computer program to search for similarities of the sentence structure and phrases used in the book and compared them to the known writings of other individuals. *Newsweek* columnist Joe Klein's published writings stood out, and Foster identified Klein as the anonymous author of the work.

The textual analysis and syntax discovered over the course of the computer search revealed Klein's favored use of adjectives like "lugubrious" and "puckish." More specifically, Foster discovered that Klein had used the phrase "tarmac-hopping" in both a column and in *Primary Colors*.[8]

It took Klein 6 months of denial before he finally admitted to authoring the book.

Though Foster was primarily a scholar, his "detective" work regarding textual analysis would eventually lead to his participation in many criminal cases, including the infamous Unabomber investigation. Originally hired by the defense to refute the FBI's analysis of Theodore Kaczynski's writings, Foster eventually confirmed their findings. He issued the opinion that he believed Kaczynski had in fact authored the Unabomber's lengthy manifesto.[9]

Foster was one of the leading authorities on the technique of "textual analysis" and Hunter may have first become aware of his expertise after his office received some correspondence from Susan Bennett, a North Carolina JonBenét Internet junkie who blogged under the alias of "Jameson."

Bennett reportedly sent a package of Internet materials to the D.A.'s office in July 1997 that included some correspondence that took place between "Jameson" and Professor Foster in an Internet chat room. It was during these exchanges with "Jameson" that Foster purportedly had mistakenly identified the writings as belonging to John Andrew Ramsey, JonBenét's older step brother. He felt that "Jameson's" writings belonged to John Andrew and that he was responsible for the murder of JonBenét, a belief he later discarded.

Foster had also written a letter to Patsy Ramsey in June 1997 suggesting that he thought she was innocent, offering his assistance in the matter.[10] Hunter decided to send to Foster the handwriting samples of a couple other key suspects in the case, "Santa" Bill and Janet McReynolds. Foster examined these samples and subsequently advised Hunter that he didn't believe either of these people were responsible for authoring the ransom note.

Hunter reportedly lost interest in the value of the professor's skills at that juncture and turned him over to Boulder Police investigators, failing to inform them of Foster's Internet involvement with "Jameson." Boulder investigators then supplied him with a variety of handwriting exemplars from other possible suspects, including those of Patsy Ramsey. For the first time he now had an opportunity to review handwriting collected from the mother of the murdered child. After a couple months of review, Professor Foster was ready to share his findings and travelled to Boulder in March 1998 to give a presentation on the documents.

As described by Detective Steve Thomas, Foster conducted a day-long presentation for police and prosecutors on his conclusions: "In my opinion, it is not possible that any individual except Patsy Ramsey wrote the ransom note" and he proceeded to "build a wall of linguistic evidence before their eyes, brick by brick."

> "He [Foster] explained that language is infinitely diverse and that no two people use it in quite the same way. They do not have the same vocabulary, use identical spelling and punctuation, construct sentences in the same manner, read the same books, or express the same beliefs and ideas. Ingrained and unconscious habits are virtually impossible to conceal, even if a writer tries to disguise his identity," he said. "Individuals are prisoners of their own language.
>
> Foster dissected the ransom note, explained that the wording contained intelligent and sometimes clever usage of language, and said the text suggested someone who was trying to deceive.

The documents he studied from Patsy Ramsey, in his opinion, form a 'precise and unequivocal' match with the ransom note. He read a list of 'unique matches' with the note that included such things as her penchant for inventing private acronyms, spelling habits, indentation, alliterative phrasing, metaphors, grammar, vocabulary, frequent use of exclamation points, and even the format of her handwriting on the page....he [Foster] pointed out how the odd usage 'and hence' appeared both in the ransom note and in her 1997 Christmas letter."[11]

Investigators walked away from the presentation with the impression that a giant step had been taken forward in the case. A nationally renowned linguistics expert, referred to them from the very office of the district attorney, had proclaimed Patsy Ramsey to be the one and only author of the ransom note. It was Foster's opinion that she had been unassisted in the construction of the wordage of the document.

The manner in which Foster became involved in JonBenét's murder investigation generated a bit of controversy however, and prosecutors left the presentation with an entirely different opinion.

While Boulder investigators had no problem with his credibility, members of the district attorney's office considered him tainted goods. His Internet exchanges with Susan Bennett, prior to his having had the opportunity to personally view the handwriting exemplars collected in the case, had sullied his stellar reputation in the eyes of the district attorney's office.

Professor Foster was a nationally recognized forensic linguistics expert who was willing to render an opinion on the matter of the identity of the author of the ransom note, and the prosecutors in the case chose to ignore his findings.

911 TAPES

Investigators had requested a copy of the tape of the 911 call placed by Patsy Ramsey as a matter of routine. 911 tapes were regularly obtained in major case investigations, and frequently their contents proved helpful as an investigative tool.

Dispatcher Kimberly Archuleta had concluded her midnight shift on the morning of December 26, 1996, with the handling of the 911 call generated by Patsy Ramsey. She had driven home that morning, having a difficult time letting go of the emotions that had developed as a result of the kidnapping call. She had spoken to her son about it later that day, uncomfortable about what she had overheard on the phone call.[12]

For some unknown reason, Archuleta was not aware of the outcome of the call she had handled that morning and didn't learn about JonBenét's death until she returned for her next regularly scheduled shift assignment at the Boulder County Regional Communications Center.

Upon hearing of JonBenét's murder, Archuleta nearly became ill. A supervisor directed her to her office where she sat and tried to calm her emotions. She could not get past the notion that something had been wrong about the 911 call and it had been there, troubling her subconscious during her days off.

Archuleta asked her supervisor if police had listened to the 911 tape and was told that they had already obtained a copy of the recording: "What about the end of the call? Have they listened to the tail end of the call after Patsy Ramsey had stopped talking?"

The supervisor looked back at Archuleta with a puzzled look on her face. "What are you talking about?" she asked.

The 911 call didn't end when Patsy stopped talking to her, Archuleta explained. The telephone line had not disconnected immediately, and she had heard a definite change in the tone of Patsy Ramsey's voice before the call was fully terminated. Archuleta explained that the hysterical nature of Patsy Ramsey's voice appeared to have dissipated, and she thought that she had been talking to someone nearby at her end of the telephone line. Investigators needed to listen to that extended part of the 911 call, Archuleta told her supervisor.

The 911 tape was subsequently sent to the Aerospace Corporation located in Los Angeles, California, and technicians determined that there was an additional several seconds of recording at the tail end of the call before the recording had been fully terminated. It was theorized that Patsy Ramsey had placed the handset of the telephone into its wall mounted cradle after discontinuing her conversation with the dispatch center, but that it had not fully settled into place to disconnect the call.

Aerospace technicians were tasked with attempting to enhance the tail end of the 911 call to determine if the voices heard there could be better understood. Through a series of electronic washings, technicians were able to reduce the background noise associated with the transmission of the telephone call and identified three distinct voices conversing at the tail end of the 911 call.

Several technicians listened to the enhanced version of the tape and compared notes on what they thought they had heard. Each technician reportedly had heard the same conversation. It was time to call Boulder authorities.

Boulder Police detective Melissa Hickman flew to California in late April 1997, and met with the technicians. She, too, was provided the opportunity to listen independently to the enhanced version of the 911 tape.

After Hickman has listened to the tape several times, she shared her observations of what she thought had been overheard with the technicians. Producing a previous set of handwritten notes, the technicians revealed their interpretation of the words spoken by the voices heard on the tail end of the tape.

They all stared in amazement. Everyone who had listened to the enhanced version of the 911 tape had independently identified the same words and gender of the people speaking them. There were 3 distinct voices heard on the tape and the conversation was identified as follows:

Male (angry):	"We're not speaking to you!"
Female:	"Help me Jesus. Help me Jesus"
Young male:	"Well, what *did* you find?"

The discovery of this conversation, taking place in the family home after Patsy Ramsey thought she had terminated her 911 call, was of significant importance. It was a piece of evidence that pointed to deception on the part of the Ramsey family. They had continued to maintain throughout their statements that Burke had remained asleep in his bedroom during the events of the morning and that they had never awakened him or asked him questions about JonBenét's kidnapping.

Proof of the Ramsey's deception was beginning to erode the foundation of the kidnapper / intruder theory in the eyes of Boulder Police investigators, and they contemplated the questions:

- Why would the Ramseys feel the need to mislead authorities about their son being asleep at the time of the 911 call?

- Were they attempting to conceal information that he may have had about the circumstances of his sister's death?

Intruder theorists seemed to discount this evidence of deception as inconsequential.

For others, those voices at the end of the 911 tape pointed to family involvement and some type of cover-up.

Lou Smit for the Defense

Ramsey attorneys continued to hold Boulder Police investigators at bay, refusing to come to terms for a follow-up interview with the family and claiming that the department was centering the entire focus of their investigation on Patsy and John Ramsey. This was not the case, but Boulder investigators were not about to talk publically about the steps they were taking in an active murder investigation.

The division between the District Attorney's Office and the Police Department had been widening, but Alex Hunter and Tom Koby mutually agreed that it would help to bring an experienced homicide investigator into the fold. From there, however, their opinions diverged.

Boulder Police wanted to bring retired Denver Police Homicide Division Chief Tom Haney on board. Haney, retiring from the Denver Police Department in January 1997, was a long-term veteran of the department and had extensive experience in their homicide bureau.

Hunter's crew wanted to hire retired Colorado Springs Detective Lou Smit. A devout Christian with an equally impressive resume, Smit was situated outside the immediate Denver-metro area and not necessarily known to all of the law enforcement community in Boulder County.

Hunter eventually prevailed, and Smit began his work at the D.A.'s office in mid-March, 1997. Smit was joined by Boulder County Sheriff's Department investigator Steve Ainsworth, and they were tasked with taking a look at the evidence in the case from the perspective of the defense team: a valuable strategy when you are trying to identify the weaknesses in a case that you might one day be prosecuting.

Smit began in earnest, and it wasn't long before he had discounted the involvement of a group of individuals in JonBenét's kidnapping and focused his efforts on proving that a single intruder, a violent pedophile, was responsible for the murder of this child.

He pointed to the back yard that concealed the grate of the Train Room window well and thought this an excellent location through which entry could be gained to the residence. Smudges in the dirt covering the exterior windowsill led Smit to believe that an intruder had used this location to enter and exit the home and a scuff mark located on the interior wall below the window further bolstered his opinion on the matter.

The odd placement of the Samsonite suitcase beneath the window was not a key element necessary for the intruder's entry to the home, but Smit felt it was a critical piece of evidence that had assisted the intruder in their escape. Given its height above the floor, something was needed to step upon in order to climb out of the Train Room window.

And then there was the impression of the poon of a "Hi-Tec" brand hiking boot found in the mold on the floor of the Wine

Cellar, next to where the body of JonBenét had been discovered. Smit theorized that the impression had been made by the boot of the intruder when he had hidden JonBenét in that obscure and remote basement room.

Photo 12 - Interior view of Train Room, Samsonite suitcase, and open window to window well, thought to be point of entry / exit by intruder theorists. Note the elongated scuff mark on the wall between the suitcase and window frame. Source: Boulder PD Case Files / Internet

A latent palm print had been lifted by CSIs from the exterior side of the Wine Cellar door and it had not yet been identified when Smit first joined the investigation. The question loomed: Had this latent fingerprint been left by an intruder as well?

It would take a couple more months of work, but Smit would see similarities in some of the marks on JonBenét's face and back and develop the theory that a "stun gun" had been used to silence her during the kidnap.

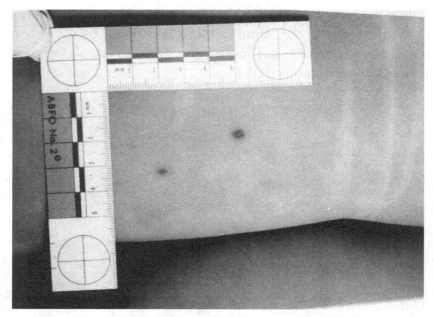

Photo 13 - Twin abrasions on JonBenét's lower left back that intruder theorists believe were created by the use of an Air Taser brand stun gun. Source: Boulder PD Case File / Internet

He reviewed the autopsy photographs of murder victim Gerald Boggs, who had been murdered in his Steamboat Springs, Colorado home in October 1993 by his wife and a male accomplice / boyfriend.

His wife, Jill Coit, would become known as the "Black Widow." She had been married eleven (11) times to nine (9) different men, and Boggs had been number eight (8). Coit and her boyfriend were eventually convicted of the murder and are currently serving terms of incarceration in the Colorado Department of Corrections.

Steamboat Springs investigators determined during their investigation that Boggs had been beaten with a shovel, shocked with a stun gun, and shot with a .22 caliber pistol.

The stun gun had been applied on the right side of his face, the electrical probes of the device making contact with his ear lobe and cheek. The deteriorating mark on his ear lobe looked strikingly similar to the orange-colored mark on JonBenét's cheek. Smit theorized that a smaller red mark closer to her mouth accounted for the location of the second probe.

It was difficult to determine the exact positioning of the stun gun probes on JonBenét's face, however, and Smit turned to the twin abrasions on her back to test out his theory of the use of this device. These marks, described as "abrasions" by Dr. Meyer when he examined them during autopsy, were much more distinct and easily measured. Smit and investigators from the Boulder County Sheriff's Department would later conduct a series of tests with a number of stun guns with the intention of bolstering the intruder theory.

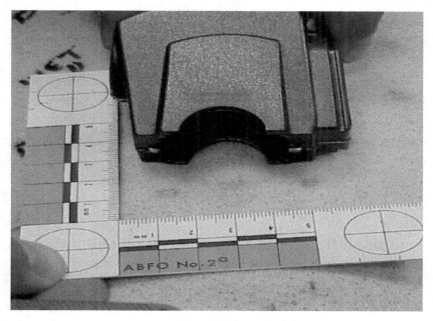

Photo 14 - Lou Smit experiments with a stun gun on anesthetized pigs. Source: Boulder PD Case File / Internet

Smit sought the assistance of Dr. Michael Doberson, Coroner for Arapahoe County, who had been involved in the Boggs murder investigation. Dr. Doberson had used anesthetized pigs to test a stun gun found in the trunk of Coit's vehicle to determine if it matched the injuries observed on the body of Gerald Boggs. He provided critical testimony about his experiments during the Boggs trial, and some thought his observations were paramount in convicting the people responsible for his murder.

Smit arranged to have the same type of experiments conducted in JonBenét's investigation, and he would eventually declare that the Air Taser brand stun gun was most likely the instrument used in this crime.

It was Smit's contention that a single intruder had entered the Ramsey home late on the night of Christmas, and used the stun gun to render JonBenét unconscious. He then carried her downstairs to the basement and physically tortured and sexually assaulted her. It was his belief that the garrote had been repeatedly tightened and loosened over the course of attack, and that the blow to her head came last, almost at the time of her death.

Boulder investigators had contacted the manufacturer of the Air Taser stun gun that Smit ultimately declared to be the weapon used in this murder, and they were told in no uncertain terms that the marks on JonBenét's body would not have been created by their device.

This did not deter Smit, or other investigators and attorneys in the D.A.'s office, however, from holding tight to their belief in the intruder theory.

Boulder PD investigators would find written materials in the Ramsey household that suggested John Ramsey may have at one time been researching the purchase of a stun gun, or that he had owned one. Nothing ever came of this lead, however, and Smit continued to theorize that the marks of a stun gun found on JonBenét pointed to an intruder being involved in her death. He felt that the parents would have no need for a stun gun to control or silence their daughter.

Smit thought that the ransom note had been written before the death of JonBenét because it referenced her still being alive when the demand for ransom was being made. He was aware that Patsy's notepad and a pen from the kitchen had been used for the note, and he considered it possible that the intruder had actually crafted the note in the home on the night of the murder.

But from there, his opinion diverged from that of the other police investigators working the case.

Document examiners had not been able to rule out Patsy Ramsey as the author of the note, but Smit was dubious about the police view that she had authored it. He didn't think JonBenét's murderer would have had the composure to write the note after having committed this brutal murder. Smit just didn't buy into the concept that the note was crafted as a part of the staging of a cover-up.

I am aware that Smit had a number of spirited conversations with Boulder investigators regarding some of the evidence collected in the case. He and Steve Thomas went round and round over the spider webs in the Train Room window well and the scuff mark located on the wall beneath that window. Boulder PD investigators didn't believe anyone used that window to either enter or exit the home, and the broken window glass and scuff mark were explainable by John Ramsey's earlier forced entry into the home.

Smit would later tell reporters that photographs of JonBenét's room showed no signs of a struggle and, more importantly, that the sheets on her bed were clean. According to him, there was no sign of urine on the sheets, and no evidence that she had wet her bed that night.

It was his theory that there had been no struggle because the intruder had used the stun gun to silence / subdue JonBenét while she was asleep in her bed.

Smit discounted observations made by the investigators and CSIs who had processed the scene shortly after the murder: the sheets on JonBenét's bed reeked of urine.

Smit and Hoffstrom would subsequently share their theory of the use of the stun gun with the Ramsey family and their attorneys in an interview conducted in June 1997. Boulder PD investigators were noticeably absent, and the Ramsey team must have felt that progress was finally being made in the search for their daughter's murderer.

The evidence that Smit believed pointed to an intruder bitterly divided the detectives. He had only been on the job for 3 days before he opined that he didn't believe the parents were involved in the death of JonBenét.

His reputation as a renowned criminal investigator was quickly dissolving in the eyes of Boulder PD investigators, and they could not understand how he so easily dismissed certain pieces of physical evidence.

For Smit, he thought Boulder investigators were spending too much time focusing their efforts on the parents and not enough time looking for an outside intruder. He could find nothing that pointed to the family's involvement in the death of their daughter. His work and his theory would eventually amass a group of "intruder believers" in certain segments of the D.A.'s office.

This division would plague the progress of the investigation for years to come.

Ramsey family ad again offers $100,000 reward

The family of JonBenét Ramsey placed a quarter page ad restating their $100,000 reward for information about their daughter's killing in Sunday's edition of the Boulder Daily Camera.

Next to a school picture showing the child beauty queen without makeup, the ad offers $100,000 "for information leading to the arrest and conviction of the murderer of JonBenét Ramsey."

The ad says the 6-year-old girl was murdered Christmas night "...in her home by an unknown person or persons."

It says the reward is offered by the JonBenét Ramsey Children's Foundation and "the family urgently requests that if you have any knowledge which can assist in solving this crime, please contact (303) 443-3535 or Crime Stoppers at (303) 440-7867."

JonBenét's body was found in the basement of her parent's Boulder home on the morning of December 26 after Patsy and John Ramsey reported finding a ransom note demanding $118,000 for the girl's return.

—Boulder Camera
April 28, 1997

"Police spokeswoman Leslie Aaholm told CNN Wednesday that Patricia Ramsey has yet to turn in a fifth handwriting sample requested by investigators, who have ruled out her 53-year-old husband as the writer of the note. But she said investigators expect her to do so."

—*CNN U.S. News,*
   April 30, 1997

CHAPTER ELEVEN

Coming to Terms

Boulder investigators were anxious to have another opportunity at interviewing the parents after they had suddenly ceased communication on Saturday, December 28, 1996. There were many unanswered questions that they wanted to ask, and they wanted to further clarify information that had been gathered on the day of the kidnapping.

The F.B.I's Behavioral Analysis and Child Abduction and Serial Killer Units, the premier federal law enforcement investigative agencies that dealt with these types of cases, were in direct consultation with Boulder Police and offering advice on how to arrange and conduct these follow up interviews.

It was apparent from the standpoint of Ramsey attorneys that they didn't want their clients walking through the doors of the police department and being subjected to interrogation style interviews. They wanted to control the environment and the setting and continuously rejected investigator's requests that the Ramseys come to the station like every other victim, witness, or suspect.

Patsy Ramsey continued to be emotionally fragile, and her attorney at one point had suggested that she be interviewed for no longer than an hour at a time and that she be in the company of her physician. The proffer was made that detectives would be allowed to see her at one of the Ramsey attorney's offices, but no visit to the police department building would be permitted.

These terms were unacceptable to the investigators. They were perplexed by the Ramsey's early decision to obtain legal counsel and felt that they were attempting to hide something. They wanted to speak to Patsy Ramsey in particular due to the similarities of her handwriting to the ransom note. This and the fact that the note had been written on a pad of paper belonging to her put Patsy in the "bucket" of suspects as Steve Thomas would later describe it.

The negotiations went on for weeks and were frequently played out in the press. Just when it seemed that everyone had agreed to a set of conditions, something would change, and the Ramsey PR team usually blamed authorities for being inflexible and insensitive to the victims of the crime.

Eventually, a date and time would be set: April 30, 1997. Investigators would be permitted the opportunity to separately interview John and Patsy Ramsey, and they could use the time in any manner they saw fit. Each would be represented by his or her attorney, of course, and a member of the D.A.'s office would also sit in as an observer.

Investigators were predominantly interested in Patsy Ramsey. In addition to her handwriting style being consistent with the ransom note, photographs that had been developed from the White's Christmas day dinner party had been reviewed, and it was discovered that Patsy had been wearing the same clothing, a red turtleneck sweater and black pants, on the morning of the reported kidnapping as those depicted in the holiday photos.

Rick French had noted his observations about the attire in his initial police report and had also observed that her hair and make-up had been done on the morning of the kidnapping.

The clothing seemed out of character for the former Miss America beauty contestant, and family friends had told investigators that Patsy had never been observed to wear the same outfit two days in a row. She was always meticulous about her appearance.

Investigators were pondering if she had ever gone to bed that night, and were anxious to hear a full accounting of her story line.

Detectives Tom Trujillo and Steve Thomas were assigned the task of interviewing Patsy and John Ramsey, and it had been agreed that the interviews would take place in a conference room at the district attorney's office.

Trujillo began the questioning by asking Patsy for some general background information and learned that she had grown up in Parkersburg, West Virginia. She pointed to some of the highlights of her upbringing, becoming a member of student government in junior high, mentioning that she had been a cheerleader in 10th grade, and had moved on and up to the "drill team" her senior year.

She attended the University of West Virginia where she obtained a degree in Journalism and graduated Magna Cum Laude. During her college years, Patsy won the title of Miss West Virginia and went on to compete in the Miss America pageant. She reported winning a $2,000 scholarship during the West Virginia competition in the category of "dramatic dialogue."

After completing college, Patsy moved to Atlanta, Georgia in the summer of 1979 where she met her future husband, John Ramsey. They were married in November, 1980.

Trujillo moved on to generic questions regarding her relationship with people in her neighborhood, her knowledge about the details of her husband's business dealings, and the types of visitors who had frequented her home. She initially did not seem to be aware of any conflicts taking place in John's work environment, but later in the interview was able to name three people who had left Access Graphics, John's Boulder business, under difficult circumstances. Two of the men had reportedly been making threats after their departure from the business.

She expressed ignorance about the $118,000 year-end bonus that John had received and any relevance it may have had to the ransom demand made by the kidnappers of JonBenét.

Investigators wanted to know if she was familiar with or suspected any of the service workers who had been in the home over the years. A number of names were run past her, and she was unable to say that she recognized anyone in particular. No one stood out as a potential suspect in her early part of the interview.

Turning their focus to the events surrounding Christmas Day, Patsy indicated that the kids had awakened her and John around six that morning. They attempted to pace themselves in the opening of presents, and when all was said and done, she made a pancake breakfast for the family.

A number of neighborhood children came over later that morning and played throughout the course of the day with Burke and JonBenét.

John went to the airport sometime after the lunch hour to check on his private airplane. They were scheduled to fly to their "second home" in Charlevoix, Michigan at seven a.m. the following morning to have a second Christmas with John's older children. John Andrew, Melinda, and boyfriend Stewart Long, were flying from the south to meet the Ramseys for a quick holiday celebration.

Another trip had been scheduled for the Ramsey family to take a cruise on Disney's Big Red Boat in celebration of Patsy's fortieth birthday, which was December 29th. Patsy advised the investigators that she had continued to do some packing for both trips after their pancake breakfast. This included some last minute present wrapping in the basement of the home.

She reported that clothing for the Disney cruise was being packed into suitcases in John Andrew's second floor bedroom.

Clothing for the Charlevoix trip was minimal and was being placed into plastic bags.

The family had been invited to Fleet and Priscilla White's home that evening to join the family and their relatives for a Christmas dinner. The kids were cleaned up after their day of play, and Patsy advised that she believed they arrived at the White home sometime around 5:30 p.m. When queried about what JonBenét may have had to eat during the party, she indicated that Priscilla had specially prepared a plate of cracked crab to ensure that she would have some to enjoy. The kids reportedly liked seafood.

Patsy believed they stayed at the party for several hours and headed home around eight or nine p.m. They made two stops on the way, delivering Christmas gifts to the homes of the Walkers and Stines.

It was revealed that JonBenét had fallen asleep in the car when the family returned home from the dinner party, and that John Ramsey had carried her upstairs to her bedroom. Following close on, Patsy turned down her daughter's bed and exchanged the child's black party pants with long-john bottoms. The sequin-starred shirt that had been worn beneath a black vest remained on her daughter as she was tucked into bed for the night.

Patsy stated on several occasions that JonBenét was "really zonked" and never awakened after returning home from the party.

Patsy would confirm during the interview that JonBenét had not had anything to eat upon returning home that evening.

Patsy thought that perhaps John had stayed up to play with Burke for a few minutes before going to bed. She indicated that she had returned to the task of trying to finish putting things together for the morning trip and was not certain how Burke went to bed that evening. She denied have any further contact with him after returning home from the White dinner party.

After spending approximately 30 minutes on last-minute packing, Patsy indicated that she believed she had washed her face, brushed her teeth, and changed into pajamas for bed.

She estimated that she turned in around ten or ten-thirty p.m. Her husband joined her not long thereafter.

Patsy stated that she rose from bed around five-thirty the following morning, December 26th, just after John had got up to shower. She reported that they had awakened without the use of the alarm. When queried about her activities upon rising, Patsy indicated that she had put on her makeup and done her hair and put on the same clothing worn from the dinner party the previous evening.

She stated that she stopped briefly in the hallway at the laundry machines located outside JonBenét's bedroom door. It appeared slightly ajar the way she had left it the previous evening, and there was no light emitting from the room. Patsy then proceeded downstairs, intending to make some coffee and prepare a little breakfast before the morning flight.

She indicated that she did not check on her daughter until after finding the ransom note at the bottom of the spiral stairs at the rear of kitchen.

As she descended the rear circular stairway, Patsy noticed some papers spread across one of the lower treads. She stepped over them and turned to see three pages spread out from left to right. There was no indication that a light had been turned on in the darkened hallway, but she said that she leaned over to read the note.

She could not recall if she had handled the ransom note, and had only read the first few lines before seeing the part about someone having her daughter. She immediately ran back upstairs to check on JonBenét.

Patsy indicated that she pushed open the door to JonBenét's bedroom and immediately saw that she was not there. The lamp next to her daughter's bed was not on, and she screamed for John.

John rushed down stairs from their 3rd floor bedroom, and Patsy told him about the note and that JonBenét had been kidnapped.

Photo 15 - Rear kitchen hallway and spiral stairs leading to 2nd floor. The Ransom Note was found on the bottom stair treads. Source: Boulder PD Case File / Internet

At some point, a quick check of Burke's bedroom was made by her husband before police were called. He had come downstairs in his underwear, and had moved the note from the stair tread to the floor near the entrance of the kitchen. John was on his hands and knees reading the note when Patsy called 911 from a nearby kitchen wall phone.

Patsy did not believe that John had gone to the basement before the first officer arrived on scene and indicated that he had run back upstairs after the 911 call to dress.

It was indicated that Burke had remained asleep throughout the entire ordeal and that he had remained in his room until Fleet White suggested that he could hang-out at his home with visiting family in south Boulder. White did eventually drive Burke to his home where he remained until after the discovery of his sister's body.

An initial suspect reported to police that morning was the Ramsey housekeeper, Linda **Hoffmann-Pugh**. Patsy mentioned that **Hoffmann-Pugh** had requested a $2,000.00 loan, and she thought that the handwriting on the ransom note looked similar to that of the housekeeper.

Patsy failed to mention to investigators during the April interview anything about Hoffman-Pugh's previous comments about "kidnapping." On the morning of December 26th, as investigators were investigating the case, it came to their attention that Linda **Hoffmann-Pugh** had once asked Patsy if she was ever concerned about JonBenét being kidnapped. **Hoffmann-Pugh** thought her to be such a pretty little girl that she might be an attractive target for someone who was so inclined.

At the close of the interview, Patsy denied writing the ransom note or knowing anything about a foreign faction or the meaning of "SBTC," the purported signatory to the ransom note. In addition, she disavowed any knowledge about, or participation in, the death of her daughter.

Trujillo and Thomas began their interview of John at three that afternoon, and he confirmed some of the details about putting JonBenét to bed after returning from the White dinner party, as had been provided by his wife.

He estimated that they had left the Whites around eight-thirty, quarter to nine and had then delivered some presents to the homes of the Walker and Stine families. They arrived home at around nine to nine-fifteen.

JonBenét had fallen asleep in the car, and John carried her to her bedroom upon their arrival home. She remained asleep throughout the process, and Patsy reportedly followed him several minutes later to prepare her for bed. That was the last time John saw his daughter alive.

Burke was interested in putting together some type of toy that he had received for Christmas, and John indicated that he spent a little time with him downstairs helping to assemble it. They spent approximately 15 minutes working on the project. Anxious to get to bed because of their early morning flight, John then had Burke prepare for bed, changing his clothes, brushing his teeth, and getting him settled in for the night.

John did not think that Burke had anything to eat after returning home that evening.

John then prepared himself for bed and took a Melatonin tablet to help him fall asleep quickly. He joined Patsy in their bed sometime around ten. He thought he may have read for a little bit and estimated that the lights were out by ten-thirty or ten-forty. Neither he, nor Patsy, were thought to have gotten up over the remainder of the night.

He rose the next morning at about five-twenty-five, before the alarm went off that had been set for five-thirty. Patsy was still in bed as he headed for the shower.

Part way through his morning ritual, he heard a scream of panic from Patsy, and he could tell from her tone that something was wrong. He ran down the back staircase and met her midway at the landing. He remembered her showing him the note, and he thought that he had run back upstairs to check JonBenét's room and then on Burke. Burke was still asleep, and reportedly had not been awakened by Patsy's scream.

John was not certain if Patsy had handled the ransom note, but recalled that it was he who moved it to the hallway floor near the entrance of the kitchen and read it as Patsy called 911. It was spread out across the floor, and he was hunched down over it so he could read it quickly.

After finishing the 911 call, John was aware that Patsy had called the Whites and the Fernies, and he ran back upstairs to finish dressing.

Officer Rick French was the first to arrive on the scene, and he reported that French directed them to the first floor solarium. He couldn't remember the exact sequence, but other police officers arrived along with the family friends who had been summoned to the home.

When asked about the security of the home, John indicated that the connecting door between the house and the garage was typically left unlocked and that he usually checked the rear door that the kids used to access the back yard.

John indicated that he believed he had checked all of the first-floor doors on the morning of the 26th. He went outside at one point to check an exterior door that accessed the garage. The interior of that door was blocked with boxes, and he couldn't get to it from inside the garage. He estimated that he was outside no longer than 30 seconds and had gone out a side door to check the security of that door. John did not report finding any other ground floor door open or unsecured.

John walked the investigators through his discovery of his daughter's body, explaining that Detective Arndt had asked that the home be checked for anything unusual. John led Fleet White to the Train Room of the basement and explained that he had broken in through that set of windows when locked out of the house the previous summer. They inspected the area for broken glass, and then John moved out of the room and down the hallway to the Wine Cellar.

He reported that he unlatched the wood block that secured the door and immediately saw a white blanket on the floor inside the room. John advised that he observed JonBenét lying on the blanket and it was "kind of folded around her legs." Her arms were tied behind her head, some pieces of black tape were on her legs, and her head was cocked to the side.

John immediately removed a piece of tape that covered her mouth and tried to untie the bindings around her wrists. He was not successful at fully removing them, and grabbed his daughter beneath her arms and carried her upright to the first floor of the house. He noted that her body was stiff, and he placed her on the floor after arriving upstairs.

The big surprise came for investigators when John revealed that he had been to the basement earlier in the morning, before being directed to check the house by Detective Arndt at approximately 1:00 p.m. that day.

John indicated that he had seen the broken Train Room window during his earlier trip. There was no glass around, and he presumed that it had not been repaired from his previous forced entry that summer. He stated that the window was open approximately 1/8" and he latched the window before returning upstairs.

When pressed for a time frame of this first undeclared visit, John thought that it had probably been before ten a.m. Investigators wondered why he would be leaving the room where a trap and trace and recorder had been established to accept the ransom call from kidnappers to explore the far reaches of the basement. To them, it seemed more likely that he had made this trip to the basement a little later in the morning when Detective Arndt first reported losing track of his whereabouts around 10:40 a.m.

John offered the theory that someone had come through the basement window and mentioned the Samsonite suitcase sitting below the window. He pointed out that someone could have gotten into the home without it, but that something would have been needed to step on in order to climb out of the window.†

He noted that the window-well grate would not have been obvious to someone walking by the home. The ground-level grate was not visible from the front, street-side of the home, nor was it readily visible from the rear alley.

John had commented shortly after the discovery of JonBenét's body that whoever had committed the crime had to have been someone on the "inside" and cited these initial thoughts as one of the reasons housekeeper Linda **Hoffmann-Pugh-** had been first named as a possible suspect. She and her husband were intimate-ly familiar with the Ramsey home and the layout of the basement.

The interview with John Ramsey concluded at approximately five p.m. on the afternoon of April 30, 1997. Patsy's interview had taken nearly six hours. His lasted a mere ninety minutes. Husband and wife left the building in the escort of a cadre of attorneys.

Investigators would learn some new things that had not been revealed during the "hours of interviews" that had been conducted with parents on the day of JonBenét's kidnapping. A number of topics were broached over the course of the day including the use of polygraphs. A later chapter will speak to that particular issue.

Patsy seemed to handle the questions with composure, but in some instances appeared to be evasive, according to the personal observations of the investigators. A number of questions were answered with "I don't remember," or "I can't recall," something that could have been reasonably expected given the time delay between the event and the date of this interview.

It was Thomas's opinion, however, that Patsy had been well-rehearsed in advance of the interview, and that a different woman sat before him than what he had experienced during the December 28th non-custodial evidence collection procedure.

Some minor inconsistencies had developed during the interview, and a few other important details were pinned down by investigators.

The initial reporting of JonBenét going to bed wearing a red turtleneck top had changed between the time of Patsy's first interview on the morning of December 26th and that conducted on April 30th. It is not clear from Patsy's April interview what became of the red sweater, but crime scene investigators had located the top balled up on the bathroom counter of JonBenét's bathroom during their processing of the crime scene.

Photo 16 - JonBenét's bathroom. Note toothbrush, toothpaste, and red sweater on right counter. (Not pictured is toilet paper in the bowl of the toilet to the left of counter.) Source: Boulder PD Case File

Additionally, Patsy was now indicating that she had found the note first *before* checking JonBenét's bedroom. This conflicted with the information that she had provided to officers on the morning of December 26th, where she indicated that she had stopped by her daughter's bedroom on the way downstairs to the kitchen. The bed had been empty at that time, and it wasn't until she continued to the kitchen that she found the note.

Was this an important discrepancy or merely hysterical confusion on the part of the mother of a missing child?

Investigators were also concerned about the statement that she had only read the first few lines of the ransom note before charging back upstairs to check on JonBenét. During the panic of the moment, Patsy had been able to tell the 911 dispatcher that the ransom note was signed off with the word "Victory," and the initials "SBTC".

How would she know that if she had never truly handled the ransom note, or read through all 3 pages? This information suggested prior knowledge of the content of the note.

John had revealed a previously unknown trip to the basement that took place before the discovery of JonBenét's body. He had never mentioned this exploration to officers on the morning of the reported kidnapping.†

John also provided specific details about immediately observing a white blanket, and his daughter's body upon opening the cellar room door that afternoon. He reported that he saw the white blanket, in which JonBenét was wrapped, the "instant" he opened the door of the Wine Cellar. This observation purportedly took place before he flipped on the light switch.

This didn't jive with details provided by Fleet White during his interviews with detectives. White had opened the cellar door earlier that morning and reported that it was too dark to see anything without a light being turned on in the room. He had stepped partially through the door and couldn't find a light switch, let alone see the blanket and body.

Investigators pondered the question: How could John Ramsey have immediately recognized the blanket and the body under the same conditions?

When all was said and done, investigators went away from the interviews with more than a few unanswered questions and continued to feel that JonBenét's parents could not be eliminated as possible suspects in the crime.

The Ramseys immediately held their own press conference the following day, May 1, 1997, and invited a select few from the Denver media stations to attend. Ramsey media publicist Pat Korten coordinated the event in a Boulder hotel conference room.

Each of the 7 local reporters had been hand-picked by the Ramsey team, and many others who had been covering the story from early on were covetous of an invitation. The Ramseys had not spoken to the media since their January 1st CNN interview, and reporters were anxious to see what they had to say, especially after their interview with Boulder Police investigators.

Carol McKinley, a reporter working for Denver KOA Radio at the time, received a last-minute invitation on the morning of the press conference. Apparently, Korten had forgotten to include anyone from the radio community, and had called McKinley not long before the Ramseys were preparing to issue their statement.

Korten provided McKinley with the *secret* location of the conference, and even gave her a *password* that she would need to gain entry to the room where the Ramseys would be speaking.

McKinley had taken the telephone call while in the company of other reporters, and they had been discussing the possible location and timing of the family press conference. Based upon her cell phone conversation, some of her peers immediately sensed that she had been granted access to the inner sanctum. She had to drive in a roundabout fashion to lose the tail of reporters who were trying to follow her to the secret location of the Ramsey press conference.

Once she arrived in the lobby of the hotel, McKinley was approached by someone who asked her to recite her secret password. She muttered the word "subtract," and she was then adorned with a bright green, circular sticker. "Don't let that fall off." she was warned. The sticker granted her access to the small conference room that contained the Ramseys.

All of the reporters present were advised of the *ground rules* for the conference. It would only last thirty minutes. John and Patsy Ramsey would make a short introductory statement, and then reporters could ask their questions. They could not, however, ask *any* questions about the murder investigation. They were not permitted to ask any questions about, or refer to other people that were in the room. These were family attorneys and friends who reportedly were accompanying the family for this endeavor.

Any violation of the ground rules would result in the *immediate* termination of the press conference.

McKinley and her fellow reporters entered a darkened hotel conference room to see John and Patsy Ramsey sitting by a well-lit table. A beautiful floral arrangement sat upon the table, and seemed to draw attention away from about a dozen people who stood in the shadows out of view of the cameras.

Photo 17 - Patsy and John Ramsey display the reward poster that had been prepared in advance of their May 1, 1997 press conference. Courtesy: The Denver Post.

As the press conference began, Patsy Ramsey held up the reward poster that had been published in the *Boulder Daily Camera* several days earlier and asked for the help of the journalists who had been invited to attend the press conference.

"I'd like to say that we would, one of the reasons we asked all of you to be here this morning is that we need your help from this moment on. I know you have been diligently covering this case and we appreciate some of what you've said...not all of what you've said. We need to all work together as a team and we need your help."

The reporters were a little gun-shy, and stumbled through a series of innocuous questions that danced around the issue of the brutal *murder* of a little girl. True to their word, the press conference ended precisely at the 30-minute mark.

McKinley later described the environment as one of the most "bizarre" media events she had ever witnessed. Ramsey attorneys and their friends hovered behind the reporters and their cameras in the darkened corners of the room.

She felt that nothing of substance was discussed, and the conference gave the appearance of being a "fluff" piece intended to the give the family the opportunity to show their continuing effort to "cooperate" with authorities. Many had the clear impression that the Ramseys were attempting to manage the media and spin their own side of the story.

Unbeknownst to the media, however, was that by the time the Ramseys gave their first official interview with police on April 30, 1997, the thirty or so Boulder investigators assigned to the case had already interviewed nearly 400 people. The list included those who were thought to be witnesses who could provide background information, as well as those whom police considered to be potential suspects.

By that time, investigators had also collected sixty-three (63) sets of handwriting exemplars, sixty-four (64) sets of fingerprints, forty-five (45) DNA / blood samples and fifty (50) sets of hair samples.

One (1) polygraph examination had been administered to a non-familial suspect.

In spite of their assurances of wanting to continue to cooperate with authorities, John and Patsy Ramsey wouldn't participate in another law enforcement interview for another fourteen months.

The next time around, Boulder Police Department investigators would not be invited to the table.

CHAPTER TWELVE

Returning to the Scene of the Crime

It was reported that sometime after Lou Smit joined the D.A.'s office in March of 1997, he began to hold a prayer vigil outside the 15th street Ramsey home. Sitting in his van, Smit prayed for JonBenét and her family. As a devoted Christian, I presume that he also prayed for guidance in his effort to find the killer of this little girl.

At one juncture, the family reportedly came by the home as Smit was engaged in his personal vigil. They were invited to join him in the Lord's Prayer, and some investigators came to suspect that this became a fairly regular occurrence over the late spring, and summer, of 1997.

It was mildly aggravating to some of the detectives, because it appeared that Smit was becoming a little too familiar with the Ramsey parents. Smit may have been trying to become better acquainted with the family so that he might learn something new about the murder, but the Boulder cops thought he was losing his objectivity in the case.

Boulder Police investigators returned to the home in July 1997, with another purpose in mind. By that time, they were trying to reconcile Fleet White's accounting of events with those stated by John Ramsey. White had told investigators that he had not been able to see a thing when he opened the door of the Wine Cellar on the morning of the kidnapping. Ramsey had told them that he had spotted the white blanket on the floor immediately upon opening the door.

Investigators wanted to see for themselves what exactly could be seen, or not seen, when the door of the Wine Cellar was opened under similar lighting conditions.

Additionally, the neighborhood canvass had produced a witness who reported hearing a child scream on the night of the murder. Investigators wanted to verify whether or not this was feasible, and whether this scream could have been heard from within the confines of the home.

Though Boulder Police had originally requested a search warrant to return to the premises, the D.A.'s office secured the consent of the family and their realtor for the investigators to conduct their inquiries. As was typical of the time, a swarm of media vehicles camped outside the residence as police and D.A. investigators went about their business.

The interior of the old, 1920's Tudor-style home had changed fairly significantly since detectives had last been through the home. Much of the furniture and personal belongings of the family had been removed. Carpet had been replaced in some areas, and the smell of fresh paint hung in the air. A "For Sale" sign adorned the front yard where there last had stood Christmas decorations.

Not long after arriving in the home, investigators noted something unusual. Small wiring ran from several motion detectors and they seemed to lead to a locked closet beneath the basement stairs. Though the house was old and had been subjected to extensive remodeling, the detectives thought it odd that the wiring to these devices would not have been concealed in the ceiling or walls.

Upon closer inspection, the motion detectors appeared to contain small camera lenses.

Sergeant Wickman kicked in the door of the closet and observed that a VHS recorder was actively recording 4 different rooms of the interior of the home. He directed Detective Gosage to collect the tape and later confirmed that members of the BPD investigative team had been recorded on the tape as they had moved around the home.

Closer examination of the recorder revealed that it was not set to record upon the activation of a motion detector, but had to be *manually* turned on to enter a record mode.

Neither the realtor, nor the Ramsey attorneys mentioned a word about the damages sustained to the locked closet door, or the removal of the VHS tape from the recorder. Their team of private investigators later took responsibility for the placement of the recorders, citing burglary concerns for the empty home. No one ever admitted to activating the recorder before the investigators had arrived on the scene that day.[13]

Investigators spent nearly a week moving through the three floors of the 7,000 square foot home. Police and D.A. investigators debated back and forth the likely scenarios that may have played out on the night of the kidnap and murder. They took turns wiggling through the basement bathroom, and Train Room windows, to determine the type of effort it would have taken to enter the home through those locations.

Debris from outside the bathroom window was dragged along with the *faux intruder* to the inside of the home, and was not consistent with the crime scene photos that showed an interior shelf below the window to be in pristine condition. The photos had also shown the bathroom window to be securely locked and there were no signs of forced entry at this location.

This particular window was eventually discounted as a possible point of entry, and it was perhaps the *only* thing that BPD and DA investigators would agree upon after leaving the home that week.

More time was spent debating the possibility that an intruder had made entry through the window-well of the Train Room. Lou Smit held to the belief that this was the perfect location for an intruder to have entered the home. The three strands of spider web anchoring the window grate to the foundation walls of the well seemed to play no significance in his theory of events, and he pointed to foliage between the metal grate and foundation as evidence that the grate had been lifted sometime recently.

Steve Thomas pointed out that the grate did not sit flush to the cement foundation and that it was a natural occurrence for foliage to grow into that space. They continued to argue about the other signs, or lack of signs, of possible entry observed in the dirt silt that covered the exterior windowsill and frame.

A black scuff mark located on the wall beneath the Train Room window also generated some discussion, and Smit thought for certain that it belonged to the intruder who had climbed into the home at that location. The theoretical debate regarding possibilities and probabilities went on all week long.

Detectives sometimes stayed into the wee hours of the night, listening to the creaks and groans of the old home. It seemed that one could not move about the house without being heard from another area of the home. Nearly every step taken seemed to cause some type of audible response from the floor joists of the structure.

Moreover, investigators found it difficult to move around in the darkness, and observed that a descent of the spiral staircase by use of the ambient light was a dangerous proposition. How had a perpetrator managed to do this while carrying a forty-pound child in his arms?

Detective Gosage had moved around to different parts of the home to see if shouting could be heard from the third-floor master suite of the parents. Investigators were trying to determine if the family would have been able to hear the same scream that neighbor Melody Stanton had claimed to hear. BPD investigators reported hearing Gosage's shouts from various locations of the home, including the basement.

A partially open, street-facing, basement window was thought to have been responsible for Stanton's ability to hear a scream emanating from the basement. An electrical cord had been run through this window over the Christmas holidays to provide power for the decorations displayed on the front lawn of the residence. This window was of insufficient size to have permitted anyone to have entered or exited the home from this location.

An expert was used to help construct the lighting conditions that would have been present when Fleet White and John Ramsey reported opening the door of the Wine Cellar. A white blanket was placed on the floor where JonBenét's body had been found and sensitive photographic light meters were used in an attempt to duplicate the conditions of December 26th.

John Ramsey had stated that he observed the white blanket immediately upon opening the door. Investigators noted that the room was pitch-black when they re-created the same drill, and the blanket was unobservable to them.

Gosage noted in his reports that even with the interior lights on, he couldn't see the blanket until he stepped into the room and had sufficiently cleared the short wall located to the left of the door.

After spending nearly a week exploring the scene of the crime, Boulder Police and D.A. investigators parted company. The many theories that had been discussed and debated during their time together in the home had only served to solidify their earlier positions on the matter.

Law enforcement investigators would not be the only people interested in visiting the scene of the crime. During the one-year anniversary of JonBenét's murder, a number of people would gather outside her home to offer a prayer, light a candle, or place a stuffed animal on the lawn of the residence in memory of the little girl who once lived there.

The presence of one particular participant would catch the eye of Smit, however, and convicted sex-offender Gary Oliva[14] would soon become the object of his inquiry. Smit would eventually discover that Oliva had written a poem about JonBenét. The fact that he owned a stun gun turned him into even more of a viable suspect as Smit continued his search to identify the intruder responsible for this crime.

Oliva, like many of the other registered sex offenders living in Boulder County, would be carefully scrutinized for possible involvement by police investigators working the case. He would be neither the first, nor the last of the pedophiles who were either intrigued by, or who fantasized about the death of this little 6-year-old girl.

Mystery Man

Autopsy protocols in this type of investigation calls for the collection of fingernail scrapings that might help identify trace evidence that would link a suspect to the crime. In many instances, a struggling victim may have scratched a perpetrator during the assault, and skin cells or blood from the assailant is left beneath the fingernails.

Scrapings from the fingernails of JonBenét's hands revealed miniscule samples of DNA that belonged to two different male subjects, and one unidentified female. The samples were too small to identify their biological origin, i.e. blood or skin cells, and investigators came to theorize that the unknown DNA samples had been transferred from contaminated fingernail clippers used in the post-mortem examinations of other bodies processed through the morgue prior to her homicide.

Investigators were able to obtain the DNA samples from eight (8) of the autopsy examinations that preceded that of JonBenét.

These samples were analyzed, but none of these matched the unknown male and female samples collected from JonBenét's fingernails. Perhaps more disappointing, was the fact that the unknown samples lacked sufficient identifying markers that permitted their entry into the state and national DNA databases.

For purposes of education and clarification, the NDIS (National DNA Index System) is one part of the CODIS[15] (Combined DNA Index System). It is the national level of several parts that contain DNA profiles that are contributed by federal, state, and local participating forensic laboratories. NDIS was implemented in October 1998 and all 50 states, the District of Columbia, the federal government, the U.S. Army Criminal Investigation Laboratory, and Puerto Rico participate in the NDIS program.

DNA that is authorized by law to be maintained at NDIS includes profiles from convicted offenders, arrestees, legal, detainees, forensic (casework samples), unidentified human remains, missing persons and relatives of missing persons.

The database is maintained by the FBI, and there are minimum requirements for the submission of certain DNA samples to the program. Generally, the 13 core CODIS loci are required for the submission of convicted offender, arrestee, detainee, and legal profiles.

A minimum of 10 core loci are required for the entry of unknown, forensic DNA profiles.

For our purposes here, the CODIS system uses two different indexes to generate investigative leads in crimes where biological evidence has been collected from a crime scene. The *convicted offender* index contains DNA profiles of individuals convicted of certain crimes ranging from certain misdemeanors to sexual assault and murder.

The *forensic index* contains DNA profiles obtained from crime scene evidence, such as semen, saliva, or blood. This is trace, biological DNA evidence that is believed to belong to the perpetrator of a crime who has yet to be identified by law enforcement personnel.

An example of how the CODIS DNA system works is as follows:

During their investigation of a sex assault, detectives will collect an evidence kit from the victim's medical examination conducted at an emergency room. Swabs from the kit will be submitted to a state laboratory to determine if trace, biological evidence, i.e. semen, was left by the perpetrator. If such evidence is present, the forensic unknown DNA profile of the assailant is then searched against the state and national DNA databases *Convicted Offender and Arrestee Indexes.*

If there is a candidate match of someone in the DNA system, a laboratory will conduct further follow-up examinations to confirm the identity of the perpetrator.

A simultaneous search is made of the *Forensic Index* for a possible match. This database contains the DNA profiles of unidentified perpetrators, and matches in this index may link two or more crimes together.

Rapists are frequently serial offenders, and an unknown subject's DNA profile may be collected from the evidence of many different crime scenes, as well as from many different jurisdictions. Tying cases together through the forensic DNA database has proven to be a valuable tool to law enforcement, and matches of unknown profiles often open up new investigative leads.

Lab technicians turned their attention to the underwear that had been worn by JonBenét at the time of her death to see if they could locate any DNA evidence left by her murderer. Two splotches of blood had been observed in the crotch of her panties, likely deposited there from the vaginal injuries inflicted during the assault, and at the time of her death.

As noted previously, some type of smearing had been observed on her thighs, and technicians and investigators had initially thought that this trace evidence may have been semen left behind by the perpetrator. This was eventually determined to be blood that belonged to JonBenét.

Sampling of the blood in the underwear, however, revealed the mixed presence of male DNA. This was a significant and puzzling discovery. How did male DNA find its way into the underwear of a murdered 6-year old girl? Had this evidence been deposited there by the murderer of JonBenét?

The male DNA sample, subsequently identified as Distal Stain 007-2, only contained 9 genetic markers, and like the DNA collected from beneath JonBenét's fingernails, was of insufficient strength to be entered into the state and national databases. Moreover, the sample was so small that technicians were not able to identify the *biological origin* of the exemplar. Regrettably, they could not tell police investigators if the biological source of the male DNA was derived from blood, semen, epithelial skin cells, or some other genetic material.

The challenge to technicians was enhancing the DNA sample so that it could be entered into the state and national DNA databases, and it took a while for this technology to develop. As noted above, the FBI requires that 10 out of 13 genetic markers be identified in order for a sample to be entered into the Forensic Index database.

DNA replication technology was utilized in the Denver Police Department's crime lab, and the 10th marker was eventually strengthened to the point that the unidentified male sample discovered in JonBenét's underwear was able to be entered into the state and national databases. This laboratory success didn't take place until 2002, nearly 6 years after the murder of JonBenét.

The presence of unidentified male DNA in JonBenét's underwear was evidence that led some investigators and attorneys to believe that an intruder had been responsible for her murder. What other possible explanation could there be for the presence of this evidence at the scene? Coupled with the other evidence discovered by Lou Smit, many thought it compelling evidence that pointed to someone *outside* the family as the perpetrator of the crime.

This partial DNA profile has been entered into the ever-growing national database of felony offenders. Weekly comparisons are run against new, known samples of convicted and arrested offenders, and other unidentified forensic samples collected from unsolved crime scenes around the country.

As of February 2012, this sample has been cross-checked against 10,560,300 known DNA offender profiles located in the CODIS data base.

There are now 417,200 unknown forensic profiles in the database. *Monster's* partial DNA profile is one of these, and thus far, the contributor of this genetic material has not been identified.

Additionally, there have been 173,500 CODIS "hits" through February 2012, and this information has assisted law enforcement in over 166,700 criminal investigations.

All things considered, DNA profiling is still thought to be a relatively new science and technology is continuously being developed and refined. The DNA database continues to grow in numbers, and by comparison, there are over 71,000,000 fingerprints on file with the FBI for criminal arrests that date back to the early 1920's. Inked, or electronically scanned, fingerprints continue to be collected from nearly every person arrested in the United States, and are used as a primary means of identification by law enforcement agencies across the nation.

It may only be a matter of time before DNA databases catch up to the number of fingerprints on file, and perhaps one day the DNA profile of an intruder who murdered JonBenét will be collected during an arrest, or from another crime scene.

If we can one day identify him, then maybe we could also learn the identity of other purported co-conspirators who participated in this crime.

CHAPTER FOURTEEN

Prelude to Resignations

1997 had been an all-consuming year for the detectives working the murder investigation. The stress of trying to solve the murder of a *child* was difficult enough, but the relentless coverage of the media presented additional pressure and challenges.

Nearly 4,000 hours of overtime were logged by the end of the first year and many of the detectives working the case had spent more time in the office, and on the road, than they did with their own families. The division that had developed between the DA's office and the BPD investigators brought an entirely new level of frustration to the men and women who were striving to uncover the truth of the matter.

The Ramseys had conducted one follow-up interview with investigators in the spring and it didn't look like they were willing to return to the table anytime soon.

Test results were trickling back from the crime labs and detectives were still awaiting the arrival of clothing articles that had been requested of the family. In some instances, they needed the clothing worn by the family on the night and day of the murder to compare against trace evidence found at the scene, and on the body of JonBenét.

In the fall of that year, the FBI had invited the Boulder authorities to Quantico to present a review of the elements of their case. Detectives were excited about the opportunity to share the information that had been gathered up to that point in time, and had hoped that the insight of the federal investigators would provide them some leverage with the intruder theorists in the Boulder DA's office.

As teams from both agencies prepared to head to Virginia, *Vanity Fair*[16] ran an article on the status of the investigation. It was highly critical of Alex Hunter's handling of the case, and a retired federal agent quoted in the article expressed the opinion that the DA's release of police reports to the Ramsey team in advance of their April 1997 interview was tantamount to *prosecutorial malfeasance.*

The former agent, Greg McCrary, had served 25 years with the FBI and indicated that he had at one time been recruited by one of the Ramsey defense investigators to join their team.

McCrary did not hesitate to decline the offer, and cited his reasons in the article: "Because on a ratio of 12 to 1, child murders are committed by parents or a family member. In this case, you also have an elaborate 'staging' – the ransom note, the placement of the child's body – and I have never in my career seen or heard about a staging where it was not a family member – or someone very close to the family. Just the note alone told me the killer was in the family or close to it."

With regard to the ransom note and practice note found on Patsy's notepad, McCrary went on to say that "Kidnappers do not spend hours at a crime scene after murdering their victims composing letters."[17]

Hunter and his team reportedly were not very happy with the article's portrayal of his office that was now spreading across the country. He ultimately decided not to attend the Quantico presentation and sent senior members of his command staff in his stead.

Boulder investigators spent a couple days sharing the details of their case, discussed the theories that had been proposed, and listened to suggested avenues of investigation as proposed by the experts who comprised the CASKU team.

Members of the FBI had been in fairly regular consultation with Boulder detectives throughout the course of the investigation, but this was the first opportunity they had had to participate in a detailed overview of the evidence collected thus far in the case.

The FBI agents continued to point out that statistics and case histories pointed to parental, family, or insider involvement, when a child was murdered in the home. Stranger abductions were far and few between, and their cumulative experience suggested that authorities needed to continue to take a hard look at the parents.

In reviewing similar cases, there had only been one instance in which a child had been taken for ransom and then found murdered in the home: it was the JonBenét Ramsey homicide investigation.

The agents also expressed the belief that Patsy had authored the ransom note *after* the death of JonBenét as a means of covering up the murder. Although it was possible, they considered it highly unlikely that an intruder would have spent the time to have written the note while in the home.

The additional evidence of a staged crime scene led them to further discount the intruder - kidnapper theory.

Boulder prosecutors reportedly were adamant in their denial that either John or Patsy Ramsey could have been involved in the murder of their daughter. It was reported that voices had been raised, and that the table had taken a pounding during the heated debate.

Cutting short his attendance at this meeting, Lou Smit went off to collect a potential *intruder* suspect from a jail in Tennessee. The man was brought back to Boulder on unrelated charges and eventually cleared as the perpetrator of JonBenét's murder.

Boulder investigators went away from the Quantico presentation with the feeling that not much ground had been gained during their review of the case. Prosecutors had not been swayed in the least by the FBI's professional assessment of the case, and they appeared to be dead set against *any* theory of the crime that involved the parents.

The first-year anniversary of JonBenét's murder came and went, and investigators continued to plug away at a series of "tasks" that the DA's office wanted completed. It seemed like the task list was never ending, and continuous additions were being made as time slipped by.

It was reported that the Ramseys had attempted to arrange an interview with BPD investigators in January through an intermediary, Father Holverstock from the family church in Boulder. Defense attorneys were purportedly not involved in the outreach, but after some discussion, police decided not to pursue the get-together. The conditions set forth by the Ramseys were not to their liking. They wanted to see more police reports and evidence collected in the case in exchange for the interview.

The Ramsey attorneys subsequently issued a press release indicating that police had declined another interview with the parents of the murdered child. BPD Investigators looked at the event as one in a series of media releases that were attempting to paint them as the uncooperative bad guys, and felt that the offer to interview had been insincere.

Over the course of that winter, both the DA's office and Boulder Police sought the assistance and advice of additional experts. Alex Hunter brought on several metro-Denver area prosecutors to consult and advise him on the case. These men were seasoned prosecutors who handled many more homicide cases than what Boulder had experienced. They included Adams County DA Bob Grant, Denver DA Bill Ritter, and Jefferson County DA Dave Thomas.

Hunter also arranged to have Dr. Henry Lee, and Barry Scheck review the DNA evidence that had been collected during the case. Both Lee and Scheck had been involved in the O.J. Simpson murder trial and were considered experts on the topic of DNA evidence.

Frustrated by the perceived lack of cooperation they had been receiving from their own DA's office, Boulder Police sought their own set of experienced prosecutors. Denver attorney Dan Caplis had initially been approached for assistance, and he eventually recruited the services of three attorneys working in the Denver area. They included Rich Baer, a former New York prosecutor; Dan Hoffman, a former dean of the Denver University Law School and former state public safety commissioner; and Bob Miller, who had served as a U.S. Attorney.

This group of attorneys would subsequently be referred to as the Boulder Police Department's prosecutorial *Dream Team,* and would offer investigators invaluable insight and advice on how to proceed with their investigation.

The publicity the case was attracting seemed to serve as a magnet for some of the more disturbed individuals consumed by this little girl's death. In one instance, someone bound and duct-taped a nude Barbie doll and left it on the front lawn of the vacant 15th street Ramsey home.

In another instance, a male had been arrested by police for the theft of some pages of the morgue log located at Boulder Community Hospital. Following his release from jail on this charge, he found his way to the Ramsey home and spent the night sitting on the back patio, staring at the house.

Later that night, he tried to set fire to the home by pushing lit papers through a mail slot located near the front door. He called Detective Gosage late the next morning to confess his crime.

Investigators responded to the home following this revelation and confirmed that an attempted arson had occurred, and booked him into the Boulder County Jail on felony charges.

The man was subsequently sentenced to two years in the county jail in January 1998.[18]

The media continued to pound at the division that had developed between the police and prosecutors, and in an effort to put a positive face on the matter, Alex Hunter and Mark Beckner agreed to join forces and moved their teams of investigators to a "secure" room in the Boulder County Criminal Justice Center. It was dubbed the "War Room," and BPD investigative files and computers were set up to serve as a central location from which to conduct the inquiry into JonBenét's murder.

Although the idea of a "task force" is not a unique idea when it comes to handling the investigation of major crimes, the successful use of one almost always requires that its members share the same vision and goals. In this instance, the two teams of investigators who had been forced by their superiors to share investigative quarters were diametrically opposed to one another in their interpretation of the crime.

By the time the teams had joined forces in the War Room, there were firmly held beliefs about where the inquiry needed to go, and countless discussions failed to dissuade either side of their position on the matter. It was akin to an effort of mixing oil and water. Try as hard as you want, it just wasn't going to happen.

The death knell of the effort to combine forces came when a BPD investigator returned to the War Room after days off to discover that his computer was not functioning properly. It appeared that someone had tried to hack into the secure investigative files of the case from his workstation. The computer contained a number of files, but one particular item of concern was that it held the results of *preliminary* DNA testing. (It is important to note, that in this period of time, DNA testing often took *months* to see any return of lab results. In today's environment,

DNA results can be turned around as quickly as 24 hours from submission.)

The DNA test results were something that Boulder police had held back from the DA's office because of alleged leaks to the media, and they suspected that someone from their team had been responsible for compromising the computer of the detective who managed that information.

A search of the security card-reader system for the door to the War Room revealed that one unauthorized entry had been attempted over the weekend. The security card belonged to a deputy DA who had been involved with the investigation, but who had *not* been granted security clearance to enter the room.

The security system indicated that, in fact, no entrance had been gained through this attempted card-swipe, but BPD investigators wondered why the attempted entry with the use of this card had been made at all.

No one who had legitimate access to the War Room admitted to *hacking* the detective's computer, and the police department subsequently requested the assistance of the Colorado Bureau of Investigation's computer technology team. The hard drive of the computer was examined for signs of unauthorized access and it was subsequently publically announced that the malfunction had been attributed to an *equipment problem,* and had not been the result of an unauthorized breach of the computer.

Detectives had been told by their own IT wizard that the computer had, in no uncertain terms, been compromised. Despite CBI's press release, they continued to believe that someone with the DA's office had hacked the computer in search of the DNA information.

The alleged breach of the computer had taken place within only a few days of the War Room being opened, and set the tone for the interactions that BPD investigators would have with their counter parts in the coming weeks. After only one and a half months, Boulder investigators would abandon the secure room at the Justice Center and move back to the environs of their own building.

There had been serious deliberation in the PD about pushing for a grand jury after the FBI had spoken to the issue, and this continued to gain momentum through the spring of 1998.

Hunter indicated he was willing to consider the use of the grand jury, but he first wanted to see what Boulder PD *had* that would establish the threshold he needed for a successful prosecution. Investigators were tasked with putting together a presentation for the DA's office that supported the *need* for convening the grand jury inquiry.

Over the course of two days in early June, 1998, Boulder investigators, and other forensic experts, proceeded to outline the evidence that had been collected and examined in the case. Lead investigators who presented during the briefing included Detective Sergeant Tom Wickman, and Detectives Steve Thomas, Tom Trujillo and Jane Harmer. Opinions were offered as to the possible interpretation of some of the evidence, and conclusions that could be inferred therefrom.

The presentation took place at the Coors Event Center located on the University of Colorado Boulder campus. Approximately forty people attended, representing agencies from the Colorado Attorney General's Office, the Colorado Bureau of Investigation, the FBI's Child Abduction Serial Killer Unit, BPD's Dream Team, Hunter's group of consulting DA's and members of his staff, along with Dr. Lee and Barry Scheck.

Media trucks with satellite dishes camped in the surrounding parking lot.

A detailed analysis was provided regarding key pieces of evidence, which included opinions on the authorship of the ransom note, evidence that pointed to prior acts of *chronic sexual abuse,* the pineapple found in JonBenét's digestive track, and the fingerprint evidence linking Patsy and Burke to the fruit.

Additional information was provided on the paintbrush found in the paint tray located outside the room where JonBenét had been discovered, and its use in the garrote that had been used to end her life.

The trace samples of DNA that had been analyzed thus far were discussed, with Lee and Scheck weighing in with their expert opinions. The conclusion was reached that more work was needed with regard to this evidence.

The long-delayed examination of fibers found on the sticky side of the duct tape used to silence JonBenét had finally returned from the lab. Only days before the presentation, BPD investigators had learned that fibers from Patsy Ramsey's black and red Essentials jacket were consistent with those found on the duct tape.

This suggested to some investigators that Patsy had been in direct personal contact with the duct tape used to cover her daughter's mouth, an element believed to have been used in the staging of the crime. She purportedly had never been to the basement on the morning of the kidnapping when the tape had been recovered. How could the transfer of this fiber evidence take place if it was the *intruder* who had brought the tape to the home during the kidnapping?

Sergeant Wickman was tasked with presenting information that discounted the suggestion that an intruder had been responsible for the crime. A series of theoretical questions were posed that challenged the logic behind an intruder's involvement. BPD investigators believed there were too many illogical, conflicting behavioral elements in the case to have involved an outside perpetrator.

It was stressed that the evidence of *prior vaginal trauma* suggested that either the intruder had the opportunity to visit JonBenét on many occasions prior to her murder, or that the person responsible for the sexual abuse and her homicide were different people altogether.

A synopsis was provided that detailed the BPD's efforts to clear all of the registered sex offenders who resided in the area, and other suspects who had come to attention of authorities during their investigation.

In their view, all evidence collected up to that point in time had pointed to family involvement. Boulder investigators were pinning their hopes on the weight of this evidence, and were confident that their presentation would convince Hunter to convene a grand jury.

They closed the presentation with a list of things they believed should be pursued through the investigative subpoena powers of the grand jury.

Hunter spoke to the media at the conclusion of the two-day presentation.

"This is all about finding the killer of JonBenét and justice... We do not have enough to file a case, and we have a lot of work to do. I will go back to my people and analyze what we heard over a number of hours and make sure it is sensible to spend the time it takes to run a grand jury."[19]

The investigators who had been leading the charge for a year and half went home to their families and awaited the DA's decision. They had put every ounce of energy into the preparation of the argument for the convening of a grand jury, and now there seemed to be nothing left for them to do. The case had effectively been turned over to the DA's office at the conclusion of the Event's Center briefing.

They would subsequently learn that the Ramseys had agreed to participate in another round of interviews with the DA's office, but Boulder Police would not be involved. In fact, the DA's office wouldn't even reveal the location of the interviews that would take place with the parents in Colorado. They were told to stay away from Georgia, which is where Burke was to be interviewed.

The interviews took place over the course of three days in late June, 1998, and BPD investigators were granted the opportunity to review the videotapes of the Q and A sessions during the evenings between interviews. It was not the most ideal set of circumstances for the investigators who wanted to ask their own questions of the family, but it was better than nothing.

Hunter seemed to be dragging his feet on announcing his decision as to whether or not he would convene the grand jury, and Steve Thomas had had enough. Not long after the conclusion of his agency's presentation on the murder case, he submitted a request for unpaid leave from the department. After months of enduring grueling work and frustration, he needed time away to recuperate and gather his thoughts.

As Hunter postured on the use of the grand jury, it was announced that Boulder's lead investigators wouldn't even be sworn on the case. It was possible that only *one* representative from the police department would be authorized to participate as a grand jury investigator.

This meant that the majority of the detectives who were most familiar with the evidence in the case would be prevented from sitting in on the testimony of witnesses called before the jury. Additionally, they would not be able to see or review any of the documents and records that would be returned by subpoena. This proposed course of action left more than a few scratching their heads in wonderment.

Thomas timed the submission of his letter of resignation to coincide with JonBenét's August 6th birthday. She would have turned 8-years-old that summer.

In an 8-page letter addressed to Chief Mark Beckner, recently appointed as police chief after Tom Koby's forced departure, Thomas spelled out the frustrations he experienced as a lead investigator in the murder case. He specifically blasted Alex Hunter and the members of his office for their incompetence and "mishandling" of the investigation. He detailed a litany of things the DA's office had failed to do that he felt had only served to obstruct the police inquiry into the matter.

In the end, Thomas indicated that he could no longer be a part of the *game* that the murder investigation had become. Until such time as a special prosecutor was appointed to take over the case, the Boulder detective wanted nothing more to do with the investigation.[20]

The media managed to get their hands on a copy of the letter and additional pressure was brought to bear on the investigation. A week later, Hunter officially announced that his office would present the case to the Boulder County Grand Jury. He declined to share the details of exactly when, and where, the inquiry would begin.

Fleet and Priscilla White, who had been trying to get a special prosecutor involved in the case since December 1997, authored a second letter to the media that was published on August 17, 1998. It expressed similar sentiments of the letter that had preceded it in January of that year.

The Whites expressed dismay at the recent departure of Detective Thomas, and went on to espouse a complicated theory of conspiracy involving the DA's decision to delay the use of the grand jury. They apparently believed that if the grand jury failed to indict anyone in the family that Hunter could then ask them to issue a report that would vindicate the family, and point the finger of blame at police for a botched investigation.

It was a lengthy and complicated discussion of changes that had taken place to Colorado grand jury laws, which had been set in motion prior to JonBenét's murder. Nonetheless, it was clear that the Whites thought Hunter's office had mishandled the investigation and they were asking Governor Roy Romer's office to intervene, and appoint a special prosecutor to move the case forward.

They closed the letter by blaming the Ramsey's refusal to cooperate with police as the "first cause" of the reason for the failure of the investigation.[21]

Though the murder investigation was now destined to be reviewed by a new set of eyes and ears, the summer of 1998 had not yet witnessed the last of the resignations of Ramsey investigators.

Not happy with the direction he thought the case was taking, DA investigator Lou Smit tendered his letter of resignation to Alex Hunter on September 20, 1998.

"Dear Alex,

It is with great reluctance and regret that I submit this letter of resignation. Even though I want to continue to participate in the official investigation and assist in finding the killer of JonBenét, I find that I cannot in good conscience be part of the persecution of innocent people. It would be highly improper and unethical for me to stay when I so strongly believe this…

At this point in the investigation the "case" tells me that John and Patsy Ramsey did not kill their daughter, that a very dangerous killer is still out there and no one is actively looking for him….

The case tells me there is substantial, credible, evidence of an intruder and lack of evidence that the parents are involved."[22]

Smit had worked on the case for the DA's office for nearly 19 months. His letter of resignation did not signal the end of his participation in the case, however, for he would go on to work for the Ramsey family, and their attorneys, as he proceeded to chase leads of the elusive intruder thought responsible for murdering JonBenét.

CHAPTER FIFTEEN

Co-opting the Investigation

Prior to his resignation, Smit had continued to pursue the defense leads that pointed to an outside intruder being involved in the murder of JonBenét. The Ramsey family, having become acquainted with him through the regular prayer vigils he held outside their Boulder home, must have felt that a savior had finally come to their rescue.

This was the man who had discovered evidence that suggested an intruder had used the Train Room window well to enter and exit the home, and he supported this theory by pointing to the odd placement of a suitcase directly beneath the window of this basement storage room.

Smit had also launched the hypothesis that a stun gun had been used to silence and subdue JonBenét during her abduction from her bedroom. The use of this instrument had left the tell-tale marks of its electronic probes on JonBenét's body, and in his opinion, it was declarative of the existence of an intruder.

It was Smit's strongly held belief that a family member would not have required the use of a stun gun to control JonBenét, and thus the evidence that pointed to its existence effectively cleared the family of any involvement in her death.

There were a number of prosecutors and investigators in the sheriff's department who believed in Smit's theory, and the separation between these agencies and Boulder PD investigators continued to widen. Boulder investigators could not understand how Smit and others in his camp excluded certain key pieces of physical evidence and behavioral clues that pointed to family involvement.

In other instances, intruder theorists outright dismissed the opinions of the outside experts who had continued to consult on the case. This included insight provided by members of the FBI's venerable Behavioral Analysis and Child Abduction Serial Killer Units. Their interpretation of the circumstances involved in the case led them to counsel BPD investigators to continue their inquiry into the family.

Despite these contrary opinions, Smit pursued Alex Hunter's charge of investigating the case from the defense perspective. His continuing efforts to run a parallel investigation are revealed in a letter that John Ramsey sent to him dated December 18, 1997. A copy of this letter was subsequently forwarded to Boulder investigators by the D.A.'s office and received on January 6, 1998.[23]

In 2 ½ pages of typewritten format, Ramsey spells out possible theories that would have prompted an intruder to target his family, and the names of other people who could have had motive to harm his daughter.

Ramsey points to two events that preceded the Christmas holidays that may have triggered someone to commit the crime. The first event was the article that had been published in the *Boulder Daily Camera* in early December 1996, announcing that his company, Access Graphics, had surpassed the 1 billion-dollar mark in sales. He states that he had a "strange gut feeling" about the publishing of the article and wasn't sure it was a good idea. There were concerns because it mentioned him by name.

He ultimately approved the go-ahead for the article and, in hindsight, seemed to be suggesting that this article painted him as a wealthy target of opportunity. Ramsey would later suggest that the ransom demand exhibited the possibility of religious over-tones, which arguably, would negate the financial motive for this crime. From the outset, many friends of the family thought the $118,000.00 demand was meager when compared to Ramsey's relative wealth.

The second event was JonBenét's public appearance in the Boulder Christmas Parade that took place on or around December 6th, 1996. Ramsey indicated that JonBenét had ridden on a car float with 2 or 3 other girls, and that her name had been attached to the side of the car. He described her as looking very pretty and was voicing reluctance for having permitted her to participate in the event. He thought that perhaps the intruder had seen her there.

Ramsey then addressed the reference in the ransom note to his "southern" heritage and pointed out that he had been raised in Michigan and Nebraska. He had only moved to the south, Atlanta, Georgia, after completing his service in the U.S. Navy, so anyone who was close enough to be familiar with his background would have known that he was not a true southerner.

Potential suspects then became the focus of the correspon-dence and Ramsey began with an assessment of Bill and Janet McReynolds, also known as "Mr. and Mrs. Santa Claus." He stated that he didn't think he could "discount" the two as possible suspects and indicated that Bill McReynolds had played Santa Claus at two previous holiday parties hosted at his home. He advised that a dozen or so friends would come to the house, and then Santa would show up as a special treat for the children.

JonBenét reportedly was fascinated with Santa and during one party took him on a tour of the house that included her bedroom and the basement. Ramsey indicated that the basement was usually full of Christmas decorations and presents.

The Ramseys had not planned a Christmas party for the 1996 holidays due to the fact that there had already been a surprise 40th birthday party celebration for Patsy, and because the family intended to go on a Disney cruise after spending some time at their vacation home in Michigan. There was a lot going on with the family that season and another holiday party had not been scheduled for the calendar.

McReynolds was reported to have called Patsy Ramsey to see if he could again play Santa for her holiday party. McReynolds indicated that Charles Kurault was in Boulder doing a special program about his portrayal of Santa and thought that he might come to the Ramsey party to film the event. He alluded to how nice the family home appeared.

Ramsey thought that McReynolds had made a point of calling his wife and inviting himself to their party.

Patsy Ramsey reportedly decided to go ahead and put together a party on short notice, inviting their regular group of friends and children. Santa was accompanied for the first time by his wife, who played the role of Mrs. Claus. Ramsey indicated that everything seemed normal at the party, although Mrs. Claus had not been particularly "cheerful" in portraying her holiday persona.

Ramsey stated that Santa "acted very frail" and needed the assistance of his wife during the evening. He noted that Santa didn't seem to be playing his role very well either, but he wrote it off to McReynolds' "feebleness."

He contrasted this behavior with what he reportedly witnessed later that December when McReynolds was observed to be acting "quite spry" when standing outside a televised broadcast of the *Today* show.

Ramsey referenced the bizarre past he would later hear about the McReynolds family and when he put it all together, he wondered if they somehow could have been involved in the murder of his daughter. He went on to state that "whoever had done this was quite clever and that they seemed to have been trying to be overly clever."

Ramsey thought that the crime had been "well thought out" and referenced Janet McReynold's fictional play that she had written about a child's murder. He thought perhaps that she had wanted to "try the real thing."

Ramsey alluded to McReynold's presence at his holiday party as being a precursor to the alleged secret visit that Santa was going to make to JonBenét on one of the days bracketing Christmas day. JonBenét reportedly told a childhood friend that Santa was going to pay her a special visit in addition to Christmas morning.

Two verses of Psalms had been circled in a bible located in his home, and he pointed to these as additional clues left by the intruder. He reported that neither he nor Patsy had ever marked a bible in their home and wondered why an intruder would leave a ransom note, except for the purpose of leaving "clever little clues."

Ramsey also indicted that he had read that Psalm 118 was located exactly in the center of the bible, and that this perhaps accounted for the $118,000.00 ransom figure.

He concluded his assessment with the McReynolds involvement by opining that perhaps the real signature on the ransom note was "SBJC", rather than "SBTC". He suggested that it could be interpreted as an acronym for "Santa Bill and Janet Claus."

Former employees of Access Graphics became the next focus of Ramsey's list of possible "suspect" leads and he mentioned two people that he himself had a hand in terminating from the company. He then named men who had been mentioned early in the inquiry, people who might have been indirectly angry with him as a CEO who had permitted their firing.

Jeff Merrick, Jim Marino, and Mike Glenn had been introduced into the company by Ramsey, but eventually terminated. Each of the men apparently thought that Ramsey should have intervened in their personnel matters.

Ramsey indicated that he found it difficult to believe that any of these men would have been involved in the murder of his daughter, but of all of the three, he was suspicious of the wife of Merrick. He thought that she could have been angry with him over her husband's situation.

The last suspect named in Ramsey's letter was the woman with whom he had had an affair. He indicated that he had not seen or heard from her in 20 years and that it was difficult for him to imagine that she could have been involved.

He provided the names of a couple people who might be able to determine her current whereabouts, and concluded by indicating that it might be possible that she had been "vengeful" about his meeting and subsequent marriage to Patsy.

John Ramsey signed off this personal correspondence expressing the hope that Smit and his family were well, and that he would be able to spend time with them. Further, he expressed his and Patsy's thanks that Smit had come into their lives at that time.

Boulder investigators were growing increasingly frustrated with the lack of any real progress in their investigation. It seemed that certain members of the D.A.'s office were bent on crippling their efforts to pursue leads in the case. Routine search warrants for records had been denied, and evidence that had been unearthed by investigators that pointed to family involvement was deemed insignificant by prosecutors, the very people who were supposed to have been their allies in the pursuit of the truth of the matter.

The media leaks continued, and the men and women of the Boulder Police Department were portrayed as inexperienced, incompetent, and biased in their singular opinion that the evidence collected in the case continued to lead them to believe that a family member had been involved in JonBenét's murder.

The leadership of the department remained silent on the public front, not able to compromise the details of an ongoing criminal investigation, but that did not assuage the demoralized investigators who worked tirelessly to solve the murder of a six-year old girl. The media would not hear of all of the other intruder leads that Boulder investigators would be pursuing in their search for answers.

Boulder investigators had been asking for a grand jury investigation from the early onset of the case, as early as January 1997. There was a need to compel testimony from people who were refusing to cooperate, and to secure the information of witnesses while it was still fresh in their memories.

It was not a novel idea. Many judicial districts brought murder cases before their sitting Grand Juries because of the broad reaching powers associated with their investigative authority. Witnesses, adverse or otherwise, could be compelled to testify, and subpoenas could be issued that directed the production of records deemed probative to the inquiry.

For some unknown reason, the D.A.'s office balked at the idea. Apparently, Hunter's office preferred to the let the gulf widen between his agency and the members of the police department who were statutorily charged with the investigation of the murder. Law enforcement agencies *investigated* crimes committed within their jurisdiction. District Attorney's offices were responsible for *prosecuting* defendants who were ultimately charged under the legal threshold of "probable cause."

Hunter seemed content to let confusion reign, and the animosity between police investigators and his office continued to build. As noted in Steve Thomas's letter of resignation, the level of frustration amongst BPD investigators was reaching epidemic proportions. The Ramseys had not been charged in any crime, and yet their cadre of attorneys were making demands exclusively reserved to the rights of a criminal defendant.

The analysis of physical evidence that could have moved the case forward was put on hold, and investigators were constantly reminded that the politically influential team of Ramsey attorneys were a power unto themselves. From an outsider's perspective, it seemed that the D.A.'s office was afraid to go head-to-head with the defense team that had been assembled in this case.

Tom Wickman was a friend and former colleague of mine, and he had come to Telluride on many occasions over the years to work as a reserve officer for me during the summer music festivals. As a detective sergeant, he had assumed responsibility for overseeing the murder investigation after Larry Mason had been removed from the case, wrongly accused of leaking information to the media.

Wickman was tightlipped about the inquiry, but he once shared with me that frustrations had run to the boiling point on one particular day. The men and women under his command had been running their tails into the ground, working untold hours, and in their minds their efforts had been fruitless.

Taking in the disparaging look on the faces of his team, Wickman decided to close the doors of the unit for the afternoon. Submitting their leave requests, the team snuck out the back door of the department and reconvened at a movie theatre. They took in a matinee movie, the topic of which was an uplifting crime drama that depicted the good guys triumphing over evil, something that doesn't always happen in the real world.

I can't tell you how impressed I was by Tom's willingness to make a command decision and retreat from the front of the battle for a short period of time. Boulder Police had been continually berated and hounded by the press, and they risked being followed whenever they left the building. His decision served to lift up the spirits of his fellow investigators and gave them the hope of starting anew the next day.

Having secured a sympathetic ear in the prosecutor's office, John Ramsey took the next step to further distance the Boulder

Police Department from the lead role they held in the investigation of the murder of his daughter. He crafted a personal handwritten letter to Alex Hunter on April 11, 1998, that purportedly bypassed his team of attorneys.

It was one of the documents that I would eventually review during my participation in the case, and it had been forwarded to the Boulder Police Department on May 4, 1998.[24]

Mark Beckner, then a commander with the department, had assembled the investigators assigned to the murder case and explained some of the exchanges that had apparently been taking place between the Ramsey team and District Attorney's Office.

A copy of Ramsey's letter, unknown to the team prior to that time, was effectively entered into the record.

The correspondence reads as follows:

4/11/98

Dear Mr. Hunter,

I am writing this letter because it seems difficult at times to communicate through attorneys who are focused on protecting my rights as a citizen.

I want to be very clear on our family's position.

1.) We have no trust or confidence in the Boulder Police. They tried, from the moment they walked in our home on December 26, 1996, to convince others that Patsy or I, or Burke killed JonBenét. I will hold them accountable forever for one thing — not accepting help from people who offered it in the beginning and who could have brought a wealth of experience to bear on this crime.

2.) We (myself, Patsy, Burke, John Andrew, Melinda) will meet anytime, anywhere, for as long as you want, with investigators from your office. If the purpose of a grand jury is to be able to talk to us, that is not necessary. We want to find the killer of our daughter and sister and work with you 24 hours a day to find "it."

3.) *If we are subpoenaed by a grand jury, we will testify regardless of any previous meeting with your investigators. I'm living my life for two purposes now: to find the killer of JonBenét and bring "it" to the maximum justice our society can impose. While there is a rage within me that says, give me a few minutes alone with this creature and there won't be a need for a trial, I would then succumb to the behavior which the killer did. Secondly, my living children must not have to live under the legacy that our entertainment industry has given them based on false information and a frenzy created on our family's misery to achieve substantial profit.*

It's time to rise above all this pettiness and politics and get down to the most important mission — finding JonBenét's killer. That's all we care about. The police cannot do it. I hope it's not too late to investigate this crime properly at last.

Finally, I am willing and able to put up a substantial reward, one million dollars, through the help of friends if this will help derive information. I know this would be used against us by the media dimwits. But I don't care.

Please, let's all do what is right to get this worst of all killer in our midst.

Sincerely,

John Ramsey

This letter was effectively signaling the end of the Boulder Police Department's primary and statutory role in the murder investigation of JonBenét Ramsey.

The following year, in May 1999, Hunter would publically announce that Burke Ramsey was not a suspect in his sister's death. It was reported in the Denver media that he was prompted to make this announcement after supermarket tabloids had pointed the finger at Burke as being responsible for the murder of JonBenét.

In this same time frame, it was announced that the Ramsey family had hired civil attorney L. Lin Wood, of Atlanta, Georgia, to represent their interests in pursuing legal action against the media outlets who were slandering the family.

Wood eventually filed a number of lawsuits on the behalf of the family in the years that followed.

"If I could speak to John and Patsy Ramsey I'd tell them to quit hiding behind their attorneys, quit hiding behind their PR firm, come back to Colorado; work with us to find the killers in this case, no matter where the trail may lead."

—Colorado Governor Bill Owens, quoted during a Barbara Walters interview aired on *ABC News*, March 17, 2000

Behind Closed Doors

L ead investigators in the case had begun to contemplate the use of a grand jury as early as January, 1997, when members of the immediate family and many other potential witnesses began to *lawyer up*, as it is sometimes called in the street-language of police officers. They also began to experience this phenomenon with those who were refusing to speak on the official record due to the publicity the case was attracting. No witness with credible information wanted to be subjected to the experience of a news crew being stationed outside their home or business for days on end.

After many debates and arguments over the issue, BPD investigators were belatedly granted their wish on March 12, 1998, when the City of Boulder issued the following press release:

> *Boulder Police Chief Tom Koby and Commander Mark Beckner today requested and recommended that the Boulder*

District Attorney convene a grand jury investigation into the homicide of JonBenét Ramsey. While there is still some investigation left to be done, both Chief Koby and Commander Beckner believe the investigation has progressed to the point at which the authority of a grand jury is necessary in order to have a complete investigation. A grand jury can be utilized to obtain sworn testimony, to obtain other items of evidentiary value not otherwise available through routine investigative methods, and to review the case for purposes of seeking an indictment after the person or persons responsible for the death of JonBenét.

Commander Beckner has worked closely with the District Attorney's Office in recent weeks in preparation of the commendation for a grand jury. According to Beckner, "We only make this request / recommendation after 14 grueling months of investigation, much consideration and thought, and after consultation with attorneys familiar with, and experienced in the use, of grand juries. We believe the investigation has reached the point at which a grand jury will be very helpful in completing the investigation, thus, our recommendation to the District Attorney."

As the investigation progressed in recent weeks, the direction the investigation should take became very clear. As stated at the Dec. 5, 1997 news conference, the police were working one of three options:

- *Seek an arrest warrant and prosecution*
- *Ask for a grand jury investigation, or*
- *Inactivate the case until such time that additional information becomes available*

Out of a task list that has grown to 90 tasks, 64 tasks have been completed or worked on as thoroughly as possible. "The longer we worked on the case, the clearer it became that inactivating the case would not be appropriate," said Beckner.

"The appropriate step at this time is to ask for a grand jury to assist us in gathering additional admissible evidence."

The next step will be for the police to assist the District Attorney's Office in the review of the case files and evidence. Given the volume of information gathered to date, it is expected that it will take some time for the District Attorney's Office to complete its review of the case files prior to any decision being made. "We have worked well with the DA's Office in the last five months and I expect to work even closer with in the months to follow," added Beckner.

City of Boulder, Press Release #65

As noted in a previous chapter, District Attorney Alex Hunter responded to this public request by saying that he needed the Boulder Police Department to present the details of their investigation to his staff before he was willing to convene a grand jury in the matter. This presentation took place over the course of two days in early June 1998.

The Ramseys apparently decided it was time to get their story on the record as well, and agreed to participate in another round of interviews that the DA's office arranged later that month. It would be the first formal law enforcement interview they had participated in since speaking to Boulder detectives in April 1997.

On August 12, 1998, Hunter announced that he was now ready to present the JonBenét murder case to a Boulder County Grand Jury. Fleet and Priscilla White responded to this news by authoring a second letter to the public, dated August 17, 1998.[25] It called for the appointment of a special prosecutor in the case. Their first letter had been published in January, 1998, and had urged then-Governor Roy Romer to appoint the Colorado Attorney General as a special prosecutor in the case, citing malfeasance on the part of Hunter's office.

Governor Romer declined to intervene in either instance, but prior to the publication of the White's August letter, Hunter's office had engaged the services of a former grand jury specialist from the Denver District Attorney's Office to serve as lead attorney in his grand jury inquiry. Michael Kane, working as the deputy director of taxation in the Pennsylvania State Department of Revenue after leaving the Denver DA's office, had returned to Colorado in time to observe Boulder PD's two day presentation in early January. He would also personally participate in the Ramsey interviews that took place over three consecutive days at the end of June 1998.

Kane supplanted two of Hunter's key prosecutors, Pete Hoffstrom and Trip DeMuth, when taking the lead role in the grand jury inquiry in the investigation. Veteran prosecutors from adjoining jurisdictions were selected to serve as advisory consul, and they included Mitch Morrissey of the Denver DA's Office, and Bruce Levin of the Adams County DA's Office.

A series of questions were posed to 60 potential jurors in open courtroom proceedings that took place during the summer of 1998. By September 16th, a panel of 12 grand jurors and 4 alternates were seated, and they began to hear the first hours of testimony in the JonBenét murder investigation. Nearly eight hours of procedural briefings and introductory testimony consumed their first day on the case.

The news media was encamped in the parking lots fronting the Boulder County Justice Center, and their cameras would come to life every time a potential witness entered or exited the gray stone building. Their vigil would continue for longer than anyone expected.

Given the history of this case, it would not have been possible for the opening day of the grand jury murder inquiry to have passed without some type of controversy. In the first hour of its birth, a Boulder man summoned to the Justice Center as a potential juror in an unrelated case, reportedly walked past a retinue of Ramsey reporters and photographers with his middle finger raised in salute, muttering a slur of epithets.

After a couple of attempts, he apparently was successful at grabbing and smashing the camera of one of the photographers covering the scene. The man was subsequently charged with Harassment and Disorderly Conduct. It is unknown at this writing if he was ever chosen to serve as a juror on the case for which he had received a jury summons.

In additional "news," the *Denver Post* reported that the newly impaneled grand jury was expected to review "fiber evidence" that linked clothing of Patsy Ramsey to the duct tape found on her daughter's body. "The fiber was discovered in recent months, long after the killing, sources said."[26]

The article proceeded to cover the legal complications involved in the late discovery of the evidence, and chastised the police for their inability to have uncovered the fiber earlier in the investigation.

An Atlanta TV station was also cited as reporting that Boulder authorities had been considering the exhumation of JonBenét's body for further forensic testing. Boulder city officials denied the report, indicating that police "knew of no court order, or court order in progress" that would direct the exhumation of JonBenét's body.

The article pointed out, however, that Alex Hunter had stated in January 1998, that he would consider exhuming JonBenet's body "if that is what is necessary in the search for the truth."[27]

The details surrounding this report were not fully disclosed, but there had been some discussion amongst investigators and prosecutors at the time as to whether the body should be exhumed to conduct microscopic examination of the skin cells at the site of the suspected stun gun injuries. It was eventually determined that the forensic examination of these injuries would not have been probative to the inquiry.

The grand jury met twice a week in the early stages of their investigation. At times, witnesses would enter and exit through the front doors of the Justice Center in plain view of anyone present.

On other occasions, witnesses were driven to the building in the rear of unmarked vehicles with tinted windows. Their entry and exit to the proceedings took place through the underground parking garage of the building, and the back hallways of the secured interior of the Criminal Justice Center complex.

It was a game of *cat and mouse* for the journalists attempting to cover the progress of the case. They were frequently attempting to determine the identity of the person(s) who had appeared before the grand jury that day, and what relevant facts they had to offer in the inquiry into the murder of an innocent 6-year-old child.

Speculation and rumor often led the headlines of the day.

It only took 15 minutes for the media to arrive at 755 15th street on the morning of October 30th, 1998, after grand jurors had been delivered to the Ramsey home to inspect the scene of the crime. Prosecutors lingered in the yard, as reporters and photographers observed from an approved distance of 100 feet, the *finders of fact* meander through the curtilage and premises of JonBenet's last abode.

Nearly two hours and twenty minutes (2:20 hours) had elapsed as the men and women of the Boulder County Grand Jury explored the scene where a brutal murder had taken place 22 months previous. Concluding their individual inspection of the home, the jurors silently boarded the Boulder County Sheriff's Department transport vans, and departed the scene with a different perspective.

The media reported on two different aspects of this visit to the crime scene. The *Rocky Mountain News* quoted the views of two separate "legal experts" on the matter.[28] One expert thought the visit to the crime scene "very unusual," and went on to proclaim that if the jury had 'enough to indict, you don't need to tour the house.'

A contrasting opinion was offered by a local University of Colorado Law School instructor, who opined that there was "nothing startling about the visit."

"This gives them an idea how isolated the various rooms are from each other, that it would be easy for noises to happen in the vicinity of JonBenet's room that the parents wouldn't necessarily hear. And it's good for them to get a feel for that."[29]

On December 28, 1998, Boulder's *Daily Camera* reported that the grand jury would be taking a month-long break until January. Ramsey attorney Hal Haddon expressed disappointment at the pace of the investigation. "We were hopeful it would move faster...but, I have no idea why they have recessed. So, I'm not critical of it."[30]

Haddon went on to state that no member of the Ramsey family had received a subpoena to testify before the grand jury.

It wouldn't become public information until more than a year later, but in February 1999, Alex Hunter obtained a court order seeking to prohibit Lou Smit's request to testify before the grand jury about his intruder theory. With the assistance of former El Paso County District Attorney Bob Russel, and former Public Defender Greg Walta, Smit overturned the court order that prevented him from voicing his opinion on the matter.

The Rocky Mountain News reported on the matter: "Smit's attorney accused Hunter of not wanting to give the grand jury all of the facts in the case, according to court documents. Authorities have named only JonBenet's parents, John and Patsy Ramsey, as suspects in the case."

"The prosecution is either intentionally or unintentionally emphasizing and focusing upon evidence which points to involvement of the Ramsey family and is not presenting clear evidence of involvement of an intruder in the murder of JonBenet Ramsey," attorney Greg Walta argued in court documents." [31]

A source close to the investigation explained Hunter's reasoning for seeking the prohibition of his former investigator's testimony: he was concerned that Smit would only offer his *theories* about the case, and no *factual* evidence to the grand jury.[32]

Smit eventually presented his intruder theory to the grand jury in March 1999. He later stated that he quit the DA's office in part, because "he believed Boulder Police and prosecutors had developed tunnel vision and were focusing only on the Ramsey family and not on other suspects."[33]

The Boulder Grand Jury was reported to have ended their spring session of 1999 not long after hearing the testimony of Burke Ramsey, JonBenét's brother, who was 9 years old at the time of the murder. Jurors took a summer hiatus of nearly 4 months after their May 25th meeting.

Late in September 1999, *Rocky Mountain News* staff writer Charlie Brennan reported that the 18-month term of the grand jury was due to expire on October 20th, and that it was unclear who would be next testifying before the panel.[34]

Brennan reported that former FBI profiler John Douglas had previously stated that he believed the crime had been committed by someone outside the family, possibly by someone with a "business-related grudge against John Ramsey."

Brennan noted, however, that interviews with executives of Ramsey's former employer, Access Graphics, revealed that no one from the company had been called to testify before the grand jury. Denver media legal analyst Scott Robinson thought that information relevant, and he believed that the investigation was focused "elsewhere in the search of JonBenét's killer."[35]

Some of the witnesses who were reported to have testified before the grand jury up to that point in time were listed as follows:

- Mike Archuleta, Ramsey pilot
- Lind Arndt, BPD detective
- Dr. Francesco Beuf , JonBenet's pediatrician
- Debbie Chaves, CBI forensics expert
- John Douglas, retired FBI profiler
- Michael Everett, BPD CSI

- John and Barbara Fernie, friends of Ramsey family
- Rick French, BPD officer first on scene
- Ron Gosage, BPD detective
- Pam Griffin, Ramsey family friend and beauty pageant seamstress
- Jan Harmer, BPD detective
- George Herrera, CBI fingerprint expert
- Linda **Hoffmann-Pugh**, Ramsey housekeeper and accused suspect
- Reverend Rol Hoverstock, Ramsey pastor
- Larry Mason, BPD detective sergeant
- Dr. John Meyer, Boulder County Coroner
- Fred Patterson, BPD detective
- Carol Piirto, JonBenet's 3rd grade teacher
- Merv Pugh, husband of Ramsey housekeeper Linda **Hoffmann-Pugh**
- Burke Ramsey, older brother of JonBenet
- Lou Smit, Boulder DA investigator
- Tom Trujillo, BPD detective
- Chet Ubowski, CBI handwriting analyst
- Barry Weiss, BPD CSI
- Fleet and Priscilla White, Ramsey family friends
- Tom Wickman, BPD detective sergeant

On October 1, 1999, the *Denver Post* reported that the grand jury was preparing to hear from people considered to be Ramsey supporters.[36] Private investigator Ellis Armistead, working for Ramsey attorneys from nearly the outset of the case, had been observed walking into a grand jury "prep room" and walking from the 'direction of the Boulder District Attorney's Office' about an hour later.'

Close family friend and supporter, Susan Stine, was said to have testified the week prior. The Ramseys had delivered a Christmas present to the Stine residence after leaving the White party on Christmas night. Susan was described as a *staunch defender* of Patsy Ramsey, and she and her husband had moved to Georgia with the Ramseys when they left Boulder.

The paper also reported that John Ramsey's older children, John Andrew and Melinda, were expected to testify on Thursday of that week. Though not in the home on the night of the murder, they could possibly answer questions about other relationships with the family.

Legal analysts theorized that the appearance of witnesses friendly to the Ramseys suggested that investigators were looking for suspects *outside* the family. Friends might be able to point to things that aroused their suspicion and provide detectives with new leads.

Though they were prepared to testify in the matter, neither Patsy nor John Ramsey was reported to have appeared before the grand jury during their investigation.

On October 13, 1999, thirteen months after being convened, Alex Hunter held a press conference and stated that the grand jury had concluded its inquiry into the murder of JonBenét Ramsey, and that "no charges have been filed." He went on to indicate that prosecutors "do not have sufficient evidence to warrant the filing of charges against anyone who has been investigated at the present time."

The panel of grand jurors investigating the murder had been dismissed and no report had been issued by their body. Hunter reportedly vowed that the proceedings would remain secret forever and jurors were prohibited from speaking about the details of their participation in the investigation.

Mark Beckner, now the police chief of Boulder, issued a statement two days later. He thanked the grand jurors for their service to the community, and went on to praise the special prosecutors who had led the grand jury through its work.

Commenting on speculation that charges had not been filed because of reluctance on the part of the District Attorney's Office, Beckner noted that 3 experienced prosecutors had worked on the grand jury investigation. In his opinion, none of them would hesitate to take the case to trial once the evidence was sufficient to do so.

Beckner indicated that despite the lack of an indictment being issued, progress had been made during the grand jury inquiry and that the murder investigation remained an open and on-going case.

Michael Kane, the special prosecutor who had led the grand jury inquiry, returned to his home in Pennsylvania a tired and frustrated man. In an interview conducted nearly two years later, Kane told *Rocky Mountain News* staff writer Charlie Brennan that he still thought about the murder case every day.

"And at least once a week, when I'm out running or something, this case will be running through my head, and I'll think, 'What if we did this now?' Or, 'What if that happened?'"[37]

Kane had the opportunity to interview the Ramseys on two occasions: the first when he joined Hunter's team in June 1998 and he assisted Lou Smit with the family interviews arranged by the DA's office. The second occasion took place in August 2000, when he traveled to Atlanta with Mark Beckner to participate in interviews taking place in the offices of Ramsey attorney, Lin Wood.

Kane indicated that he had spent many hours questioning the Ramseys and believed they had 'yet to give him the straight story.'[38]

It was his impression that he felt like he was talking to a "press secretary who was giving responses with a spin." "I felt like their answers were very careful and, in some cases, scripted. And that caused me a lot of concern."

The August 2000 interviews had been arranged so that police could explain the evidence that placed the Ramseys under suspicion, and explore whether the family had any explanations for some of the evidence. [39]

Kane and Wood went head-to-head on one or more occasions during the interviews. Kane took exception to Wood's interjections during some questions and accused him of obstructing his questioning. Wood responded by calling Kane's line of questioning as irrelevant, and referred to one particular question about Burke's school security as "the disgusting tactic of an overzealous prosecutor."[40]

Kane had encouraged Wood to accompany him to a judge's chambers, and seek public disclosure of the grand jury records. Wood responded affirmatively to the suggestion, but there was never any follow-up on the proposal.

The August interviews were characterized by both police and Wood as non-productive, and marked the end of Kane's official involvement in the murder investigation.

He told Brennan in his 2001 interview that he thought a major problem with the case was that prosecutors had failed to initiate a grand jury inquiry early in the investigation. He felt that the grand jury should have been impaneled promptly, not necessarily with the intent to seek a quick indictment, but to use its broad-ranging subpoena powers. Reluctant witnesses could have been compelled to testify, and records of a personal and business nature could have been obtained in a more timely fashion.

Kane indicated that, despite the numerous books and media stories that had covered the investigation, the public was not fully aware of the real facts of the case. There remains 'dozens of secrets and what the public thinks is fact is simply not the fact.'[41]

After a year and a half spent focusing on nothing but the murder case, Kane indicated that he was burned out from the *cat-and-mouse* aspects of the case. He found it rewarding, but was glad to have been able to take a break from the frustrations of the investigation.

To Tell the Truth

The polygraph has been a tool used by law enforcement investigators for decades, and it is an instrument that relies upon the physiological responses of an individual who undergoes questioning while attached to the machine. It is intended to tell an examiner whether or not someone is being truthful during the testing process.

The polygraph machine tests three aspects of the human physiology:

- Respiration
- Changes in skin resistance / skin conductance
- Relative blood volume and pulse rate

The *lie* is purportedly detected by physiological changes taking place in the body when a person is not being truthful. The premise being, that when a person is deceptive, there are numerous physiological changes that occur, such as an increase or decrease in blood volume being pumped through the body; an increase or decrease in the heart rate; and changes in respiration and perspiration.

When a person is being truthful, the body functions within its normal patterns with no significant changes. The polygraph examiner helps determine this baseline of physiological behavior by asking questions for which a truthful response is expected: i.e. How old are you? Do you live at 123 Oak Street, Anywhere, USA? What is your name?

Changes in physiological conditions are graphed throughout the questioning, and alteration or significant and consistent changes in a person's responses may be indicative of deception.

It is important to note that many studies have taken place over the years to help determine the reliability and veracity of polygraph testing. There are many different factors that come into play when deciding whether the results of a polygraph test can be relied upon to determine the truth of the matter.

Despite the studies that have been completed to date, there continues to be a debate about the *accuracy* of polygraph exams. While it is has been stated that the polygraph technique is highly accurate, it must be recognized that it is not infallible, and errors can and do occur when an examiner is interpreting the data collected during a test.

Like the situation in which an inexperienced physician can misdiagnose an x-ray, so too can a polygraph examiner misread a chart if there is insufficient experience coming into play. Most errors point to inexperienced polygraph examiners.

And despite the evidence that points to the credibility of polygraph testing, there are many people who claim to be able to teach methods and techniques that will help someone successfully beat the machine. The Internet is full of websites that claim to offer this service.

The American Polygraph Association notes that the admissibility of polygraph test results vary from state to state and from one federal circuit court to another. A judge is usually the final arbiter when it comes to admitting polygraph test results in a court of law. Most frequently, both sides must stipulate in advance of any test, that polygraph results will be permitted to be entered into the record of the case being heard before the court.

In Colorado, it is extremely rare to see polygraph results considered during the prosecution of a criminal case. The polygraph is more typically used as an investigative tool, and test results are frequently utilized during the interview that immediately follows an examination. The subject of the interview may be questioned more thoroughly about indications of deception on certain questions that were asked during the testing process.

The success of rooting out the deception that has been uncovered during the polygraph examination is often determined by the experience, and skill of the trained police interrogator. An admission of guilt must accompany a deceptive polygraph exam, for it is not possible to waive the test results of a lying suspect in front of a prosecutor and expect that criminal charges will be filed. It just isn't going to happen in today's environment.

Boulder investigators were fully conversant with this situation when they had their first opportunity to conduct follow-up interviews with John and Patsy Ramsey in April, 1997.

Treading lightly in his approach to the topic, Steve Thomas indicated that he was attempting to take possible suspects *out of the bucket* so that he could focus his efforts on those who declined to clear themselves of involvement in the crime. He didn't specifically ask either of the parents during their interview if they would submit to polygraph testing, but wanted to know *how* the test results would turn out if they did take a test.

John Ramsey indicated that he had been told that he should not take a test because of the tremendous amount of guilt he was harboring for failing to protect his daughter. This feeling of guilt, and the strong emotions he was experiencing, might impact his test results. He went on to say that he had not killed JonBenét, and that if the polygraph was accurate, he would "pass it 100%."

Thomas pressed the issue, and asked Ramsey if he would, at some point, take a polygraph.

Ramsey replied that he would be "insulted" if asked to take a polygraph, and though he was willing to follow any recommendations made by his attorneys, he objected to the way he thought police were trying to characterize him and his wife in the matter. He expressed the opinion that police were on a course of "tragic misdirection" by spending time investigating him and Patsy for possible involvement in the murder of their daughter.

Patsy was asked a similar set of questions regarding a polygraph examination, and indicated that she was "telling the truth." She stated that she didn't know how polygraphs worked, but that if they "tell the truth," then she would be "telling the truth."

When asked specifically if she would pass a test, Patsy replied by saying, "Yes, I would pass it. I'll take ten of them, I don't care, you know. Do whatever you want."

The topic of polygraphs remained dormant for the 40 months that followed the death of JonBenét, and it was not until after the grand jury had concluded their inquiry into the matter that Ramsey attorneys considered using the lie detector for their clients.

When answering questions posed by the media during the release of their book, *The Death of Innocence*[42], in March 2000, the Ramseys indicated that they had never taken a polygraph in relation to the murder investigation of their daughter. At one point during the interviews, however, they stated that they were now willing to do so, provided that the polygraph examiners had no connection with the Boulder Police Department.

Chief Beckner decided to take them up on the offer not long thereafter, and after consulting with the DA's office and FBI, indicated in an April 11, 2000, press release that he was willing to accept their conditions. Beckner indicated that Ramsey attorneys had been notified of the acceptance of the offer and was awaiting a reply to schedule a date for the exam.

Negotiations appeared to have broken down in the interim, and the City of Boulder issued another press release on April 25, 2000.

After several discussions with Boulder Police, an attorney for John and Patsy Ramsey today informed police Chief Mark Beckner that the Ramseys will not take polygraph examinations.

On April 11, the Boulder Police Department accepted John and Patsy Ramsey's public offer to take polygraph exams regarding the death of their daughter, JonBenét. The department agreed to the conditions as set forth by John Ramsey in a March 23 television interview as follows:

- *The exam be conducted by an examiner independent from the Boulder Police Department*
- *The exam be conducted in Atlanta*
- *The results of the exam be made public*

Boulder Police arranged to have FBI specialists conduct the examination in Atlanta. After consulting with others in law enforcement, Boulder Police selected the FBI polygraphers specifically for their international reputation in criminal polygraphs and their independence from the Boulder Police Department. Other factors that weighed heavily in selecting the FBI were the specialist training received by FBI examiners, the quality control implemented in their examinations and supervisory oversight that is provided for every exam.

During subsequent discussions, Ramsey attorney Lin Wood told Boulder Police that the Ramseys were reluctant to take an exam administered by the FBI, as they believed involvement of the FBI and FBI laboratories in the JonBenét Ramsey murder investigation prevented them from being "independent" examiners.

As a compromise to the Ramsey's concerns, the FBI agreed to assign an examiner who had no prior knowledge or involvement in the Ramsey case, and the Boulder Police Department agreed not to be involved in selecting the specific FBI examiners.

This did not satisfy Ramsey concerns with the FBI involvement, and the Boulder Police Department is not willing to further compromise the issue, so there will be no polygraph exams at this time.[43]

Beckner was quoted as saying that he was disappointed that the Ramseys had declined to take the polygraph examinations, after publically saying that they would.

Ramsey attorney Lin Wood was hesitant to accept Beckner's offer when he learned that the FBI's protocol for a polygraph examination typically involved *pre* and *post-testing* interviews. Subjecting his clients to another series of interviews was not part of his agenda, and he countered by offering to have the Ramseys tested by someone other than the FBI. He claimed that the Bureau had been assisting the Boulder Police Department throughout the entire course of their investigation and he didn't consider them to be neutral parties in the matter.

Wood didn't trust the federal authorities, based upon his prior experience with the FBI when defending accused Atlanta bomber, Richard Jewel. He thought the Boulder Police Department's conditions for polygraph testing was unfair. Further, he was insisting that the Boulder Police take the parents off the suspect list if they were able to successfully pass their tests.

Mark Beckner balked at the idea. Investigators believed it was important to carefully craft the types of questions that would be posed to each of the parents during an examination, and there were too many variables to consider if someone unfamiliar with the details of the investigation were to run the test.

Besides, there were just too many things that had been uncovered in the investigation to remove the parents from the *umbrella of suspicion*. Their passing of a polygraph test was not likely to convince investigators of their innocence.

The ball was now in Wood's court. His clients had volunteered to take a polygraph examination and had offered to make the details public. Some in the media quietly debated whether the

Ramseys had been experimenting with polygraphs before the topic was ever raised during the press conference that announced the release of their book.

Wood declined Beckner's offer to participate in an FBI test, but was now beginning to feel the heat that was building with the media. He had to do something, and outside the scope of public scrutiny, proceeded to hire a private examiner from New Jersey to carry out the testing.

Wood subsequently held a press conference about a month later on May 24, 2000[44], pointing out that his clients had never actually been asked by police investigators to take a polygraph during the interviews being conducted in the death of their daughter. Wood quoted portions of the April 30th, 1997 interview transcripts of the Ramseys, during which time they had only been asked *how* they might do on a test *if* taken. (Relevant portions of those questions are referenced above.)

Wood seemed to be trying to make the point that police had never asked the Ramseys to submit to polygraph testing, and that it had been *their* idea to clear themselves of involvement of the crime by taking a lie-detector exam.

Wood pointed out that the topic of polygraphs had not been raised at all during the family's second set of interviews, arranged by the D.A.'s office in June 1998.

Wood reported that the polygraph examiner who conducted the first tests on John and Patsy, Jerry Toriello, determined the results to be "inconclusive." Toriello reportedly didn't think he should conduct follow-up tests, and pointed Wood to Edward Gelb, a man recognized nationally as an expert in the field of polygraphs.

Toriello's absence at the press conference was explained by Wood to be due to a recent medical procedure, and he proceeded to introduce Gelb to the Press Corp gathered for the conference. He let Gelb speak to his area of expertise and outline the testing procedures that he had used in his examination of the Ramseys.

Gelb cut to the chase and listed the questions that had been individually posed to John and Patsy Ramsey.

Conclusion: Based on the numerical scoring of the examination in this series, John Ramsey was telling the truth when he denied inflicting the injuries that caused the death of his daughter, JonBenét. Series 2, John Ramsey, Question 1. Do you know for sure who killed JonBenét? Answer: No.

Regarding JonBenét, do you know for sure who killed her? Answer: No

Are you concealing the identity of the person who killed JonBenét? Answer: No.

Conclusion: Based on the numerical scoring of the examination in this series, John Ramsey was telling the truth when he denied knowing who killed JonBenét.

Patsy Ramsey's examinations: The first polygraph examination was unusable due to distortions. Appropriate cautions were suggested to eliminate the artifacts so that conclusive results could be obtained. Three series of single-issue examinations were conducted with Patsy Ramsey. The first examination was conducted to determine if Patsy Ramsey had direct involvement in the murder. In other words, whether Patsy inflicted the injuries that caused the death of JonBenét. The second examination was conducted to determine whether Patsy knew who killed JonBenét. The third examination was conducted to determine if Patsy wrote the ransom note that was found at the scene.

The questions asked during the three single-issue examinations follow with Patsy Ramsey's answer:

Series one, Patsy Ramsey: Did you inflict any of the injuries that caused the death of JonBenét? Answer: No.

Regarding JonBenét, did you inflict any of the injuries that caused her death? Answer: No.

Were those injuries that resulted in JonBenét's death inflicted by you? Answer: No.

Conclusion: Based on the numerical scoring of the examinations in this series Patsy Ramsey was telling the truth when she denied inflicting the injuries that caused the death of her daughter, JonBenét.

Series two, Patsy Ramsey. Do you know who inflicted the injuries that caused the death of JonBenét? Answer: No.

Regarding JonBenét, do you know for sure who killed JonBenét? Answer: No

Are you concealing the identity of the person who killed JonBenét? Answer: No.

Conclusion: Based on the numerical scoring of the examinations in this series, Patsy Ramsey was telling the truth when she denied knowing who killed JonBenét.

Series three, Patsy Ramsey: Did you write the ransom note that was found in your house? Answer: No.

Question 2: Regarding the ransom note, did you write it? Answer: No.

Following the initial disclosure of these test results, Wood introduced Cleve Baxter, another veteran polygraph examiner, who served as the quality control monitor to Gelb's testing procedures. Baxter went on to state:

Now the quality control of polygraph examinations, a lot is dependent upon the adequacy of your case information, the strength of the issue concerned, and distinctness of the issue concerned, in order to try to eliminate inconclusive polygraph examination results.

Baxter spoke a little about comparison questions compared to relevant questions and went on to advise that he felt the case information for this testing process was adequate. There was some brief discussion about two different types of polygraph testing: one involving "zone comparison" testing, which Gelb had developed during his career, and one that was referred to as "guilty knowledge" testing. This second type of examination reportedly involved "evidence connecting questions," that were asked about a case. Wood indicated that this type of polygraph was "extremely difficult to prove truthful."

Wood advised that portions of the testing processes had been video and audio-taped, and that he had offered to have the FBI observe the examinations. The offer had been declined by the Boulder Police Department.

Copies of the test results had been faxed to the Boulder D.A.'s office, as well as to Chief Beckner, and Wood indicated that he was waiving the attorney privilege and would allow investigators to question Gelb about his testing procedures. In total, Wood indicated that Gelb had administered five separate polygraph tests to John and Patsy Ramsey and declared that they had passed them all.

Within a few hours of the Ramsey press conference, Chief Beckner told the media that the investigation into JonBenét's murder would proceed unaffected. The fact that the parents had passed an examination conducted by a private professional in the field of polygraph tests held little sway in the minds of the law enforcement officials who were directing the inquiry into the murder of JonBenét Ramsey. Neither positive, nor negative test results would ever make their way into a criminal court of law.

In spite of this response, the Ramseys and their attorney were pleased that they could point to positive test results that seemed to suggest that they had no personal involvement in the death of their daughter.

≖ ⊕ ≖

On June 3, 2000, the Ramseys posted a psychic's composite sketch of a possible suspect in the murder of JonBenét on the website of the foundation they established in 1997. The sketch was based on the work of psychic Dorothy Allison, who had passed away in 1999. Allison was reported to have developed her vision of the perpetrator during a 1998 appearance on a network television program.

The website reportedly asked: *Have you seen this man? This man may have been in the Boulder area in December 1996...We firmly believe that this most horrible of killers will be caught based on information provided by people who care about right and wrong...Please help, so another innocent child will not be a victim and another family will not suffer unbearable grief.*

CHAPTER EIGHTEEN

A New Direction

Topic: December 17, 2001 City of Boulder Ramsey Expense Memo

On the above captioned date, Chief Mark Beckner released a summary of expenses as they related to the JonBenét Ramsey homicide investigation. The department had been providing this information on an annual basis to the media and the following is a year-by-year summary of total expenditures:

1996:

Overtime Expenses	$20,340.80
Travel Expenses	$ 248.38
Investigative Expense	$ 788.55
Total Expenditures	$21,377.73

1997:

On-duty Salary Expense	$308,630.81
Overtime Expense (3,929.5 hours)	$134,621.66
Travel Expenses	$ 57,392.46
Investigative Expenses	$ 30,830.08
Total Expenditures	<u>$531,475.01</u>

1998:

On-duty Salary Expense	$562,149.72
Overtime Expense (954 hours)	$ 37,541.46
Travel Expenses	$ 11,319.01
Investigative Expenses	$ 19,946.74
Total Expenditures	<u>$630,956.93</u>

1999:

On-duty Expenses	$220,780.16
Overtime Expenses (218.75 hours)	$ 10,554.11
Travel Expenses	$ 3,842.91
Investigative Expenses	$ 3,010.70
Total Expenditures	<u>$238,187.99</u>

2000:

On-duty Expenses	$133,648.28
Overtime Expenses	$ 4,898.78
Travel Expenses	$ 3,157.00
Investigative Expenses	$ 4,369.25
Total Expenditures	<u>$146,073.31</u>

2001:

On-duty Expenses	$133,624.66
Overtime Expenses	$ 3,005.59
Investigative Expenses	$ 550.00
Total Expenditures	<u>$137,180.25</u>

The report indicated that total expenditures related to the Ramsey homicide investigation for the years 1996 through 2001 were $1,705,251.21.

The conclusion of 2002 brought a decision that would significantly change the direction of the investigation. In a December 20th press release issued by the City of Boulder, it was announced that Chief Beckner and DA Mary Keenan (later to become Lacy) had agreed that the Boulder County District Attorney's Office would assume responsibility for following up on new leads and other information developed in the murder case.

"The primary reason for this change is an attempt to further the investigation in a positive manner," said Chief Beckner. "The interests of the Boulder Police Department have always been to do what is in the best interest of the investigation. This is a strategy to address concerns expressed by the Ramseys and their attorney that the Boulder Police Department is not following up additional leads. This may provide the Ramseys and their attorney greater comfort in forwarding what they believe is new information or leads that need to be investigated."

"It is our hope that by changing the dynamic of the investigation, information maintained by the Ramseys will be forwarded to the DA's Office for follow-up," stated Chief Beckner. "Obviously, it is impossible to investigate information you do not have access to.

We also realize that a fresh look at the case from time to time is healthy and could lead to new progress in the investigation."

Beckner went to say that he didn't care *how* or *who* solved the case, and if this change in the investigation helped, then it was the right thing to do.

On June 14, 2003, the *New York Times* provided a brief update on the status of the JonBenét Ramsey murder investigation.

"The Boulder district attorney, Mary Keenan, has hired a retired police detective, Tom Bennett, to lead her office's investigation into the 1996 death of 6-year-old JonBenét Ramsey. Ms. Keenan's office took over the investigation in January, and in April she said that she believed an intruder might have killed the girl. An earlier investigation by the Boulder police focused on John and Patsy Ramsey, JonBenét's parents."[45]

The fact that the *New York Times* decided to print a brief update on the changing status of the Ramsey investigation only served to illustrate the continuing nation-wide interest in the case.

Primary responsibility for the investigation into the murder of JonBenét would remain in the hands of the Boulder County District Attorney's Office for eight years.

PART
TWO

Taking the Lead

On October 11, 2000, Ramsey attorney Lin Wood sent a Confidential Facsimile Transmission to Bill Wise at the Boulder County District Attorney's office. The correspondence included a 4-page attachment of an Affidavit that Wood had prepared for Alex Hunter's consideration. The Affidavit essentially declared that the Boulder District Attorney's office didn't consider Burke Ramsey to be a suspect in the murder of his sister.

Wood suggested in the cover letter of the fax that, "While there are no guarantees, hopefully this Affidavit will minimize or negate any further appearances by Alex or a representative of the D.A.'s office in the Burke Ramsey litigation."

Wood had filed a libel / slander lawsuit against the *Star* tabloid on the behalf of Burke Ramsey at the time of this request, and apparently thought he could benefit from a sworn declaration of this type.

Hunter reportedly reviewed the draft Affidavit provided by Wood, and after striking some of the language contained therein, signed off on the edited document.

AFFIDAVIT OF ALEXANDER M. HUNTER

STATE OF COLORADO
COUNTY OF BOULDER

Personally appeared before the undersigned officer duly author-ized by law to administer oath, ALELXANDER M. HUNTER, who being duly sworn, deposes and says as follows:

1.

My name is Alexander M. Hunter, I am over twenty-one (21) years of age and I am competent to make and give this Affidavit, and do some from personal knowledge.

2.

I am an attorney duly licensed in the State of Colorado. Since January 9, 1973, I have been the elected District Attorney for the Twentieth Judicial District, County of Boulder, State of Colorado.

3.

On or about December 26, 1996, JonBenét Ramsey, a six (6) year old minor child, was murdered in her home in Boulder, Colorado.

4.

Since the date of her death, I have been continuously involved in the investigation of JonBenét Ramsey's homicide.

5.

As part of the investigation into the murder of JonBenét Ramsey, questions about any possible involvement by her brother, Burke Ramsey, who was nine (9) years of age at the time of his sister's murder and who was one of the individuals present in the house at the time of her murder, were raised and investigated as part of standard investigative practices and procedures.

6.

[Draft language was struck from this paragraph]

7.

In May of 1999, I was made aware that tabloid newspapers had indicated that Burke Ramsey was a suspect in the murder of JonBenét Ramsey or was believed to be her killer. As a result of these articles, I was contacted by media representatives and I instructed my office to release a press statement which publically and officially stated that Burke Ramsey was not a suspect in connection with the murder of his sister and that stated in part, "almost a year ago (Boulder) Police

Chief Mark Beckner stated during a news conference that Burke (Ramsey) was not a suspect and that we are not looking at him as a possible suspect. To this day Burke Ramsey is not a suspect." The information contained in the May 1999 press statement was true and correct.

8.

From December 26, 1996 to the present date, I have never engaged in plea bargain negotiations, talks or discussions with anyone in connection with the investigation into the murder of JonBenét Ramsey based in whole or in part on the premise that Burke Ramsey killed his sister. From December 26, 1996 to the present date, no member of my office has ever engaged in plea bargain negotiations, talks or discussions with anyone in connection with the investigation into the murder of JonBenét Ramsey based in whole or in part on the premise that Burke Ramsey killed his sister.

9.

[Draft language struck from this paragraph]

10.

I am aware that this Affidavit may be used by counsel for Burke Ramsey in connection with libel litigation brought on his behalf in various jurisdictions.

FURTHER AFFIANT SAYETH NOT.
This 12th day of October, 2000
Signed by Alexander M. Hunter

Documents obtained from the lawsuit indicated that Hunter struck the following language, as drafted and proposed for his consideration by Lin Wood, from two paragraphs before signing off on the final version of the Affidavit. The deleted language reads as follows and a copy of the original affidavit with the changes, and handwritten notes in the margin may be viewed in the appendix.[46]

6.

"All questions related to Burke Ramsey's possible involvement in the murder of JonBenét Ramsey were resolved to the satisfaction of the investigators and Burke Ramsey has never been viewed by investigators as a suspect in connection with the murder of his sister.

Handwritten notes in the margin next to paragraph 6 appeared to modify Wood's proposed language to the following:

From December 26, 1996, to the date of this affidavit...

When combined with the remaining language of Wood's affidavit, paragraph 6 read as follows:

From December 26, 1996, to the date of this affidavit, no evidence has ever been developed in the investigation to justify elevating Burke Ramsey's status from that of witness to Suspect."

Paragraph 9 appeared to be struck in its entirety.

9.

"From December 26, 1996 to the date of this Affidavit, Burke Ramsey has not been and is not at present, a suspect in the investigation into the murder of his sister, JonBenét Ramsey."

Winds of Change

I had been in Telluride for nearly eleven years and the last two had been a little frustrating. I had been struggling to put a cocaine trafficking investigation to bed since an attempted homicide of a street peddler had taken place in 1998. In the year prior, street level dealers were leaving town after allegedly being assaulted / threatened with baseball bats, and in at least one instance, a rivalry occurred between warring factions that involved a felony menacing with a knife.

The 1998 incident that set me into high gear involved a "hit" that had been ordered on a street-level dealer who had sold cocaine to a cooperating undercover informant just two days before he was shot in the front passenger seat of a car. The hit was ordered because he had fallen behind in his payments. It was a meager $350.00, but it was the principal of the matter and he was to be made an example for those who transgressed.

The shooter, another foot soldier in the cocaine trade from Montrose, had fired three shots into the target of his contract before his gun malfunctioned. A struggle ensued and the victim was able to flee on foot from the scene of the shooting, a lone county road surrounded by nothing but rugged terrain, pine trees and pitch black night. Bleeding profusely, he eventually found his way to the porch light at the front door of an unsuspecting county resident who immediately dialed 911.

In the months that followed that attempted homicide, agents of the Colorado Bureau of Investigation worked in conjunction with my office to get a handle on what was happening in my jurisdiction. It seemed that the "cocaine cowboy days" of my previous Boulder narcotic unit experiences were returning.

At one juncture, a couple of the local street dealers attempted to turn one of my patrol officers to their side of the fence. He played along for a short period of time, but it wasn't long before I pulled the pin on that particular course of action.

The investigation was broad, ranging from Hispanics who were making a move to control the cocaine trade in southwestern Colorado to a highly placed group of local individuals, some of whom appeared to have been involved in the distribution of cocaine in Telluride for upwards of twenty years.

The lyrics of Glenn Fry's "Smugglers Blues" that described how they "hid it up in Telluride" was no joke.

My wife, an E.R. nurse at the local medical center, had become embroiled in a series of personality conflicts at work. As one of the more senior and respected nurses at the clinic, a number of people came to her to express their dissatisfaction with the way things were being handled, and she became a spokesperson for those unwilling to say it out loud to management.

Events eventually came to a head, and a house cleaning was initiated by management at the clinic. My wife, apparently viewed as a troublemaker for her willingness to help carry the voice of the disenfranchised, was one of the casualties and found herself unemployed for the first time in nearly 30 years. No good deed goes unpunished. Isn't that how it usually goes?

If memory serves, she only collected one unemployment check. A dozen or more people wrote letters to the editor expressing their dismay at her dismissal. Many in the community had been treated in the emergency room over her decade of service, and she was held in high esteem, due to the manner in which she dealt with her patients and her display of life-saving medical expertise.

It was perhaps 6 weeks later that her position was reinstated. Management admitted that perhaps some of their decisions were ill-conceived, but it was too late. The damage had been done. Having given her heart and soul to the medical center for ten years, she was hard pressed to muster the enthusiasm she had previously felt for her place of employment.

Some events in our lives have a way of changing things, and during the days she spent at home as one of the unemployed, my spouse began exploring the possibility of going back to school. I was supportive of that idea, but didn't expect that ultimately she would be moving back to Boulder to pursue a Master's degree in Transpersonal Psychotherapy.

The time frame for completing this project, that involved finishing up a Bachelor's degree before post graduate studies even began, left me with the responsibility of raising the last of our children (a 9th grader at the time) and living without a partner for five years.

I waved goodbye to my spouse in August 2003 and pondered the realities of a long- distance relationship. On a good day, a one-way trip to Denver's Front Range involved approximately 7 hours of driving. Needless to say, I found myself in a rather discouraging mood and turned my attention to surviving the on-going battle taking place in my front yard.

In 2001 - 2002, certain members of Town Council seemed to have become motivated to de-motivate everyone within their employ. My department, in particular, seemed to bear the brunt of their hostility, and I found myself repeatedly in front of their number, fighting for the very existence of an agency whose sole purpose and function was to protect the health, safety, and welfare of the community.

I was begging for a full-time investigator who could handle the myriad of cases that were overwhelming my department during the fall budget hearings. I had personally spent a full 6 weeks of my time that summer investigating a case that involved an embezzlement of public funds from a housing complex that totaled thousands of dollars in lost revenue to the city.

Yet my arguments fell on deaf ears. Some felt that my budget was out of control, in spite of the fact that I pointed out that public safety agencies frequently comprised the larger percentage of any city's budget. Unlike other departments, public safety was open for business 24 hours a day, 7 days a week, 365 days a year. There was a logical reason why our staffing and budget was larger than some of the other departments operating in town, and why the utility bills for our building were greater than others. Our lights and computers stayed on after 5:00 p.m. when everyone else went home.

The truth of the matter, however, is that some people just don't like cops and are not hesitant to say it during a public meeting. Overtones of that sentiment played itself out over the course of 2002 and 2003. In one particular instance, a council member suggested that the employees of my department forego a pay raise, so that other town employees could benefit from that savings and receive a higher cost of living increase.

I was fast approaching 28 years of service in the law enforcement profession and nearing 11 years as a chief of police in a mountain resort community. A sense of isolation seemed to envelope me, and I was feeling increasingly alone in more ways than one.

Depression and frustration had become my bedmates, and over the course of that long, cold winter I struggled to see what the future held for me.

A lifeline appeared out of nowhere when I noted an employment advertisement placed in the *Daily Camera* during a visit to Boulder in the early spring of 2004. The Boulder County District Attorney's office was looking for a criminal investigator to join its ranks.

The winds of change had shifted direction once again, and I soon found myself announcing my retirement.

It may become apparent that I am averse to leaving loose ends to their own design. Before departing for the environs of the Twentieth Judicial District Attorney's Office, I was determined to bring closure to the cocaine trafficking investigation initiated in 1998. It had been a long, arduous, and complicated set of affairs that involved many disappointments but a series of search and arrest warrants were finally issued in the spring of 2004.

Regrettably, not nearly as many people were arrested as I had hoped, and while a few had escaped our efforts to take down an on-going criminal enterprise, I was finally satisfied to see at least some type of conclusion to what had become a five-year narcotic trafficking investigation. I would like to think that it sent the message that it was no longer safe for those who desired to hide and peddle poison in Telluride.

It was not long thereafter that I stepped through the doors of the Criminal Justice Center located at 1777 6th Street, Boulder, Colorado. It was the building that had once housed the Police Department where I had begun my professional career.

Like the circumstances surrounding the death of JonBenét, the first case assigned to me on that first day of June, 2004, coincidentally involved a death by strangulation. Jeffery Scott Gutiérrez had murdered his fiancée, Belinda King over the Memorial Day holiday weekend, and I was to serve as a liaison between the district attorney's office and the law enforcement agency handling the investigation.

Jeffery was a little vague on the details of what had happened, but he told investigators that some type of argument had taken place over the holiday weekend between himself and his betrothed. It was a verbal argument that got out of hand.

Surveying the scene later that day, it appeared that the physical altercation had begun in the living room. I took note that a television appeared to be missing from a small entertainment center, and although there were several VHS rental tapes and boxes scattered about, there was no VHS player present.

There were a few things knocked over or looked to have been thrown around in the living room, and clumps of blonde colored hair were observed to trail down the floor of the hallway.

More hair and pieces of a shattered 70's-style blue and white Corning Ware coffee pot were on the floor of the bedroom and on the bed. The coroner would discover blunt force trauma to Belinda's head, and it was presumed that she had been struck with the heavy coffee pot during the altercation. This blow did not render her unconscious, however, and Belinda fought back during the assault.

Jeffery was able to eventually force Belinda to her back on the floor of the bedroom and, straddling her body, manually strangled her to death. It is my recollection that she had broken fingernails and had bit her tongue during her struggle to survive.

Jeffery told investigators that the argument had taken place Sunday evening but it had taken him some time to work up the nerve to call his relatives and tell them about the death of his live-in fiancé. He had covered her head and the upper part of her torso with a blanket and left her body on the floor of the bedroom overnight before calling anyone.

Verbal arguments don't typically end with someone being strangled to death, and though police had obtained a remorseful confession from Jeffery, I was tasked with trying to better under-stand the motive behind the argument and murder. It certainly looked like "heat of passion," but I was interested in the underly-ing dynamics of the situation.

While walking through the crime scene that afternoon, I would locate a piece of documentary evidence that would help put it all together. It was a small paper receipt from Walmart that was crumpled up on the rear floorboards of Jeffery's car. It was dated on the Saturday afternoon of the holiday weekend.

CHAPTER TWENTY

Taking the Lead

Mark Beckner had turned over the Ramsey case to the D.A.'s office in 2002 when he decided that his department had finally exhausted every viable lead available to them. He once explained to me that he felt they were building the defense team's case by continuing to chase down dead-end perpetrator leads. In his opinion, the D.A.'s office could either file the case or take over responsibility for chasing down all of the weird stuff that continued to stream into his office.

The media painted the story a different color at the time, suggesting that the D.A.'s office had taken the case *away* from the Boulder Police Department for a variety of reasons, but primarily because they had mishandled the investigation. I thought that story line laughable, for it must be pointed out that Mary Lacy's office had no statutory authority to take away anything from the Boulder Police Department.

But I don't think that Beckner cared one way or the other. After all of the meetings and presentations that his office had arranged over the years, it was obvious to him that the D.A.'s office would never bring charges against any family member involved in the death of JonBenét. He was ready to chalk up his losses and move on to other things.

A search was initiated to locate an investigator who would take over the lead role for the D.A.'s office, and Lacy chose retired Arvada, Colorado Police Department investigator Tom Bennett. Tom had initially started out part-time in his role as chief investigator in the case, but it was not long before he was working a full caseload and supervising the other investigators in the office.

He had been working for the D.A.'s office for nearly a year when I arrived on the scene, and I worked by his side for another 12 months. It wasn't long before I began to take note of the signs that his workload and the Ramsey case had been taking a toll. He would frequently disappear behind the locked doors of the office dubbed the "Ramsey Room" and spend hours checking phone messages left on the tip line, checking email, and collating other leads that had been sent to the office.

When he finally emerged from the room, he would sometimes mutter references about the necessity to keep on "whacking moles." It was a private joke shared between the two of us that referenced the "whack a mole" game. This was played in pinball parlours before the advent of electronic gadgets, where gophers would randomly poke up their head through a hole in the gameboard and the player was charged with "whacking" as many of them as they could with a bludgeon before they disappeared back down their hole. Points were scored by direct hits landed on the heads of the quick little critters.

Tom apparently thought the nature of the game reflected the environs of the criminal justice system. The criminals just kept popping up, no matter how skilled we had become at knocking them down.

His frustration with the case first came to my attention in the late summer of 2004, not many months after I had joined the D.A.'s office. Tom advised me that John and Patsy Ramsey had scheduled a visit to the office and were requesting copies of the D.A.'s investigative files. He asked me confidentially what I thought about the matter.

I was dumbfounded. "Aren't John and Patsy still considered possible suspects in the death of their daughter? How did Mark phrase it…the parents remain under an 'umbrella of suspicion'?"

Tom nodded.

"Then why in the hell would anyone in their right mind consider handing over confidential files from an active investigation to a potential defendant!?"

Tom shrugged his shoulders wearily and thanked me for sharing my thoughts.

The Ramseys came for their visit, and Tom spent some time updating them on the status of his inquiry. He later told me that he had prevailed upon Mary Lacy, and no files were reportedly copied for the Ramsey family or their defense team.

In the meantime, I continued to work on a variety of cases that included Belinda King's homicide. I had obtained Jeffery's cell phone records and discovered that he liked to talk on the phone. He liked to talk a lot. Not having full time work, he seemed to spend a lot of time on the phone, and some of the folks he was talking to had arrest records for trafficking in cocaine and weapons offenses.

Belinda appeared to be the primary wage-earner in the family at the time, and they were having a difficult time financially. She had started a relatively new job, but had a positive outlook on life and was looking to improve her situation.

Things had been a little rocky over their 5-year relationship, but Jeffery and Belinda had finally picked out an engagement ring. A deposit of approximately $75.00 had put it on layaway at Walmart. Belinda had intended to pay off the balance quickly, so they could move forward with their plans of marrying. At some point, however, Jeffery's plans took a turn south.

The Walmart receipt discovered in the back seat of his car revealed signs of Jeffery's duplicity. He had withdrawn the cash down-payment for the ring on Saturday afternoon. Video surveillance at the jewelry counter, coupled with his cell phone records, documented him calling a man who had an arrest history of trafficking in cocaine, from inside the Walmart store.

By all appearances, Jeffery was cashing in his fiancé's engagement ring for a line or two of coke.

We were unable to determine exactly when the television and VHS player went missing, but these presumably also went to feed Jeffery's drug habit. I suspected that they were part of the package that made up the difference for a $100.00 price tag for a gram of cocaine.

We never had another opportunity to interview Jeffery after police took his initial confession, but putting two and two together led me to some conclusions about what may have happened between him and Belinda that holiday weekend.

The argument started when Belinda came home from work to discover the electronic equipment missing from the apartment. There was a verbal confrontation, and it came to light that Jeffery had funded his cocaine purchase by pulling the ring deposit from Walmart.

Cashing in the engagement ring became the last straw for Belinda. I suspect that she told Jeffery she was leaving him for good and told him to get out. That sparked a heated confrontation and what followed was a knock-down, drag-out fight that resulted in Belinda's demise.

Jeffery's cell phone records revealed that he frequently was up late at night conversing with people, and the call detail indicated he had been up until nearly 2:00 a.m. on Friday night. He began again late the next morning, and by Saturday afternoon we were able to pin down his exact location for one telephone call: the jewelry counter at Walmart.

His use of the cell phone ceased around 7:00 p.m. on Saturday evening – unusually early based on the track record of his cell phone records. I believed that this signified the end of Belinda's life, and the beginning of a long weekend, where Jeffery attempted to muster up the courage to call his mother and tell her that he had killed his girlfriend.

Neighbors reported seeing him chain-smoking outside the apartment on several occasions over the course of the weekend, but he had not been overly communicative.

Authorities were eventually summoned to the home after Jeffery called his parents on Monday morning, Memorial Day. He had called them to report that something bad had happened to Belinda.

They responded immediately to discover the body of their future daughter-in-law laying supine on the floor of the guest bedroom. The blanket remained in place over her upper torso.

Criminal profilers will tell you that the placement of the blanket over Belinda's upper torso and face was most likely due to Jeffery's feelings of shame and remorse. He was unable to deal with the consequences of the violent actions directed toward his fiancé, and though he left her body in its final resting place on the floor, he was compelled to hide the results from view.

The use of a blanket in JonBenét's murder took a different meaning, and will be discussed a little more in detail in a later chapter.

Jeffery would subsequently enter a guilty plea to the charges of murder, and was sentenced to 30 years in the Colorado Department of Corrections.

It was a sad and tragic affair for all involved, and I counted it as another one in the books for those who don't believe illegal drugs destroy people's lives.

≍ ⊕ ≍

It was late June 2005 when Tom Bennett pulled me aside one morning and asked if I was interested in taking over the chief investigator's position for the office. He indicated that he wanted to spend more time with his wife and was ready to "hang up his spurs" for the second time in his lengthy law enforcement career.

For the most part, Tom had been fairly tight-lipped about the Ramsey leads that streamed into the office, but, based on several conversations we had had over the year, I knew that he felt most of the things coming into the office were a colossal waste of time.

Tom was now asking if I would be interested in taking over that lead role in the Ramsey investigation and run the team of investigators who worked for the Twentieth Judicial District Attorney's office. In my wildest dreams, I had never imagined that I would one day be responsible for overseeing this investigation. I considered it to be a tremendous responsibility, and it took only a moment of consideration before I said "yes."

I found myself having lunch with D.A. Mary Lacy and her first assistant Pete Maguire within a few days of that decision, and she shared her thoughts on how she wanted to see the Ramsey investigation proceed. The primary message was that she wanted to scale back the time spent by her staff on the case, and we discussed several different options to accomplish this task.

During a follow up meeting with Tom and First Assistant District Attorney Bill Nagel, Tom proceeded to advise that the volume of information (letters, email correspondence, telephone calls, and walk-in interviews) that was being received was extremely large and a time consuming to process. He characterized most of the information coming from the public as being of little value in moving the case forward and suggested that it was impossible for one investigator to manage a caseload and pursue Ramsey leads at the same time.

He advised that there were approximately two-dozen frequent callers and writers who had nothing material to offer to the case and indicated that he had specifically requested a handful of those individuals to cease their calls and correspondence. Despite those requests, telephone calls, letters, and emails continued to pour into the office.

It was eventually decided that the first thing to be cut was the responsibility of returning phone messages left on the tip line. We determined that one way to cut down on the amateur closet detectives was to deny them access to the time of a working criminal investigator. The message on the telephone tip line was changed to inform callers that if they believed they had a viable lead to present in the case that they reduce it to writing and submit it via the U.S. Mail or other carrier.

The second thing to go was the email. A generic email address was established on the D.A.'s website that was designed to provide the same message as that left on the telephone tip line. People who wished to provide information on the case were instructed to reduce it to writing and were informed that all leads would be evaluated on an individual basis.

A memorandum outlining these changes was circulated through the office and to the Boulder Police Department. Receptionists were advised to instruct citizen callers to forward their information in written form. They were also instructed to inform walk-in visitors that unannounced visits would not be granted interviews: that their information should be sent to the Investigations Division in written form and that after review and evaluation, it would be up to the chief investigator to determine if a follow-up interview would be conducted.

Law enforcement personnel calling with information were to be forwarded directly to my telephone extension.

All correspondence received in the matter would continue to be logged into the system that had been established by Tom when he first came to the office in 2002. I prepared a generic letter that would be sent back to those individuals submitting information that acknowledged receipt of and thanking them for their tendered lead in the case.

Letters of introduction were prepared and sent to Ramsey attorneys Lin Wood and Bryan Morgan advising them of the change in investigative assignment. I also spoke to Denver CBI Supervisory Agent Ron Arndt and Denver Police Department Crime Lab Director Greg Laberge to advise them of my new assignment. Both labs had been involved in the collection and analysis of the DNA involved in this case.

Tom set about the task of briefing me on the status of the investigation and the leads that he had pursued over the course of his involvement in the case. A few weeks later, I was being sworn as a grand jury investigator so I could review materials gathered in 1998 and 1999 when there had been a grand jury inquiry into the murder of JonBenét.

Tom took me on a tour of the Ramsey room and explained how the materials and binders had been stored in the cabinets lining the walls. It was my first glimpse into the "library" of investigative documents that had been compiled by the Boulder Police Department. It would be an understatement to say that I was awestruck by the sheer number of binders that filled the room.

The "murder book" that documented the investigation into the death of this little girl had evolved into a full-blown mini-library of materials. The last count of pages, revealed during the Cold Case Task Force meeting held in February 2009, indicated that approximately sixty thousand (60,000) pages of documents had been collected during the course of the investigation.

Tom proceeded to show me how to operate the I-Legal computer program that contained all of the investigative files. Every piece of paper in the case had been scanned to this program, and it held an incredible search engine that permitted an investigator to find anything in the massive file by just entering a few keystrokes on the computer screen. It would prove to be an incredible time-saving resource as I began to familiarize myself with the details of the case.

It seemed a blink of the eye before Tom had parted company with the office and I was filling his shoes as chief investigator for the D.A. in the Ramsey case. I was continuing to carry a full felony caseload for the prosecutors in our office, supervise the other members of our investigative unit and soon began to learn of Tom's frustration. The leads that streamed into my office on JonBenét were nothing less than goofy and bizarre:

A woman sent in a child's craft kit for a small loom that made kitchen hot-pads. No explanation provided.

Lengthy, indecipherable audio tapes were accompanied by dozens of unreadable chicken scratches of handwriting.

What could only be described as "manuscripts" were submitted that outlined intruder theories, identified traders of child sex pornography, and participants engaged in kinky sex rings.

The names of ex-boyfriends and spouses were provided because they were acting "weird" around the 1996 Christmas holidays.

I could go on, but I think you probably get the nature of the majority of "leads" that were being sent to our office.

There were a few things that came in that seemed to deserve further inquiry, however. In one instance, a local merchant called my office to explain that a customer had left some papers with him during a business transaction. I can't recall the exact details at this writing, but he described handwritten notes on the back of the papers that described details about the death of JonBenét. They apparently were disturbing, and he thought he should report the information to our office.

I subsequently contacted the author of the notes, an elderly gentleman living in a retirement complex in south Boulder. It turned out he was thinking about writing a book about JonBenét and had been scribbling notes about his theory of events. He didn't have all of his facts straight. The lead was a dead-end, but one of those that I felt deserved a little more attention than just surrendering it to a file box after applying a date stamp.

There were a couple of other leads that were generated by the public, but none that were particularly noteworthy once they had been chased down.

In any event, what is important to note is that when I first inherited the responsibility of handling this case, I felt it was necessary for me to become fully acquainted with the details of the investigation. I believed that I needed to know these details first-hand and not fall into the trap of assuming something based on a previously held perception. Moreover, I felt it was my responsibility to fully understand all of the elements of the case so that I would be in a position to fully evaluate all of the leads coming into my office.

I decided to get a fresh start by reviewing events that began at day one.

≡⊕≡

Journey of Discovery

From the outset of my involvement in this case, I felt it was absolutely critical that I bring an objective viewpoint to the inquiry into this matter, and I did not take that responsibility lightly.

Despite my previous affiliation with the Boulder Police Department, I felt it was my professional obligation to fully evaluate all of the evidence that had been gathered over the course of the investigation into JonBenét's murder, and to reach my own conclusions as to who may have been involved in her untimely death. To have moved forward in any other fashion would have been irresponsible.

Stepping into this role, I was aware that there existed two different and contrasting theories that accounted for the events surrounding JonBenét's death. The first theory outlined her mother's obsession with perfection, and her anger with JonBenét for returning to a pattern of bed-wetting. In a fit of anger, Patsy was purported to have struck out in rage, killing her beloved daughter. A cover-up of the circumstances then followed in an attempt to lead investigators away from the embarrassment of family involvement. The ransom note, for which Patsy could never be eliminated as authoring, became a focal point for this hypothesis.

The other camp favored the intruder – pedophile theory. A clever man, intimately familiar with the family, had entered the Ramsey home on Christmas night and sexually assaulted the object of his desire. To throw investigators off his trail, he took the time to craft a ransom note from writing materials found in the home, pointing police to a disgruntled group of foreigners who had originally intended to take John Ramsey's daughter for ransom. A stun gun had been used to render JonBenét unconscious during the kidnapping, and this is why no one else in the household had been alerted to her abduction.

There may have been some other theories floating around out there at the time, but these seemed to be the two primary and prevailing theories that explained the circumstances surrounding JonBenét's death.

I determined to set aside any misconceptions, and prior thoughts I may have had about the case, and began the task of reviewing the investigative files that had accumulated over approximately nine (9) years' worth of effort. It was my intention to review and evaluate the evidence that had been gathered up to that point in time, with the primary objective of becoming sufficiently familiar with the details of the case so that I could intelligently and properly screen the new leads regularly streaming into my office.

I began the process by reading the reports of the officers and investigators who were first on scene that morning. I wanted to know first-hand what they saw and what they did. This included the reports completed not only by uniformed officers, investigators, and crime scene technicians, but the recorded statements of the Victim Advocates and civilians who were present in the home that day...the family friends who had been summoned to the Ramsey home for a "family emergency" by Patsy.

Though not all inclusive, the following were the additional documents that I intended review in order to gain a baseline acquaintance with the investigation:

- The Boulder Police Department Case Synopsis (February 2001)
- Bill Nagel's draft summary of the facts known in the case, complete with annotations from the various investigative reports.
- Analysis and review of the autopsy report
- Analysis and review of the reports and interviews of the expert witnesses who consulted with the Boulder County Coroner's Office on the autopsy protocol and its related documents.
- Analysis and review of the previous medical treatment of JonBenét.
- Analysis and review of the physical and trace evidence that was collected over the course of the investigation and the forensic analysis of items submitted to government laboratories.
- Analysis and review of crime scene photographs and videotapes.
- Analysis and review of the statements supplied by family and key witnesses to the event.
- Specific topic: Review of polygraph results
- Specific topic: Review forensic examination of duct tape; neck and wrist bindings, analysis of handwriting on ransom note, latent fingerprints
- Review of the behavioral analysis opinion offered by the FBI Child Abduction Serial Killer Unit (CASKU)

- Review of the behavioral analysis opinion offered by retired FBI agent John Douglas, a consultant hired by the Ramsey family.

Given the size of the investigative file, the task of becoming familiar with the details of the case seemed daunting. Nevertheless, I set about the process of pulling binders from the library and began to read. I somehow found time to review materials during the workday when caught up on my caseload. I frequently would sit at my desk over my lunch break and pour over reports and interviews. It was not unusual to remain after-hours to finish up an interview or report, and I sometimes took binders home on the weekends.

I scribbled questions and notes to myself, and attached sticky notes to various binders indicating the dates of my review. It was not long before I was leaving different colored sticky arrows in various binders that corresponded to different questions I had about the case: i.e. Suspects marked for further inquiry, pieces of physical and trace evidence that I had questions about, witness statements that contained questionable information, or observations that seemed to be "key" to the inquiry. It was a quick way of cataloging and marking information for further follow up.

The more I read, the more questions I had about the details of the case. I became a voracious reader, and continued to try to focus my attention on what I considered to be the "core" documents that contained the key elements of the offense.

There was a box in one of the cabinets that contained a handful of VHS video tapes. I scanned a number of these and found them to contain some video clips of JonBenét's beauty pageants, news media coverage of the murder investigation, and what appeared to be a surveillance video of the Ramsey neighborhood dated from the day of the kidnapping. Boulder investigators were recording vehicles parked in the area.

One particular news media video caught my attention, and it featured Lou Smit speaking to NBC news anchor Katie Couric in a multi-part series for *The Today Show*. He was pointing to the remote and isolated location of the window well in the back yard of the residence, declaring it to be a perfect place for an intruder to enter the home undiscovered.

Photo 18 - Ramsey Home: Rear South West entrance. Den is pictured to the left, JonBenét's bedroom and balcony is located above the Den; Train Room window grate is located behind the grill on right. Source: Boulder PD Case Files / Internet

Smit demonstrated the actions of the intruder by pulling up the metal window grate, and sliding into the window well, continued through the frame of the middle window on the backs of his legs and buttocks. Smit was not a large man, and I noted that his legs and hips totally filled the space of the small window frame as he scooted into the basement room.

The image of Smit's entry through the basement's Train Room window well stuck with me, and I would review the video clip on a number of occasions over the course of my investigation.

Over the coming weeks, I would learn that some of the evidence that Smit had pointed to as belonging to an intruder had been explained. For example, the latent fingerprint found on the outside of the Wine Cellar door, still unidentified when Smit first joined the case, had subsequently been identified by CBI technicians as a palm print belonging to Patsy Ramsey.

Photo 19 - Exterior view of the window grate above the Train Room window well. Source: Boulder PD Case Files / Internet

One other latent print from the same door had also been identified as belonging to her, and another belonged to John Andrew.

A latent print lifted from the frame of the Train Room window was identified as belonging to John Ramsey. There were no other unknown latent fingerprints collected from that window.

One particular sample of hair collected from the blanket that had been wrapped around JonBenét's body had initially given the appearance of being a pubic hair. Investigators thought this might belong to a male perpetrator. The FBI was later able to identify this as an axillary hair (underarm, back, chest) and determined it did not come from the pubic region of the body.

Mitochondrial DNA tests were run on this hair, and the FBI technicians determined that the hair shaft did not belong to an unidentified stranger. Patsy Ramsey could not be excluded as the source of the hair, and it was noted that it could have come from either her or someone else in her maternal lineage.

During a meeting with Sgt. Tom Trujillo, I was shown a handful of Polaroid photographs of hiking boots collected over the course of the investigation. One such pair had been collected from Ron Walker, the Denver FBI supervisory agent who had responded to assist Boulder Police on the morning of the kidnapping.

Agent Walker had accompanied Sgt. Mason to the basement to inspect the Wine Cellar after the discovery of JonBenét's body. He had been wearing a pair of Hi-Tec hiking boots at the time, and it was thought that the poon of his boot could have been responsible for the intruder's footwear impression in the mold of that room.

Though I hadn't read the reports yet, Trujillo told me that they believed Burke had also owned a pair of Hi-Tec brand hiking boots, and he could have been responsible for the intruder *footprint* evidence in the Wine Cellar.

BPD investigators had been contacted by a store clerk in Vail who believed Patsy Ramsey had purchased a set of Hi-Tec brand hiking boots before the murder. They had also been told by one of Burke's playmates that he owned a pair of this brand of boot.

These were significant pieces of information, but didn't lend themselves to helping investigators identify the *exact* set of boots responsible for the evidence located in the Wine Cellar. The boots purportedly owned by Burke were never recovered. Moreover, the imprint of the poon of the boot bore no distinguishing wear marks that would have allowed its comparison to *any* set of boots collected in the investigation.

As I moved forward in my examination of the evidence in the case, it seemed plausible that an explanation for the boot imprint in the Wine Cellar had been established, and that it didn't necessarily belong to an unknown intruder.

Trujillo shared some other information regarding trace evidence collected from the home and JonBenét's body. He advised that investigators had been asking for the clothing articles worn by John and Patsy on December 25th since the first days of the investigation. Christmas photos had depicted the items worn by the family, and investigators needed the items for elimination purposes.

It would take a year before the black and red Essentials brand jacket Patsy was photographed wearing was finally delivered to them. It was frustrating. The clothing articles seemed to trickle into their office a piece or two at a time. In one instance, a sweater – that Patsy was said to be wearing under the jacket – was delivered that looked like it had just come off the shelf of a retail clothing store. The fold marks were crisp and clearly present, suggesting it had never been worn.

Trujillo advised me that lab technicians had identified eight different types of fibers on the sticky side of the duct tape used to cover JonBenét's mouth. They included red acrylic, gray acrylic, and red polyester fibers that were subsequently determined by laboratory examination to be microscopically and chemically *consistent* to each other, as well as to fibers taken from Patsy Ramsey's Essentials jacket.

Further, fibers from this jacket were also matched to trace fibers collected from the wrist ligature, neck ligature, and vacuumed evidence from the paint tray and Wine Cellar floor.

Some intruder theorists thought that the transfer of Patsy's jacket fibers to the duct tape may have taken place after John had removed it from JonBenét's face, and placed it on the white blanket in the cellar. They believed it possible that prior contact taking place between the blanket and jacket could account for the transfer of these fibers to the tape.

Lab technicians had conducted experiments with the same brand of duct tape, by attempting to *lift* trace fibers from the blanket recovered in the Wine Cellar. Direct contact was made in different quadrants of the blanket. There was some minimal transfer of jacket fibers made to the tape during this exercise, but Trujillo told me lab technicians didn't think that this type of transfer accounted for the *number* of jacket fibers that had been found on the sticky side of the tape. It was thought that *direct* contact between the jacket and tape was more likely the reason for the *quantity* of fibers found on this piece of evidence.

BPD investigators looked to the other jacket fibers found in the Wine Cellar, in the paint tray, and on the cord used to bind JonBenét as physical evidence that linked Patsy with the probable location of her daughter's death – the basement hallway and Wine Cellar.

The paint tray was reported to have been moved to the basement about a month prior to the kidnapping, and investigators doubted that Patsy would have been working on art projects while wearing the dress jacket. The collection of jacket fibers from *all* of these different locations raised strong suspicions about her involvement in the crime.

Investigators also learned that fibers collected from the interior lining of the Essentials jacket did not match control samples from the sweater that had been provided to police by Ramsey attorneys. Investigators thought that this suggested she had been wearing some other article of clothing beneath the jacket.

But there were still other trace fibers that had yet to be accounted for. Brown cotton fibers had been found on four items closely associated with the body of JonBenét and implements used in her murder. Lab technicians thought the fibers similar to a pair of cotton work gloves.

Had the gloves gone the way of the cord, duct tape, practice notes, and stun gun when the perpetrator left the home that night?

I returned to my office and contemplated the sheer size and volume of the Ramsey *library* of materials awaiting my review. I realized that coming to understand it all was going to be one of the biggest challenges I had ever faced.

It would be an understatement to say that I was genuinely surprised by what I eventually discovered.

Revisiting the Point of Entry

I reviewed the same 35 mm photographs in the files that Lou Smit had reportedly studied, and I think we only agreed on one point. It appeared to me that there were fresh smudge marks in the dirt on the exterior windowsill of the north, ground floor bathroom window. The interior photographs of this window revealed it to be locked and no debris or other signs that this may have been a point of entry were present.

Smit had pointed to a baseball bat being present on the ground just a few feet from this window, and I think he may have been suggesting that this might be linked to JonBenét's head injury. Another bat was found in another part of the yard, and I thought these the remnants of childhood play and explainable. I thought it possible that some of Burke's playmates were responsible for the smudges observed on the sill of this window due to the close proximity of the baseball bat.

Our opinions diverged considerably at that point.

In his Power Point presentation, Smit spent a significant amount of time pointing out smudge marks, leaves, vegetation, and other debris located in and around the Train Room window well. The smudges he pointed out in these photographs did not appear to be as fresh as those observed on the exterior of the north bathroom windowsill, and it was my opinion that these had been created that summer when John Ramsey had broken into the house. Yes, there were definite signs of disturbance in the area of this window but there appeared to be a film of dirt on this sill that was not present at the bathroom window.

Photo 20 - Smudging on exterior window sill of Train Room window well. Source: Boulder PD Case Files / Internet

More importantly, there was no way to properly date the placement of the mark on the wall below the window, and I believed it entirely possible that John Ramsey was responsible for that "intruder" evidence. Ramsey told investigators during his April 1997 interview that he had stripped down to his underwear before climbing through that window, but had worn his dress shoes.

The darkened mark on the wall looked like it could have been created by the sole of this type of shoe.

For the sake of clarity, I think it is important to understand the positioning of the Train Room window well, and the relation of the window bank to the interior of the storage room of the basement.

The window grate sits level with the ground and is located just outside a south facing door that opens to the rear south-west yard of the home. This door provides access to the rear kitchen hallway and can be viewed from the windows of the den. The grate is difficult to see from the alley running behind the residence, and a large covered bar-b-q grill further obscured its view from the rear of the home.

The metal grate was not secured to the foundation and one could easily lift it and drop into the narrow window well, thus gaining access to a series of 3 windows that provided subterranean light and air to the basement Train Room. The window well was a confined space, measuring 77 inches in length, 16 inches in width, and 45 inches deep.

From the interior view, there were a series of 3 wooden windows that ran horizontally across the face of the west wall of the storage room, and they butted up against the ceiling of the room. The bank of windows extended across approximately 6 feet of the wall and was situated approximately 4 feet above the floor. Each window contained 4 separate panes of glass.

It was the middle window that John Ramsey had chosen when forcibly entering his home the previous summer, and the upper left window pane had been partially broken out when he had unlocked the window, and climbed into the basement. The BPD diagram showed that the exterior width of this window frame was 20 inches.

This particular window was hinged on the right side and swung to the interior of the room when opened. Each window was secured by an old-fashioned latch that turned 90 degrees to latch into hardware attached to the frame.

The interior dimensions of these windows were not generous, but an adult could maneuver in the tight spaces of the window well and manage to scoot through the frame and drop to the floor of the room. The dimensions of each window, as documented by Boulder CSI's, measured approximately 25 inches high by 20 inches wide.

With regard to the intruder's access through the window grate, Smit specifically pointed to vegetation that was growing between the cement foundation of the wall and the metal frame- his premise being that the grate had been lifted by the perpetrator to gain access to the basement and had pinned the plant material beneath it. Yet, in the same photograph, he ignored clusters of pine needles that were sitting atop the grate. These certainly would have been displaced if the grate had been recently lifted as he was theorizing, and I didn't understand how he could dismiss evidence that was clearly in plain sight.

Photo 21 - Window grate depicting leaves and pine needles above, and vege-
tation growing beneath. Source: Boulder PD Case Files / Internet

I found it puzzling that he didn't present any photographs of the cobweb situated in the lower left hand corner of the window frame. My review of the 35 mm still photographs suggested this triangular-shaped web to be of significant size and very likely would have been destroyed by someone climbing through the window. I couldn't fathom why he neglected to include this as a part of his presentation of the intruder theory.

Up to that point, I had only studied the 35 mm still photographs of the crime scene and had not been able to locate a device to play the mini-cassette video recording taken by CSIs during the execution of the search warrant. BPD came through again and was able to copy the crime scene video to a CD / DVD for my examination.

The crime scene video documented the return of the Boulder Police Department to the Ramsey home at approximately 2036 hours on the evening of December 26th, 1996, after having secured a search warrant for the premises. I reviewed the video on a number of occasions, but in this particular instance the recording of the Train Room window drew my attention.

It is a commonly shared experience by all of us in this past century that a "still" photograph represents a very minute slice of time. We have all gazed in amusement at our childhood pictures and tried to remember what was going through our minds at the moment that the snapshot momentarily captured our image and our essence. We have similarly contemplated the same things when viewing historical photographs that reach beyond our life span.

And it goes without saying that the film that captures our physical movement has captivated our imagination since the early 1920's, and Hollywood has turned this technology into a billion dollar industry. Strips of celluloid have permitted us to visit the places of our dreams.

The crime scene video of December 26th, 1996, proved to be equally hypnotic and most assuredly took me firmly into its grasp.

I watched as the CSI pointed their camera and followed them as they proceeded to tour the Ramsey home. It was as though I was standing over their shoulder as the camera turned here and there.

It was disheartening to see the lifeless body of JonBenét stretched out upon the floor of the living room near a decorated

Christmas tree, and I was reminded of the cruel tragedy that had been visited upon this family.

The lens of the camera eventually reached the basement of the home, and I was intrigued as it tracked the route that had been described in the interview transcripts of John Ramsey and Fleet White. A flashlight illuminated a closet that was blocked by a fireplace grate, one and the same that Fleet had described searching during one of his three interviews with police investigators.

I stepped through the doorway of the Train Room housing a table that displayed the imagination of a 9-year-old boy. Train track and its attendant vehicles encircled miniature buildings and the figures of townspeople who seemed oblivious to the nature of their surroundings. Loose track was scattered across the floor, and I proceeded into what appeared to be a cluttered storage room, taking in a space filled with shelving and the detritus of a family's existence that was spread across the floor.

A hard-cased suitcase stood erect beneath an open window, and upon closer inspection, a small kernel of glass sat upon the top of the suitcase. The interior sill of the window was clear of any glass, and I thought it possible that the wind had blown open the window, knocking White's *small kernel of glass* to the top of the suitcase before the crime scene video had captured the scene. [47]

The video continued to explore the condition of the window and a light breeze gently teased the remnants of additional cobwebs that clung to the lower portion of the window frame.

My vision blurred as I focused my attention on the window that was standing halfway open on the exterior wall of the home. A series of three windows stretched across the wall, and the center window was comprised of four panes of glass. The upper left pane exhibited fractured glass that had never been replaced and fulfilled the description of John's entry into his home that previous summer.

The torn remains of a broken, and dusty cobweb floated gently from portions of the broken and jagged glass.

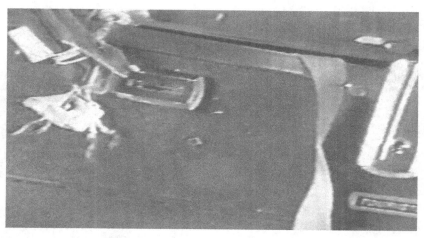

Photo 22 - Small kernel of glass resting on top of Samsonite suitcase. Source: Boulder PD Case File / Internet

My attention turned to a triangular-shaped silken web clinging tenuously to the lower left window frame, and it fluttered in the winter breeze. To its right, near the midsection of the exterior sill, was balanced a small rectangular-shaped piece of glass. It had in some fashion come to rest on the sill in this precarious position.

Photo 23 - Spider web and debris tangled in lower left hand corner of the Train Room window. Source: Boulder PD Crime Scene Video / Case File

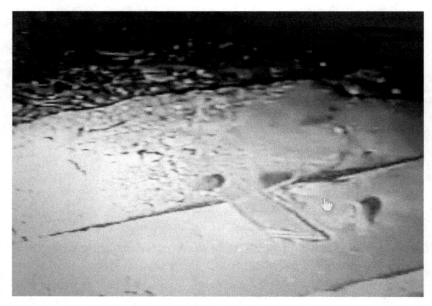

Photo 24 - Close up view of alleged point of entry, and rectangular shaped piece of glass resting on the exterior Train Room window sill. It was located near the middle of the sill. (Note the window screen eye bolt to the right of the glass shard) Source: Crime Scene Video, Boulder PD Case Files

I took several deep, cleansing breaths.

It was difficult to extricate myself from the intimate experience of exploring the Ramsey home that evening.

Crime scene videos, by necessity, are intended to provide the viewer with an objective and un-biased view of the cold, bare facts of an investigation. Photographs and videotape help us to discern fact from fiction.

My previous viewing of Smit's Prime-time televised exhibition of his intruder theory immediately came to mind – it revealed that his small stature entirely filled the bottom sill of the window as he demonstrated how an intruder could have gained entry to the Ramsey home on Christmas night. Taking into consideration the location of the fragile spider web in the corner of the window frame, and the rectangular glass fragment visible in the crime scene video, I reached my first investigative conclusion:

It was extremely unlikely that anyone climbed through this window on the day that JonBenét was kidnapped and cold-bloodedly murdered.

I came to the realization that my work had only just begun.

Photo 25 - Detective Smit, interviewed by Katie Couric, demonstrates the "intruder" entry through the Train Room window on NBC. Note how the width of his hips and legs fill the entire base of the window frame. The author doubted the cobweb, depicted in crime scene video in the bottom left corner of this window, would have survived this activity. Or, similarly, that the rectangular piece of glass centered on the exterior window sill would have remained in its precarious position. Source: Single frame from NBC news program

A New Focal Point

The late summer and fall of 2005 had been a busy time in the office. I seem to recall that I had helped one of the Deputy D.A.'s prepare a couple of sex assault cases that went to trial, and my felony caseload was burgeoning with other active investigations. I was sifting through cell phone records obtained in the Gutierrez homicide and was trying to clarify motivation in that death by strangulation. In spite of those demands, I somehow managed to find the time to press forward on the Ramsey case and explored a number of additional questions that needed resolution.

I had been particularly interested in Lou Smit's intruder theory and was aware that a number of elements comprised the basis for his hypothesis. The following is an overall synopsis of these elements:

1. Given the fact that no forced entry had been discovered on any of the exterior doors and windows of the residence,

Smit thought the secluded window well of the basement
Train Room an ideal location for a suspect to gain entry to
the house.

2. The window had been broken by John Ramsey when
    locked out of the home the previous summer and it was
    simple enough for an intruder to reach through the broken
    glass to unlock the window for entry.

3. There was a scuff mark on the wall beneath the window
    and Smit theorized this had been left by the perpetrator.

4. There was a Samsonite suitcase sitting upright directly
    beneath this window. He felt that the height of the window
    above the floor required the use of this as an aid to climb-
    ing back out through the window well.

5. There was the impression of a boot print in the Wine
    Cellar near JonBenét's body. It was identified as the poon
    of the sole of a Hi-Tec brand boot and Smit thought this
    was left by the perpetrator while concealing the body.

6. The duct tape placed over JonBenét's mouth was evidence
    of the intruder's intention to silence her during the kidnap.

7. The bindings tied to JonBenét's wrists were utilized to
    restrain her during the assault.

8. The garrote tied around her throat was used to torture her
    during the sexual assault. This included the penetration of
    her vaginal orifice through the use of the broken handle of
    the paintbrush tied into the cord of the garrote.

9. A ransom note was left by the perpetrator with the inten-
    tion of misleading authorities about the true nature of the
    crime: Smit believed a lone sexual predator was responsi-
    ble for the kidnap and murder of JonBenét.

10. Photographs of marks on JonBenét's face and her back
    appeared to Smit to have been created by a stun gun. It
    was his theory that this weapon had been used to render
    her unconscious during the kidnapping.

Smit was not shy about sharing his theories and he prepared a Power Point presentation that outlined the evidence that purportedly supported this hypothesis. It was my understanding that he used this presentation to point to the involvement of a sexual pedophile in this crime. He had prepared a shorter version for Lacy to utilize during her presentations on the case.

I reviewed both of these presentations during my exploration of his theory, and the underlying premise appeared to be this:

- There had been no recorded history of bad conduct, of physical, or sexual abuse located in the family's background, and Smit could not identify a motive for either parent that pointed to their being responsible for the brutal murder of their daughter[48]

- Failing that, the lack of a viable theory for this crime of violence then pointed to the involvement of a sexual predator

- Some of the implements used in the crime were not found in the home after the discovery of JonBenét's body, and he, therefore, presumed that they had been carried away from the scene by the perpetrator.

- The use of a stun gun was the cornerstone of the intruder theory. The parents would not have required the use of this type of instrument to control and silence their daughter.

As noted previously, Smit had appeared on national television and explained his thoughts about the point of entry, demonstrating how the intruder gained access to the home through the basement window well of the Train Room. I thought that the photographic and video evidence presented a compelling counter-argument to his theory, and a portion of this video clip would subsequently play a key role in my presentation about the intruder theory to ranking D.A. officials in January 2006.

I should note that I first met Smit during the summer of 2004 when Tom Bennett was still the lead investigator in the case. He was very pleasant, and he would usually spend a little time with Tom when visiting the office to check on leads. He would sometimes bring a checklist of things that he thought should be pursued in the case. I think I may have seen him in the office on approximately four to five separate occasions before I took over the investigation.

I specifically remember the last time I had seen him, and it was in the last week of September 2005, after I had returned from working as a reserve officer for a Telluride music festival. I had been in the lead role for several months by that time, and my head was still swimming as I tried to get a handle on all of the details of the case.

Smit took a seat in my office and we spoke briefly about the progress of the investigation. He told me that he had recently returned from Atlanta, where he had spent time visiting the Ramsey family. Patsy had been in the hospital, battling a return of cancer, and he described her as being on her "deathbed".

I expressed my sympathy for Patsy and the family. They had been through hell.

Smit told me that he had spent some time with Patsy in the hospital, holding her hand and looking into her eyes. He told me that this experience led to him believe that she was "innocent."

He advised me that he had also looked into the eyes of John Ramsey and didn't feel that he had been involved in his daughter's death either.

Smit reported that Patsy had been in and out of the hospital undergoing chemotherapy and had been staying at her parents' home.

After several minutes of conversation, he indicated that it had taken him about a week to discover the evidence that pointed to an intruder being involved in the murder. He had formed this theory after studying the crime scene photographs, and it was my distinct impression, based upon his statements, that he spent little or no time reading any of the police reports that had been prepared by the initial responding officers, detectives, and crime scene technicians.

I wasn't quite certain how to respond to that revelation. Smit was informing me that it had only taken him a week to develop his theory of the crime. I was several months into my review of the evidence collected in the case and couldn't commit one way or the other to an opinion about who may have been responsible for the murder of JonBenét.

I chalked it up to his extensive experience as a homicide investigator and decided that I still needed some time to reach any firm theory about the circumstances of the crime.

That was the last time I saw Smit, and I regret not having been in a better position to have debated the merits of the case with him before he passed away.

Steve Thomas spoke to me on several occasions about his own conversations with Smit, and it was apparent that he was entirely committed to the sexual predator theory. The two had gone round and round about the feasibility of the window well being used as a point of entry and exit to the home. The spider webs played a central role in these discussions, as well as the suitcase and scuff mark on the wall.

Smit was not to be swayed and held steadfast in his belief that John and Patsy were not responsible for the death of their daughter. He could discern no motive that directly tied them to JonBenét's brutal murder.

<hr />

Tom Wickman was adamant that no stun gun had been used in the murder, and it was clear from my review of the autopsy report that the coroner believed that the marks on JonBenét's back were "abrasions" versus "burn marks." Boulder investigators had also sought the opinion of the manufacturer of the Taser stun gun thought to have been used in the crime. In no uncertain terms, they declared that the marks on JonBenét were not created by their stun gun.

It came to light during my read of the opinions of the medical consultants in the case that the marks on JonBenét's face were believed to have been caused by something other than a stun gun. Michigan Pathologist Dr. Werner Spitz opined that the mark on her cheek had been caused by the imprint of a small object versus a deteriorating burn mark from a stun gun.

Dr. Spitz offered some additional expert opinions on the injuries sustained by JonBenét that are referenced in Chapter Six of this book.

Smit was determined to nail down the stun gun theory, and with the assistance of Boulder County Sheriff's Department (BCSO) investigators, proceeded to conduct experiments on pigs under the influence of anesthesia. The most likely brand of stun gun that matched the distinct marks on JonBenét's back was the Air Taser, and a series of photographs were taken of the marks left on the skin of the pig by the Taser.

I studied these photographs, and they depicted a series of marks in succession that marched up the side of the belly of the pig. A scaled BCSO business card was held next to these marks, but I could not locate any photographs of one-to-one comparisons of these marks to those found on JonBenét.

According to the scaled card, the measurement between marks on the pig appeared to be consistent with the coroner's written report that stated the abrasions observed on JonBenét were approximately 3.5 cm apart. Smit's Power Point stated that the marks appeared "close" in measurement, but had not been officially scaled to JonBenét's injuries.

Scaled photographs of the electronic leads of the Air Taser were taken by investigators, but again I could not locate any one-to-one comparisons to the abrasions on the back of JonBenét.

I contacted Tom Trujillo, now a detective sergeant in Boulder's Detective Bureau, and asked him if he had any one-to-one photographs that compared the electronic leads of the Air Taser to JonBenét's injuries. I thought I had read that Lakewood Police had prepared a set of one-to-one photos early in the investigation for Boulder Police. Trujillo asked me to come by his office and he would show me what he had.

A thick binder of 35 mm photographs was produced, and Trujillo thumbed to a tab containing several enlargements of different views of the Air Taser, one of which included a front view of the electronic leads on the head of the instrument.

There was no one-to-one photograph comparing the electronic leads to the marks on JonBenét's back, but Trujillo had fashioned a clear plastic overlay that depicted the same scaled representation. Holes had been cut in the plastic that illustrated the location of the electronic leads of the Taser and placed over the photograph of the injuries.

I leaned over to take a closer look at the plastic overlay. The holes cut in the plastic representing the electronic leads did not appear to match JonBenét's injuries.

I asked Trujillo if any photographs had been taken of these materials, and he shook his head. These had been prepared back around 2000 when investigators were exploring the possibility that a stun gun had been used in the crime. No further work had gone into the materials since that time frame and especially because Chief Beckner had handed the case over to the D.A.'s office in 2002.

Technology had made giant strides in that period of time, and I asked Trujillo if he could arrange to have some scaled one-to-one photographs completed of his materials for a Power-Point presentation.

Within a week, a CD disk prepared by BPD Criminalist Shelly Hisey arrived at my office, and it contained a series of Power Point slides that depicted a graphic overlay of the stun gun to the injuries on JonBenét's back. I pulled up the file on my computer and hit the play button.

I must have watched the presentation several times before I leaned back into my chair and felt a chill crawl down my back.

It was strikingly clear that the electronic leads of the Taser purported to have been used by an intruder in this murder did not align with JonBenét's injuries.

Lou Smit's representation that these marks were a "close match" were exactly that, "close", but not the *exact* match you would expect to see from the direct physical contact that would have been required in these circumstances.

It was an opinion that Boulder Police investigators had been expressing privately for years.

In my view, the theory of the lone intruder, and his use of a stun gun, was beginning to unravel.

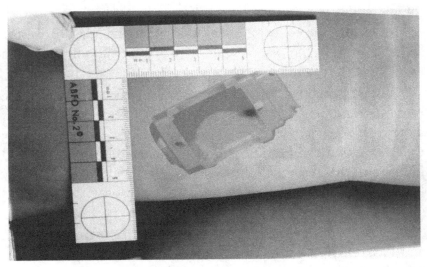

Photo 26 - One-to-one scaled Power-Point overlay photograph showing that the electronic leads of the Air Taser stun gun do not align with JonBenét's injuries. This was the "close match" that led intruder theorists to believe a stun gun had been used in the kidnapping. Source: Power-Point series prepared at request of author and completed by Boulder PD criminalist Shelly Hisey

" The killer had a stun gun. I am sure the killer had a stun gun...

There is no reason at all for the parents to have used a stun gun to help stage the murder of their daughter."

—Former D.A. Investigator Lou Smit during an interview
aired on *48 Hours Investigates–Searching for a Killer.*
October 4, 2002

"If you're like most Americans you probably think that John and Patsy Ramsey are hiding something in the murder of their daughter, JonBenét. In fact, a new poll for 48 Hours Investigates, 52 percent say they believe one or both parents were involved in the murder in some way."

—Television Journalist Lesley Stahl during a *48 Hours Investigates* program: "Searching for a Killer", aired October 4, 2002

Stepping Off The Fence

I had taken several binders home with me over the 2005 Thanksgiving holiday weekend, and they included the first at-length police interviews conducted with John and Patsy Ramsey on April 30th, 1997. I had read in police reports what had been ascribed to them over the course of their inquiry, but was now at a point that I wanted to spend some in-depth time reviewing the details of these statements. One of the binders also included the June 1998 interviews of John and Patsy that I would learn had been conducted by members of the D.A.'s office.

Most of the weekend was spent in a lounge chair where I sat in the relative warmth of the sunny weather outside my cottage in Chautauqua Park. I was into the first few pages of John Ramsey's April 30, 1997, interview when I nearly fell out of my chair. I was dumbfounded to read that the Ramseys had been provided copies of police investigative reports in advance of their sit-down with detectives.

It certainly seemed an unusual move when viewed as an investigative technique. Police investigators don't usually share their reports with people who are about to be questioned, especially when they are still under suspicion of being involved in a criminal case. I would later learn that the D.A.'s office had agreed to the release of these reports to the Ramsey team in exchange for their participation in the interview. This would be one of *many* concessions that the D.A.'s office would make over the course of the investigation.

My review of the June 1998 interviews held yet another surprise.

The opening pages of John's interview, led by Lou Smit, highlighted the fact that Boulder Police investigators were not present and considered "persona non-grata." I had seen a copy of a handwritten letter authored by John Ramsey in the spring of 1998, during my search of the I-Legal files, and Smit read into the record this same letter requesting an independent meeting with members of the D.A.'s office outside the scope of BPD involvement.[49]

Present with Smit and representing the D.A.'s office was special prosecutor Mike Kane. John Ramsey was accompanied by attorney Bryan Morgan and their private investigator David Williams. Morgan expressed the desire of wanting to continue to cooperate with the D.A.'s office, but there was a caveat. Morgan stated that the family felt the need to withhold certain medical records from the criminal inquiry, claiming that they deserved an "island of privacy" when it came to the investigation into JonBenét's murder.

The following is an excerpt from that interview:

Morgan:

"I have a real problem with certain kinds of medical records. These people are entitled to an island of privacy to try to recover what they've been through."

"I think you will get virtually everything you've described with the possible exception of personal medical records that

I think John and Patsy are at least entitled to make a reasonable decision on...."

"I've already discussed these matters with Hoffstrom and he knows how we operate."

There was additional reference to a "first" letter that Lou Smit apparently had sent to the Ramseys prior to this June interview. Based upon my reading of this transcript, it seemed that there was a movement afoot to segregate and distance the Boulder Police Department from further involvement in the investigation.

It seemed to me that the Ramseys were looking for a sympathetic ear in the law enforcement community.

There had been a number of occasions in the preceding months when I turned in for the night, contemplating the details of the case. It was a method of problem solving that had developed over years of police work, letting my subconscious evaluate all of the angles of an investigation while my physical body was rejuvenated by a night's rest.

There were many times when I awoke the following morning with a different perspective, and this allowed me to pursue a new course of action. On a few occasions, thoughts would emerge in the middle of the night, and I learned to keep a notepad by my bedside to record these transient images. My research into the details of the Ramsey case was no different.

By that juncture, I had been scouring police reports and interviews for nearly five months, and something I read in the files that Thanksgiving weekend triggered a similar event. I awoke at 3:00 a.m. on one of those mornings for no apparent reason. I was suddenly and completely awake, and sat upright for a moment before moving into the living room.

It seemed a simple realization, but it dawned on me that Patsy had reported that she had never finished reading the ransom note before rushing upstairs and screaming for John. Yet, she was able to recite the name of the kidnappers during the panicked and hysterical 911telphone call to police that morning.

She explained in her April 1997 interview that she had looked at the note when the dispatcher asked her if the kidnappers had identified themselves. I wasn't buying the explanation.

John Ramsey, according to his statement, was on his hands and knees hovering over the note as he tried to read through it.[50] He was facing **south** and the note was spread from left to right. Patsy was on the phone about four – five feet away and would have been required to read the note upside down - that is, if she had been able to look *through* her husband.

It was a significant turning point for me and could be described as one of those "ah haa" moments when the truth has finally been revealed to the seeker.

It had taken a number of months of intensive examination of investigative files before I came to believe that the family was somehow involved in the death of JonBenét. I did not quite know how or why, but at that juncture, I no longer felt it was likely that an intruder had participated in this crime.

I returned to the office from the holiday weekend with a renewed energy and an expanded viewpoint. While continuing to evaluate the new leads that continuously streamed into our office, I began to narrow the focus of my review on the family, and observed a number of behavioral clues that seemed out of sync.

Suffice it to say, the more I scrutinized the Ramsey family, the more I came to believe that the likelihood of involvement by a kidnapper – intruder was becoming extremely remote.

I was aware that investigators had discovered that the 911 tape contained a few extra seconds of recorded telephone conversation that was captured when Patsy had failed to fully terminate the call. A number of people had independently listened to the tail end of the call and described hearing the same voices and words on the tape. It piqued my interest because it was reported that a young voice, thought to be that of Burke, had been recognized on the tape.

If that was the case, and Burke was in the vicinity of the kitchen and speaking to his parents when the 911 call was made, why were the Ramseys continuing to insist that he was asleep in his bedroom?

I had listened to the CD of the 911 call and couldn't quite make out the voices that others had heard, so I decided to contact the California lab that had worked on enhancing the tape. (I have to admit that my hearing has somewhat degraded over the years due to the many hours spent on firearms ranges.) I wanted to know if there was any new technology that could further clarify the voices caught on the tail end of the recording.

I had called Mike Epstein at the Aerospace Corporation just prior to the Thanksgiving holidays, and he advised me that he had not completed any additional work on the tape since first being contacted by Boulder investigators in 1997. He indicated that he didn't think they had missed a word that had been said on the tape and was willing to send another master copy of the CD for my review. I was not certain which generation of recording was in my hands at the D.A.'s office, and it was my desire to have a cleaner, fresher generation that could be reviewed.

I was disappointed to hear during my gathering of information that technology had not changed and that the same "tool set" being used in the entertainment industry in 1997 was still state of the art in 2005.

In the meantime, while awaiting the arrival of the new Aerospace CD, I continued to work the regular caseload that was ever present in the office. If memory serves, the DA's office handled nearly 2500 felony and misdemeanor filings in any given year, and many of those cases required additional follow-up investigation once police had cleared their case by arrest. Preparing those cases to the threshold of "beyond a reasonable doubt" frequently fell to the investigative unit of the DA's office.

I continued my review of the Ramsey case file whenever a spare moment presented itself, and further explored the possibility of family involvement in the weeks that followed.

The Evolution of John Ramsey's Statements†

As noted in previous chapters, investigators were concerned about the discrepancies showing up in the statements being provided by the family. I was interested in tracking the history of the statements to see exactly how they had evolved over time.

The following is a synopsis of the statements made by John Ramsey with regard to some of the actions taken on the morning of the discovery of the ransom note. Included are his thoughts about the intruder and the suspected point of entry used to access his residence.

A more detailed analysis of some of John Ramsey's statements is addressed in a later chapter.

The Chronological History of John Ramsey's Statements
<u>Initial Police Investigation: December 26, 1996:</u>

- John advised officers / investigators that he believed the house to have been locked on the evening of December 25, 1996.
- He indicated that he observed no signs of forced entry to the home.
- He advised that upon learning of JonBenét's disappearance, he checked on Burke's welfare and determined him to be safely asleep in his bedroom.
- John did not ask Burke if knew the whereabouts of JonBenét or if he'd seen or heard anything during the night.
- John stated that he conducted a cursory search of JonBenét's bedroom after reading the ransom note, but there was never any mention of a trip to the basement.
- During questioning by police investigators about possible suspects, John and Patsy provided names and possible motives for suspects, but John did not say anything about his observations and suspicions regarding a possible entry / exit point to the residence.

Follow-up Police Interview: December 27, 1996

- Sergeant Larry Mason and Detective Linda Arndt responded to the Fernie residence on the evening of Friday, December 27th in attempt to arrange a follow-up interview with the Ramseys but were told that Patsy was too distraught to answer questions about the death of her daughter.

Ramsey friend / attorney Michael Bynum, present at the Fernie residence that evening, wouldn't permit an interview to take place at the police department.

Sergeant Mason asked John about the broken window in the basement and was told that he had broken it during a forced entry to his home the previous summer when he had left his keys behind.

Police investigators were subsequently advised on December 28th that members of the Ramsey family were now being represented by legal counsel. Any questions investigators wished to pose to them would have to be routed through the district attorney's office.

CNN Interview: January 1, 1997:

- Not yet having participated in a formal police interview, the Ramseys decided to involve the national media by providing an interview with CNN in Georgia.
- John Ramsey stated that he had 'shared his thoughts with the police' and that he intended to return to Boulder and speak to investigators.
- John Ramsey reported that they were "now ready to cooperate."
- John Ramsey stated that he / family were "not angry" about JonBenét's death but he / they were interested in finding out "why" this had occurred.
- John and Patsy pointed to the involvement of an intruder in the death of their daughter but, other than mentioning the ransom note, provided no other details about an intruder's activities in their home.

Police Interview: April 30, 1997

- Having negotiated the terms of their first official police interview, John Ramsey advised investigators that the garage door was typically used to enter and exit the house.

- He reported that he had checked the 1ˢᵗ floor doors and they appeared to have been locked.
- John stated that he would usually check the back hallway door because it was typically used by the kids to enter and exit the house when playing in the back yard.
- John reports that he checked on Burke "fairly quickly" after the discovery of the ransom note and that he was still asleep.
- John reports that he had been to the Train Room sometime early that morning and observed the broken window but that he didn't see any glass. (The exact timing of this visit is not made clear during the interview but it was described as being later in the morning, after the 911 call to authorities.)
- When he did visit the basement, John assumed that the window was broken from his summer 1996 forced-entry to the basement.
- He reported that the Train Room window was open approximately "1/8 inch."
- John stated that he closed and latched the window
- John reports that he didn't return to the basement until at the direction of Detective Arndt. This took place at approximately 1:00 p.m. and he led Fleet White to the Train Room and informed him of his previous forced entry into the room. They inspected the window and looked for window glass together.
- John states that the unlatched window 'probably struck him as a little unusual…but it wasn't dramatically out of the ordinary'.
- He didn't bring it to anyone's attention.
- John went on to state: "My theory is that someone came in through the basement window…because there was the blue Samsonite suitcase also sitting right under the window…" "[He]…could have gotten into the house without that but you couldn't have gotten out that window without

something to step on"…"Those windows weren't obvious to somebody just walking by…"

Denver News Media Interview: May 1, 1997

- In response to the criticism of the father of murder victim Polly Klaas regarding their lack of cooperation with authorities, John Ramsey reports to the media that they (the Ramsey family) had 'spoken with police investigators for approximately eight (8) hours on December 26th, 1996; another two (2) hours on December 27th, 1996 and that they had supplied them with every piece of information they had.'
- John stated, "And we have all along, through our investigative group…communicated every piece of information we had that we felt was relevant to the case."

Boulder County District Attorney's Interviews: June 23, 1998

- John thinks he checked JonBenét's room before Patsy called 911.
- He stated that… "there was just a lot of running around going on.
- John "just looked in [Burke's room] he was in bed and was asleep…I knew he was there and he was ok." "I mighta looked around the house some more."
- "I know I looked in the refrigerator, we have this walk-in refrigerator we're always worried about the kids getting in there…"
- John was "perplexed" at how they got in. 'Later in the morning…wondering if anyone was watching the house…went to Burke's room with binoculars…' "There was a truck parked in the alley across the road [behind the Barnhill residence] that

I never noticed before…" "There was a white Ford Fiesta driving by more than once."

- John reported that he had gone to the basement earlier and found the door to the Train Room 'kinda blocked…there was a chair in front of the doors…window was cracked open…maybe an inch.'

- John stated a "Samsonite suitcase was against the wall directly under the window"… "I don't think I looked anywhere else…at that point I was still trying to figure out how they got in the house."…"The window was sort of explainable…but the suitcase was unusual, that shouldn't have been there."

- Regarding his trip to the basement: "Well, when I came down, one of the things I noticed was, ok, that door is still kind of blocked"…"There were some boxes and there was a stool kind of thing sitting there"…"It wasn't obvious to me that someone had gone through there cause I had to move the chair to get in which I did."…"the window was partially open, but the suitcase just kind of jumped out at me."

- John states "I absolutely did not put it [suitcase] back there [in the Train Room].

Continuation of District Attorney's Office Interview: June 24, 1998

- Detective Lou Smit and John Ramsey review photograph #71, which depicts the entryway to the Train Room:

John Ramsey: 'What is different, the door is blocked only by this drum table. Here's the chair I said was blocking the door…I moved the chair to get into the door.' 'When I went down, that chair was kind of blocking that entrance right there [Train Room door]. 'There was something else on the other side…but all I had to do was move that chair and I walked into the room.'

Lou Smit:	"So do you think that the chair would block the door in an attempt that nobody would have gotten in there without moving it?"
John Ramsey:	"Correct."
Lou Smit:	"In other words, let's say that the intruder goes into the Train Room and gets out, let's say, that window...would he get that chair to block the door..."
John Ramsey:	"I go down...I moved that chair and went in the room."
Lou Smit:	"So you couldn't have gotten in without moving the chair?"
John Ramsey:	"Correct.
Lou Smit:	"I'm trying to figure out, if an intruder went through the door, he'd almost have had to pull the chair behind him...that would have been his exit."
John Ramsey:	"Yeah, it was blocked. He had to move something to get in the room."
Lou Smit:	"And he would have had to have moved it back, if he was in there, to get out."
John Ramsey:	"Yeah."
Lou Smit:	"So that's not very logical in terms of doing that."
John Ramsey:	"Yeah, I think it is, if this person is bizarrely clever to have not left any good evidence, yet left all these funny clues around, they certainly are clever enough to pull the chair back when they left."

ABC News Interview: March 17, 2000

- During a nationally televised interview with Barbara Walters, John Ramsey shares his thoughts regarding the open Train Room window: "I was a bit alarmed, but I was more alarmed with the Samsonite suitcase that was standing up below the window." "That looked wrong. That suitcase did not belong there…it was out of place."

- John's first impression was that the kidnapper had gone through the window.

Excerpts from the Ramsey's Book, *The Death of Innocence*, published March 2000

- Sometime that morning while awaiting the ransom call, John recalls breaking into the basement Train Room when locked out of the house that previous summer.
- While waiting for the ransom call, he remembers that the note indicates the kidnappers will be watching. Hoping to catch them looking at the house, he races upstairs to find binoculars.
- He observes a strange vehicle in the alley across the street behind the Barnhill residence. After several minutes, nothing has happened and he returned downstairs.
- The ransom call does not come by 1000 hrs and John's desperation increases.
- "That entry point needs to be looked at…the pane is still broken and the window is open, with a large old Samsonite suitcase sitting under it. Odd, I think. This doesn't look right."
- "This suitcase is not normally kept here. Maybe this is how the kidnapper got in and out of our house. The window ledge is a few feet off the floor, so a person would need something to stand on in order to get up and out."

Videotaped Deposition of John Ramsey in Civil Case 00-CIV1187(JEC) 'Robert C. Wolf v. John Ramsey. Atlanta, Georgia: December 12, 2001

- John Ramsey testified that he went to the basement on one occasion before Detective Arndt asked him to check the residence. He did not remember the time that he made the first trip to the basement.
- When asked what he remembered seeing in the basement when he went down there, John states, "I saw a partially opened window with broken glass and a suitcase beneath the window."
- When asked if he saw anything else there, John responded: "Not that looked out of the ordinary."
- Questioned as to why he went to the basement, John states: "I was trying to determine how someone could have gotten into our house."
- John advised that no one directed him to check the basement and doesn't know if anyone saw him go there.
- He had a vague recollection of mentioning the broken window to Detective Arndt, but had explained his earlier summer entry to the house.

What I found disturbing about the chronology of these statements is that John had failed to mention his observations, and suspicions, about the suitcase to investigators on the morning of the kidnapping. He had the opportunity to tell Detective Arndt about this after his exploration of the basement. This was a crucial bit of information, especially in light of the fact that everyone in the house was puzzled about how kidnappers had gained entrance to the home that morning.

He also neglected to mention these observations to Sergeant Mason the following evening, on December 27, 1996, when officers visited the family at the Fernie residence.

Moreover, investigators didn't learn about John's observation of the 'suspicious' vehicles in his neighborhood until June 1998. I am aware that BPD investigators were driving through the neighborhood in unmarked vehicle(s) on the morning of the kidnapping, and they could have easily checked on the identity of the people occupying these vehicles.

And then came the 1998 revelation that a suspect was believed to have moved a chair in the basement before escaping the residence. This chair could have yielded latent fingerprints for comparison against the seventy-one million (71,000,000) known offenders maintained in the national IAFIS FBI database. This database is more than 7 times the size of the DNA database and I would suggest that this would have improved the chances of identifying a suspect if latent fingerprints had been collected from the chair.

Despite claims that the family had shared all of the information they had with law enforcement authorities, it was discouraging to bear witness to the wasted opportunities presented in the events chronicled above.

Assuming the intruder theory to be valid, it is entirely possible that the case could have been significantly advanced by identifying the people in the vehicles observed by Ramsey, and by the processing of critical evidence that might have been handled by suspects while in the home.

CHAPTER TWENTY - SIX

The Christmas Gift

The 2005 Christmas Holidays were fast approaching, and for some reason I felt the necessity of "gifting" the discoveries of my work in the Ramsey case to District Attorney Mary Lacy. By that time, I felt that my reexamination had discredited the evidence that suggested an intruder had been responsible for this crime, and indeed, that compelling visual evidence pointed the investigation in an entirely new direction.

I couldn't understand how Smit so easily dismissed physical evidence that discounted the window well as a point of entry. Spider webs attaching the grate to the foliage and window well wall, as well as cobwebs in the corner of the frame, and the placement of the rectangular piece of glass on the exterior windowsill, appeared to preclude anyone's entry or exit from this location. A collection of pine needles and leaves on the top of the grate further bolstered this observation.

More importantly, the sequencing of the injuries sustained by JonBenét were entirely inconsistent with Smit's version of events. It was his belief she had been repeatedly strangled with the garrote and then had suffered the blow to her head at or near the time of death. The lack of blood from an external wound apparently accounted for this hypothesis.

But it should be noted that the first strike involved in a blow to the head doesn't always break the skin of the scalp and cause immediate external bleeding.

JonBenét's injury gave the appearance of one massive strike to the top right side of her skull. There did not appear to be any follow-up blow, and the severity of her injuries could not be interpreted from a viewing of the external autopsy photographs alone. The severity of the injury to her skull was not realized until *after* her scalp had been redacted to inspect the internal aspects of her head. It only *then* became apparent that she had suffered a crushing blow to her skull.

Internal bleeding normally does not occur once the heart stops beating. According to the forensic examiners who studied the evidence, the presence of such bleeding revealed that JonBenét had lived for some period of time after receiving the blow to her head.

Moreover, it appeared to me that the garrote had been applied in one singular fashion and not repeatedly tightened during an orgy of torture. Dr. Spitz's opinion about the collar of the shirt causing the other abrasions on JonBenét's neck seemed consistent with the appearance of those injuries. Although I thought it possible that the perpetrator could have repeatedly tightened and loosened the garrote during an episode of torture, I wondered why someone would do that to an unconscious child. This activity would not have resulted in the victim regaining any semblance of consciousness, and would not likely have provided the intruder any degree of satisfaction. The intent of torture is to see the victim's fearful reaction to pain, and physical torture, and that was not possible in this set of circumstances.

It was a matter of speculation on my part, but I believed the cord of the garrote had been tightened during one single application. The hair that was caught in the knot of the garrote located at the base of her neck would likely have been torn free from JonBenét's scalp during a repeated loosening and tightening of the ligature. As noted by the coroner, the final application of the garrote was the proximate cause of her death.

I couldn't help but wonder if Smit had ever reviewed any of the forensic findings when he constructed his theory of the intruder. His hypothesis was contrary to the forensic science developed over the course of the investigation. My interpretation of some of the physical injuries suggested that an entirely different series of events had taken place, and they were in direct contradiction to what Smit was proposing.

There were other aspects of the "kidnapping" that didn't quite ring true, and it was my belief that careful consideration of all of these pieces of evidence and clues would help steer the investigation back on course.

A fairly substantial Power-Point presentation was nearing completion, and I was preparing to sit down with my boss to spell out the details of my efforts. I was patently aware that I was wading into dangerous territory. Mary Lacy didn't believe that the parents had been involved in the death of their daughter.

And then my phone rang.

Jay Harrington, Town Manager of Telluride and my former employer, was calling to see if I had I tired of my current position. He indicated that the chief of police in Telluride, in place for less than a year, was preparing to move on to bigger and better things. Harrington wanted to know if I was willing to consider the possibility of returning to my old desk.

Here I was, on the eve of committing political suicide, being offered an opportunity to return to the safe haven of the mountains of southwestern Colorado. I couldn't help but laugh at the irony of the situation.

I could be fired the next day for expressing my professional opinion about a murder investigation and out of the blue came another job offer. How fortuitous was that?

I ended up postponing my presentation to Lacy and her staff, scheduled for the next day, so that I could add a few more video clips that would help round out my case theory.

When I ultimately presented my theory on January 30, 2006, I wasn't terminated. I didn't really think that was going to happen, to be honest, but the events that followed seemed to suggest that I had fallen out of favor.

CHAPTER TWENTY - SEVEN

January 2006 Presentation

I had been working on a Power-Point presentation for approximately two months and was finally prepared to share my findings with Mary Lacy and her command staff at the end of January 2006. It had been a long haul, but I felt that I had prepared a fairly comprehensive investigative piece that placed the lone-intruder theory into question.

There were a number of elements that comprised the foundation of my theory and key to these discoveries was the belief that I had effectively discounted the evidence that suggested an outsider was responsible for this crime. The core documents / photographs compiled by Boulder investigators had eventually revealed their secrets. My presentation consisted of a number of still 35mm photographs and video segments that would help illustrate my hypothesis.

Closer examination of the crime scene video completed by Boulder Crime Scene Investigators on the evening of December 26th, 1996, virtually eliminated the possibility that entry had been made to the Ramsey residence through the Train Room window well. This video provided more detailed information about the condition of the window well than what had been depicted in the 35 mm still photographs.

I then moved forward to examine the theory that a stun gun had been used to silence JonBenét. Notwithstanding the fact that Boulder County Coroner John Meyer reported the undetermined marks on JonBenét to be "abrasions" versus burn marks, D.A. investigators conducted their own comparison of the most likely brand of stun gun alleged to have been used in the assault.

One-to-one photographs comparing the stun gun probes to the injuries on JonBenét had not yet been prepared, however, and I asked that this be done. A series of Power Point photographs were completed that revealed the measurements of the electronic probes did not match the injuries on the body of JonBenét.

It was related to me that the Hi-Tec boot print in the Wine Cellar was potentially from a number of sources and not necessarily left by an intruder.

Additionally, by the time I arrived on the investigative scene, the FBI laboratory had already conducted random DNA tests on underwear purchased off the shelf. They determined that DNA samples could be obtained from new, unopened packages of children's underwear, suggesting the possibility that the genetic material deposited there had come from the manufacturing / packaging end of the line.

I thought it would be a small step from there to conduct additional tests that simulated a coughing, sneezing, spitting seamstress / handler of similar items to verify this type of DNA could be collected from fresh off-the-shelf clothing articles.

Under those circumstances, I believed that there may have been a plausible explanation for the DNA found in the underwear and that its presence may have had nothing whatsoever to do with the death of JonBenét.

Its presence was puzzling, but I felt that this single piece of DNA evidence had to be considered in light of all of the other physical, behavioral, and statement evidence that had been collected over the course of the investigation.

Having eliminated the Train Room window as a likely point of entry and exit and ruling out the use of a stun gun in this abduction, I was left pondering the question of motive. If an intruder was not responsible for the murder of JonBenét, then what possible reason could the Ramseys have had for brutally murdering their daughter?

I didn't quite buy the hypothesis that Patsy had lost her temper and struck JonBenét. She had not been eliminated as the author of the ransom note, which certainly left open the possibility that she had involvement in the crime. I just couldn't reconcile the fact that Patsy was, by all accounts, a loving and doting mother, and I had difficulty envisioning her ever brutalizing either one of her children.

Nevertheless, that was one of the questions I contemplated as I began to study the behavioral aspects of the family. A necessary part of that process required an examination of the motives presented in the crime. On the face of it, this was a crime that involved mixed motives, and the slide presentation I produced for Mary Lacy and her command staff was entitled "A Tale of Two Motives."

I cited materials from the FBI's Crime Classification Manual and the National Center for the Analysis of Violent Crime to spell out the details of these motives.

The first involved the crime of Kidnap and was a motive identified as "Criminal Enterprise." There had been the taking of a hostage that was to be held for ransom.

Aside from the missing victim, the ransom note was the most obvious element for this motive, and it spelled out the monetary figure demanded by the perpetrators.

But then things took a different twist. The object of the kidnap was never removed from the home. Additionally, the lengthy note suggested an intimate knowledge of the family, and it seemed reminiscent of a "Hollywood" version of the crime.

Agents of the FBI consulting on the case thought the note extremely unusual. It had been their experience that kidnappers didn't typically want to reveal details about themselves. Ransom notes were short and sweet: "We have your kid and want one million dollars. Wait for our call." Period.

The FBI had also advised Boulder investigators after the discovery of JonBenét's body that they needed to take a close look at the family. Statistically, a child found murdered in the home usually involved a family member.

FBI agents shared another word of advice. The circumstances surrounding this crime led them to believe that two hands were involved in this murder.

The second motive present, quite obvious due to the violence perpetrated against JonBenét, was identified as "Sadistic Murder – Sexual Homicide." The injuries inflicted upon JonBenét left little doubt about this motive.

All things considered, these were entirely different and contrasting motives that seemed to defy explanation.

If there truly was a group of people intent on extorting ransom from John Ramsey, why would they murder the object that held value in their cause? If JonBenét had been killed by accident, why not remove her from the home and follow through with the ransom call? They could have collected their money, and the family would never have been aware that their daughter was already dead.

The other question posed addressed the sexual sadist. If the motivation for this crime involved a lone sexual predator, why would he not remove the object of his desire from the home? Pedophiles who abduct children typically take them somewhere private where they can take their time abusing their prey. He instead took the risk of being discovered and trapped by assaulting JonBenét within the confines of the residence.

And for what purpose did he take precious time to craft a ransom note?

Based upon a neighbor's observations, it appeared that he may have written the note beneath the dimmed lights of the kitchen.

From there I outlined the factors that pointed to a "mixed offender" profile, a technique used to help police narrow down the pool of suspects possibly involved in a case.

The confusing circumstances present in this crime suggested that we had both an "organized" and "disorganized" offender(s) responsible for its commission.

Some of the clues present suggested that an organized offender was responsible for this crime. He / they were methodical and had appeared to have conducted surveillance of the home before the kidnapping. According to the ransom note, they also appeared to be familiar with the family. Implements used in the crime, i.e. the cord and duct tape, were not found in the home after the discovery of the body, so it was presumed that they had brought these items with them: a sign that thought had gone into the process of pre-planning this event.

On the other hand, the disorganized aspect of the case involved the use of Patsy's notepad and pen in the construction of the ransom note, as well as the use of the paintbrush handle in the garrote. These were items collected from the scene, perhaps at the last minute, and suggested that no planning or forethought had gone into this process. Taking the time to craft this note unnecessarily exposed the perpetrator to discovery and capture, the sign of an unsophisticated and disorganized mind.

I felt that the presence of these mixed motives and offender profiles raised doubt about the involvement of a lone-sexual predator.

An additional part of the presentation included an examination of the crime scene characteristics that raised the issue of "staging" and the behavioral analysis aspects of "undoing."

The Crime Classification Manual describes staging as activities that someone may engage in when they purposefully alter a crime scene prior to the arrival of police. Elements of staging raises "red flags" for the investigator because an offender who stages a crime scene usually makes mistakes because they prepare it the way they *think* a crime scene should look.

Law enforcement officers respond to hundreds of crime scenes over the course of their careers and have developed that "sixth sense" that sends off alarm bells when something doesn't look or sound right.

They recognize that a crime scene will often contain these red flags in the form of inconsistencies.

There are two reasons someone may engage in staging a crime scene:

1. They wish to redirect the investigation away from the most logical suspect, or to

2. Protect the victim or victim's family. (This could include a motive to avoid embarrassment, or criminal charging based upon the underlying circumstances present in a crime.)

The specific acts committed by the perpetrator in this case that gave the impression of staging were the circumstances surrounding the application of the wrist bindings and duct tape.

By their very nature, wrist bindings are presumed to be used for restraint and control, especially in a situation involving a kidnapped hostage.

Yet the wrist bindings were applied so loosely that John Ramsey was able to remove one in a matter of seconds upon discovering his daughter's body. Moreover, her wrists were not bound together, and the length of cord, fifteen (15 ½") inches, that separated her hands offered no protection from efforts that may have been made to remove the duct tape.

Dr. Meyer, the coroner conducting the autopsy, noted that the binding remaining on one of JonBenét's wrists was loose enough for him to slip a finger beneath the cord.

It seemed apparent that these bindings were not intended to restrain JonBenét, but may have been applied for another purpose.

To demonstrate the nature of a true binding utilized in a kidnap, I obtained photographs of the injuries sustained to the wrists of Tracy Neef, a 7-year-old child abducted on March 16, 1984, from the exterior of her school in Thornton and whose body was recovered later that day in Boulder County.

In this instance, there were ligature marks found on Tracy's wrists, right elbow, and face. The bindings used to create these marks had been removed prior to the discovery of her body.

Investigators noted that there were linear marks along her cheeks that suggested she had been gagged, and there were distinct marks on her wrists that indicated she had been bound by some type of rope or cord.

The purpose of this comparison was to point out the distinction between bindings that had been applied for the brutal purpose of control and restraint and those that may have been applied for another reason. Tracy's wrists bore the marks of rope that had been applied with significant force.

In JonBenét's case, the bindings were so loose that they inflicted no marks upon her wrists. Were these utilized for restraint and control or in the staging of a crime with the intention of misleading investigators?

Duct tape placed over the mouth of a victim performs the function of silencing them and preventing them from calling out for help. Autopsy photographs reveal mucous on the face of JonBenét in the area beneath the placement of the tape.

The interpretation of these observations and the physical symptoms that would have accompanied her death, suggest that the tape had been placed on her face after her death. Conceivably, this was another potential aspect of staging.

The psychology behind the concept of "undoing" specifies that certain acts taken at a crime scene are usually based on an attitude of caring and remorse. Undoing is an action taken by an offender who has a close association with the victim, and they try to symbolically "Undo" the homicide.

Examples of such actions have included washing a victim, placing a pillow under the victim's head, and covering the victim with a blanket.

JonBenét had been found wrapped in a blanket, bundled like a "papoose" according to her father. Her favorite pink Barbie nightgown was with her.

The violent blow to her head, taken in combination with her strangulation and vaginal assault, suggested that a ruthless, cold-hearted individual was responsible for her murder.

The caring manner in which JonBenét had been wrapped in a blanket, however, stood in direct contrast to these acts of violence. Whoever took the time to wrap her up like a papoose was expressing care and compassion for this child.

I believed that these were additional elements that conflicted with accepted assumptions about circumstances surrounding JonBenét's death. I entirely understood the FBI opinion that more than one person had participated in this crime.

The most significant piece of evidence that suggested this crime scene had been staged was the ransom note. Boulder investigators were not willing to let go of the fact that Patsy could not be eliminated as the author, and I was right there with them.

Strengthening their suspicions was the peculiar fact that it had been written on *her* notepad kept in the kitchen. A pen found in the same area was identified as the instrument used to write the note. Moreover, there were remnants of what appeared to be a practice note and missing pages from the tablet.

In considering the components of this theory, I took into consideration Lou Smit's perspective regarding this loving, Christian family. I asked the following:

- Did John or Patsy have any motive to intentionally murder their daughter?

I believed the likely answer to that question was No.

I then pondered the theory that the death had been an accident:

- Was it possible that Patsy had lost her temper during an argument with JonBenét, and struck her with an object?

It was clear that *someone* had struck a blow to the head of JonBenét, and that it had not been self-inflicted. If it wasn't Patsy, then who?

The next questions that had to be considered were then the following:

- If the parents didn't intentionally kill their daughter, and if there was no intruder, then why go to all of the effort of staging a cover-up?
- Who would benefit?
- Who was being protected?
- Why?

It has been my experience that the interpretation of a crime involves an understanding of the dynamics and psychology of human behavior. As humans, our behavior tends to reveal our motives, and we all behave for specific intent and purpose. We are driven by our desires and objectives.

Determining motive demands more than the simple task of following the physical evidence. Uncovering motive involves careful evaluation of all of the elements associated with a crime.

Solving a crime requires a comprehensive, objective interpretation of both the physical evidence and the human behavior associated with the events under investigation.

The presentation of my Power-Point theory began at 1300 hours on the afternoon of January 30, 2006. Materials contained within the presentation included crime scene photos, a variety of video clips from police interviews and media coverage, as well as a discussion of some of the physical evidence that had been collected over the course of the investigation.

A significant number of slides detailed statements that had been made by the family and other witnesses. The behavioral aspects of motive and opportunity were discussed at length.

The clock was closing on 1900 hours. Mary and the members of her command staff, Pete Maguire and Bill Nagel, had listened attentively and asked pertinent questions over the course of the afternoon.

But I could tell their attention was fading. We had not taken a break during the entire six hours, and there were approximately fifty slides of material yet to be shown. I decided that it was time to cut to the chase.

I pointed out that Ramsey attorneys had effectively withheld medical records from the prosecution during the investigation, and I specifically referred to John Ramsey's interview of June 1998.[51] I felt, that given the above information, we should be revisiting and intensifying our investigation of the involvement of the family. Among other things, we should be seeking the psychiatric records of Burke to determine if he had had any knowledge of the death of his sister, either through a grand jury or by asking the Ramseys for the information.

I believed wholeheartedly that this was a viable investigative lead that deserved pursuit. If nothing came of it, then at least we could say that we had covered all of our bases.

Mary Lacy's response is something that I will have difficulty ever forgetting.

She told me that she was unwilling to pursue that lead because she 'didn't want to harm her relationship with the Ramsey family.'

This response left me speechless, and it effectively ended the presentation. At that juncture, I felt that nothing more could be said, or done, that would sway Lacy from this position.

As I was packing up my computer and projector, she told me about something that Tom Wickman had purportedly observed during the execution of the search warrants at the Ramsey home. He reportedly had observed the impression of someone's buttocks in the carpet of the hallway outside JonBenét's second floor bedroom. It appeared that someone had been sitting on the floor with their knees up around their chest, leaning against the wall / cabinets.

Wickman purportedly told her that he thought it was where the intruder had been waiting while the family was at the White dinner party. I was aware that some intruder theorists believed it possible the perpetrator had entered the home while the family was away that evening, and that he had written the ransom note while awaiting their return. Apparently, Lacy thought that Wickman was suggesting the intruder had found some time to sit on the floor outside JonBenét's bedroom after penning his note.

I didn't recall seeing anything like that in any of the police reports I had read and subsequently asked Wickman about it.

He told me he had no idea what I was talking about.

CHAPTER TWENTY-EIGHT

Black Sheep

My last days with the district attorney's office were fast approaching. It wasn't official yet, but at the time that I presented my theory to Mary Lacy and her command staff, it seemed likely that I would be returning to the West Slope. Had Lacy opted to pursue the leads I was proposing, I had decided that I would stick around long enough to see it through. But it was clear that was no longer likely.

As her chief investigator, I felt that it had been my obligation to inform her of my findings and had proceeded with fingers crossed, hoping that the essence of my argument would carry the day. Perhaps some of the things I presented that day were too esoteric.

January 30th happened to fall on a Monday, and late Tuesday morning I stopped by Lacy's office on another matter. While there, she informed me that her daughter had actually run into John and

Patsy Ramsey at a Boulder restaurant the previous evening. They spoke briefly and indicated that they might stop by the D.A.'s that week for a visit.

How coincidental was that? The lead investigator in their case had just come off the fence and taken a position opposite that of his employer. I wondered if they really would come by the office to visit and if I'd have an opportunity to meet them.

The following afternoon I attended the case staffing at the weekly SART meeting which, as usual, took several hours to complete.

I returned to my office and was asked by an investigator in the neighboring space if I had been with the Ramsey family. No, I replied. I had been otherwise engaged.

I checked my desk phone and saw that I had no voicemail messages or missed calls. The cell phone at my hip displayed the same information.

Mary Lacy caught me at the end of the day and told me that the Ramseys had stopped by the office, and she had spent an hour or so visiting with them. She indicated that she had looked for me that afternoon to no avail.

I subsequently asked my neighbor if anyone had come looking for me while I was gone that afternoon: Not that she had seen.

It has been said that timing is everything, and it seemed apparent that timing was against me in this instance.

I had missed my opportunity to meet the parents of the little girl whose murder investigation had been entrusted into my care.

Bill Nagel stopped by my office the following week. He apparently had been giving my theory some additional thought. Bill advised me that no one had really taken a very close look at Burke and that Ramsey attorneys had campaigned Hunter's office to publically clear him of any involvement in the case. All eyes were focused elsewhere, and Hunter eventually caved on the request.

It made sense to me. I recalled having seen a handwritten note on attorney letterhead that had been faxed to the D.A.s office.

It was my impression that Hunter's subsequent announcement to the media, which cleared Burke Ramsey as a potential suspect in the case, read nearly verbatim to the content of the note sent to him by Ramsey attorneys.

I was writing reports up to the last day that I occupied my desk at the D.A.'s office and had been unable to find the time to translate my theory into the form of a written document. The Power-Point had been crafted over time using sticky notes scattered through numerous binders, and there wasn't always an explanation that accompanied some of the slides. I felt that a written investigative report was a necessary component of the presentation.

It was a matter, I believed, of quid-pro-quo. Tom Bennett had permitted me to travel to Oregon in the early days of my employment with his office in order to execute an arrest warrant I had obtained prior to leaving Telluride. The warrant had been issued as one in a series in the cocaine trafficking investigation I had been leading, and this subject had disappeared on the eve of our roundup.

He was a key witness that needed to be turned state's evidence, and Bennett let me go on company time. I felt that I would return the favor and finish the written report after returning to Telluride. I told Tom that I thought I should be able to finish the project before the summer festival season kicked off in June.

The best of intentions...

≡ ⊕ ≡

April 2006 witnessed my return to the mountains of southwestern Colorado. The "sabbatical" I had taken in Boulder had been interesting and rewarding, but I was happy to be back. I didn't realize how much I had missed the majestic beauty and solitude of the hills surrounding my log home.

Tom Bennett had been recruited to return to Lacy's office yet again, and in this instance, it seems that the timing of events had spared me from the humiliation of one enormous fiasco. I was unaware of it at the time, but shortly after my departure Bennett was assigned the unfortunate task of dealing with Michael Tracey, a journalism professor and movie maker who had become focused on the Ramsey investigation. He wanted us to help him track down a pedophile who was claiming by email to have been the person responsible for JonBenét's abduction and murder.

April and May were occupied with a move to a new headquarters building for my department, and Bennett was fully engaged in the Tracey mess. Unbeknownst to me, he was working seven (7) days a week on nothing but that case.

June brought the death of Patsy from a second bout with ovarian cancer, and a media frenzy once again surrounded the family. I should not have been surprised to see Mary Lacy attending the funeral services.

The summer festival season demanded my attention, and my thoughts of the Ramsey case fell further from my mind. I had begun to debate whether it was really necessary to pursue the course I had suggested to Lacy given all of the pain and suffering the family had endured that year.

Then all hell broke loose. It was soon broadcast all over the media in August of that summer that there had been an arrest in the Ramsey case. John Mark Karr had been identified as the person responsible for corresponding with Tracey via email, and he was to be brought back to Colorado from Thailand for further investigation.

There were not a lot of details released in the first hours of Karr being taken into custody, and I thought to myself, "Damn, they've finally caught the son of a bitch." I shot a quick email to Bennett congratulating him on the arrest.

His response was less than enthusiastic. Bennett didn't think this was the guy.

Perhaps half a dozen reporters called my office in search of details. I was asking questions too because there was not a lot of information being reported about the things Karr had disclosed to Tracey in his emails. I wondered what it was that had been said that led authorities to seek his arrest.

Within a few days, the details of his writings began to publically emerge. I told a friend in the media that John Mark Karr was no doubt a pedophile, but he wasn't responsible for the murder of JonBenét. His written explanation of events was pure fantasy and didn't match the forensics of the case.

FOR IMMEDIATE RELEASE
August 16, 2006

Statement of John Ramsey
On Today's Arrest in Connection with Murder of His Daughter,
JonBenét Ramsey

"I want to have only limited comment on today's arrest because I feel it is extremely important to not only let the justice system operate to its conclusion in an orderly manner, but also to avoid feeding the type of media speculation that my wife and I were subjected to for so many years." said John Ramsey. "I do want to say, however, that the investigation of the individual arrested today in connection with JonBenét's death was discussed with Patsy and me by the Boulder District Attorney's office prior to Patsy's death in June. So Patsy was aware that authorities were close to making an arrest in the case and had she lived to see this day, would no doubt have been as pleased as I am with today's development almost 10 years after our daughter's murder. Words cannot adequately express my gratitude for the efforts of Boulder District Attorney May Lacy and the members of her investigative team."

Patsy Ramsey lost a 13-year battle with ovarian cancer and passed away on June 24.

"The Ramseys and I have been totally amazed and impressed with the professionalism of law enforcement under the direction of Boulder District Attorney Mary Lacy. This was obviously an incredibly complex task but one that has been carried out in almost textbook fashion with the investigation of this individual going on for several months, without any leaks in the case," said L. Lin Wood, attorney for the Ramsey family and partner at Powell Goldstein in Atlanta. "I want to express my heartfelt thanks to the many people who have stood by the Ramseys, believing in them and their innocence these long and difficult years."

John Ramsey will not be providing interviews at this time. Requests for future interviews should be directed to Lin Wood, attorney for the Ramsey family, at:

Mr. L. Lin Wood

Powell Goldstein LLP

One Atlantic Center, 14th Floor

1201 West Peachtree Street NW

Atlanta, Georgia

Press Release issued by John Ramsey and attorney Lin Wood following the Boulder District Attorney's office arrest of John Michael Karr in Thailand, August 2006.

CHAPTER TWENTY - NINE

"Karr-mic" Reality

I watched with interest the continuing news coverage of Karr's extradition proceedings. It was reminiscent of the feeding frenzy from the early days of the investigation, and I couldn't help but read Tom Bennett's displeasure of having to stand in the wings behind his boss as they spoke about the circumstances leading to the arrest of the man thought responsible for JonBenét's murder.

We'd had no further correspondence about the case since that brief email exchange, but Bennett's expression and demeanor seemed to say it all. This was not a time of celebration, and he held no illusion that this was the intruder we'd all been chasing for years.

The photographs and videotape of Karr sipping champagne on his flight to the U.S. was almost too much to bear. Oh, this was not going to end well, I thought.

It didn't take long for the media to pull up their archived files on the case and locate Dorothy Allison's composite sketch of her vision of the murderer. Side-by-side photographic comparisons were displayed for the public that revealed Karr's uncanny resemblance to Allison's psychic rendering of the perpetrator.

There were more than a few who seemed to consider the similarity of Karr's features to that of the man portrayed in the psychic sketch as proof that the D.A.'s office had finally found their man. In many corners, and in spite of the fact that DNA tests had not yet been completed, people were celebrating the fact that JonBenét's killer had finally been caught.

Some went so far as to renew their criticism of the Boulder Police Department's previous handling of the investigation, apparently thinking that Karr's DNA would seal the case against him.

In response to some of these comments, the members of Boulder PD's legal *Dream Team* prepared a statement that was released on August 31, 2006. It read as follows:

Police Response to Allegations:

Recent events in the nearly 10-year- old homicide of JonBenét Ramsey have rekindled the firestorm of accusations about how the Boulder Police Department handled the investigation into her death. The department had remained silent in recent years, as the effort to correct inaccuracies seemed futile.

In the fall of 1997, three prominent Denver-area attorneys, Dan Hoffman, Robert Miller, and Richard Baer, assisted the Boulder Police Department with the investigation. After reading comments made by Trip DeMuth in today's Rocky Mountain News, all three felt compelled to contact the police department to provide support. They have authorized the Boulder Police Department to release this statement on their behalf:

> *We assisted the Boulder Police Department in their investigation of the murder of JonBenét Ramsey. Throughout our involvement and to this day, we have never spoken to the media about*

this case because we feel that comments by anyone involved in the investigation could only compromise the ability to prosecute the perpetrator or perpetrators of this horrible crime. However, we are compelled to respond to the irresponsible statements of one of the deputy district attorneys who worked on the case, Trip DeMuth. Some ten years after the fact, DeMuth claims that he was somehow prevented by the Boulder Police Department from pursuing leads in the investigation. Based on our knowledge of this matter, DeMuth's claim is ridiculous. Mr. DeMuth's assertion that the Boulder Police Department refused to pursue a variety of theories is also ludicrous. In our opinion, the Boulder Police Department, as well as Michael Kane, an experienced prosecutor, conducted an exhaustive and wide-ranging investigation of this matter. If Mr. DeMuth truly cares about seeing justice done, he should act responsibly and refrain from making inaccurate statements that could further jeopardize this investigation.

The Boulder Police Department, over the years, investigated more than 160 potential suspects in the case.

"A few people have accused the department of focusing too narrowly in its investigation of this homicide when that was not the case" said Chief Mark Beckner. "People who have spoken out that way have relied on the department's inability to discuss case specifics, but I cannot allow the misperceptions to go unanswered any longer."

Daniel Hoffman has practiced law in Colorado since 1958 and he was the dean of the University of Denver, College of Law from 1978 to 1984. He is now in private practice at a firm in Denver. Robert Miller was the U.S. Attorney for Colorado from 1981 to 1988. Before that, he was the Weld County district attorney for 10 years. He is now in private practice in Denver. Richard Baer was a state prosecutor in New York before joining a law firm in Denver. He is now the executive vice president and general counsel for a large corporation in Denver.

—Julie Brooks, PIO
City of Boulder

It was painful to watch the follow-up press conference declaring John Mark Karr innocent of this crime. Though Lacy had initially cautioned the public not to rush to judgment about Karr's arrest in the matter, the time had finally come to announce that his DNA did not match the genetic materials found in JonBenét's underwear. Mary Lacy reported, that despite their best efforts, they had not found their man.

I was embarrassed for the Boulder County District Attorney's Office and for the Boulder Police Department. Chief Beckner apparently had only been told about this lead in the hours before Karr's arrest, and no investigator from his agency had participated in the investigation that brought Karr back to U.S. soil. Nevertheless, Beckner had issued a press release the day after Karr's arrest, stating that the department was pleased with the recent development in the case, and that his investigators were hopeful that the arrest of John Mark Karr would lead to closure in the case.

Beckner went to state that he knew there were still many questions that needed to be answered in the case, but that his department stood ready to assist the D.A.'s office in tracking down those answers.

It was reported that approximately thirty-five thousand ($35,000.00) had been expended in pursuit of this lead. I later learned that Tom Bennett had worked approximately three (3) months straight putting this thing together for Lacy. He took not a solitary day off in that entire time frame. He was ever still the dependable workhorse.

I wondered if the results would have been different if Lacy's office had been willing to put forth the effort in pursuing the direction I suggested to her earlier that year. In my humble opinion, there was much more substance present in the details I had shared with her than in the delusionary musings of this particular child molester.

I decided that I really needed to finish my written analysis of the theory I had developed earlier in the year and set about in earnest.

I delivered a single binder to Tom Bennett on October 8, 2006, that contained a detailed synopsis of my findings, accompanied by the supporting materials that made up the Power-Point presentation.

As was my practice when writing investigative reports for the D.A.'s office, I presented copies of my work product to the law enforcement agency holding primary jurisdiction for the crime. I hand-delivered a copy of the binder to Mark Beckner.

While my interest in the Ramsey case may have waned during the summer, it had become re-energized after the completion of my written synopsis. Among other things, I was genuinely convinced that there was merit to the exploration of Burke's psychiatric records.

I had received no word from Bennett that my materials had been reviewed or that my efforts in completing this task for Lacy's office were even appreciated. Based on my view of her efforts in the Karr debacle, I felt that it was unlikely that anyone had cracked the cover on my work. She seemed unwilling to consider any lead that would explore family involvement.

I decided to query her office with a request to have the materials / theory presented to the prosecutors who had been most familiar with the details of the case and who had participated in the 1998 grand jury investigation. I was politely requesting an objective review by these distinguished attorneys.

The following is a redacted version of the correspondence I sent to D.A.'s office in the fall of 2006:

October 31, 2006

Honorable Mary Lacy
District Attorney
Twentieth Judicial District Attorney's Office
1777 6th Street
P.O. Box 471
Boulder, CO 80306

Dear Mary,

As you may be aware, I recently provided chief investigator Tom Bennett with the final version of a written outline of my analysis of the investigation and circumstances surrounding the death of JonBenét Ramsey. This outline was completed for the purposes of accompanying the Power Point presentation of the case theory that I provided to you in January of this year. The underlying premise of this theory suggests that no intruder participated in the premature death of JonBenét Ramsey.

I would advise you that I did not arrive at this decision casually, nor was it due to preconceived notions held prior to my involvement in the investigation of the case. It was my responsibility to acquaint myself with the details of the investigation when I assumed the lead investigative role for your office in July 2005 and I set about reviewing what I considered to be the core documents of the investigation. I felt I needed to get 'up to speed' with the facts of the case so that I could properly evaluate new leads that were continuously streaming into our office.

I have to admit that the circumstances surrounding the death of JonBenét were very perplexing and it presented as a very complicated and unusual case. Nevertheless, I was intent on bringing an objective viewpoint to the inquiry and I continued my research into the circumstances of this crime. In search of motive, opportunity and a better understanding of the events, I pursued many questions that led to dead-end. I took another look at suspects who had previously been cleared and I continued to examine the statements and behavior of the Ramsey family.

It was only after approximately 5 months of intensive examination of these documents did I come to believe that the family was somehow involved in the death of JonBenét. I did not quite know how or why, but at that juncture, I no longer felt it was likely that an intruder had participated in this crime. While continuing to evaluate new leads coming into our office, I began to narrow the focus of my review on the family. Over the course of the following months, I began to discover things that tended to support my belief and as I evaluated behavioral clues, statements and physical evidence, a plausible theory of family involvement and cover-up began to take form.

Although I left your office in the late spring of this year, the details of this investigation have ever been in the forefront of my mind and the written outline presented to Tom Bennett several weeks ago is a culmination of the deliberative process that has been ongoing since the day I first reviewed a Ramsey homicide report.

As a distant observer to the events surrounding the arrest of John Mark Karr, I initially was cautiously optimistic that he might prove to be the intruder who was responsible for the murder of JonBenét. By all accounts he was presenting as a dangerous pedophile and, until a case is solved, all things should be considered possible. Unfortunately, it soon became apparent to me, based upon statements attributed to him by the media, that Mr. Karr did not know what he was talking about. When his correspondence with Mr. Tracy was finally revealed, it was clear that his stated version of events were inconsistent with autopsy findings and physical evidence discovered during the processing of the crime scene.

From the perspective of a 30-year veteran of law enforcement, I can understand that you wanted to be absolutely certain that Mr. Karr was not the perpetrator of this offense and felt it necessary to eliminate him by comparing his DNA to the forensic sample found in this case. Nevertheless, I would suggest that the DNA in this case is only one artifact of evidence and its evidentiary value must be considered in light of all of the other pieces of physical, testimonial and behavioral evidence that have been collected and analyzed over the course of this investigation. Technological advances in science now allow us to collect and identify microscopic evidence that had once not been available to the criminalist. As you know, this type of evidence can be very helpful in identifying a perpetrator or solving a crime, but I am concerned that one piece of trace evidence, to the exclusion of everything else, is dominating the theory and the investigative construct of this crime. If I am correct in my assessment, there may be a plausible explanation for the presence of the DNA in the underwear and it may have nothing whatsoever to do with the death of JonBenét.

Therefore, after much reflection and having enduring many sleepless nights, I am requesting that I be permitted the opportunity to present my case theory to Mitch Morrissey and Michael Kane, the special prosecutors who were most familiar with the investigation when the case was presented to the grand jury in 1998. I believe there are specific records and testimony that were not sought during the first inquiry that are key to solving this case and these are things that could be obtained through the investigative powers of the grand jury.

For that reason, I am forwarding a copy of this letter to Governor Bill Owens and Colorado Attorney General John Suthers, in that there is a state grand jury already sitting that could hear this matter. It would be my hope that, at least initially, an inquiry at the state level would allow prosecutors to avoid the media attention that accompanied the first announced inquiry that took place in Boulder. I am of a mind that the criminal investigation into this death should not be played out in the media on an hourly basis.

In closing, I have to indicate that I find myself in a very uncomfortable position for I have a great deal of respect for your office and the people employed there. I was once the chief investigator for that office and had the opportunity to serve as the lead investigator in one of the most bizarre murder investigations this country has ever witnessed. What I discovered during my review of this case leads me to believe that it is solvable. With that said, I fully realize that my theory is in direct contradiction to your stated belief that the Ramseys were not involved in the death of their daughter…yet I am resolved to move forward and seek resolution to a matter that has endured nearly a decade of speculation and frustration.

As a criminal investigator, I believe it is our duty to pursue all viable leads developed during the course of a homicide inquiry. Furthermore, I hold to the belief that investigators and prosecutors are obligated to seek the truth, regardless the difficulty of the task and no matter where the course may lead. I would propose that there are sufficient grounds to revisit the possibility of family involvement and would like to think that this theory and these leads warrant the same degree of attention, effort and resources that were recently expended in the pursuit of John Mark Karr.

Thank you for your consideration of this matter and I patiently await your response. As a former JonBenét Ramsey homicide investigator and private citizen…

Respectfully,

A. James Kolar

ajk

Cc: Chief Mark Beckner, Boulder Police Department

Governor Bill Owens, State of Colorado

Attorney General John Suthers, State of Colorado

My pursuit of that request would most certainly turn me again into the *black sheep* of my former family.

PART THREE

A Family Affair

Federal Judge: 'No Evidence' That Ramseys Killed JonBenét

"U.S. District Judge Julie E. Carnes, a former federal prosecutor, ruled that there is "abundant evidence" to support assertions by JonBenét's parents, John B. and Patricia P. "Patsy" Ramsey, "that an intruder entered their home at some point during the night of Dec. 25, 1996, and killed their daughter."

Carnes' order stem from a 2000 case filed in U.S. District Court in Atlanta by Robert Christian Wolf, a Boulder, Colo., journalist who has written for Colorado Daily and The Boulder County Business Report. Wolf, who had been questioned by Boulder police as a potential suspect in JonBenét's murder, sued the Ramseys. He claimed that Patsy Ramsey and her husband, as a way of directing police suspicion away from Patsy, had hired private detectives to investigate Wolf and others "in hope of encouraging the authorities to arrest the plaintiff for the murder of her daughter".

On March 31, Carnes dismissed the case against the Ramseys on a motion for summary judgment. Noting that if Wolf could not prove "by clear and convincing evidence" that his theory that the Ramseys killed their daughter was true, "he cannot demonstrate that their statement concerning his status as a suspect was made with the requisite malice."

'It is the first time that a judge has reviewed all the evidence pertaining to JonBenét's murder and released a public analysis of the case,' said the Ramsey's Atlanta attorney L. Lin Wood Jr.

'I just find it, from A to Z, a total, unequivocal victory for John and Patsy Ramsey, Wood said. 'The court has done what I've urged the public to do from day one. Look at the evidence…If you look at the evidence, you will reach the same conclusion Judge Carnes reached. This is a family that has been horribly and wrongly accused of the murder of their child.' Wood said that since Boulder County District Attorney Mary W. Keenan took office, she has rejuvenated the investigation into

JonBenét's murder. Characterizing Keenan's investigation as 'very active,' Wood said investigators 'are doing things in that case that have never been done before,' including testing foreign, male DNA that was found in JonBenét's underwear."

R. Robin McDonald
Fulton County Daily Report
April 07, 2003

New Questions Emerge

As noted in other chapters, I had been researching the official family statements made over the course of the investigation and these included those that had been provided by Burke. Some things said by him had set off faint alarm bells, and I was continuing to look for things that could help clarify questions I had about his behavior.

Having explored the window well and stun gun, thought to be specific elements that pointed to the existence of an intruder, I turned my attention to the DNA evidence found in the underwear worn by JonBenét at the time of her death.

I met with the man who had worked so diligently to enhance the DNA sample identified as Distal Stain 007-2. Denver Police Department crime lab supervisor Greg Laberge met me for lunch in early December 2005 and advised me that the forensic DNA sample collected from the underwear was microscopic, totally invisible to the naked eye. So small was it in quantity, consisting of only approximately 1/2 nanogram of genetic material, equivalent to about 100 – 150 cells, that it took him quite a bit of work to identify the 10th marker that eventually permitted its entry into the CODIS database.

DNA samples generally consist of 13 Core loci markers, so it is important to note that Distal Stain 007-2 is not a full sample of DNA, and the FBI requires at least 10 markers be identified before an unknown sample can be entered into the national CODIS data base.

Laberge indicated that the sample had flashed the color of *blue* during CBI's initial testing of the sample, suggesting that *amylase* was present. Amylase is an enzyme that can be found in saliva, and it had been theorized by other investigators in the case that someone involved in the production phase of this clothing article could have been the source of this unknown DNA sample. It was thought that this could have been deposited there by coughing, sneezing, or spitting or through a simple transfer of saliva on the hands of a garment handler.

Laberge confirmed that no traces of semen had been present in the underwear or clothing articles worn by JonBenét upon the discovery of her body.

Laberge advised, confirming what Tom Bennett had previously shared with me, that some random DNA tests had been conducted in 'off-the-shelf' children's underwear to determine if trace biological DNA samples could be obtained from brand new clothing that had been shipped from the manufacturer.

He indicated that DNA samples had been located on the articles of new clothing, but that they had been approximately 1/10 the strength of the unknown sample found in JonBenét's underwear. The male sample identified in Distal Stain 007-2 was weak, and degraded to begin with, and weaker samples of the same genetic material were found in the waistband and leg bands of the underwear. It was observed that these were areas of the clothing that would have been handled more strenuously during the production phase of the clothing article.

Laberge indicated that it was his opinion that the male sample of DNA could have been deposited there by a perpetrator, or that there could have been some other explanation for its presence, totally unrelated to the crime. I would learn that many other scientists held the same opinion.

We talked about some other aspects of the case, and he pointed out that he was only a scientist and not familiar with the details of the investigative side of the case.

It was my understanding that the Bloomies brand of underwear, worn by JonBenét at the time of the discovery of her body, was manufactured and produced in Taiwan, making it entirely possible that this article of clothing was produced in a garment sweatshop.

Sweatshops have historically employed child labor, and as there is currently no scientific method available that allows us to determine the *age* of a contributor, I had thought it feasible that the unknown forensic sample of male DNA found in JonBenét's underwear could belong to a Taiwanese boy.

Furthermore, there is no scientific method to determine *when* a biological specimen was placed at the scene of a crime.

Under those circumstances, I believed, as did many of the other investigators working the case, that there may have been a plausible explanation for the DNA found in the underwear and that its presence may have had nothing whatsoever to do with the death of JonBenét.

The presence of this DNA is a question that remains to be resolved, but it continues to be my opinion that this single piece of DNA evidence has to be considered in light of all of the other physical, behavioral, and statement evidence that has been collected over the course of the investigation.

Realizing that there could have been a rational explanation for the unidentified male DNA being found in JonBenét's underwear did not deter me from continuing to assess new leads that were continuing to stream into the office.

Around this same time period I took a call from an FBI agent in the Midwest who wanted to pass along information she had received from an individual who had a track record of cooperating in other criminal investigations.

The CI had told her that a subject known to them had once worked and lived in the Boulder area and that they had returned to their Midwestern farm home very shortly after JonBenét's death. The CI told the agent that the subject had become very reclusive and was acting out of character. Apparently the decision to return home was very spontaneous and although a long shot, the CI thought that it bore mentioning to authorities.

I obtained the name and date of birth for the suspect and ran a criminal history to check for an arrest record. I don't recall that there had been any history of arrests for this subject but I did locate a traffic citation when querying his driving history in Colorado. The ticket had been issued in a mountain resort county approximately 7 months after JonBenét's murder. The timing of this citation placed the subject in Colorado for considerably longer than what the CI was indicating as a return date to the Midwest.

I proceeded to obtain a photocopy of the traffic ticket to check out the handwriting of the defendant. I recognized that the block handwriting of the ransom note would likely be different when compared to the actual signature of an individual, but observed that neither bore any resemblance to the other.

Some other minor details were explored with this lead, and I didn't believe that they pointed to the need for a trip to the Midwest. It joined the file of many that didn't appear to hold any true promise.

In the fall of 2005, I had decided to take another look at the theory proposed by retired FBI Agent John Douglas. He had the opportunity to interview John and Patsy Ramsey in early January 1997, at a time when they were still holding BPD detectives at bay, and I wondered what type of insight he may have gained through his face-to-face encounter with the parents. He had devoted an entire chapter to his participation in the JonBenét investigation in his book, *The Cases That Haunt Us*.[52], and I spent some time reviewing his analysis of the details of the case.

Douglas noted that he had not been hired by Ramseys to provide a profile of a possible offender, although, based upon his initial review of the circumstances during his interview with the parents, believed that the perpetrator was someone who was familiar with John, and who had harbored *ill feelings* toward him. It was thought that the killer had been in the Ramsey home sometime prior to the murder.

A "Personal Cause Homicide" was believed to have been the motive for the murder, and Douglas pointed to the elements of *revenge* and *retaliation* that had been voiced in the ransom note as the basis for this opinion. Following this brief interview with John and Patsy, he had told their attorneys that he didn't believe the parents had murdered their daughter.

Ramsey attorneys would subsequently arrange to have Douglas meet with BPD investigators to share his thoughts about the case. Though they had already been consulting with the FBI from the outset of the investigation, lead detectives in the case listened politely to his early analysis of the crime. This took place the day after he had interviewed the parents.

When all was said and done, the investigators thanked the former FBI profiler for his time, and continued the process of chasing leads in their case. Despite the generosity exhibited by Ramsey attorneys to share the opinion of their "expert witness," the BPD elected to continue their dialogue with the men and women of the FBI's specialized units that were fully conversant with the active, and emerging details of the investigation.

As further outlined in his book, Douglas advised that it was his belief that the motive for the crime was *personal* and directed specifically at John Ramsey. He didn't believe this was the work of

a serial killer and thought the person responsible was an "inexperienced, mission-oriented offender." For that reason, he didn't
anticipate that there would be a repeat of this specific "signature
crime" that would capture the attention of authorities.

. The ransom demand of $118,000 matched a year-end bonus
that Ramsey had received and Douglas thought that the perpetrator has somehow gained access to this information, and used it in
the kidnap note.

The "UNSUB" (unknown subject) was thought to be a white
male in his 30's or 40's, with some type of business background,
although Douglas indicated that he would later revise the age of
the perpetrator downward. His final profile suggested that the
killer was "relatively young," and that he carried a "personal
grudge" against JonBenét's father. The act of murdering this little
girl had served to rob John Ramsey of the most valuable thing to
him in the world: his daughter.

Despite the presence of a ransom demand, Douglas did not
believe that this was a crime of *criminal enterprise,* which would
have relied upon the motive of financial gain. There was some type
of personal motive involved in the planning and commission of
this crime, and apparently, the demand for money was mentioned
only as a ruse.

Like the FBI agents who had already been working with BPD
detectives, Douglas thought that the crime scene and crime,
exhibited signs of both an *organized* and *unorganized* offender.
This suggested to him that the individual responsible for this
crime was "criminally unsophisticated."

In his book, Douglas spent some time analyzing the opposing
theories as proposed by Detectives Thomas and Smit, and posed
a few rhetorical questions of his own about some of the elements
involved in the crime. He provided, based upon his experience,
some answers to the questions that had been posed.

I noted that Douglas had indicated that he had *not* been
provided full access to the entire range of police investigative

reports, and witness statements, that his former colleagues at the FBI BAU / CASKU units were considering as they consulted with BPD detectives. He was forced to rely *only* upon the information that had been provided to him by the parents of the murdered child in order to establish his offender profile. I considered this significant when it came time to evaluate his opinion on the matter.

As Douglas went through his analysis of the case, he cited Sherlock Holmes's investigative dictum that states, "When you have eliminated the impossible, whatever remains, *however improbable,* must be the truth."

I would eventually think it apropos that he would offer this investigative theorem as a basis for his analysis of the JonBenét homicide investigation. It is something that would also be argued at the conclusion of my investigative journey into the murder of this little girl.

Before I had ever become involved in the investigation of this murder, I had contemplated Smit's theory regarding the use of the stun gun by an intruder. It was his opinion that the stun gun had been used as a means of controlling JonBenét. Douglas had covered the use of the stun gun when reviewing Smit's theory, and I once again gave this aspect of the crime some thought.

It is important to note that a stun gun, also known as an Electronic Control Device (ECD) in today's nomenclature, does not render a person unconscious. It delivers approximately 600,000 volts of electricity to its victim and disrupts the body's neurotransmitters, which essentially physically incapacitates a person *while* the electronic charge is being delivered. Muscular control is virtually non-existent during the activation of the device and a person is incapable of fighting back or resisting during the event.

Depending upon the device used, the duration of a normal electrical charge is 5 seconds long and neuro muscular incapacitation ceases when the ECD has finished doing its job. It is important to note, however, that a person can fight back *after* the delivery of an electronic charge, and those under the influence of narcotics or alcohol frequently may require more than one electronic dose before they are ready to submit to arrest or control.

There are two methods utilized to deliver an electronic charge to an individual, depending on the type of device used. One involves the discharge of two barbed probes that are shot from the head of an ECD. The barbed probes are capable of being shot of a distance of up to 35 feet and remain connected to the device by thin wires. The probes must properly imbed themselves on the individual being targeted, and if sufficiently anchored, the circuit is completed and an electronic charge is then delivered by the ECD. As noted above, the initial dose usually lasts 5 seconds, but this can be cut short by the operator, or additional, follow-up doses may be delivered.

A second method involves *direct* contact with the head of the ECD and the subject being targeted. The twin electronic contact leads on the head of the ECD are placed flush on the body and the operator activates the device to deliver the electronic charge. This type of contact is referred to as a "drive-stun" in Taser nomenclature. It was this type of device that Smit believed was responsible for the marks on JonBenét's body.

The problem I had with Smit's theory is that the use of this device would not have knocked JonBenét out, nor do I think that it would have made her more compliant with her kidnapper. The delivery of this electronic charge is extremely painful and most people scream uncontrollably when they have been at the receiving end of this *less- lethal* law enforcement tool.

From a law enforcement point of view, an ECD is used to temporarily incapacitate and induce *pain compliance* when confronting a violent, out-of-control subject, or in situations where lethal force might otherwise be legally employed. The idea being, by way of example, is that an incapacitating dose from an ECD may temporarily disable a knife-wielding suspect long enough so that we may disarm him without having to resort to shooting him with a firearm. The *distance* that can be maintained by an officer from an armed subject under these circumstances is what makes this tool so effective.

I don't want to make this sound overly simplistic. There are many circumstances that come into play when an officer has to make a split-second decision regarding the use of deadly force. I am merely attempting to provide some background on the use of a device that was developed to help law enforcement personnel better do their job.

It was not clear to me as to *when* Smit thought the stun gun had actually been used during the kidnapping, but it is my belief that JonBenét would have screamed bloody murder if it had ever been used on her. Moreover, it had been his opinion that the stun gun had been used *twice* during her abduction – once on her face, and once on her back. Sound asleep or otherwise, I don't believe she would have ever been able to have controlled herself vocally if confronted with the excruciating pain of this device.

The need for the use of a stun gun in the torture and murder of Gerald Boggs may have very well played some significance in that crime. On the other hand, to have used this device on a small, 6-year-old girl, within earshot of the family, seemed extremely improbable from my point of view.

It didn't quite make sense to me that an *adult male*, presumably the person responsible for this kidnapping, would require this type of device to control a 45-pound, 6-year-old girl. The use of duct tape or a hand over JonBenét's mouth would have easily sufficed.

There was one additional lead that had come into the office in the closing weeks of my tenure that I had intended to try to track down. Someone had suggested that a couple of construction workers had also been acting strange around the time of JonBenét's murder and were purportedly involved in the remodel of a garage somewhere in her neighborhood.

It was a very vague lead, and no names were provided for the construction workers, or for the people whose home was being remodeled.

"Acting strange" and "being somewhere nearby" were frequently key words that prompted people to write and call the office, but I was trying to remain open to the possibility that one tip might eventually pay dividends.

I had considered the FBI's early opinion about more than one individual being involved in this crime. Certainly, the possibility existed that the remodel of a garage in the area of the Ramsey home might point to two construction workers who had become infatuated with a 6-year old girl living nearby.

I had thought I might canvass the neighborhood to see if any such project were actually taking place at the time of the murder, but time was not on my side. I left the D.A.'s office before I was able to find the time to knock on any doors.

It probably would not have mattered in any regard. By the time I parted company with the D.A.'s office, I was convinced that there was no significant possibility that an intruder had been involved in the death of JonBenét. Subsequent events would only serve to solidify that opinion.

"We could find the killer tomorrow, he could be arrested, convicted and you know, jailed, and there'd still be 20 per cent of the population would think that we had something to do with it."

—John Ramsey during an interview aired on *48 Hours Investigates–Searching for a Killer*
October 4, 2002

"I don't give a flying flip how scientific it is. Go back to the damn drawing board.

I didn't do it. John Ramsey didn't do it, and we don't have a clue of anybody who did do it.

Quit screwing around asking me about things that are ridiculous and let's find the person that did this."

—Patsy Ramsey's response to an investigator who indicated that trace evidence appeared to link her to the death of her daughter. Boulder District Attorney interviews, June 1998

Red Flags and Behavioral Clues†

The essence of our daily existence is comprised of some form of constant thought, movement, and behavior. As human beings, we are motivated to achieve certain things in our lives, and we take specific steps and actions to accomplish these goals and objectives. The things we say and do when moving toward realization of these goals are observable, and sometimes they help point an investigator to a better understanding of the motivation behind an individual's actions.

In some of the preceding chapters, I have marked things that popped up as a "red flag" for me as I poured through the investigative reports that had been compiled over the course of this thirteen- year investigation. The pages or paragraphs are marked with a symbol (†) that identify a statement, piece of physical evidence, or behavioral clue that seemed out of sync with the elements that were supposed to point to a crime being committed by one or more intruders. They were the initial signs that alerted me to the possibility that all did not seem right within the reported construct of this crime, and I continued to come back to these time and time again as I tried to sort out the events and comprehend the motive for the commission of this murder.

Some of the same things may have jumped out at you as you read through the events that transpired over the course of this inquiry. I will leave it to your discretion if you wish to review their history before continuing to explore this chapter, but it is here that a discussion of these behavioral clues will be presented.

I would note that this is neither an all-inclusive listing of things that raised questions about the existence of an intruder, nor are they presented in the chronological history of their discovery. And let me make it clear, many of these red flags were the same things that troubled Boulder Police investigators during their investigation into this matter.

The evolution of John Ramsey's statements make for an interesting study and will be analyzed in a later chapter, but one of the first things to catch my eye were his comments made during the January 1, 1997, CNN interview. In response to a question from CNN correspondent Brian Cabell about the family's decision to hire a defense attorney, John indicated that he was "not angry" about JonBenét's death but he / they were interested in finding out "why" this had occurred. He stated that they could not go on until there was an answer as to "why" his daughter had "died."

I was puzzled by this statement and could understand that he would be asking *why* someone had chosen his daughter to murder, but the part about not being *angry* was confounding. The emotional aspect of this statement didn't make sense to me. I would have thought that of all the emotions flowing through a family victimized by a violent murder, surely anger would have been one of them. As a parent of three, I believe I would have been extremely angry if a stranger brutally took the life of one of my children.

And then, in the context of this same sentence, he referred to JonBenét's "dying" as opposed to her being "murdered." This selection of language may be inconsequential, but the choice of this word seemed to soften the circumstances of this crime.

To whom, I wondered, was this response being directed?

The Ramseys received quite a bit of criticism for the perception that they were attempting to manage the media. As noted in Chapter Seven, a national public relations firm had been retained early in the investigation and a family spokesperson regularly issued press releases and responded to media reports that covered the progress of the investigation.

I thought it interesting that John Ramsey tried to divert some of the criticism about the decision to do the January 1, 1997, CNN interview to his former friend, Fleet White. Ramsey stated in a 1998 sworn deposition taken during the Steven Miles law suit (Miles, a local photographer who had been charged but not convicted of sexual exploitation of children, sued John Ramsey and the National Enquirer for pointing to him as a likely perpetrator of the crime) that it was White who had insisted that the family go on CNN to plead their innocence.

My review of the records didn't support Ramsey's claim of White's involvement. According to Mary Ann Kaempfer, she had overheard Patsy Ramsey participating in a telephone conversation on the morning of January 1, 1997. Patsy was on a conference call from a phone in Kaempfer's bedroom, and they talked once the call had ended.[53]

Kaempfer reported that family friend Rod Westmoreland was a close friend with the president of CNN and that he (Westmoreland) had suggested that the family do an interview on the cable news network. It was felt that the family had to make some type of public statement to stifle all of the other media reports that were speculating about family involvement in the murder of JonBenét.

John and Patsy Ramsey subsequently responded to the CNN studios that day, and the interview was broadcast later that night. Nearly everyone in the Paugh household stayed up to watch the broadcast, including Kaempfer. The following day, Kaempfer indicated during her interview with Boulder investigators that the CNN interview had included a short video clip from inside the Atlanta church that had been recorded during JonBenét's funeral services.

Kaempfer remarked that she had seen the camera set up in the balcony of the interior of the church. It looked to be a commercial grade camera, versus a smaller hand-held unit that she had seen present in the Boulder services.

It is uncertain if this was a family photographer recording the services for posterity or if a CNN cameraman had been granted access to the interior of the church to record the events. If that were the case, it would seem that the negotiations for a CNN interview had been on-going for a little longer than originally indicated, and this footage of the services had been arranged with the intent of being aired during the January 1st interview.

John Ramsey's attempt to point the finger of blame at Fleet White for recommending the CNN interview did not appear to be supported by the record. It also appeared that this discussion had been taking place soon after their arrival in Atlanta for JonBenét's services, and material for the interview was being prepared almost immediately.

I had also labored under the impression from the beginning of my involvement in the case that the Ramsey family had not hired attorneys and private investigators until after Lt. Eller had attempted to withhold the body of JonBenét in exchange for a family interview.

I had reviewed a VHS video tape in the investigative files that featured an interview with Ramsey family friend and attorney Mike Bynum. Acting as a spokesman for the family, Bynum was speaking on national television in September 1997, and being interviewed by news correspondent Diane Sawyer, who had asked why the Ramsey family had obtained a lawyer. [54"]

Bynum indicated that he, as a family friend, felt they should have "legal advice" in the matter concerning the police investigation into the murder of their daughter. He had mentioned this to John Ramsey because, as a former prosecutor, he knew where the attention of the police would be focused – the parents and family.

Sawyer commented that by Saturday, two days following the murder, police were "openly hostile" toward the family. Bynum was reportedly told by the D.A.'s office that the police were refusing to release the body of JonBenét for burial unless the parents would provide interviews with investigators.

He wasn't sure if this course of action was legal or not, but pointed to this action as being "immoral and unethical." Bynum indicated that he just was not willing to have the family participate in that kind of situation, and told the DA / police that not only would the family not give an interview under these circumstances, but he told them "Hell no, you're not getting an interview."[55]

Investigative files revealed that Eller had not even considered this option until Saturday, December 28th, around the time that non-testimonial evidence was being collected from the immediate family. Even then, it was reported that his thoughts of holding on to the body of JonBenét was not for the intention of holding her for "ransom" in exchange for a family interview, but to determine if there were any other forensic examinations that could have been conducted that would help shed light on the mechanics of her murder.

When Eller was discussing this possibility with the D.A.'s office, it was Pete Hoffstrom who coined the phrase "ransom the body," and this term eventually was espoused by Ramsey attorneys in later public statements.

I found it noteworthy that Bynum specifically stated in the Primetime interview that it was he who suggested to John Ramsey that attorneys should be brought in to consult with the family. He expressed the thought to John that there were some 'legal issues that needed to be taken care of.' Bynum went on to indicate that he did not think that it had occurred to the family to do this prior to his conversation with John.[56]

Bynum's inference to the national audience during the September 1997 interview, however, was that legal representation had not been retained until *after* Commander Eller had performed this act of desperation.

So you can imagine my surprise when I learned that Ramsey attorneys and their investigators were working the case on Friday morning before the autopsy of JonBenét was even underway.

Even more intriguing was the identity of the person selected for their first interview. It was not housekeeper Linda **Hoffmann-Pugh**, the woman whom Patsy had named as a possible suspect –a person who needed money and who had previously mentioned concerns about the kidnapping of JonBenét.

Ramsey attorneys instead chose trusted family friend Fleet White: one of the few who had immediately been summoned to the Ramsey home on the morning of the kidnapping, and the only individual who had accompanied John Ramsey to the basement in search of JonBenét.

Of all the people initially named as possible suspects by the Ramseys, what could Fleet White possibly know about the kidnapping and murder of JonBenét? Moreover, why would it be so important that he, a material witness to the discovery of JonBenét's body, be interviewed before the cause and manner of her death had even been determined?

I realize that attempts to interview the housekeeper could have interfered with the police investigation, but it did not preclude the Ramsey team from running their own parallel investigation and interviewing other material witnesses.

John Ramsey continued to shield that information, and conveniently side-stepped a question about attorney involvement posed by Lou Smit during their June 1998 interview. They were discussing events that were taking place on the evening of Friday, December 27, 1996, when the Ramsey family was staying at the

Fernie residence. According to John Ramsey, Mike Bynum had been delivering food to the residence while Sergeant Mason and Detective Arndt were there attempting to arrange a follow-up interview with the family.

Smit asked if that had been the first time that he, John Ramsey, had contacted a lawyer. Ramsey replied that Bynum just happened to be there, delivering food from Pasta Jay's and called a "time-out" when police were trying to "haul" them down to the station for questioning.

Bynum, according to John Ramsey's statement to Smit, reportedly took him aside and asked him if he would allow him to do some things that he thought were necessary. Ramsey agreed, and Bynum and Ramsey claimed that it was after this conversation that Bynum reportedly brought attorneys Bryan Morgan and Pat Burke into the case.

This statement clearly does not account for the fact that Ramsey attorneys had actually been attempting to reach Fleet White on the very afternoon of the discovery of JonBenét's body, and were seeking to interview him first thing the next day, on Friday morning.

According to White, he had driven to Denver on Friday morning to conduct some personal business. His wife, Priscilla, advised him upon his return early that afternoon that Ramsey attorneys had again been trying to reach him that morning, and wanted to speak with him. The interview was held later that day in the Boulder law offices of Bryan Morgan, and private investigator David Williams was present taking notes.

More recently, John Ramsey provided a description of how attorneys became involved in his book, *The Other Side of Suffering*[57], which significantly differs from the explanation he provided to Lou Smit, and what Mike Bynum reported during his Primetime Live television interview.

In the latest version, Ramsey states that he received a *telephone call* from a friend at his office on the day after JonBenét was murdered. This person told him that they had been asked to get a message to him, and the message was as follows: "The police are out to get you...the police think you murdered JonBenét."[58]

Ramsey went on to state that the person warning him had received a call from a reliable person "inside the system," and that they had recommended he get the best defense attorney to represent him as possible.[59]

Ramsey indicated that the idea that police would suspect him of being responsible for the murder of his daughter was "insane," but was now offering this as a reason why criminal defense attorneys had been hired by the family so early in the investigation. In his opinion, the caller had been correct, and he believed Boulder Police began to focus their attention on him from the early hours of the investigation. It was this insider's tip that forced him to engage the services of attorneys to defend him, and his family.

This latest explanation of how attorneys became involved again appears to be in conflict with the information I had reviewed about the matter. If this information is taken at face value, however, it opens up a Pandora's Box of other issues.

The day after JonBenét's murder, the coroner's office spent most of the day performing the autopsy on her body. A break in the autopsy protocol took place that afternoon when Dr. Meyer called together the Boulder County Child Fatality Review Team. As noted in a previous chapter, the team had collectively established a list of things for Boulder Police and DSS investigators to pursue in their search for possible explanations of the evidence that suggested prior sexual abuse.

At that stage of the game, anything was possible, and I didn't see anything in the official reports that suggested the focus of the investigation was centering on John Ramsey. So, from my perspective, his reference to a *telephone call* made to him on the day *after* his daughter's murder raises some additional questions:

- Who was the 'reliable insider' who purportedly wanted to get this urgent message to John Ramsey?

- At what point, from their *insider's* view of the matter, did they decide that John Ramsey needed a criminal defense attorney? Was it when search warrants for the home were being drafted on the afternoon of the discovery of JonBenét's body? Or was it when evidence of prior sexual abuse became apparent during her autopsy the following day?
- Moreover, if he, or she, truly does exist, is it the same individual who was sharing Lou Smit's intruder evidence with the Ramsey defense team in advance of the Ramsey's April 1997 interview?

This situation gave me pause, and raised the following red flags:

- Why would John Ramsey feel the need to conceal the details about the timeline of his attorney's first involvement in this investigation?
- Why would his original explanation of attorney involvement change between 1998 and 2012?
- Was he compelled to safeguard this information from the public because he believed it would somehow be detrimental to his cause?

Additionally, I found it difficult to swallow the Ramsey's response to a question raised during their April, 1997, interviews with BPD investigators. Both John and Patsy had been asked during their interviews if they had the opportunity to review the police reports that had been provided to them in advance of the interview.

Patsy indicated that she had not reviewed the materials, and John stated that he had only "scanned" the reports prior to his sit-down with authorities. I found these responses implausible under the circumstances. Five-hundred-dollar-per-hour defense attorneys don't negotiate and demand copies of police reports and witness statements prior to an interview, unless they intend to go through them with a fine-toothed comb as they prepare their clients for questioning.

By the time the Ramseys sat down for their first uninterrupted interview with the detectives investigating the death of their daughter, you can rest assured that each of them was very well-rehearsed and prepared for the questions that would be posed to them.

There were a couple of other behavioral clues exhibited by John Ramsey on the morning of the kidnapping that appeared out of sync with the circumstances at hand.

At one point that morning, while the family and police investigators still awaited the ransom call, pilot Mike Archuleta volunteered to fly to Minnesota to intercept the commercial jet carrying Melinda and Stewart - the suggestion being that he could quickly meet the kids and ferry them back to Boulder, thus avoiding the hassle of their having to arrange a new commercial flight into Denver.

John Ramsey nixed the idea, and I wondered why he didn't want to take advantage of his pilot's offer to shortcut the uncertainty of the availability of flights that would divert the kids to Colorado. I gave thought to the idea that perhaps he had declined this offer because he wanted to be assured of his private plane being accessible for a quick departure from the state. What came later seemed to confirm that piece of speculation.

It seemed incomprehensible to me that John Ramsey, within less than an hour of the discovery of the body his daughter, would be making arrangements to take his family and leave the state by private plane. When overheard making these arrangements with his pilot, Ramsey told Detective Bill Palmer that he had an important business meeting to attend in Georgia.

Like many of the Boulder investigators, I pondered the question:

How could a business meeting in Georgia outweigh the need to work with authorities in their attempt to identify the person who had just murdered his daughter?

Red flag: Why was John Ramsey so anxious to leave the state?

I subscribe to the notion that, for the most part, as human beings we tend to act instinctively in certain situations. It is part of the survival instinct of the human "fight or flight" response that has been programmed into our genes over the millennia.

There was one other major discrepancy discovered by investigators as they continued to evaluate John Ramsey's behavior, and statements. Stewart Long had arrived at the Ramsey home in a taxi with his fiancé, Melinda, and John Andrew, just as police were clearing the house for a search warrant following the discovery of JonBenét's body. All three of the older kids joined the family in a vehicle that was headed to the home of John and Barbara Fernie.

As they departed the area, John Ramsey told Long that he had found JonBenét's body at 11:00 a.m. that morning. Long recounted this conversation to Detective Thomas when interviewed as a part of the follow-up investigation.

Thomas, knowing that Ramsey had gone to the basement at the request of Detective Arndt at 1:00 p.m. that day, pressed Long on his recollection of the time of discovery as stated by John Ramsey. Long was adamant that Ramsey had stated that he had found JonBenét at eleven o'clock that morning.

Considering the time-line of events, this was smack dab in the middle of the time frame during which John Ramsey had disappeared from Detective Arndt's view, and a full two hours *before* she had directed him to search the house.

The red flag here was John Ramsey's stated timing of the discovery of the body of his daughter. If this was not just a miscommunication and he had truly found her body two hours before he had been directed to check the home, why didn't he immediately reveal this critical discovery to the police detective on the scene?

What could have accounted for his decision to delay telling authorities about his finding the body of JonBenét?

Barbara Fernie had raised another flag when she decided to contact investigators in early January, 1998. She and her son had seen photographs of golf clubs in a tabloid story about JonBenét while shopping in a grocery store and her son recognized the set of clubs as belonging to Burke. The sight of the golf clubs spurred her memory about an odd comment that John Ramsey had made to someone while the family was staying at the Fernie residence, after the discovery of JonBenét's body.

It was in this time frame that authorities had granted permission to Pam Paugh, Patsy's visiting sister from Georgia, to enter the Ramsey home and retrieve a number of JonBenét's personal belongings. This was during the time that investigators were still processing the crime scene for evidence, and the Ramsey family was permitted access to gather some items that were intended for the funeral services being arranged in Georgia.

Mrs. Fernie recalled that John Ramsey had asked a strange question of the person stopping by her home one evening: He asked if they had remembered to "get his golf bag" from his house.

Mrs. Fernie recalled that the individual replied that they had not been able to retrieve the bag, as the police would not let them downstairs.

Given the emotional condition of everyone in her home after JonBenét's murder, John Ramsey's request for his golf clubs seemed out of the ordinary to her. His daughter had just been murdered and it was the dead of winter in Colorado. For what purpose would he be asking that his golf bags be retrieved from his home?

The red flag waving for me was this: I doubted Ramsey was planning to play a round of 18 holes at any time in the near future, even in Atlanta, and I wondered if he were interested in the retrieval of the golf bag because it contained something *other* than sporting equipment.[60]

Mrs. Fernie shared one additional tidbit of information with investigators that had been bothering her. She indicated that late in the summer, or early fall of 1996, she had observed damages to the latch area of an exterior screen door located on the rear, south side of the Ramsey home. Mrs. Fernie was concerned that perhaps a burglary attempt had been made to the home, and shared this information with Patsy.

They inspected the door, and determined that the interior door exhibited no damages whatsoever. Patsy expressed no concern about the damaged screen door and suggested that perhaps John was responsible for the marks. He reportedly was always forgetting his keys and had broken into the house on other occasions.

Mrs. Fernie indicated that she had seen a photograph of this same screen door displayed in an advertisement running in one of the Denver newspapers shortly after the murder. The advertisement, placed by Ramsey attorneys and taking up at least half of the page of the newspaper, purported that this may have been a possible point of entry used by the kidnapper of JonBenét.

This did not sit well with Mrs. Fernie, because Patsy was fully aware that these damages had been inflicted upon the screen door weeks or months prior to the murder of JonBenét. The use of this particular photograph seemed to be an attempt to mislead the public about the evidence associated with the crime and the Fernies indicated that they severed their contact with the family following their observation of that advertisement.

There were other behavioral aspects of Patsy Ramsey's actions that didn't ring true to me and that seemed out of sync for the circumstances.

For example, Patsy indicated during interviews that she initially was confused about whether the ransom note was referring to JonBenét or John's oldest daughter, Beth. This didn't quite make sense because Beth had been killed in a traffic accident a couple years prior to the kidnapping.

In any event, Patsy stated that she never finished reading more than the first few lines of the ransom note and immediately went to check on JonBenét. Opening the door of the bedroom, Patsy stated that she did not see JonBenét in her bed, and had immediately screamed John's name.

It did not make sense to me that a mother would not have screamed her daughter's name and searched the room for her.

In spite of the presence of a ransom note, maternal instinct and the stress of the moment should have sent her beyond the threshold of the door, and into the entire bedroom and bathroom. Not finding her there, I would have expected a search to have been made of Burke's room, and that he would have been awakened and asked if he knew his sister's whereabouts.

The Ramseys stated publicly on more than one occasion that Burke was asleep, and they never asked him if he had seen JonBenét, or whether he had heard anything unusual that night.

More importantly, what parent would not be screaming their child's name as they searched the house for her?

It was only Fleet White who stated that he had called for JonBenét as he checked the house after being summoned to the home that morning. This specific behavior on the part of the parents lacked a certain legitimacy for me, and I couldn't quite put my finger on it, but Patsy's accounting of these events on their first nationally televised interview seemed scripted.

I was also perplexed by Patsy's behavior exhibited upon the discovery of JonBenét's body. As noted in police reports, Fleet White charged up from the basement shouting for someone to call an ambulance after he and John Ramsey had found JonBenét's body in the Wine Cellar.

In this setting, I think it is reasonable to presume that most of us would be thinking that someone was *injured*, and in need of immediate medical attention. Why else would White be shouting for an *ambulance*? Apparently, Barb Fernie and Priscilla White thought the same thing, for they immediately rushed out of the solarium to see what was going on.

Not Patsy Ramsey, however. According to Detective Arndt's reporting of events, the mother of the missing and kidnapped child remained in the solarium during all of this commotion, and it was not until she directed John to retrieve his wife did she enter the living room to encounter the lifeless body of her daughter.

In Patsy's interview conducted on April 30, 1997, she stated that she had heard White's screams for an ambulance. She kept asking, "What is it? What is it?", but never took the initiative to leave the room to find out. She claimed to have been restrained in the solarium by family friend Barb Fernie.

A big red flag flew up the pole on this particular behavioral clue. I would have expected a mother to have rushed into the fray to determine if her child had been found, and be asking why an ambulance was being called to her home. I didn't believe *anyone* would have been able to hold back a mother under these circumstances.

To me, Patsy Ramsey's actions in this specific instance were counter-intuitive.

So, under those circumstances, I had to ask myself:

- Why did Patsy remain behind in the solarium when Fleet White was shouting for an ambulance?
- Was it because she already knew that her daughter was dead?
- If that was the case, how did she come to know that information?
- Further, if she already knew of her daughter's death, did she play a role in that crime?

In our constitutional system of jurisprudence, people are presumed innocent until proven otherwise. It is the responsibility of the defense attorney to represent their client's best interests, and this necessarily requires them to make the prosecution prove their case beyond a reasonable doubt.

One of the tactics commonly used by the defense bar is to counsel their client to deny at the outset, any and all accusations of criminal conduct. In their attempt to divert attention away from the actual *conduct* and *behavior* of their client, defense attorneys are forever searching for plausible deniability and circumstances that will muddy the waters.

When the facts are in dispute, the first line of defense is frequently to deny, deny, deny.

When the facts are incontrovertible, then it is time to move to the next tactic, and raise questions about the process by which those facts were established. It is their intention to undermine the foundation of the presentation of the physical evidence that would be used at trial. Succeed at throwing out the defendant's bloody fingerprint found at the scene of the crime, and it is likely that no conviction will follow.

If those first two tactics are not successful, the next strategic move is to attack the honor and credibility of the men and women who are tasked with seeking the truth of the matter. Evidence linking the defendant to the crime was "planted," and the cops are lying about investigative procedures.

Or, as witnessed in JonBenét's case, Boulder Police lacked the expertise to investigate a murder case on their own.

We witnessed the successful implementation of these tactics in the O.J. Simpson trial, and I thought it curious that Patsy Ramsey would specifically refer to the O.J. "situation" during her CNN interview[61].

To place this in perspective, Brian Cabell had offered the following observation during the interview:

Cabell: "Inevitably, speculation on talk shows will focus on you. It's got to be sickening…"

John Ramsey: "It's nauseating beyond belief."

Patsy Ramsey: "You know, America has just been hurt so deeply with the...this...the tragic things that have happened. The young woman who drove her children into the water, and we don't know what happened with the O.J. Simpson...and I mean, America is suffering because we have lost faith in the American Family.

We are a Christian, God-fearing family. We love our children. We would do anything for our children."

Patsy Ramsey's reference to high-profile murder cases was intriguing, and I wondered why she had chosen these two cases in particular. Why not summon remembrances of the horrific crimes committed by the likes of the Son of Sam, Jeffrey Dahmer, or Theodore Bundy?

The public sentiment following O.J.'s acquittal seemed to be one of astonishment. The "dream team" of defense attorneys had completely twisted the physical evidence collected in the case, and focused their attention on the destruction of the credibility of the investigators of the crime. Their arguments ultimately set O.J. free, but a civil jury would not be so easily misled.

In the case of Susan Smith, Patsy was calling into her court the cold-blooded details of a South Carolina mother who had intentionally driven her two young boys into a lake, and left them to drown. Susan then concocted the story of a carjacking, and proceeded to blame a mysterious black man for the crime. She shed plenty of tears during her broadcast-television interviews, and pleaded with the public to help track down the kidnapper who had taken her children from her.

The deception of Susan Smith would not survive the skepticism of investigators, however, and she ultimately confessed her sins to Union County Sheriff Howard Wells. The black "carjacker" who had kidnapped her children was non-existent, and it was Susan who had driven her two young boys into the lake, and left to drown.

In my viewing, Susan Smith's tearful pleas for help were strangely reminiscent of Patsy Ramsey's accounting of events on CNN, and I couldn't help but feel that there was a similarity between the two events.

Patsy Ramsey's proclamation of innocence due to her God-fearing, Christian status seemed too convenient. It was the type of alibi often used by those attempting to divert attention from their guilt, and was classic material drawn from the text of police interrogation manuals: The argument being that a loving, Christian family would be incapable of committing horrendous crimes of violence. For those crime historians among you, I suspect that this line of reasoning holds little weight, for our prisons are full of Christians convicted for their participation in similar crimes of violence.

More to the point, Patsy's spontaneous reference to these two murder cases gave me pause. In her prescription-induced, medicated state, was she subconsciously aligning herself with people who had brutally murdered members of their own family?

I looked to the possibility that this dialogue consisted of a "spontaneous utterance," the unguarded words we speak that sometimes reveal the workings of our internal thoughts.

Detective Steve Thomas had made note of an additional utterance made by Patsy during the collection of non-testimonial evidence on Saturday, December 28, 1996. To put the statement in perspective, I cite the entry from his book, *JonBenét – Inside the Ramsey Murder Investigation*.[62]:

Patsy was unsteady as I had her lift the sleeves of her loose denim blouse so I could check her for bruises or scratches on the fronts and backs of her hands and arms. Then I checked her face and neck and found nothing unusual. We were standing in a row at the counter, with Patsy in the middle, when she shifted slightly and whispered to [Detective] Gosage, "Will this help find who killed my baby?"

He carefully replied, equally softly, "I hope so."

Patsy looked at her inked fingers and spoke again. "I didn't kill my baby." The [Ramsey] lawyer apparently did not hear her, but my head snapped around as if on a swivel. Colorado Revised Statute Procedure 41.1 spelled out that we couldn't ask investigative questions during this evidence collection, but we could certainly listen if anything was said voluntarily, and the mother of the murder victim had blurted out something totally unexpected. I directed my comment to Gosage. "What did she just say?"

Patsy Ramsey repeated, to me this time, "I didn't kill my baby."

The lawyer lurched away from the wall, placed his hands on her shoulders, brought his face to within inches of her ear, and whispered emphatically. She didn't say another word during the entire session, but what she had already said hung like thunder. I didn't kill my baby.

No one suggested that she had.

There were a couple red flags raised in this instance, the first being that John Ramsey and his attorneys had continued to characterize this December 28th meeting with Boulder Police as an "interview" and evidence of their continuing "cooperation" in the investigation.

For the lay public, it is important to understand that this collection of non-testimonial physical evidence could be viewed as *cooperation,* but in no way should it be construed as an *interview* with authorities.

The attorneys and private investigators accompanying the Ramseys on that day made certain no interview or testimonial evidence would be collected by police investigators, and I viewed the Ramsey's representations of cooperation as a continuing part of their media spin.

Why would they strive to buttress the perception that the parents had been cooperating with authorities, when clearly, they halted any productive communication with Boulder investigators as soon as they left their home on the afternoon of December 26, 1996?

Secondarily, Patsy Ramsey was stating to investigators that she did not kill her baby. At that point in time, Boulder investigators were still gathering facts, and had no clue as to who had actually been involved in the murder of JonBenét.

A ransom note had been left by her kidnappers, and evidence of her restraint and abduction were readily apparent. Why would Patsy feel it necessary to proclaim her innocence in the death of her daughter?

Spontaneous utterances can take many forms, and by way of further example, I refer to the well-publicized California murder investigation involving the family of Scott and Lacy Peterson. Scott had uttered an interesting question during his conversations with the detective who was investigating the disappearance of his pregnant wife.

When advised that the police department had been using K-9 teams to assist in the investigation, Scott asked if they "had used cadaver dogs yet."[63]

The question gave the detective pause: Why would Scott ask if a dog trained in the recovery of dead bodies was being brought into the investigation? At that early point in their inquiry, Lacy Peterson was only thought to be overdue and missing. What possible benefit would a cadaver dog bring to the investigation?

This spontaneous utterance was a red flag for the investigator, and this statement, combined with many of the other behavioral clues discovered during their investigation, proved to be instrumental in helping prove Scott Peterson's consciousness of guilt at trial.

Another illustration of a spontaneous utterance involves a sexual assault investigation that I directed in the early 1990's. I refer to some aspects of this investigation in other portions of this book, but the specific reference to be made here is with regard to statements made by the suspect who became the primary focus of our pursuit for the perpetrator.

We had obtained a court order for the collection of non-testimonial evidence in the case, i.e. blood samples that would be compared against DNA evidence left at the scene of the assault. When served with notice of the 41.1 Court Order demanding his compliance in the collection of this physical evidence, the suspect read the cover page of the warrant and uttered the following words:

"First degree sex assault? No way, first degree!"

I viewed these spontaneous comments as representative of his consciousness of guilt. Though not stated, he apparently thought that the commission of this residential burglary and rape constituted the crime of a Second or Third Degree Sex Assault, and that our warrant had it all wrong.

There was good reason that this suspect had flunked out as a self-sponsored student of a police academy, and the evidence collected in our court order eventually sealed his fate. He subsequently entered a plea of guilty to this crime and served eleven years in the Colorado Department of Corrections.

We are all creatures of habit, and the fact that the ransom note had been written on Patsy's personal notepad served to drive this home for me as one more red flag that needed to be considered.

Under the stress of the moment, confronted with the sudden and violent death of her daughter, I wondered whether Patsy, if she were the writer of the note, had failed to consider the possibility of finding a *different* pad of paper and pen when it came time to craft the evidence of a kidnapping. She would have been acting as she normally did when writing something down –grabbing her own pad and a felt-tip pen that she frequently used over the course of her daily activities. While thought was being given as to how attention could be diverted away from the family, another key detail was overlooked as the staging of the crime scene took place.

I don't know exactly how many pads of paper were available in the home that day, but I had to wonder what the odds would be that an intruder had located *her* pad of paper to write the ransom note, and then that handwriting experts would be unable to eliminate Patsy as the author.

Boulder investigators had located the pad in the rear kitchen hallway, and the Sharpie pen that was eventually identified as the instrument used to write the note was in a cup below the kitchen phone Patsy had used to call 911. They thought the note had been crafted shortly before the 911 call to authorities, hence the placement of the pen near the phone.

I am certain that many of those in the reading audience could think of the many habits and routines that have become a part of your daily experience. Do you always start shaving on the same side of your face? Does the right shoe always go on before the left? Do you drive the same path to work every day, even when another route may be available? It takes some conscious effort to alter those activities, but when stress is added to the equation, we frequently fall back on what we are used to doing – primarily because the habit has served us well.

Take for example police firearms training. There is an old axiom that has developed over the years, and it is this: we are likely to perform in the field as we train in the classroom.

Several decades ago investigators were sometimes confronted with trying to figure out why an officer involved in a shooting incident took the time to retrieve the spent shell casings dumped from their revolvers - all while engaged in the heat of a gunfight with bad guys. In a number of instances, officers fatally wounded during the exchange of gunfire were found to have their own empty shell casings in their pockets.

Investigators were stumped. What could possibly be the reason for an officer engaged in a deadly gun battle to take the time to collect his empty brass? It soon became apparent that the officers, acting under the duress of the moment, had merely been acting on behavior that had been ingrained during many hours of firearms training. In some jurisdictions, it was routine to immediately collect your empty brass after you had fired your weapon at a paper target. It made for easier clean-up at the end of the day at the range.

Training soon adapted to this realization, and spent brass stayed where it fell until the end of the day. Officers fatally wounded in shootouts no longer were being found with empty shell casings in their pockets.

It was my thought that the combination of things taking place in regards to the ransom note pointed to a matter of habit and routine. As hard as Patsy may have tried to alter the crime scene, she had not been able to overcome the habit of using her own notepad when it came time to craft the ransom note left behind by the *intruder.* The same could be said of her punctuation, use of language, and style of handwriting.

Investigators frequently look to "post offense" behavioral changes when attempting to narrow a list of suspects believed responsible for a crime. In this instance, BPD investigators could not understand why the Ramsey family had taken refuge behind a wall of attorneys so early in the investigation. They had expected the family to be pounding down their doors wanting information about the status of the search for their daughter's killer.

Soon after the burial of her daughter, Patsy seemed to be suggesting that she was interested in learning where investigators stood in their progress. During a conversation held with Mary Kaempfer, who had played "nanny" to Burke and her son, Anthony, during the funeral services held in Atlanta, Patsy stated that she wanted know why they had not heard from Boulder Police about the case. She wondered what progress had been made and was frustrated about not knowing anything.

A day or so later, after watching their CNN interview on television, Patsy commented on the news coverage that reported a group of Boulder detectives were boarding flights for Atlanta. Patsy was reportedly observed to turn to her husband and ask: "So, are we going to have company tomorrow?"[64]

John responded, "I guess."

I thought it ironic that she was voicing frustration about her lack of knowledge of the status of the investigation, and could have easily made arrangements to receive a briefing from Boulder authorities after their arrival in Georgia. Instead, John and Patsy Ramsey quietly slipped out of the state and took refuge in the Colorado home of family friend "Pasta Jay" Elowski.

Patsy's interest in learning about the status of the progress of the investigation, and her husband's willingness voiced during the CNN interview to return to Colorado and work with police, seemed to have quickly dissipated.

Another piece of post-offense behavior noted by investigators centered on Patsy Ramsey's sudden change in handwriting techniques. In April 1997, Detectives Steve Thomas and Ron Gosage paid a surprise visit to the Georgia home of Nedra Paugh, Patsy Ramsey's mother. Mr. and Mrs. Paugh were not particularly happy to see the investigators, and they reportedly gave an earful about how they thought Boulder Police were persecuting their daughter.

At one point the discussion centered on the ransom note. Detective Gosage indicated that if Mrs. Paugh believed her daughter had not authored the note that perhaps she'd be willing to provide some handwriting examples to help investigators clear her of possible involvement.

Mrs. Paugh responded by thrusting a piece of paper into the detective's hands, stating that her daughter had just written on it that morning.

After departing the residence, Gosage noted that the piece of paper contained a list of handwritten names, addresses, and telephone numbers. Gosage further observed that the second letter "a" in the name of Barbara Fernie had originally been written in the *manuscript* style, but had been written over with a black felt tip pen changing it to a *cursive* style of letter.

Investigators noted that the ransom note contained a total of 376 words, and the small letter "a" had been printed in manuscript style 109 times, and written in lowercase cursive style only 5 times. This was clear evidence that the author of the note was attempting to conceal his or her handwriting style in order to be precluded from being identified.

Unwittingly, Nedra Paugh had provided investigators with a sampling of Patsy Ramsey's handwriting that indicated she was consciously making attempts to change her handwriting style. Investigators noted that in Patsy Ramsey's *pre-homicide* writings that she had consistently used the lower case manuscript style "a" in her handwriting.

In her *post-offense* samplings however, Patsy Ramsey's writing of the manuscript style of the letter "a" disappeared entirely. Investigators believed the evidence pointed to a conscious effort on her part to obscure her style of handwriting.

It is this type of post-offense behavioral change that investigators are looking for when evaluating evidence of a subject's possible involvement in a criminal offense. Patsy Ramsey's conscious effort to alter her handwriting style suggested she wrote the ransom note and had some type of participation or knowledge about the circumstances of the death of JonBenét.

There had been another discrepancy in one of Patsy Ramsey's law enforcement interviews that caught my attention. Investigators had noted that the wrapping paper on a pair of Christmas presents observed in the Wine Cellar at the time of the discovery of JonBenét's body had been torn. She told the detectives that she couldn't remember what was contained in the presents, and hence the need to tear back part of the paper.

I learned, over the course of my inquiry, that it was Burke who had actually been responsible for tearing back the paper of the presents while playing in the basement on Christmas Day, and I wondered why Patsy would claim responsibility for doing this. Patsy had also told investigators that the unwrapped box of Lego toys in the same room was being hidden for Burke's upcoming January birthday.

I didn't give much thought about the presence of the Christmas presents in the room at the time, but would later think these played a role in some of the events that took place on Christmas day.

Photo 27 - Torn Christmas presents in the Wine Cellar next to the body of JonBenét. The wrapping on these presents are the same as those depicted in photographs of JonBenét and Burke in front of their Christmas tree on the morning of December 25, 1996. Source: Boulder PD Case File / Internet

It was reported that information about investigative steps being taken by Boulder Police investigators was leaking like a sieve to both the Ramsey camp and media. It seemed that any tidbit of information, whether it had substance or not, was being devoured by the press. In one instance early in the investigation, a tabloid offered thirty thousand dollars ($30,000.00) for copies of the ransom note that had not yet been released to the public.

Information about one critical piece of evidence was in Patsy's hands before she interviewed with the D.A.'s office in June 1998. It is not clear how she came to know this, but it was apparent she was aware that pineapple had been found in the digestive track of her daughter. Armed with this knowledge, she denied feeding pineapple to her daughter, or knowing how it may have entered her system.

Through questioning, Patsy had indicated that she had cleaned up the kitchen and dining room after their late Christmas morning pancake breakfast. She didn't think the family had had lunch that day due to the late breakfast and the fact that they were going to the White's that afternoon for a dinner party.

Shown photographs of the dining room table that held a glass with a tea bag and a bowl of pineapple and spoon, Patsy declared that someone else had to have placed those items there. Her reasoning for believing this was that she "would never put a spoon that big in a bowl like that..."

Photo 28 - Bowl of pineapple and empty glass of tea discovered on dining room table: Fingerprints belonging to Burke and Patsy Ramsey were recovered from these objects. Source: Boulder PD Case File / Internet

At first view of the photographs, she stated that she couldn't tell what the contents of the bowl were, suggesting that they were "grits, or apples, or cereal."

Patsy continued to maintain that JonBenét was sound asleep when the family returned home from the White dinner party, and that she had not served pineapple to her daughter.

There was some brief discussion about the White's not serving pineapple at their party, so the investigator was trying to pin down the time and location that JonBenét may have had access to the fruit.

Patsy stuck by her story, and further stated that she did not believe it possible that either of her kids would have got up that night to fix themselves a snack, because she would have heard the kitchen cupboards being opened and closed.

She suggested that the person who had murdered her daughter was responsible for feeding her the pineapple, and that this had actually happened while he was in the home that evening. I took this to mean that she believed the intruder had been a little more careful about opening and closing the cupboard doors as he prepared this snack for JonBenét.

Patsy had at one point asked if the bowl and glass had been fingerprinted, and when told that latent prints had been identified as belonging to one of them (John and Patsy), she continued to deny knowledge about the dinnerware found on the dining room table:

> "I did not feed JonBenét pineapple. Okay? So, I don't know how it got in her stomach and I don't know where this bowl of pineapple came from. I can't recall putting that there. I can never recall putting a tea bag like that in a cup."

It is important to note that investigators determined that the Whites had not served pineapple during their dinner party.

Moreover, by the time of this interview, investigators had developed latent fingerprints on the drinking glass on the dining room table that belonged to Burke. Latent fingerprints found on the bowl of pineapple were identified as belonging to Patsy.

Assuming the bowl had been washed before use, this was proof that linked Patsy to a tangible piece of physical evidence that played an important role in this murder. The timing of the ingestion of this piece of fruit placed JonBenét at home after the White dinner party, having consumed it within approximately two hours before her strangulation at approximately 1:00 a.m.

JonBenét may very well have been asleep when the family arrived home that evening, but is it plausible to believe that she had ventured downstairs sometime later that night?

The red flag in this instance addresses Patsy's adamant denial of having anything to do with the glass of tea and bowl of pineapple discovered on the dining room table. And yet the physical evidence in this instance suggests that she served a bowl of pineapple to Burke after returning home from the White dinner party.

Was Patsy denying this activity because the pineapple in JonBenét's digestive system provides evidence of contact between Burke and his sister at a critical time?

I believe she gave voice to a specific motive on the day she accompanied Burke to the DSS interview that was conducted on January 8, 1997. Speaking with Detective Arndt as Burke was being interviewed by Dr. Bernhard, Patsy stated that she would have *nothing left to live for if she lost Burke.*

Was this a spontaneous utterance that betrayed a motivation for a lack of candor about this crime?

In my view, these were questions that required further consideration. In fact, from my perspective, the entirety of this investigation was awash in a sea of red flags.

And yet, remarkably, there were additional discoveries that would be made more than thirteen years after the murder of this little girl.

"You know, America has just been hurt so deeply with the tragic things that have happened. The young woman who drove her children into the water, and we don't know what happened with the O.J. Simpson – and I mean, America is suffering because (people) had lost faith in the American family.

We are a Christian, God-fearing family. We love our children. We would do anything for our children."

—Patsy Ramsey during the January 1, 1997 CNN interview

CHAPTER THIRTY - TWO

Enigma

As I became convinced that involvement of any intruder in JonBenét's murder was not a viable possibility, I focused my attention on members of the Ramsey family who were present in their home at the time of the murder. In the preceding chapter, I have narrated my thoughts on statements and circumstances that suggest John or Patsy may have been involved.

My review of the investigation revealed that little attention had been paid to Burke Ramsey's possible involvement in the events of December 25th and 26th. In this and the ensuing chapters, I address what we know about Burke and his circumstances at the critical times. My in depth examination of that information, I believe, shows that to reach the truth in this investigation requires a full inquiry into Burke's family and mental health history, and his knowledge and conduct on December 25th and

26th, 1996. My analysis of what we know now provides the beginning, but by no means the end, of that inquiry.

From the outset of this investigation, the Ramsey family appeared to have gone to great lengths to distance Burke from Boulder Police investigators. Rick French attempted to speak to him on the morning of the kidnapping as he was departing the residence with Fleet White. John Ramsey intervened and told the officer that Burke had been asleep and didn't know anything.

Well, how would Ramsey know that? The family has repeatedly stated that they never woke him up that morning to ask him *anything* about JonBenét's disappearance.

Boulder investigators did get one preliminary opportunity to speak with Burke, however, and Detective Fred Patterson had the foresight to scramble to the White residence not long after the discovery of JonBenét's body. This interview took place at approximately 1500 hours on the afternoon of December 26, 1996, and a woman at the residence, identifying herself as Burke's grandmother, sat in on the interview. The transcript of the recording was the first glimpse I had into Burke's thought processes.[65]

It is not clear whether Burke was aware that JonBenét had been found at the time that this interview was conducted, but throughout the questioning, I found it odd that he never once expressed concern for his sister or asked about the status of the search for her.

Quite the opposite was observed. Detective Patterson had to stop his interview at one point in order that Burke could finish eating a sandwich. Here was a police detective, asking him about the disappearance of his sister, and he was so engrossed in the act of eating that he couldn't articulate his words with a mouth full of food.

Patterson was able to elicit some details about events leading up to the kidnapping and was informed that Burke had played at home until around 1630 – 1700 hours on Christmas day and had put on a sweater before heading to the White dinner party.

He played and ate some sandwiches while there and stated that the family went directly home after the party.

This conflicted with statements offered by the parents who reported that they had made two stops on the way home to deliver Christmas presents to family friends.

Burke stated that he put on his P.J.'s, brushed his teeth, and went to bed upon arriving home. He estimated this time frame to have been between 2030 and 2100 hours.

The only noise he reported hearing after going to bed was the "squeaking water heater." He did not hear any "scream, cry, yell or any raised voices" during the night.

Burke provided conflicting information about waking: in one instance he advised that he woke and his father told him about JonBenét being gone. In another instance, he advised Detective Patterson that his dad had awakened him and told him that his sister was missing and that they were going to find her.

At the close of the interview, Burke again stated that he didn't hear any arguing between anyone the previous night.

A red flag fluttered when I noted that Burke concluded the interview, not with a question about the welfare of his missing sister, but with a comment about his excitement about going to Charlevoix. The anticipation of being able to build a fire at the family's second home apparently held some appeal to him.

It was an odd comment, and I concluded my reading of the last page of this transcript with more questions than what I had going in at page one. How could Burke not be inquiring about the status or welfare of his missing sister? Was it conceivable that he was already aware of her fate?

Detective Patterson's interview was the first of several that would eventually be conducted with Burke over the course of the investigation and each provided some new insight into the enigma of this little boy.

Sgt. Mason had attempted to arrange another interview with Burke during his brief visit to the Fernie residence on the evening of December 27th, but as with Patsy, Dr. Buef refused to allow that to occur. When the second interview was subsequently scheduled, it was conducted by a member of the Department of Social Services (DSS), and not a law enforcement officer.

As I write this chapter, it occurs to me that I never asked anyone involved in the investigation how it came to pass that Burke was interviewed so early in the investigation and at a time when his parents were refusing to participate in follow-up interviews with police investigators.

As noted previously, however, this interview had been one of the recommendations made by the Child Fatality Review Team that had been convened by the Coroner on the afternoon of JonBenét's autopsy. So I have to presume that it had something to do with DSS protocols that required the removal of siblings from the home in the event of a child's death. I suspect that the Ramseys capitulated to this second interview because they didn't want to give up temporary custody of their son to the Department of Social Services.

At the family's insistence, the interview, conducted on January 8, 1997, was performed only by personnel from DSS, and Dr. Susanne Bernhard was the sole adult in the room with Burke. She later provided her assessment of his reaction to events surrounding the kidnapping and murder of his sister to one of the Boulder investigators.

There had been no transcript prepared for this interview, but a brief synopsis was written up by Detective Jane Harmer after she spoke with Dr. Bernhard. I read through the outline of the dialogue that had been exchanged between Dr. Bernhard and Burke and her assessment of the interview. She had expressed concerns about Burke's "affect" during the interview and indicated that he showed little emotional connection with his family. I came away wanting to know more.

It took some time, but I eventually obtained a copy of the video of this interview, and I reviewed it on many occasions. I was troubled by what I saw.

At one point during the interview, Dr. Bernhard asked Burke if he felt safe in his home. There was no hesitation when he responded that, yes, he felt safe at home and was not worried about an intruder returning.

I thought it unusual that he would feel safe about his circumstances following the death of his sister. Here he was, probably 30 feet down the hall from her bedroom, when an intruder silently crept into his home and snatched his sister from her own bed and brutally tortured and murdered her within earshot of his family. There were other children and families in Boulder who were terribly afraid that they could be the next target of this monster, and Burke seemed not to give it a second thought.

When asked key questions about sexual contact, his body language exhibited signs of anxiety, and at one point, he picked up a board game they were playing and was rubbing it on his head. The display of this body language contrasted to the behavior exhibited as a baseline throughout other parts of the interview.

On another occasion, Dr. Bernhard had mistakenly taken a sip from Burke's soda can. He seemed to bristle at the intrusion of his personal space / property and indicated that he couldn't drink from the can anymore.

I was taken aback at another comment offered during the playing of a board game. The nature of the game involved guessing the features of faces hidden on the opponent's side of the game board. Burke had mistakenly flipped down a face on his side of the board and then returned it to an upright position, commenting: "Oops, you're not dead yet." This off-hand comment seemed extremely callous and suggested little care or concern for the circumstances at hand. I would later think that this comment might have its source in the events surrounding the death of JonBenét.

Dr. Bernhard had also expressed concern about the family portrait Burke had been asked to compose during the interview. She noted that JonBenét was conspicuously absent from the picture.

It was Dr. Bernhard's experience that many similarly situated children included dead relatives in their family portraits for years after their passing. It was an interesting contrast because it was reported that many of JonBenét's classmates had drawn pictures of her into their artwork when they attended a grief and counseling session hosted at her elementary school a couple days after her death.

In Burke's situation, however, a week and a half after the brutal murder of his sister, he was now moving forward with his life and JonBenét was no longer of importance. She had not been drawn into the family picture. Hardly the response I would have expected from a 9 year-old-boy who had just lost a sibling to a violent death.

Dr. Bernhard also made note of the size of the figures representing Burke's parents and suggested that their small stature in the picture possibly signified an issue with emotional attachment.

His father was pictured in the window of the cockpit of a distant plane, and she interpreted this to mean that Burke's father didn't play a significant role in his life and was viewed as distant and remote.

His mother was smaller than the figure representing Burke's self-portrait, and Dr. Bernhard thought that she didn't hold much sway or influence over him.

I also thought it interesting that Burke admitted to having *secrets* during the interview, but wouldn't reveal them to Dr. Bernhard because then they would no longer be a *secret*.

I had interviewed Dr. Bernhard, (now going under the name of Pinto) on the first of December, 2005, because I was intrigued by the composition of the family portrait Burke had been asked to draw and wanted to see it first-hand. Unfortunately, she did not have it in her possession, so I never was able to see it, or secure a copy for the investigative files.

We spoke of many things during our interview, but what concerned me the most was her continuing impression of the nine year old. She remembered that Burke had presented a flat, unemotional affect, that he was closed down and that she had a difficult time drawing information out of him. He seemed reticent to talk about his family, and she thought him very protective of them.

It was her experience that kids usually talked more about their family relationships, and Burke was not displaying attachment to either his sister or parents.

She commented on the fact that he had shed no tears when speaking about JonBenét's death.

She went on to explain that it was sometimes difficult for children to distinguish what to say and what not to say, especially when they are trying to hide something.

I inquired about the picture that Burke had drawn of his family during their interview. She advised that it was difficult to interpret. The drawing represented a family that was not attached, and it raised questions for her about the typical behavior taking place in the household.

I asked further about indications of childhood personality disorders, and Dr. Bernhard explained that anxiety such as that displayed by Burke at points in his interview comes from caring and that this type of behavior is not typically observed in sociopathic personalities. She indicated that some of Burke's behavior could more likely be indicative of a dysfunctional environment.

While discussing the topic of childhood development, Dr. Bernhard advised that bedwetting usually ends around the age of 3 - 4 years. If it continues into the 5th year, it is usually indicative of medical or emotional issues being involved.

Dr. Bernhard had expressed concerns about having follow-up interviews with Burke because of the "affect" he was exhibiting toward his family. These never took place, however, and apparently the one interview that DSS conducted with him on January 8, 1997, got the family off the hook. Burke was able to remain in the custody of his parents.

There was one other troubling aspect to Burke's DSS interview that bears mention, but I need to provide another piece of information to place it into proper perspective.

During my review of police reports, I came across a transcript of an interview conducted with Mary Ann Kaempfer[66], whose son Anthony Pecchio was a classmate and friend of Burke. Anthony and his mother had been invited to accompany the Ramsey family to Atlanta for JonBenét's funeral services, Anthony to be a playmate for Burke. Kaempfer, not knowing anyone in attendance, assumed the duty of being a nanny to the boys throughout the course of their stay in Georgia.

Boulder Police investigators, interested in a first-person account of what had transpired in Atlanta, interviewed Kaempfer on the evening of her return from Georgia.

She described Burke as being a "very withdrawn little boy", who didn't care much for hugs and would "rather you leave him alone."

While attending the memorial services in Boulder, and while playing with Anthony in Atlanta, Burke was described by Anthony as acting like "he kind of knew what happened and trusted that people would find out."

Anthony indicated that Burke may have appeared "confused" at times, but was not acting upset and indicated that he was not scared. When asked how he was doing, Burke said he was "fine." Anthony told investigators that he never saw Burke cry during their stay in Atlanta.

Kaempfer advised that the only time she had seen him display some emotion and sadness was at the cemetery after the graveside services. He had left a group of people and went to the side of JonBenét's casket, patting it gently.

After that brief display of caring, Burke and Anthony went exploring, skipping through the headstones in the cemetery.

Upon returning from Atlanta on January 2, 1997, Kaempfer spoke to fellow parent Susan Stine and was told about a conversation Stine had overheard taking place between Burke and her son, Doug. This was reported to have taken place on the afternoon following the grief counseling session that had been hosted at JonBenét's school on the morning of Saturday, December 28, 1996.

Stine appeared to Kaempfer to have been disturbed by the conversation and had listened to Burke and Doug talk about how JonBenét had been strangled. Based upon Kaempfer's statement, it appeared that Stine had over overheard the boys discussing whether or not manual strangulation had been involved in JonBenét's death.

Stine described the conversation as being "very impersonal," and it struck her that the discussion about the details of JonBenét's death was like the boys were "talking about a TV show." This discourse between Burke and Doug had taken place no more than 2 days following JonBenét's murder and apparently had such an impact upon Stine that she brought it up in conversation with Mary Kaempfer at the first opportunity.

As I reviewed the video of the DSS interview between Dr. Bernhard and Burke, he was asked if he knew what had happened to his sister or if he had talked to his parents about it. Burke stated that he knew what happened and indicated that he had asked his father where he had found JonBenét's body. His father had told him that she had been found in the basement.

During the initial exploration of this topic, Burke again appeared to be exhibiting signs of discomfort and stress. As displayed during the question about sexual contact, he began rubbing the board game on his head and was holding it in front of his face. He eventually put the board down.

When asked again what he thought had happened, Burke advised without hesitation that he knew what had happened to

JonBenét and that she had been killed. He stated that he thought someone had quietly carried her downstairs to the basement and that person had then either stabbed JonBenét or struck a blow to her head with a hammer.

A chill ran down the back of my neck as I watched Burke twice physically imitate the act of striking a blow with his right arm during his casual discussion of this matter.

I stopped and replayed that section of the video several times.

It seemed absolutely incredible, but Burke was replicating exactly the type of an over-the-arm blow that would have been responsible for the head injury sustained by JonBenét.

It is difficult to describe what I was experiencing. I flashed to the scene of a photograph that I had seen depicting John Ramsey standing next to JonBenét and Burke on a sandy beach. The three of them were standing next to one another, nearly arm-in-arm, and they appeared to be enjoying a summer vacation.

Burke stood head and shoulder above his little sister, and it was the difference in their height that struck me at that moment. JonBenét seemed so petite standing next to her brother, and the mechanics of the delivery of a lethal blow to her head appeared to be within the realm of possibilities.

I leaned back in my chair and contemplated the scenes I had just witnessed on the DSS video. There were red flags popping up all over the place, and I wondered why, assuming Burke had not been misled himself, he apparently would feel it necessary to mislead Dr. Bernhard about his knowledge of the circumstances surrounding the death of his sister and the possibility that a stabbing was involved.

As I reviewed the video time and again, I found it noteworthy that Burke never once mentioned the fact that he knew that JonBenét had been strangled during this conversation with Dr. Bernhard.

As noted, Burke's interview with Dr. Bernhard took place a little more than a week and a half after JonBenét's murder on

January 8, 1997. The fact that JonBenét had been strangled was common knowledge in Boulder by that juncture.

The *Daily Camera's* first published article that reported on the news of the kidnap and murder of JonBenét was released to the public on the morning of December 27th, 1996. It was noted in the article that the autopsy of JonBenét had not yet been conducted, but was expected to be performed sometime that day.

Chief Tom Koby told the reporter that "although the official cause of death was not yet known… the case was considered a homicide."

Detective Sergeant Larry Mason was quoted as saying that the child "had not been shot or stabbed."

The fact that JonBenét had been strangled wouldn't be released by the papers until the following day, on December 28th, but the exact details about the manner in which the strangulation had taken place were not released.

I thought it noteworthy that neither one of these first two newspaper articles mentioned any blow to JonBenét's head, and I wondered how Burke could have known about that injury.

I would later find through research of the news media coverage that the *Boulder Daily Camera* would make passing comment about a head injury a few days later, but full details of the depressed skull fracture wouldn't be revealed to the public by the Boulder County Coroner until July 1997.[67]

The first public mention of any type of head injury appeared to have been reported by the *Daily Camera* in an article published on January 6, 1997, and read as follows:

John Ramsey and a friend later found JonBenét strangled in the basement. The killer had sexually assaulted the girl, covered her mouth with duct tape, looped a nylon cord around her neck, and fractured her skull.

I considered the possibility that this early release of information could have been the source of Burke's speculation about the
"hammer" strike to his sister's head, but he had combined
this comment with his mention of a "stabbing" as well. Why
speculate about two methods of injury if he was truly conversant
with his sister's injuries.

I spoke to media people who were more closely associated
with the daily reporting of events at the time and became aware
that some minor references regarding the injury to JonBenét's skull
had also been discussed by retired FBI agent John Douglas on
Dateline NBC on the evening of January 28, 1997.[68]

As noted previously, Douglas had been hired by the Ramsey
family, and subsequently provided a profile of the person believed
responsible for the abduction and murder of their daughter. The
Dateline NBC interviewer, Chris Hansen, attributes the following
statement to John Douglas during a voiceover on the program:

> Hansen: "Douglas says JonBenét was brutalized, that she had
> duct tape on her mouth. *She suffered severe head wounds.* And
> she was strangled and sexually assaulted."

The late date of this public broadcast didn't explain Burke's reference to the head injury, however, and I attempted to determine
what exactly had been known by the family in advance of Burke's
DSS interview.

The Ramseys were not conversing with Boulder investigators
at the time, so I reached the conclusion that, as the parents of
a murdered child, members of the either the Coroner's Office or
D.A.'s office were probably sharing this information with Ramsey
attorneys. I thought it likely that they were advised of this
information fairly early in the investigation and long before it
became general public knowledge.

The parents had maintained that they never spoke to their son
about the circumstances surrounding JonBenét's death, and had

indicated over the following months that they had made every effort to limit his exposure to the media coverage taking place about the murder. At one point, Patsy had actually asked the manager of a supermarket to remove the tabloid newspapers from the racks of the business. She didn't want her son to be confronted with that type of sensationalist coverage of the murder while waiting in the checkout line of the grocery store.

I again thought it feasible that he may have overheard his parents talking between themselves about the head injury. Or, similar to the conversation he had with Doug Stine about the strangulation, Burke may have been conversing about the details of the investigation with playmates and learned of the head injury prior to the DSS interview.

This was certainly within the realm of possibilities, but I was still asking myself the following questions:

- Why would Burke tell Dr. Bernhard that he knew what had happened to JonBenét and not mention her *strangulation*? He clearly was aware that strangulation had been involved due to the conversations he was overheard having with Doug Stine not more than two days after the murder of his sister.

- Additionally, if Burke had truly become aware of the circumstances surrounding the murder, why would he be mentioning a *stabbing* when there had been no such injury sustained by his sister?

- As illustrated here, the first media report issued on the murder *specifically* stated that JonBenét had *not been stabbed*.

Those were troubling questions, and I wondered whether Burke deliberately misled Dr. Bernhard regarding the exact knowledge he had of the circumstances surrounding his sister's death, and why he would feel the need to do so.

Taking all of those things into consideration, I wondered if perhaps this was merely another strange coincidence that would continue to muddy the waters of the investigation.

On the other hand, I couldn't help but contemplate the possibility that Burke had just physically demonstrated first-hand knowledge of the lethal blow that had been struck to the head of JonBenét.

$$= \oplus =$$

Boulder Police investigators were effectively being sidelined by the late spring of 1998, and the D.A.'s office had successfully negotiated another series of interviews with the Ramsey family. The fact that a grand jury investigation was looming seemed to play a role in getting the Ramseys back to the interview table, but this time the man who had given birth to the intruder theory would be directly involved.

Boulder Police were aware that interviews were going to take place, but the D.A.'s office would not reveal where they would occur. Investigators were provided the opportunity, however, to review the videotapes between the interviews that had been scheduled over the span of three days in June, 1998.

Transcripts of the interviews conducted with John and Patsy Ramsey had subsequently been prepared, but I couldn't find any written record of the interviews conducted with Burke. I was eventually able to obtain DVD copies of these videotapes.

It was my impression that Burke continued to display a distant and detached attitude toward the events surrounding JonBenét's death, and he frequently appeared bored by the investigator's questions. When queries finally began to center around the details of his sister's disappearance, Burke retreated into his chair in a fetal-like position, and he seemed to become agitated and nervous.

Again, I thought that this body language seemed to suggest anxiety and distress. I had initially thought that he might have been withdrawing unconsciously into a position of fetal protection, but later observed that he was calling out that the hour of the interview was nearing an end. This to me resembled the behavior of a reluctant psychiatric patient monitoring the clock for the conclusion of a counseling session.

I was not able to review the third and final segment of these interviews due to a faulty DVD disk, but I was advised by Tom Wickman that, at the conclusion of the last interview, Burke was asked if he had any questions regarding the investigation into the death of his sister. Provided this opportunity, did Burke inquire whether police were any closer to catching the person who had brutally murdered his sister?

No. He asked instead if the brand of wristwatch being worn by the detective was a Rolex.

The demeanor, and continued lack of "affect" exhibited by Burke during this series of interviews was unsettling. It appeared to me that he had no interest whatsoever in the progress of the investigation regarding the death of his sister.

Another item of interest that came to my attention were issues that related to Burke's late age of bed-wetting. A short-term housekeeper had reported to police investigators that Burke was having problems with urinating in bed in 1993, and the parents were having problems with him at the time. Burke seemed reluctant to acknowledge the extent of the issue to Dr. Bernhard during the DSS interview in early January 1997.

Let me again make it perfectly clear. I was not proposing that what little we knew demonstrated that Burke was sociopathic or had a personality disorder. I fully realized that more than this was needed to prove any theory of his involvement, but at the time, those were red flags that began to pique my attention as I continued my review of investigative files.

I had discovered during my review of case files that, with the apparent consent of prosecutors, there were medical records that Ramsey attorneys withheld from the District Attorney's Office in 1998, and I believed it conceivable that they spoke to the very issue of family involvement and a cover-up regarding the circumstances of JonBenét's death.

If the family was involved in any fashion, I believed those records were key to solving the mystery of this child's death, and it was one of the leads I had attempted to convince Mary Lacy to pursue in January 2006.

There was one more peculiar aspect of Burke's outward behavior that left me uneasy. At one juncture during my tenure at the D.A.'s office, I had met with Tom Trujillo, and we were going over some materials in one of the investigative binders at his office. We happened upon three individual Polaroid photographs of Burke and his parents. I had previously seen duplicates of these in the D.A.'s files.

I asked Trujillo about them, and he informed me that he had taken the photographs on the afternoon of Saturday, December 28th, 1996, when he was collecting non-testimonial evidence from members of the family.

I took a few moments to silently study each of the photographs.

John Ramsey looked tired, haggard, and despondent.

Patsy Ramsey was hard to recognize. Her hair was pulled back tightly against her head; she was pale and without makeup and looked as though she had aged a hundred years. The beautiful woman I had seen in many other photographs was barely recognizable, and there was no doubt in my mind that she was consumed by anguish.

Like his parents, Burke was seated in a chair and he leaned back slightly, with his right arm slung casually over a nearby table.

Burke looked directly into the lens and smiled for the camera.

It was puzzling. Here he was, providing handwriting exemplars, fingerprints, and DNA samples to police investigators in their investigation into the murder of his sister. It had to be a stressful and extremely painful time for everyone.

I couldn't help but wonder why Burke was smiling.

CHAPTER THIRTY-THREE

SBP and Beyond

There were several significant developments that took place over the late fall of 2006 and early winter of 2007.

One of them was a tip I had received from a reporter who called from time to time. He had shared some fairly interesting things with me during my work on the case, and he was now informing me that the FBI was considering taking over the investigation. It was reported that there might be a federal angle of some sort that would permit their entry into the case, and they were determined to prevent a repeat of the Karr disaster.

Call me a Doubting Thomas, but this didn't seem very likely to me. I couldn't fathom *any* law enforcement agency wanting to step in and take responsibility for this homicide investigation. Nevertheless, he insisted on giving me the name and telephone number of an agent in the Bureau's Behavioral Analysis Unit (BAU) located in Quantico, Virginia and urged me to call.

There would be many occasions over that winter when I would ask myself what the hell I was doing. I had left the D.A.s office nearly eight months previous and was somehow still involved in this damn case.

I had already gone out on a limb when I had written Mary Lacy at the end of October 2006 and asked her to permit me the opportunity to present my theory to a set of outside prosecutors. I had requested that members of the BAU participate as well, so it didn't seem to be out of line to call this agent and chat with him. In for a penny, in for a pound I figured.

I ended up speaking with FBI Supervisory Special Agent James Fitzgerald. I identified myself and work history to the agent and made it clear that I no longer had any investigative authority or responsibility in the matter and that I was calling as a private citizen who once played a lead role in the case.

It didn't take long to confirm my suspicions. The FBI had no interest in taking over the JonBenét Ramsey murder investigation from Colorado authorities.

We started talking about current events and my attempt to get the D.A.'s office to pursue what I considered to be a handful of viable leads. He soon had me fleshing out the details of my discoveries, and then he dropped the other shoe.

SSA Fitzgerald informed me that, along with being a criminal profiler, his particular area of expertise in the BAU was forensic linguistics and that he had testified as an expert witness in state and federal courts on a number of occasions. One of the investigations he had participated in was the Ted Kaczynski "Unabomb" case.

Though he was aware of Professor Foster's work on the Ramsey ransom note, and had reviewed the written opinion of the professor's findings, he had not been provided the opportunity to personally evaluate the note and writing exemplars collected from any of the suspects in the matter.

We spoke about the elements of crime scene staging, and references in the note to the lines of dialogue that were in headliner movies before, or at the time of JonBenét's murder. Like agents Gregg McCrary, and John Douglas, he felt that the use of movie script dialogue suggested an amateurish attempt to misdirect the course of the investigation. This was not how kidnappers operated in the real world.

SSA Fitzgerald agent expressed his personal views about the contents of the ransom demand, but the extensive analysis required to issue a professional opinion on the possible identity of the author of the note had not yet taken place.

During several discussions with the agent, he expressed disappointment over the outcome of Professor Foster's involvement in the investigation. Foster had developed a reputation as a literary detective and made some interesting discoveries during his academic research. But the professor was not a trained law enforcement officer, and the letter he sent to Patsy Ramsey before being asked to officially become involved in the investigation had potentially jeopardized his objective standing in the matter. SSA Fitzgerald was not aware of the earlier letter to Patsy Ramsey until notified by the Boulder P.D., after Foster's report was received by them.

Professor Foster apparently didn't recognize the need to disclose the previous correspondence, and the agent felt that this probably should have precluded his involvement in the analysis of the writing samples gathered in the case.

SSA Fitzgerald was very interested in my theory and wanted to know if I'd be willing to come to Quantico to share it with the members of his team. The opportunity sounded very attractive, but at that juncture, I was not comfortable with taking that step. My allegiance was still to the Boulder D.A.'s office, and I wanted to give them every opportunity to be the ones who would break this case wide open.

I would have several more conversations with the BAU supervisory staff over the course of that fall and we talked about the manner in which their participation in the case might be accomplished: An official request needed to come from the law enforcement agency of primary jurisdiction, and it had to originate with the FBI's Denver field office. Only then could the Quantico office participate in the investigation.

I kept Mark Beckner informed about my progress, or lack of progress that winter, but could never convince him to invite the BAU in for another consultation on the case. He had turned over primary investigative authority for the case to the D.A.'s office in 2002, and he seemed to be only mildly amused at my efforts to budge Mary Lacy from her fortified position on the Ramsey case.

One could only imagine the level of my frustration.

[Author's note: I spoke again to SSA Fitzgerald in March, 2012. He had since retired from the FBI and indicated that he had written to Chief Beckner in early 2009, not long after Boulder Police had taken back the case from the DA's Office. He was offering to put together a small team of forensic linguistic experts from around the nation to take another objective look at the ransom note. One of his peers from the United Kingdom had volunteered to participate as well, and it was posed to Chief Beckner that the analysis work would be performed pro-bono. Chief Beckner reportedly thanked the agent, but for unknown reasons, turned down the offer.

Fitzgerald continues to practice as a forensic linguist, and went to work for the Academy Group, Inc., located in Manassas, VA following his retirement from the FBI. He has been involved in a number of high-profile cases since leaving the BAU that have involved the field of threat assessment, and textual analysis.[69]

There have been many intervening cases over the years that have validated the foundation for this type of criminal investigative work, and notwithstanding Chief Beckner's decision to decline Fitzgerald's earlier offer, I think it would be interesting to see what a new panel of experts would determine as far as authorial attribution of the ransom note.]

The second important event to occur that winter involved additional discoveries that were related to the behavioral symptoms of a childhood disorder.

While working on the written case outline that was completed in October 2006, I became aware of a childhood behavioral disorder that revolved around the issue of *sexually aggressive children*. I learned about clinical research that had been conducted on the topic of children with a behavioral disorder commonly referred to as "Sexual Behavior Problems", or "SBP."

I had obtained a copy of the book, *Sexually Aggressive Children: Coming to Understand Them*,[70] and other research materials on that topic late that fall and began to review them in my spare time. Araji's book, in particular, provided a comprehensive overview of national research that had studied sexual abuse perpetrated by children 12 years of age and younger.

Approximately two months had passed since the mailing of my letter to the D.A.'s office, and I had finished my study of the SBP text book. It was incredibly enlightening, and the case studies only served to strengthen my belief that developed from my analysis of the case that indicated some form of family cover-up.

This information is not all-inclusive but provides an overview of the behavioral symptoms seen with this childhood disorder:

- Research into sexually aggressive children was described as being in its "infancy" in the mid1990s. (It appears that the earliest studies on this topic only dated to 1980.)

- The average onset of preadolescent sexual behavior problems (SBP) are between the ages of 6-9 years

- Although the term "sexual" is used, the children's intentions and motivations for these behaviors may be unrelated to sexual gratification.

- Children act out for many varied reasons. Some may have been the prior victims of sexual abuse. Some may act out due to other behavioral problems related to PTSD, anger, fear, or emotional detachment. Sexual acting out has been linked to anger, rage, loneliness, and fear.

- FBI UCR reports in 1979 revealed 249 rape arrests for children less than 12 years of age. Sixty-six of those children were under the age of 10.

- Early research conducted in the 1980s provided evidence that preadolescent children's behaviors can be as aggressive and violent as those of adolescents and adults.

- FBI UCR discontinued reporting the age of offenders in 1980, but the National Center for Juvenile Justice reported a forcible rape rate of .02 per 1000 for 10 and 11 year olds in 1988.

- 1990 FBI and media reports in this time period indicate that among adults convicted of sex crimes, approximately 30% said they began offending before they were 9 years old.

- A 1991 study revealed that some children engaged in behaviors that involved fire-setting, bed-wetting, animal mutilation, and scatological behaviors- (disturbed bodily functions related to urination and elimination).

- A 1993 nationwide survey of SBP therapists identified preadolescent behaviors in 222 children that ranged from voyeurism to coercion: The more serious offenses involved digital penetration, penile intercourse, anal intercourse, bestiality, and ritualistic or sadistic sexual abuse.

- Another 1993 survey conducted in the Northwest revealed that some offenders used physical coercion that included tying up their victims.
- Offenders lack compassion, empathy, and exhibit inadequate social skills.
- A victim may be the object of revenge or anger and could be viewed as the parent's "favored child" by the perpetrator.
- Families frequently attempt to portray themselves to the world as the "perfect" family.
- Co-morbidity: SBP patients have a higher incidence of psychiatric disorders that include, but are not limited to, attachment disorder and separation anxiety.

Revelation of these clinical case studies and the emerging national recognition of this childhood behavioral disorder was in its infancy at the time of JonBenét's death, but confirmed what I had occasionally witnessed in the District Attorneys' weekly SART meetings: Children of Burke's age had been proven capable of sexually abusing their siblings and others.

Moreover, these studies confirmed that children of his age were capable of committing horrendous acts of physical violence typically thought to have been reserved to adults.

It had been stated repeatedly that there had been no prior recorded history / incidents of abuse that would have suggested parental involvement in JonBenét's death. As I pointed out in the case analysis report and Power Point outline completed in the fall of 2006, Burke had already exhibited one prior incident of violence against JonBenét.

The incident that involved a blow to the head with a golf club that took place in Michigan was claimed to be an "accident" by the Ramsey family, but it is interesting to note that this incident took place within a day or two of JonBenét's birthday in August 1994.

One can only wonder whether sibling jealousy or envy may have played any part in that instance, and whether these feelings spilled over into the events of the Christmas holidays in 1996.

I had also found it interesting that the Paughs had reportedly purchased several books on childhood behavior for the Ramsey family. The titles of the books were intriguing:

- *The Hurried Child – Growing Up Too Fast*, by David Elkind;
- *Children at Risk*, Dobson / Bruer;
- *Why Johnny Can't Tell Right From Wrong*, Kilpatrick.

When exploring the nature of the content of these three books, I wondered what might have been taking place in the home that prompted the grandparents to purchase these types of childhood behavioral books for the family.

I had reviewed an investigator's report that documented a 1997 interview with former Ramsey nanny – housekeeper Geraldine Vodicka, who stated that Burke had smeared feces on the walls of a bathroom during his mother's first bout with cancer. She told investigators that Nedra Paugh, who was visiting the Ramsey home at the time, had directed her to clean up the mess.

There were other police reports in the files that documented what I thought could be viewed as related behavior. CSIs had written about finding a pair of pajama bottoms in JonBenét's bedroom that contained fecal material. They were too big for her and were thought to belong to Burke.

Additionally, a box of candy located in her bedroom had also been observed to be smeared with feces. Both of these discoveries had been made during the processing of the crime scene during the execution of search warrants following the discovery of JonBenét's body.

I wondered whether fecal material observed in pajamas thought to belong to Burke, and smeared on the box of candy in his sister's bedroom, could have been related to the symptoms of scatological behavior associated with SBP.

I also contemplated the reasons *why* a box of JonBenét's candy would have been smeared with human excrement.

As noted previously, Linda **Hoffmann-Pugh** had also mentioned finding fecal material in JonBenét's bed sheets. It raised the question as to who may have been responsible for the deposit of that material in her bed – had it been JonBenét or was it Burke?

I readily admit that I am not a trained psychologist – psychiatrist, having taken only the most basic of courses during my college studies. But these observations pointed to indicia of some type of behavioral issue that had been taking place in the Ramsey household, and they appeared to have been taking place over some period of time. Incidents like these would not likely have become known to those outside the family, but could have been an underlying reason for the grandparent's purchase of the childhood behavioral books discussed previously.

I eventually conducted a brief telephone interview with Dr. Araji in the late winter of 2007. I did not divulge the details of the investigation that I was working on, but wanted to know what more she could tell me about the treatment of children diagnosed with the symptoms of SBP.

Dr. Araji advised that treatment for young patients exhibiting signs of this behavioral disorder could be successfully concluded in as little as three to four months. Sessions frequently involved other family members, and appropriate role-playing exercises were part of the treatment curriculum.

I inquired whether treatment for SBP would last a year or more. Dr. Araji indicated that it was possible, but that treatment going on for an extended period of time might be due to the involvement of some other type of behavioral disorder problem. She advised that SBP symptoms could be intermixed with other childhood behavioral disorders, thus requiring greater lengths of treatment.

Once again, I came away with more questions than what had been answered. Though some described Burke as being a little withdrawn, the reports that I reviewed about his conduct and work at school appeared to be representative of a normal child in his age range. But these records didn't correspond to the impressions Dr. Bernhard had formed during her interview with him, and I couldn't help but wonder what had been going on behind closed doors at the Ramsey home.

It wasn't clear from his parent's interviews exactly how long Burke had been seeing a psychiatrist, but it seemed safe to assume that some type of treatment and psychological testing had been taking place after JonBenét's death. Otherwise, neither of his parents would have made reference to his counseling sessions during their interviews.

I contemplated the demeanor that had been exhibited in the transcript of the first interview conducted of Burke by Detective Patterson, and the "affect" that had been described by Dr. Bernhard during the interview she had completed with him a couple weeks later. My review of the videotape of that particular interview raised concerns, and I wondered whether the co-morbidity of an attachment disorder should be considered in the grand scheme of things. It was something that Dr. Bernhard had expressed concerns about, and it had been an underlying reason for her thoughts that follow-up interviews should be conducted to further explore the matter.

In my review of all of the official interviews recorded with this boy, not once had he expressed concern about the welfare of his sister, nor had he ever asked investigators how their search for her killer was progressing.

The stress of his mother's battle with a deadly disease could have accounted for a fear of being abandoned, and very well could have contributed to the emotions associated with separation anxiety. It is important to note this illness took place when Burke was at an early and impressionable age.

In considering all of these circumstances, it seemed plausible to me that there were a whole host of things taking place in the home environment that could have influenced the events that eventually unfolded on the evening of December 25, 1996.

As a criminal investigator who was attempting to make sense of the clues that were presenting themselves in this inquiry, the question that arose is this:

- Under currently accepted behavioral science lore, was it reasonably possible for a nine-year-old, who was several weeks from turning ten years of age at the time of this murder, to have committed this type of crime without having exhibited symptoms of some type of behavioral disorder to teachers and others outside the home before and after the death of JonBenet?

The observations of family friends and Dr. Bernhard notwithstanding, I explored the Internet for updated studies on the topic of sexually aggressive children following my call to Dr. Araji, and observed that there were a number of more recently published articles on the disorder.

The U.S. Department of Justice, Office of Juvenile Justice and Delinquency Prevention, authored a fairly extensive article in March 2001 that provided a comprehensive overview of research on the matter.

Juveniles Who Have Sexually Offended – A Review of the Professional Literature[71] pointed out that sex offenses committed by juveniles continued to be a serious problem. The researchers who authored the article provided a comprehensive and annotated account of the many research projects that had documented the characteristics of juveniles who commit sex offenses. The article also explored the types of offenses committed, and the characteristics of the families of juvenile offenders.

Discussions regarding the characteristics of offenders included Offending Behaviors, Child Maltreatment Histories, Social and Interpersonal Skills and Relationships, Sexual Knowledge and Experiences, Academic and Cognitive Functioning, and Mental Health Issues.

Other headings of interest included Types and Classifications of Offenders and provided an outline of behaviors related to Sibling Incest, Girls Who Have Committed Sex Offenses, Young Children Who Have Committed Sex Offenses, Juveniles with Developmental Disabilities and Mental Retardation Who Have Committed Sex Offense, and Juveniles Who Have Committed Sex Offenses Versus Other Types of Offenses.

And lastly, of course, the article covered the results of research on the critical aspects of the Assessment and Treatment of this childhood disorder.

There were numerous articles and research studies that had followed on the heels of Dr. Araji's comprehensive publication and some of the articles I reviewed included the following:

- The California Social Work Education Center published an article titled *Child Sexual Abuse* in 2002.
- *The National Center On Sexual Behavior Of Youth* published a Fact Sheet on the topic of "Sexual Development and Sexual Behavior Problems in Children Ages 2 – 12", in January, 2004.
- The Association for the Treatment of Sexual Abusers published a report in 2006, titled *Report of the Task Force on Children with Sexual Behavior Problems*[72], which was intended to guide professional practices with children, ages 12 and under. The mission of the ATSA was to promote effective intervention and management practices for individuals who have engaged in abusive sexual behavior.

The point to be made is that the Internet offered an abundant amount of materials on articles that had documented research involving the emerging issue of children who were involved in problematic sexual behavioral.

The studies seemed to confirm Dr. Araji's initial exploration of the matter, and revealed that we are all born as sexual beings. Research on sexual behavior of children ages 2 to 12 suggests that sexual responses are present from birth, and that a wide range of sexual behaviors for this age range are normal and non-problematic. Further, sexual development and behavior are believed to be influenced by social, familial, and cultural factors, as well as genetics and biology.

It is the sexual "acting out" that falls outside the norm of human sexual development that has created the concern about child, and juvenile offenders. What I found intriguing was that children exhibiting behavior associated with SBP ranged widely in their degree of severity and potential harm to other children.

Furthermore, researchers had determined that there was no universal characteristic, or profile, that could help identify the children who were most likely to offend.

And despite concerns that children who had begun offending at an early age would continue into their later years, evidence suggested that the bulk of children diagnosed with SBP were at very low risk for committing future sex offenses, especially when provided with appropriate treatment.

While a large number of children identified with symptoms of SBP were overtly exhibiting behavior that appeared developmentally inappropriate, others showed no outward sign of sexual problems.

It was noted in a number of studies that sibling incest was quite prevalent, but it often went underreported and ignored. Contrary to the studies involving extra-familial sexual abuse, research found that it was difficult for parents to report the abuse of one of their children when it has been perpetrated at the hands of another child in the household.

One 1991 study referenced in the U.S. Department of Justice article indicated that the duration of sex offending was greatest for sibling offenders. Nearly 45% of the sibling offenders studied in the research had been committing offenses for more than a year.[73] Moreover, sibling offenders were more likely to vaginally or anally penetrate their victims than extra-familial offenders.

Research continued to find reports of scatological behavior that was associated with SBP diagnoses, and indicated that mental health issues relating to anger, depression, and anxiety were factors that offenders attempted to resolve by acting out sexually.

One particular set of studies caught my attention as I struggled with the significance of the absence of pronounced symptoms of a behavioral disorder. This body of research reported that as a group, juveniles who sexually offended typically experienced academic difficulties. One study, however, found that 32% of a sample of male juvenile sex offenders had above-average academic performance.[74]

The conclusions I drew from my review of these many studies was that coming to understand the dynamics underlying the causes of childhood sexual behavioral problems was extremely complex. Many variables figured into the equation as childhood psychotherapists, over the years, have attempted to understand and appropriately respond to the issue of this type of sexual behavior.

To me, the more pressing question to be resolved centered on the issue of whether children of Burke's age were capable of committing acts of physical violence that included murder. Additionally, having committed such an act, could we expect to see some type of specific pre-offense, or post-offense behavior, which would alert us to the child's propensity to commit this type of crime.

The FBI reported that there had been 15,848 people murdered in the United States in 1996. Seven-hundred and twenty-three (723) of those had been eight (8) years old and younger.

I conducted further research into crime statistics involving *juvenile offenders*[75] and learned that two-hundred and fifty-seven (257) children, who were fourteen (14) years of age and younger, had been arrested for murder and non-negligent manslaughter in the United States in 1996.

Sixteen (16) of those arrests had been for boys under the age of 10. Another fourteen (14) arrests involved boys aged 10 to 12 years.

The statistics for forcible rape were even more discouraging. Sixty-one (61) boys under the age of ten had been arrested for this offense in 1996. An additional three-hundred and thirty-five (335) boys had been arrested who were aged 10 to 12 years.

John Douglas's thoughts about the perpetrator being a single-time offender struck a chord when I reviewed national homicide statistics. Douglas had rendered the opinion that the person who killed JonBenét was a "mission oriented offender" and would not likely kill again.

Thankfully, people who commit serial murders are far and few between, but like those who perpetrate single offenses, offenders usually tend to blend in with the rest of us. They don't advertise their actions by tattooing a scarlet "M" on their forehead, and it frequently takes a great deal of investigative work to identify the person responsible for committing this type of crime.

Additionally, given the fact that a great number of murders are never solved, it must be presumed that many perpetrators were able to successfully elude the attention of authorities and that their outward behavior did not give them away.

Was it possible for a perpetrator in this particular instance to have taken the life of another and go forward without necessarily drawing the attention of authorities, or that of the people with whom they interacted every day?

To date, no one has been arrested and convicted for the murder of JonBenét, so I would have to say that the answer to that question is a resounding "yes."

It therefore must be acknowledged that there are many who walk among us, of all ages, sex and color, who have murdered someone at some point in their lives, and they have thus far successfully eluded identification and capture.

Whether it had been accidental, or intentional, I believed that the national statistics pointed to the real possibility that a 9 or 10-year old could have committed a crime as egregious as the murder of JonBenét. It was my belief that the possibility of Burke's involvement in the events of December 25 – 26 warranted further exploration.

In coming to understand the family dynamic, I felt it was necessary to consider Patsy Ramsey's view of the world. Striving for the image of perfection came early for her and was demonstrated through the various things she accomplished over the course of her lifetime.

As a high school cheerleader, she became drawn to being the center of attention and moved on to the competition of beauty pageants. She won the title of Miss West Virginia in 1977 and later competed for the Miss America crown.

As a wife and mother, she was forever concerned with putting the best foot forward and according to family friends, was never to be seen wearing the same outfit two days in a row. She took particular care in grooming herself when going into the public eye and was a perfectionist when it came to presenting the family image.

Opening her home to the Boulder Holiday Parade of Homes, Patsy decorated extensively and every room boasted a different type of Christmas tree. Everything was in its place and was intended to show the world the face of a happy and prosperous family.

An understanding of Patsy's internal drive to present the "perfect" image of her family is illustrated in many examples. One that surfaced during my review of reports revealed that she had once hired someone to cut her neighbor's lawn before an event was to be held at the Ramsey home. She reportedly had not spoken to her neighbors before executing this plan of action, and I thought it helped explain her mindset when it came to presenting her world to those outside the family.

Thus, I felt it was necessary to fully understand the importance of *image* to Patsy, as it was "key" to identifying a possible motive for a cover up in this crime. I thought it twofold:

First of all, I didn't think that Patsy would ever be able to live down the "loss of face" if it came to be known that JonBenét had suffered either an accidental, or intentional death, at the hands of a member of her household. It probably would not have taken long for this information to go "viral" in the competitive world of child beauty pageants. The prospect of this outcome would have been unbearable.

Secondly, I believed Patsy had given voice to a more specific motive during Burke's DSS interview. Having lost her beloved daughter, she would have nothing left to live for if her last remaining child were to be taken from her. Was she determined not to let that happen, and set about an elaborate cover-up to ensure that authorities would be misdirected?

When I took into consideration all of this information, I had to pose the following questions:

- What does it matter whether or not Burke was awake at the time that Patsy Ramsey made the 911 call to police and why would his parents wish to conceal this information?

- Furthermore, what parent would not ask their son, who slept just feet from the bedroom of their kidnapped and murdered daughter, if he had seen or heard anything during the night? This course of action defies human nature and had long been a red flag for me.

- And why would the Ramseys refuse to allow homicide investigators the opportunity to interview Burke about the death of his sister? Instead, they insisted that this interview be performed by a psychologist / psychiatrist.

- Why were Burke's parents so adamant that he was not a witness in this investigation? Was it because the family was afraid that direct contact with experienced police investigators might reveal some way in which he was involved in this case?

It was readily apparent that my request of the D.A.'s office for an objective review of my hypothesis was being ignored.

I was stepping out of my comfort zone, but I made the decision to take my case to Governor Bill Owens. I was aware that the governor's office had been asked to intervene during Alex Hunter's reign, and I thought it might be time for him to consider doing it again.

I spoke with Governor Owens on several occasions, and he was very interested in my endeavor and supportive of my cause. Having failed to receive any type of response from the Boulder District Attorney's Office, I crafted the following letter for his consideration:

January 1, 2007

Governor Bill Owens   *VIA FAX*
136 State Capital Building
Denver, CO 80203-1792

Re: JonBenét Ramsey Death Investigation

Dear Governor Owens,

As you are aware, I wrote a letter to Boulder County District Attorney Mary Lacy at the end of October 2006, requesting that I be granted the opportunity to present information regarding an alternate case theory to the former special prosecutors who conducted the 1998-1999 grand jury investigation into the death of JonBenét Ramsey. As indicated in that correspondence, I believe there are specific records and testimony that were not sought or considered during that first inquiry into the matter of JonBenét's death.

Nearly two months have passed since making this formal request and, as of this writing, I have received no response from the Boulder District Attorney's Office. I suppose this is not surprising, in that I am well aware that Mary Lacy believes an intruder was responsible for the death of JonBenét. My concern, highlighted by the events surrounding the arrest of John Mark Karr, is that the District Attorney's Office will go to extreme lengths to pursue an 'intruder' in this case but is unwilling to consider new evidence that suggests the possibility of family involvement and a cover-up.

I am writing you because I am aware that you have the authority to involve the Colorado Attorney General's Office in a matter such as this and that you had taken similar steps in 1998 when you asked several Denver-Metro area District Attorneys to consult in the case. I am convinced there are grounds for taking another look at the possibility of family involvement in the death of JonBenét and would request that the special prosecutors who were most familiar with the details of the first grand jury inquiry be asked to review the evidence that I discovered during my work on this investigation. I believe this information is key to resolving the matter and I am seeking your assistance in bringing this death investigation to a close.

In as much as the Boulder District Attorney's Office has elected not to respond to my request for an independent review of this information, I will be asking that the Boulder Police Department observe/ participate in the presentation of this case analysis. As the law enforcement agency that retains original jurisdiction over the investigation of the matter, I do not believe Boulder Police Chief Mark Beckner would withhold his consent to a review of information that had not been previously considered by investigators.

Additionally, I would also ask that consideration be given to inviting the FBI's Behavioral Analysis Unit to participate in the examination of this new evidence and case theory. The members of this unit certainly have the expertise to evaluate the merit of this information and I believe they would offer an unbiased and objective viewpoint to the overall inquiry.

In closing, I believe there is no harm to be done in examining information that could possibly move the investigation toward definitive resolution. Cold homicide cases are often solved when evidence is considered in the light of new theories. Moreover, if the family had a part in the death of JonBenét, I believe I know where the answers are to be found that will finally solve this decade-old mystery.

Thank you for your consideration of this matter and I look forward to hearing from you in the near future. Please do not hesitate to contact me should you have any questions or require further information.

Sincerely,
A. James Kolar
ajk

Governor Owens was interested in seeing this case move forward, and placed a telephone call to the D.A.'s office to inquire about the lack of a response to my October letter. I am not conversant with the details of the discussion that took place, but Tom Bennett called me some time later to see about arranging a meeting to go over the materials.

I asked him who would be invited to participate, and he indicated that it would likely be himself, Mary Lacy, and members of her command staff. No outside prosecutors, Boulder Police Department representatives, or members from the BAU would be joining in the presentation.

It seemed ironic. The Ramsey family took every opportunity to publically criticize Boulder Police for not seeking outside assistance, even though that was not the case. Now it was the D.A.'s office that was unwilling to seek the assistance and opinions of outside experts on the matter. It seemed doubtful, however, that the Ramseys would have objected to Lacy's position in this instance.

I saw no point in continuing to pursue the issue. Lacy was entirely sold on the intruder theory and continuing to hang her hat on microscopic traces of DNA. It was extremely frustrating to see this one piece of evidence dominate the entire direction of this case.

Governor Owens thought he could do more if I were willing to go public and encouraged me to give it some consideration. I thought about it for a few weeks and scrubbed the idea. I didn't particularly care for wearing a bulls-eye on my back and decided to wait for a change in regime in Boulder.

Not long thereafter, I received a letter from Lacy that more or less accused me of overstepping my authority, and being too willing to pursue leads that she did not think likely to be productive.[76] It had been her intention to scale back the investigation when I took over the case for her office and instead, I had pumped new blood into it by discounting the point of entry, eliminating the use of a stun gun, and discovering viable leads to pursue.

It was readily apparent that I no longer retained any investigative authority having left her employ, but it was to her office that I first sought permission to obtain an expert analysis of my hypothesis. I guess I could have accepted the invitation to present at the BAU, but my loyalties were still with the D.A.'s office at the time.

I subsequently drafted a response to her letter, and went to some length to further explain my unresolved suspicions about SBP and the red flags that were present in the investigative files. Resolution of the case was in her hands, and I urged her to not let it slip from her grasp.

No further communication took place after these exchanges, and one of my friends still employed there informed me that the word circulating around the D.A.'s office was that I was "obsessed with the case."

It was a discouraging time, but things began to brighten a bit when the last development finally came to fruition.

Sergeant Harry Stephens, involved in the surveillance of Jay Elowski described in Chapter One, had retired from Telluride several years prior, but continued to come back and work as a reserve officer during the major music festivals. I was in the process of completing my case synopsis in late September 2006 during one of the fall festivals, and I took the occasion to show Harry a few of the video clips of the Train Room and Stun Gun Power Point slides.

Around a month later, he called to tell me that he wanted to send me something in the mail. He thought it might be responsible for the twin abrasions located on JonBenét's back. As promised, about a week later, a rectangular box arrived, and it contained a child's toy.

It was a single piece of "O" gauge style train track, the same model of train and track depicted in the crime scene video of the basement play room. The track had three pins extruding from one end.

I called Harry, and we spoke about the track. "It has three pins," I said "and we only have two abrasions on JonBenét's back."

"The pins fall out all the time." He replied. "Didn't you ever play with trains as a kid? It's possible the middle pin was missing when this was used on her back."

Laughter. "I was an HO-3 man, and the pins weren't this sturdy."

I thought it over and said I'd take some scaled photographs of the end of the track.

I emailed a set of digital photographs to Tom Trujillo a week or so later. It took awhile, but Shelly Hisey (*see* Chapter Twenty-three) again worked her magic with the Power Point slides. In late February 2007, I received a CD from Boulder Police with a photo array of slides.

The disk loaded into my computer and took several moments before the screen came alive.

I was on the phone after my first viewing.

"Way to go Harry! I think you just found the weapon used to inflict those marks on JonBenét."

The pins on the outside rails of that piece of "O" type train track *matched up exactly* to the twin abrasions on the back of· JonBenét.

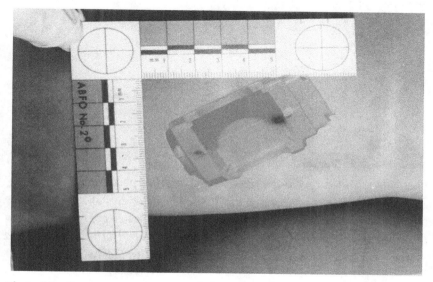

Photo 26 - Stun gun one-to-one scaled overlay

This was a toy readily accessible in the home and located only feet from where her body had been found. Crime scene photos / video had captured images of loose train track on the floor of Burke's bedroom as well.

Lou Smit's calculation of the "close" match between the Air Taser stun gun and JonBenét's injuries had effectively been marginalized. This cornerstone piece of "evidence" of an intruder's participation in the crime, already called into question, had essentially vaporized. .

One of my female officers, Christine Sandoval, volunteered to be a "beta'" tester the following week, and I videotaped her jabbing and slightly twisting the head of the track into the soft flesh of her palm.

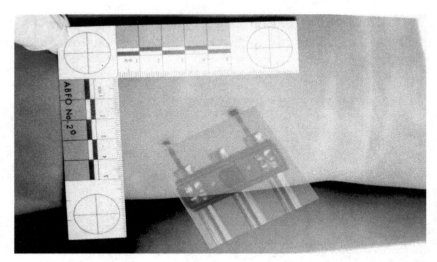

Photo 29 - Scaled one-to-one Power-Point overlay photographs of the "O" gauge type of train track found in the Ramsey home reveals an exact match to the abrasions located on the back of JonBenét (The center pin is missing from the track in this photograph). Source: Photo of train track by author, and Power-Point series prepared by Boulder PD criminalist Shelly Hisey

The pins of the track left red marks when sufficient pressure was applied, and I suspected that the twisting motion of the twin outside rails could have been responsible for the appearance of an *abrasion,* especially when considering that the target area was the soft skin of a 6-year-old girl's back. It was my observation that the twisting motion of the pins could have created the round and slightly rectangular aspect of the abrasions as noted by Dr. Meyer during the autopsy.

I believed the discovery of this toy was a significant development in the case, and I contemplated the possibilities of its use during the commission of this offense. Ultimately, I had a good cop, and an old friend, to thank for unearthing this breakthrough.

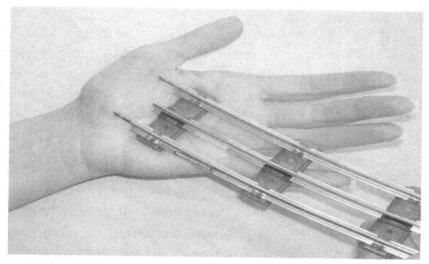

Photo 30 - A twisting and jabbing motion of the "O" gauge train track will create abrasions when sufficient pressure is applied. Source: Author photograph of Deputy Christy Sandoval

In June 2007, Mark Beckner and I found ourselves both in attendance at the annual Colorado Chiefs of Police conference being held in Ft. Collins. At the tail end of the gathering, we spent some time discussing my attempts earlier that year to stimulate interest in opening a new grand jury inquiry into the matter of JonBenét's death.

It was apparent that Beckner had not wanted to wade into the middle of that effort, and it made perfect sense. At the time, there were approximately two years remaining in Mary Lacy's term as D.A., and he couldn't afford to jeopardize the working relationship between their two agencies.

I spelled out some of the details of the childhood behavioral disorder that I had been studying and how it appeared to correspond to several observed aspects of Burke's behavior and others that were possible and called for further investigation. Beckner seemed interested in these details, and I told him that I would try to find the time to organize the information into a written document for his consideration.

I would estimate that I had been working on this for well over a year, but managing my own department had demanded the better part of my extracurricular energy. Although delayed by many months, I finally forwarded a synopsis of the studies to Beckner in October 2008. It provided an assessment of the statements, physical evidence, and behavioral clues that strongly suggested family involvement in the crime under investigation.

I pointed out that I thought it extremely significant that Ramsey attorneys were able to withhold certain medical records from the District Attorney's Office during the period of their cooperation that preceded the grand jury inquiry in 1998. At the time, Alex Hunter probably considered it a small concession to agree to a partial withholding of records that Ramsey attorneys were declaring to be an "island of privacy" required of the family.

John Ramsey noted during his June 1998 interview with Lou Smit, that he was taking medication that had been prescribed for him by Burke's psychiatrist, Dr. Steven Jaffee of Atlanta, Georgia. The fact that John was taking medication to help him through those difficult times didn't seem out of the ordinary to me. I did think it unusual, however, that Burke, who reportedly had not witnessed any of the events surrounding JonBenét's kidnapping or death, was still being treated professionally nearly a year and a half after the event.

Patsy had also made reference to Burke's treatment during her 1998 interview with authorities, indicating that they didn't want to him to wake up one day when he was forty, and have difficulties dealing with the repercussions of all that was going on with the events surrounding the murder investigation.

Purported to have witnessed nothing related to his sister's disappearance, or having nothing of import for a police interview,

I could not help but wonder why Burke would require such extensive psychological counseling.

I also referenced statements made by Pam Paugh during a nationally televised interview that had taken place around the time that the grand jury had begun its inquiry in 1998. Paugh declared during that interview that Burke had been cleared of any involvement in his sister's death by psychological testing. Worthy of note is that she felt it necessary to spontaneously provide his psychological treatment as an offer of proof that he could not have been involved in this crime of violence.

I presented the argument to Beckner that Pam Paugh's statements to the national audience about Burke's psychological counseling, and his being cleared of any involvement in the death of his sister, may have voided the doctor-patient privilege. I believed that by raising the issue of his psychological testing and treatment, she had made the issue of his mental health treatment a matter of public record, interest, and concern. I wondered whether or not her public statements had opened the door to accessing his psychiatric records, for I felt that they needed to be evaluated in relation to any possible knowledge he may have had about the death of JonBenét.

I concluded my letter to Beckner urging that he again consider involving the grand jury in the matter of JonBenét's death and was hopeful that a new regime at the District Attorney's office would consider this course of action.

It was this work that prompted an invitation to participate in the Cold Case Task Force that would later be assembled to consider the future course of the investigation. I was optimistic that some positive movement would finally be taking place.

PART
FOUR

Theory of Prosecution

"The Boulder Police would like us to go away. They would like to just close the books on it, pretend that none of it ever happened. But we are not going away. We are going to be their worst nightmare. Patsy and John Ramsey are hanging in there, until the day we die we'll be looking for the person who murdered our daughter."

—Patsy Ramsey, quoted during an interview with Barbara Walters aired on *ABC News* March 17, 2000.

CHAPTER THIRTY-FOUR

The Intruder Left Behind

In the late fall of 2008, Boulder County District Attorney-elect Stan Garnett announced that he intended to take another look at the infamous JonBenét Ramsey homicide and return primary investigative responsibility back to the Boulder Police Department. Upon receipt of that news, one of the first steps taken by Boulder Police Chief Mark Beckner was to invite a wide-ranging group of experienced local, state, and federal law enforcement investigators, forensic laboratory technicians, and prosecutors to participate in a briefing and brain-storming session that was intended to help point the 12-year-old homicide investigation in the right direction.

I had been invited to attend, not only as an advisory member of the Cold Case Task Force, but as a presenter. I had been asked to participate because during my role as a chief investigator in the JonBenét Ramsey case for the Boulder County District Attorney's Office, I had discovered credible information that discounted the single intruder theory that had been espoused in the early months of the investigation. It was my responsibility to spell out the details of that theory to the team of experts who had assembled for a briefing on the case.

Over the course of two days, on February 26th and 27th, 2009, approximately 30 law enforcement professionals assembled to receive a briefing on the status of the investigation. It had been nearly 7 years since the Boulder Police Department had relinquished their case to the D.A.'s office, and I was anxious to see where events would take the inquiry.

I had been waiting for this opportunity for nearly 3 years and was hopeful that the district attorney's office was willing to take a look at the case with a new set of experienced prosecutorial eyes.

Prior to the gathering, Beckner had forwarded to me a portion of the materials that I had prepared for Lacy's office in 2006. I proceeded to condense what originally was roughly an 8-hour Power-Point presentation to 2-hours. I was the last investigator to present on the first day of case review, and provided a condensed version of my theory to the group of experts who had been convened to review the matter.

Day two was comprised of a round-table discussion of the previous day's work, and it ended on a positive note. There was a renewed energy to clean up some old details and pursue new additional courses of inquiry.

I was exhausted from a week of anxious, irregular sleep patterns, and the two days spent reviewing the details of the investigation had been mentally and physically draining. Boulder was more than 4 hours behind me as I headed home to the mountains of southwestern Colorado.

The Escalante Canyon was coming up on the approach to Delta and the decision was made to pull off the highway to do some meditative wandering. The Escalante was a frequent stopping point for me on my return trips from the front-range, and meandering over the open rugged plain offered a brief respite of quiet and solitude. Moreover, it offered the opportunity to explore something that had been tugging at the edge of my consciousness for some period of time.

Something said during our review of the investigation had set my subconscious into overdrive. It had been there, hiding beneath the surface, since the early days of my involvement in the investigation, and I felt that a meditative hike through the backcountry might help flush out the intangible that had been lingering in the background for several years.

I contemplated the comment that had stirred my memories: a Colorado Bureau of Investigation lab supervisor had talked about looking at the chronological sequence of events. I knew there was a challenge in that because from the early outset of their response to the 911 call reporting the kidnapping of JonBenét, Boulder Police had decided to maintain radio silence so as not to alert the perpetrators to their activities. Constructing an accurate time clock from the dispatch radio logs for a number of the investigative steps that were taken on December 26th, 1996, could be challenging.

Nevertheless, the comment about establishing a time line for the sequence of events struck a chord with me. After having poured over hundreds of pages of police reports, interviews, and lab findings during my time as lead investigator on the case, I recognized that it was the nature of the sequence of events that had been hovering in the shadows of my subconscious for the previous 3 1/2 years. The missing piece gradually began to take form as I trekked in a westerly direction toward the canyon walls enveloping the Gunnison River.

It occurred to me that the answer had been voiced during my presentation regarding the analysis of John Ramsey's statements. I had held up two photographs for the group to see: one of John Mark Karr and the other a psychic rendition of what the perpetrator was supposed to look like. (Eerily similar to Karr I must note.)[77]

Holding the photos up for all to see, I had posed a rhetorical question to the group: "Where were they hiding?"

Photo 31 - Photograph of John Mark Karr at the time of his arrest by the Boulder District Attorney's Office in 2006. Source: Boulder County Sheriff's Department

Photo 32 - Dorothy Allison's psychic rendition of the "intruder" thought responsible for the kidnap and murder of JonBenét Ramsey. Source: Internet

There had been an inordinately long pause of silence after I asked the question, and some forgotten insight had momentarily surfaced, but was gone before I could fully take hold of it. The synapses had failed to fire, and it wasn't until I was hiking in the solitude of the rugged plain that the full image finally came to mind.

As the sun breaks the horizon during its rise, so did the thought slowly emerge that shed clarity on the shadow that had been plaguing me.

The realization slowly dawned that, according to John Ramsey's account, at least one of the intruders must have remained hiding in his home well after the time that police arrived on the scene to investigate the kidnapping of his daughter.

That realization abruptly halted my westerly progress, and I paused to gather my thoughts. I struggled to remember the details of the chronology of the visits to the basement that had taken place before the discovery of JonBenét's body. I knew that four people had been through various parts of the basement that morning, either looking for JonBenét or for a viable point of entry and exit from the home. The sequence of those events was significant, and I recognized that confirmation of this watershed moment was to be found in the various statements provided by those who had been in the house that morning.

From the outset of my involvement in this murder investigation, I found it interesting that John Ramsey had never mentioned his concerns about the placement of the Samsonite suitcase below the Train Room window, or his suspicions about the condition of that basement room to investigators during their initial inquiry on the morning of December 26, 1996. It seemed unusual because, after all, police officers and investigators were aggressively attempting to determine how the perpetrator(s) had gained entry to the residence to accomplish the task of kidnapping JonBenét, and it was on the minds of everyone at the home that morning.

Determining a point of entry or exit might have yielded physical evidence that could help identify the assailant(s). Yet knowing this, John not once mentioned his concerns about the placement of the suitcase, the condition of the basement, nor the suspicious vehicles he reportedly observed driving in the area and parked in the alley across the street that morning. None of this information came to light until months later when the family finally consented to their first full-length police interview and even then, John continued to withhold information that may have been helpful to the investigation.

It was the memory of these facts that provoked the realization that if John Ramsey's account was to be believed, at least one of the perpetrators had remained in the home on the morning of December 26, 1996.

For the sake of objective clarity, the reader may wish to review the chronological history of John Ramey's statement in chapter Twenty-Five so that you may better understand the following analysis.

The Chronology of Visits to the Basement Train Room

Patsy Ramsey placed a 911 call to the Boulder Regional Communications Center at 0552 hours on the morning of December 26, 1996, and Officer Rick French was the first police officer to arrive on the scene at 0555 hours. Patsy greeted him at the front door and John Ramsey was observed standing to the rear of the residence near the kitchen. Officer French was advised that the Ramsey's 6-year-old daughter was missing and shown a ransom note. He immediately took steps to sequester the parents to the first floor Solarium located in the S. E. corner of the residence.

Sergeant Paul Reichenbach is reported to be the second police officer to arrive on the scene, and after receiving a quick briefing from Officer French, he conducted an exterior / interior sweep of the residence that included the basement. He is believed to have been the first police officer to visit the basement.

Officer French remained with Patsy and John as Sgt. Reichenbach called in additional resources to assist in the investigation.

> CSI Karl Veitch arrived on scene at 0610 hours.
>
> CSI Barry Weiss arrived on scene at 0640 hours.
>
> CSI Sue Barklow arrived on scene at 0700 hours.

At some juncture, French conducted a cursory inspection of the rear ground floor doors and garage and ultimately checked the basement. Looking for a forced entry to the residence, he did not open the Wine Cellar door due to the fact that it was secured from the outside by a rotating block of wood. If someone had forced entry through that door from the outside of the residence, behind which lay the body of JonBenét, the wood block would have been damaged.

French apparently did not think the Train Room window a likely point of entry and left the basement as he had found it. He did not report placing a chair in the doorway to block the Train Room. The timing of French's visit to the basement was believed to be sometime after CSIs had arrived on the scene to begin their processing on the first floor level of the house and before the White and Fernie families arrived on scene.[78]

It was close to 6:30 a.m. when John and Barbara Fernie arrived and, from outside the rear kitchen / patio door, John was able to observe the ransom note still spread out on the floor of the hallway next to the kitchen.

Not long **thereafter**, Fleet and Priscilla White **were the next family friends to arrive** at the Ramsey home. Fleet reported that within approximately 15 minutes of his arrival he made a quick inspection of the basement of the home. He was purportedly the third person to visit the basement at that point of the morning, and I believe his observations are a key component to unraveling this mystery.

White observed a Samsonite suitcase beneath the broken Train Room window. Its side was flush to the wall, and he moved it as he closely inspected the area for new broken glass. White reported finding one small kernel on the floor that he placed on the interior window ledge. He observed the window to be closed but unlatched and left it in that condition.

Continuing his exploration of the basement, White unlatched a door and briefly looked in the darkened room identified as the Wine Cellar. Unable to find a light switch and not seeing anything in the dark, he closed the door and returned upstairs. He subsequently removed Burke Ramsey from the residence, and this was accomplished prior to the arrival of Detective Arndt at 0810 hours.

Interviewed by police on three separate occasions about his inspection of the basement, White never mentioned having to move a chair to enter the Train Room. He made it clear that he spent some amount of time inspecting the window and aside from placing a kernel of glass on the sill, he left the window in its original closed and unlatched position. He never reported placing a chair to block the Train Room doorway upon his departure from the basement.

Critical Analysis of John Ramsey's Statements

At no point does John Ramsey ever state that he visited the basement prior to the arrival of Officer French. As outlined herein, over the course of numerous interviews and public statements, he vaguely indicates that the time frames were within one to three hours after French's arrival and likely after the 10:00 a.m. ransom call had failed to materialize.

Though it was noted that Ramsey had to run to the den to answer the phone on one or more occasions, it didn't seem reasonable to believe that he would have ventured as far as the basement, or the second floor, while awaiting a call from the people who had kidnapped his daughter. I would suggest that it is more likely that he made trips to Burke's room and to the basement when Detective Arndt reported losing track of his whereabouts from approximately 10:40 to 12:00 hours.

Also to be considered were the time frames involved in his first being alerted to JonBenét's disappearance by Patsy. According to family statements, John responded downstairs in his underwear and was reading the ransom note in the back hallway as Patsy was on the 911 call. At some juncture, he had to check on Burke, search JonBenét's room, and then rush upstairs to fully dress and be back downstairs in the kitchen to be present when Officer French arrived at the scene. All of this activity would purportedly have had to have occurred within minutes of Patsy's finding the note and the 3 minutes it took French to arrive after receiving notice of the 911 call.

Based upon the historical record of his statements and the timing of events described above, it is therefore presumed that John's first visit to the basement did not occur before Officer French arrived on scene. One has to surmise that John Ramsey did not report his trip to the basement or his suspicions about the suitcase to Officer French, for otherwise the first CSI on scene would have been diligently processing the area when Fleet White arrived that morning.

If these are accurate statements, then it must be concluded that an "intruder" had to have moved the chair into a position to block the doorway after Fleet White had conducted his search of the basement. The time frame of White's trip to the basement can be estimated to have occurred between 0630 - 0700 hours. Following this testimonial evidence, this places an intruder in the home well after a number of police officers and CSIs were on scene and processing the house.

Photo 33 - The chair that John Ramsey purportedly moved to gain entry to the Train Room. Source: Boulder PD Crime Scene Video/Case File.

There is another aspect of Fleet White and John Ramsey's statements that need to be considered. During his first in-depth police interview conducted on April 30, 1997, John advises that he "closed and latched" the Train Room window during his first visit to the basement. Fleet White clearly states that he observed the window to be closed but "unlatched."

Giving consideration to the likely timing of John's first visit to the basement (after 1000 hours), this means that Fleet visited the Train Room before John was there to close and latch the window. Under these conditions, based upon John's statements, it must be presumed that the perpetrator was still concealed within the basement and didn't block the Train Room doorway until after Fleet left the basement. This again places an intruder in the basement from approximately 0700 to 1040 hours.

If, on the other hand, John was somehow mistaken about the time frames involved and visited the basement before Fleet, then the doorway blockage would have been cleared and the window latched. This could only have occurred after police had arrived.

The intruder would have to have been responsible for unlatching the window and escaping after John's visit to the basement, but **before** Fleet **concluded** his examination of the basement at 0700.

Closing Observations

The two key elements that should be considered in this analysis are to be found in the chronology of John Ramsey's statements regarding the condition of the basement Train Room and window well. His observation of the *blockage* of the doorway to that room and his *latching* of the window, when viewed in terms of the timeline of events and witness statements, places an intruder in the home long after police arrive on the scene.

Lou Smit questioned John in depth about the blockage of the Train Room door during the interviews conducted in June 1998, and it appeared to be a significant element that supported his intruder theory. But as noted above, the blockage of the doorway was never mentioned in John's April 1997 interview and after its brief appearance in 1998, it was suddenly excised from any further discussion about his theory of the intruder's actions in his home.

The chair that played such a significant role in establishing the existence of an intruder is never again mentioned following Lou Smit's 1998 exploration of matter.

As a criminal investigator, I have to consider the question: Was this an oversight on John Ramsey's part, or does the intentional absence of this key element reveal consciousness of guilt?

It begs the broader question:

- Is it possible, or even plausible, that one or more intruders were able to remain concealed in the basement during four sweeps of that area?
- If so, why would they remain in the residence hours after JonBenét's death, and how did they avoid the attention of

police officers and family friends when they eventually did escape the residence that day?

I found it noteworthy that John Ramsey never mentioned his immediate concerns and suspicions about the placement of the Samsonite suitcase to Boulder Police investigators on the morning of December 26, 1996. This information was only first declared on April 30, 1997, during his negotiated interview with police investigators.

Nor did he mention his immediate concerns about the suitcase to Fleet White when they were inspecting the train room window well together. According to White there was some discussion about the "possibility" that someone could have come through that window but Ramsey said nothing about his concerns regarding the suitcase.

I would point out that this information only materialized after the D.A.'s office had provided police reports to his defense attorneys in preparation for the April 1997 interview.

Of further interest, the theory regarding the use of the Samsonite suitcase being evidence connected with a possible point of entry and exit for the intruder(s) wasn't espoused by investigators, or the Ramseys, until *after* Lou Smit joined the investigation in mid-March, 1997. This particular aspect of the case was troubling and gave me pause.

I found it intriguing that John Ramsey did not introduce the chair into the intruder equation until June 1998, nearly eighteen months after the murder of his daughter. In concert with the suitcase, was there no thought given to the fact that CSIs may have been able to collect latent fingerprints or trace DNA from such valuable pieces of evidence?

If John Ramsey's version of events is to be believed, then one has to accept that one or more perpetrators were able to successfully remain concealed in the Ramsey home for some period of time after police had responded to the family's 911 call reporting the kidnapping of their daughter.

In this leap of faith, if one follows the evidence, it must be concluded that the "foreign faction" involved in the abduction and murder of JonBenét were truly an exceptional and clever group of criminals.

WWPWS

I regret that I cannot recall the specific circumstances of this event, but we had been ensconced in the confines of a large conference room that contained a white dry-erase board upon one wall. Black capital letters, "WWPWS", had been scrawled across the board.

Sitting with me were Mary Lacy and Peter Maguire, and we were discussing some important case that was being set for trial.

I occasioned to ask the significance of the letters displayed on the board.

My query about the letters led to a brief explanation about a guiding principal regarding the practices of governmental agencies, and apparently, the Boulder County District Attorney's Office.

The acronym stood for this: "What Would Paula Woodward Say?"

For those of you not familiar with the Denver news media, Paula Woodward was an investigative reporter for Channel 9 News, and she frequently reported on the questionable activities of government employees. What immediately came to mind was her work in an unmarked van that had exposed Denver Public Works employees sloughing off on the job. Prime time news video captured too many coffee breaks at the expense of taxpayers.

Fast forward to current events:

As noted previously, I had written Mark Beckner in October 2008 regarding my views of the case, and was soon preparing to participate in a review of the case through the efforts of a newly formed Cold Case Task Force.

Events in the case would take another twist before the task force had an opportunity to convene, however. In the waning days of her term, Mary Lacy announced the results of new DNA testing.

More than two years had passed since leaving her service, and I was mildly interested in her declaration that "Touch DNA" had effectively cleared the Ramsey family of any involvement in the death of their daughter.

She authored an official letter of public apology to the Ramsey family, and many thought that this final act in office precluded the incoming District Attorney from taking future action against family members.

Lacy Exoneration Letter

Lacy reported that the new technology of Touch DNA revealed that the perpetrator believed responsible for the kidnap and murder of JonBenét had also handled the leggings worn by her on the night of her abduction. DNA originally found in her underwear now matched microscopic traces of male DNA found in the interior waistband of these leggings.

She considered it proof positive that an intruder was responsible for this crime.

DISTRICT ATTORNEY S OFFICE
TWENTIETH JUDICIAL DISTRICT

MARY T. LACY, DISTRICT ATTORN

July 9, 2008

Mr. John Ramsey

Dear Mr. Ramsey,

As you are aware, since December 2002, the Boulder District Attorney's Office has been the agency responsible for the investigation of the homicide of your daughter, JonBenet. I understand that the fact that we have not been able to identify the person who killed her is a great disappointment that is a continuing hardship for you and your family.

However, significant new evidence has recently been discovered through the application of relatively new methods of DNA analysis. This new scientific evidence convinces us that it is appropriate, given the circumstances of this case, to state that we do not consider your immediate family, including you, your wife, Patsy, and your son, Burke, to be under any suspicion in the commission of this crime. I wish we could have done so before Mrs. Ramsey died.

We became aware last summer that some private laboratories were conducting a new methodology described as "touch DNA." One method of sampling for touch DNA is the "scraping method." This is a process in which forensic scientists scrape places where there are no stains or other signs of the possible presence of DNA to recover for analysis any genetic material that might nonetheless be present. We contracted with the Bode Technology Group, a highly reputable laboratory recommended to us by several law enforcement agencies, to use the scraping method for touch DNA on the long johns that JonBenet wore and that were probably handled by the perpetrator during the course of this crime.

The Bode Technology laboratory was able to develop a profile from DNA recovered from the two sides of the long johns. The previously identified profile from the crotch

Boulder Office: Justice Center • 1777 6th Street • Boulder, Colorado 80302 • (303) 441-3700 • Fax: (303) 441-4703
Longmont Office: 1035 Kimbark • Longmont, Colorado 80501 • (303) 441-3700 • Fax: (303) 682-6711
TDD/V (303) 441-4774 • Internet: http:/www.co.boulder.co.us/da • E-mail: boulder.da@co.boulder.co.us

of the underwear worn by JonBenet at the time of the murder matched the DNA recovered from the long johns at Bode.

Unexplained DNA on the victim of a crime is powerful evidence. The match of male DNA on two separate items of clothing worn by the victim at the time of the murder makes it clear to us that an unknown male handled these items. Despite substantial efforts over the years to identify the source of this DNA, there is no innocent explanation for its incriminating presence at three sites on these two different items of clothing that JonBenet was wearing at the time of her murder.

Solving this crime remains our goal, and its ultimate resolution will depend on more than just matching DNA. However, given the history of the publicity surrounding this case, I believe it is important and appropriate to provide you with our opinion that your family was not responsible for this crime. Based on the DNA results and our serious consideration of all the other evidence, we are comfortable that the profile now in CODIS is the profile of the perpetrator of this murder.

To the extent that we may have contributed in any way to the public perception that you might have been involved in this crime, I am deeply sorry. No innocent person should have to endure such an extensive trial in the court of public opinion, especially when public officials have not had sufficient evidence to initiate a trial in a court of law. I have the greatest respect for the way you and your family have handled this adversity.

I am aware that there will be those who will choose to continue to differ with our conclusion. But DNA is very often the most reliable forensic evidence we can hope to find and we rely on it often to bring to justice those who have committed crimes. I am very comfortable that our conclusion that this evidence has vindicated your family is based firmly on all of the evidence, including the reliable forensic DNA evidence that has been developed as a result of advances in that scientific field during this investigation.

2

We intend in the future to treat you as the victims of this crime, with the sympathy due you because of the horrific loss you suffered. Otherwise, we will continue to refrain from publicly discussing the evidence in this case.

We hope that we will one day obtain a DNA match from the CODIS data bank that will lead to further evidence and to the solution of this crime. With recent legislative changes throughout the country, the number of profiles available for comparison in the CODIS data bank is growing steadily. Law enforcement agencies are receiving increasing numbers of cold hits on DNA profiles that have been in the system for many years. We hope that one day soon we will get a match to this perpetrator. We will, of course, contact you immediately. Perhaps only then will we begin to understand the psychopathy or motivation for this brutal and senseless crime.

Respectfully,

Mary T. Lacy
District Attorney
Twentieth Judicial District
Boulder, Colorado

The media's response to Lacy's letter of exoneration was less than complimentary. It was one thing to announce the findings of new DNA testing results, but it was quite another to take the next step and publically clear the family of *any* involvement in the death of their daughter.

The *Boulder Daily Camera* wrote, "Lacy has ruined her public and professional reputation through her collective actions in the Ramsey case...The consensus, overwhelmingly, is that (the public and other attorneys) think she is incompetent. Quite frankly, I think they are stunned and confused about the entire way she has handled the Ramsey case."[79]

University of Colorado Law Professor Paul Campos declared the letter a "reckless exoneration." He went to state, "Everyone knows that relative immunity from criminal conviction is something money can buy. Apparently another thing it can buy is an apology for even being suspected of a crime you probably already would have been convicted of committing if you happened to be poor. That at least is one explanation for the letter Lacy sent John Ramsey last week, absolving the Ramsey family of any involvement in the killing of his daughter, and apologizing for contributing to the 'public perception that (anyone in the family) might have been involved.'"[80]

Craig Silverman, a defense lawyer and former Denver prosecutor, called the move to exonerate the Ramsey family "extremely unusual." "Nothing is out of the realm of possibility in this case...anything could happen."[81]

Reporter James Baetke, a staff writer at the *Boulder Daily Camera,* went on to report that touch DNA wasn't necessarily new, but technology had improved its ability test for "increasingly small genetic samples."[82]

The article included an advisory note of caution about touch DNA from an Oakland, California forensic mathematician, Charles Brenner: "Some controversy surrounds this kind of collection; the sample can be so small, it's hard to be reliable."[83]

It was not disclosed during the task force presentation the exact strength of these markers, or how they compared to other samples previously discovered on JonBenét's body (i.e. The male and female DNA collected at autopsy from beneath her fingernails), but it did not prevent the outgoing DA from exonerating the Ramsey family in this murder investigation.

Knowing the history of Mary Lacy's announcements, I should not have been surprised when D. A. Investigator Andy Horita shed further light on the Touch DNA test results during the Cold Case Task Force meeting held in February 2009.

I had supervised Horita during my stint as chief investigator at the D.A.'s office, and it was my opinion that he had a promising future ahead of him. He had no experience as a police officer, but he was an extremely intelligent young man. He looked decidedly dejected as he delivered the news about the additional DNA test results.

Horita confirmed the public announcements Lacy had made about matching DNA found in the leggings worn by JonBenét.

He went on to report, however, that *additional* samples of trace male DNA had been discovered on the cord used in the wrist bindings, and the garrote that had killed JonBenét. These trace "Touch DNA" samples were *genetically unique* from one another, and were believed to belong to different individuals.

It took several moments for this information to be absorbed by the cadre of law enforcement experts filling the room before one of the female laboratory technicians voiced her observation.

It went something like this:

"Are you telling me, based on trace Touch DNA testing results, that we are now looking at six different people being involved in this murder?"

Horita reluctantly nodded his head.

We collectively recapped the DNA evidence that had been analyzed in this investigation, and it included the following:

1.) There had been trace DNA samples collected from beneath JonBenét's fingernails of both hands during autopsy that was identified as belonging to her.

2.) There had been trace DNA samples collected from beneath her left fingernails during autopsy that belonged to an unidentified male.[84]

3.) There had been trace DNA samples collected from beneath her right fingernails during autopsy that belonged to another unidentified male, and a female. (JonBenét could not be eliminated as a possible contributor of the female DNA.)

4.) There had been trace DNA samples located in the crotch and waistband of her underwear that belonged to an unidentified male. This became known as Distal Stain 007-2.

5.) The new technology of Touch DNA identified trace samples in the waistband of the leggings that matched the unidentified male DNA (Distal Stain 007-2) in the underwear.

6.) The new technology of Touch DNA had located another sample of DNA located on the wrist bindings that belonged to a different unidentified male.

7.) The new technology of Touch DNA had located another sample of DNA located on the garrote that belonged to yet another unidentified male.

By our count, we were looking at *six separate and independent DNA samples* that belonged to unknown individuals, comprising a group that consisted of five males and one female.

But there was more.

Horita indicated that Touch DNA testing had discovered traces of genetic material on the pink Barbie nightgown found in the Wine Cellar with the body of JonBenét. This Touch DNA belonged to Patsy and Burke Ramsey.

No surprise there: they all lived in the same house.

So, what is the takeaway that we may derive from this information?

In my view, it demonstrates the advances that our scientific community has made in the application of the forensic sciences.

A hundred or more years ago it was a stretch to make people understand that the ridges on the tips of our fingers were uniquely identifiable. It wasn't long before the technology of fingerprinting exploded, however, and there are now over seventy-one (71) million sets of fingerprints on file with the Federal Bureau of Investigation.

We were only first exploring the identifying characteristics of genetic markers twenty years ago, and in many states across the nation convicted felons / arrestees are now required to provide a saliva swab so that we may compare their DNA identity to the unknown samples collected in open and unsolved cases.

It has been repeatedly demonstrated that technology frequently outpaces the slow moving constraints of the criminal justice system. This was illustrated by the case study presented in the sexual assault investigation that I oversaw in 1990's. RFLP DNA testing technology available at the time indicated that there was a statistical chance of one in ten thousand that our suspect was the contributor of the semen left at the scene of this assault.

DNA testing conducted pursuant to new PCR technology a year later advanced these numbers to one in nine-hundred billion!

The point to be made is that Touch DNA is relatively new technology, and we are still trying to understand the parameters of its capabilities.

Does the discovery of the additional samples of "touch" male DNA on implements used in JonBenét's murder truly mean that we should be searching for an entire group of individuals who participated in this crime?

Or should we interpret this trace evidence in another manner?

Is it possible that new technology is capable of identifying trace evidence, naked to the human eye, which has nothing to do with the transfer of DNA evidence that occurred during the actual commission of a crime?

Is it possible that these trace samples of DNA were deposited on these items of evidence at a time *prior* to the murder of this little girl?

There are numerous examples across the nation where courts have thrown out critical physical evidence due to some type of contamination taking place during laboratory testing. A technician forgets to change a pair of gloves, and microscopic trace evidence from one crime is transferred to the evidence of another.

I can't help but wonder, what the hell makes this case so different? Why are we not giving consideration to the possibility that all of these pieces of trace evidence were in place long before these articles came into contact with JonBenét Ramsey? Are we afraid to even consider other options in our evaluation of this case, and in our pursuit of the truth?

By way of another example regarding the collection of physical evidence at a crime scene, I again refer to the sex assault investigation I oversaw in the early 1990's.

The suspect had worn gloves during his entry to the apartment where the assault took place, but removed one of them during the assault. He unplugged the telephone when leaving, and we collected a decent latent fingerprint from the plastic covering of the phone. We thought it possible that he had handled the phone with the ungloved hand and had left us a tangible clue.

We submitted the latent print for comparison to the national AFIS database and were extremely disappointed when we received no hit. Whoever had left the print on the phone was not in the system, and had no record of arrest.

The inked fingerprints of friends and family of our survivor were collected for elimination purposes, and we gathered nearly two dozen cards for review by technicians.

Again, there was no match of the latent fingerprint to any of the known inked cards we had collected for elimination purposes. It was an extremely frustrating setback.

The latent fingerprint, thought to possibly belong to our perpetrator in the early stages of the investigation, was never identified as belonging to anyone associated with our inquiry. It was one piece of physical evidence that the defense attorney continued to point to as evidence of his client's innocence until the DNA test results came back.

Ultimately, as noted above, the case was made on the DNA evidence left at the scene. The suspect had ejaculated during the assault, and we had plenty of this type of physical evidence to link our perpetrator to the crime.

The point to be illustrated here is that physical evidence may be collected from a scene that has no connection whatsoever to the perpetrator of a crime. There will frequently be unanswered questions about this type of evidence, and each piece must be carefully scrutinized and weighed as to its probative nature. It is critical that we keep an open mind, however, and properly evaluate every piece of evidence that we have collected over the course of an investigation.

As of this writing, I have been unable to determine the strength of the genetic markers that were identified as the Touch DNA samples found in the leggings worn by JonBenét at the time of the discovery of her body. Horita reported that they were weaker than the partial sample identified as Distal Stain 007-2.

The strength of the loci (genetic markers) observed in the cord of the wrist bindings were reported to be 6 markers, and those of the male in the garrote were 7. Both of these samples were less than the partial sample of 10 markers identified as Distal Stain 007-2.

What I viewed as significant however, was the revelation that Horita had disclosed during the task force meeting held in February 2009:

- Touch DNA testing discovered the presence of two additional, unknown samples of male DNA on the implements that had been used to kill JonBenét.

- Mary Lacy made the decision to withhold this information from the public when she apologized to, and exonerated, the Ramsey family.

For what it's worth, here is my personal observation and my takeaway:

For reasons beyond my comprehension, there has been a total lack of objectivity on the part of the prosecutor's office regarding the DNA in this case, and I have a difficult time understanding why the totality of the Touch DNA testing evidence was not released to the public by Lacy when the family was exonerated in the death of their daughter.

Why was Mary Lacy's office so unwilling to look at *all* of the evidence that had been collected over the course of this investigation?

Finally, and more to the point, I can't help but wonder what Paula Woodward would say if she were conversant with all of the details surrounding these new, Touch DNA "discoveries."

CHAPTER THIRTY - SIX

Theory of Prosecution

Not yet half-way through his first term in Boulder, Stan Garnett had decided to throw his hat in the ring for the Colorado Attorney General's office. The campaign trail had brought him to the Western Slope on a couple occasions during the summer and fall of 2010, and the first time we were able to get together was over a cup of coffee in my kitchen as he was on the way to the airport. He was in the company of his chauffeur, so we didn't have an opportunity to speak confidentially about the status of the JonBenét investigation.

I emailed him later that week and asked if he thought if anyone would ever be prosecuted in this murder investigation. He replied by telling me that Boulder Police had not yet provided him with a "theory of prosecution."

I was aware that Boulder investigators had been following up on some of the leads that had been suggested at the task force meeting, and that there had been an effort to gather DNA samples from JonBenét's and Burke's classmates to determine the possibility of a match with the unknown sample in her underwear.

Garnett's last trip to Telluride was approximately two weeks prior to the November election, and this time we were able to speak for a few minutes. He advised me that he had received virtually no communication from Beckner's office about their progress on the case, and he knew of no plans for calling the task force back together.

He indicated that he, and Ryan Brackley, his first assistant district attorney, had been intending to make a trip to Telluride to chat with me further about my theory, but his first 18 months in office had been a busy time. Five full-blown murder trials had resulted in five convictions, and they just hadn't been able to find the time to drive to my far corner of the state.

Garnett suggested that we get together after the election, and we tentatively pinned down a date in mid-November when I would be in Denver on other business. Before parting ways, I told him that I would give some thought to putting together a theory of prosecution for his consideration.

The meeting we had agreed upon never took place, and I subsequently prepared a document that outlined a theoretical concept of the events that had taken place in the Ramsey household on the night of December 25, 1996, and the potential criminal charges that I believed were supported by the evidence in the case. I copied this correspondence to Chief Beckner at the Boulder Police Department.

The cover letter below is a redacted version of the correspondence I sent to Garnett's office in January 2011.

Portions of the document containing references to grand jury information and other sensitive materials have been excised from its presentation here.

January 3, 2011

Stan Garnett, District Attorney
20th Judicial District Attorney's Office
1777 6th Street
Boulder, CO 80302

Stan,

Somewhere in between your campaign visits to Telluride this last fall, I had inquired by email if you thought anyone would ever be prosecuted for their involvement in the death of JonBenét. Your response indicated that Boulder Police had not yet presented a theory of prosecution to your office.

I am aware that Mark's office has been pursuing the task of attempting to identify the contributor of the DNA in JonBenét's underwear and presumably this effort has been consuming a lot of time on the part of his investigators and laboratory personnel. Understandably, he is attempting to negate this piece of trace evidence before updating a case theory and although this seems a thorough and necessary course of action, I will be pleasantly surprised if this endeavor yields positive results.

During our last brief conversation, I indicated that I would consider putting together a working theory for your consideration.

This task has taken longer than anticipated but I am enclosing a theory of prosecution that outlines this hypothesis. It incorporates a theoretical construct of the events of the crime and is presented in a manner that might be argued before the members of a grand jury. As expected, a working theory involves some degree of speculation and for the sake of brevity I did not duplicate all of the information that has previously been documented in my investigative reports and correspondence.

From my perspective however, and it will become evident should you elect to take the time to review this theory, your predecessors have *left your office with little or no opportunity to prosecute anyone who had a hand in the murder of JonBenét or those who participated in the cover-up of the circumstances surrounding her death.*

With the recent passing of the fourteenth anniversary of JonBenét's murder I suspect that the vast majority of people have given up hope of ever seeing the case resolved. Moreover, I whole-heartedly share the opinion that you voiced during the task force meeting nearly two years ago: most in Boulder County wish to hear nothing more about the case unless it has been definitively solved.

With those sentiments in mind, I continue to argue that there is a course of action available to you that will ultimately clear this homicide. I believe that the information outlined in the attached materials provides your office with the best and perhaps the last opportunity to seek the answers that Alex Hunter and Mary Lacy were unwilling to pursue.

Ultimately, the furtherance of this murder investigation rests in your hands and I would propose that the time has come for the prosecutor's office to take back the initiative from the cadre of Ramsey attorneys who have steered the course of this inquiry for far too many years.

In closing, I have to state that I have always held to the belief that the criminal justice system would be able to bring this case to a successful resolution. And as a criminal investigator who was once responsible for the lead role in one of the most bizarre murder investigations this country has ever witnessed, I feel that I have finally fulfilled my obligation to the office where my participation first began.

Respectfully,
James Kolar
Ajk
Enclosure: Theory of Prosecution

The document prepared for Garnett, which ran to approximately 20 pages, included an opening statement that a prosecutor could use to outline the details of the case to a jury, and was followed by a theoretical construct of the events that I believe to have occurred in the Ramsey home on the evening of December 25, 1996.

The actions of each of the family members in the home that night were fleshed out in a story-telling fashion that was based upon, and supported by, information found in the investigative files I had reviewed up to that point in time.

The conclusions voiced about what likely occurred in the home that evening were based upon my analysis of the behavioral clues, family statements, and physical evidence that had been gathered over the course of the investigation. The theory outlined a suggested motive for the cover-up of JonBenét's death.

I found the totality of the circumstances comprising the investigative theory to be rather disquieting, and too disturbing, in my opinion, to express in a public forum. It was another internal debate that continued for some period of time as I went about putting the finishing touches on this work, but eventually, as the time to go to press grew near, I decided not to spell it out it, or share that written document in the body of this manuscript.

Some portions of the theory regarding the behavioral aspects of the crime were of a highly speculative nature, and I felt they are better reserved for a presentation to a trained law enforcement audience.

I realize that this situation is probably a little frustrating to the reader, but the foundation for this theory is interspersed through-out this manuscript and I will have to leave it to your imagination for the moment.

Missed Opportunities

The Theory of Prosecution that I sent to Stan Garnett and Mark Beckner also included some closing thoughts and observations on the status of the investigation, as well as a suggestion on how the case might be moved forward toward closure. These comments also included references to grand jury materials, so I decided to paraphrase the essential elements of this discussion so as not to compromise the integrity of the grand jury investigative process.

I pointed out that Ramsey attorneys and intruder theorists had continued to hail the DNA identified in JonBenét's underwear, Distal Stain 007-2, as proof that a lone sexual predator was responsible for her murder. This partial sample is microscopic, and the strongest specimen was located in the crotch of the panties with weaker samples located along the waistband and seams of the underwear.

I think it is interesting to note, however, that intruder theorists have conveniently chosen to ignore the other trace DNA evidence that suggests more than one intruder was in the Ramsey home on the evening of December 25th. From the outset, they appear to have remained silent on the evidence collected from beneath JonBenét's fingernails at the time of her autopsy.

It is uncertain whether Ramsey attorneys are aware of the two new "Touch DNA" profiles developed at the time that Mary Lacy exonerated the family in the closing days of her term in 2008, but I had given it a lot of thought after attending the Cold Case Task Force meeting held in February the following year.

If I understand the DNA evidence correctly, I would propose that this trace evidence could be interpreted in either of two ways:

1.) The intruder theory must be expanded to incorporate the existence of six perpetrators, four of whom were in the home and had direct physical contact with JonBenét at the time of her death. The DNA in the underwear and beneath her fingernails supports this proposition.

It could be argued that the DNA on the two pieces of cord could have been placed there without the necessity of these last two individuals being in the home.

These six individuals form the core group of the "foreign faction" identified in the ransom note, and the investigation must expand its scope to search for a number of co-conspirators.

To deny this physical evidence is akin to admitting that Distal Stain 007-2 is an artifact that has no correlation to the murderer(s) in this case. Intruder theorists must now explain how all of these people entered and exited the residence leaving no further evidence of their existence.

2) An opposing theory suggests that the strongest partial sample of DNA discovered in this case, Distal Stain 007-2,

was deposited in the underwear during the manufacturing process, and survived to the date of JonBenét's murder.

The technological advances in 'touch DNA' analysis have revealed the capability of forensic science to identify trace evidence that may, or may not, have anything to do with the crime being investigated.

Distal Stain 007-2, and the other trace samples collected in this case, are mere artifacts of trace genetic materials that have no bearing on the investigation, and are of no material assistance in identifying the perpetrator(s) involved in this crime. They were in place long before the crime was committed.

The totality of the circumstances, and all of the evidence gathered over the course of an investigation, must be evaluated when seeking to identify the perpetrator(s) who had the motive, opportunity, and capability of committing, or covering up this crime.

The prosecution has the opportunity to legitimately argue that the numerous unidentified DNA samples collected in this case are explainable, and that their origin has nothing to do whatsoever with the death of JonBenét.

The same theoretical principles of transfer thought to be involved in the DNA collected from beneath JonBenét's nails could be applied to the transfer of genetic material from her underwear to the leggings. "Cloth to cloth" transfer could be responsible for this new evidence.

The point to be made is that technological advances in the collection of "touch" microscopic DNA evidence has yet to be fully understood and clarified.

When the prosecution is able to discount the intruder theory, and all of its components (DNA, stun gun, window-well entry and exit, Wine Cellar foot print, and disproving that an anonymous person authored the ransom note), it is then in a position to focus its primary attention on the motivations of the family, and all of the other evidence that points to their involvement.

I expressed my belief to Garnett and Beckner, that the theory of family involvement outlined in the preceding chapters was supported by witness interviews and Ramsey statements, forensic findings, fingerprints, trace evidence, and an identifiable childhood pathology that explained the circumstances leading up to, and surrounding the death of JonBenét.

DNA theory aside, I pressed the argument to Garnett and Beckner that there continued to be a course of action to pursue through the assistance of a grand jury.

I believed that there was a reason defense attorneys had worked so hard behind the scenes to withhold family medical information, and proposed that this "island of privacy" was a viable lead that deserved the attention of investigators and prosecutors.

I am sure it has become apparent that I believe each member of the Ramsey family, home on the night of the murder, may have been involved at least as an accessory after the fact. Burke, only nine years old at the time, could not have been prosecuted for any crime because, in Colorado, a child under ten years of age is presumed incapable of forming criminal intent. The statutes of limitations for the crime of accessory after the fact have long since expired.

There is no statute of limitations for murder, but all persons in the family home the night of the murder have been formally "cleared" of any crime. Those actions by past prosecutors create a formidable obstacle to any future prosecution.

Yet clearly, the death of JonBenét remains an open murder investigation, and while no one is likely to *ever* be criminally charged with this crime, I expressed the opinion that there are proactive steps that should be taken to bring it to resolution and closure.

In our pursuit of truth and justice, not only for this little girl, but for all of the other innocent people wrongly accused by her family, isn't it our responsibility as criminal investigators and prosecutors to go in search of it?

"Smit says he is only interested in finding the truth, wherever it takes him.

'If the Ramseys did this and I found out, I'd be the first one standing in line at the Boulder Police Department,' he says."

—*CBS:* "Searching for a Killer: The Stun Gun Theory"
David Kohn
February 11, 2009

One Last Lead

Lou Smit was often heard to say that we should "follow the evidence," and presumably, it would lead it us to the people responsible for this crime. Smit was a true gentleman in the classic sense of the word, and I regret that we never had the opportunity to have debated the evidence in this inquiry. So I will have to be content with leaving this last lead for the intruder theorists who yet remain.

It always makes sense to revisit your theories when you are working a case. New evidence comes to light that must be considered, and sometimes this completely alters your concept of the crime.

In this instance I looked back at the significance of the discovery that John Ramsey had made when he had alerted Smit to the chair that blocked the entrance of the Train Room doorway. This important piece of the puzzle placed at least one or more of the intruders in the residence long after police and friends of the family had stormed the home.

What if I was wrong about excluding the window well as being a possible point of entrance and exit? Smit had demonstrated on national television how someone could have entered the home through that window, and Boulder Police investigators also conducted trial runs of sending someone in and out of that window in attempts to evaluate it as a possible part of the crime.

They conducted the same tests on the window of the basement bathroom and, for a variety of legitimate reasons, quickly ruled it out as a possibility.

The Train Room window well was a small space, and it seemed unlikely that a single intruder, let alone six of them, would be able to enter / exit that window and not disturb the cobweb that was in the lower left corner of the window frame - or similarly, that the rectangular shaped piece of glass balancing on the sill would not have been jostled from its position during this activity.

And then there were the additional spider threads that anchored the metal window grate to the surrounding vegetation and cement foundation of the window well.

The bug experts had stated that the spiders responsible for these webs were in hibernation at that time of year, and that the stringer portion of the web attached to the grate would only stretch about ten inches before breaking. If these had been destroyed by an intruder(s), the webs would not have been reconstructed that day.

Smit had adjusted his theory after being told that information, and he suggested that perhaps the grate had been swung "forward" to permit entry to the window well versus being swung "up," as he had demonstrated on television. This would permit entry to the window without breaking the stringer lines.

That didn't account for the remaining web in the corner of the window frame, however, and I continued to think about how it was possible that someone could have used that window for their entry and exit. According to the Ramseys, every other door of the residence had been locked that day.

The suitcase didn't belong below the Train Room window well according to John Ramsey, and he should know. He was the owner of the house. That suitcase certainly may have played a role in the crime.

It dawned on me that someone physically fit and agile could possibly maneuver through that narrow window, and not disturb the glass and spider webs.

I thought back to the clues that had been presented in the ransom note. The kidnappers had stated that they were members of a foreign faction that didn't care for the way John Ramsey did business. Perhaps it was someone from overseas that was responsible for this crime, and we should take the note at face value.

Amsterdam. John's company conducted business in the Netherlands, and to my knowledge, this was a lead that had not been considered or pursued during the course of this investigation. His company also operated out of Mexico City, but it was fairly evident that the ransom note had been written by folks fairly familiar with the English language, so I decided that we could rule out this country as a possible home base for the perpetrators.

Furthermore, based on the DNA samples collected in this case, I suspected we were looking for at least six individuals who had conspired to commit this crime. For some reason, this group of individuals had been greatly offended or harmed by something undertaken by John Ramsey's company in the Netherlands.

Follow the evidence, I continued to remind myself. Who really could have been responsible for the kidnapping and murder of JonBenét?

It was the consideration of all of this evidence that prompted me to craft the theoretical construct of the actions of the team of kidnappers outlined in the opening chapter of this book, "Foreign Faction." Given the trace DNA evidence present in this case, it seemed entirely reasonable to propose this new theory, and the explanation of the activities of those who invaded the Ramsey home certainly appears to fall within the realm of possibilities.

So, based upon some of the evidence, we were looking for a group of six individuals (five men and a woman), who likely lived overseas, and who were incredibly athletic and agile – skilled enough perhaps to get through the window well without disturbing anything, and leaving no other trace of their existence.

Images suddenly conjured of the scene from the movie, *The Great Escape*, where prisoners of war slowly crept out, one by one, through the narrow hole of an underground tunnel to gain their freedom. If I recalled correctly, well over a hundred of them made it clear of the tunnel before a Nazi guard stumbled to their endeavor. Perhaps that was possible in this instance.

As I contemplated the possibilities that followed this evidence, I again looked to the contents of the ransom note. As the Ramseys liked to phrase it, there were all of these "funny little clues" left around the house that seemed to taunt investigators at their every turn. No one could make sense of the manner in which this kidnap and murder had been committed.

If I was right, and the kidnappers had left some additional *funny little clues* as to their identity, maybe there was something else in the note that had been deliberately written to challenge and further confuse investigators. In plain sight for everyone to see, they had declared themselves to be the members of a *foreign faction,* which I deduced to mean that they were not claiming to be U.S. citizens.

I contemplated this information for quite some time, and it was another one of those midnight awakenings when a possibility finally dawned on me. I got out of bed and quietly stepped out onto the deck of my home to view the pitch-black night. There was no moon, and the twinkling lights of the milky-way gazed back at me.

Victory! Victorious.

I guess the kidnappers could claim their "victory" although it could be viewed as hollow. They exacted their revenge by killing JonBenét, but went home with an empty attaché case. The ransom money was never collected. I wouldn't necessarily count that as a victory.

SBTC. SBTC...something there... Got to follow the evidence...

A coyote, the trickster of the night, barked not far beyond the limits of my night vision. I stifled a yawn as a star streaked through the sky, and then there was light.

People have been guessing at the meaning of the acronym since the day it became public, and it seemed not a tremendous jump in logic to think that the group had signed off the ransom note with another funny clue as to their identity. SBTC: I thought that perhaps they were declaring themselves to be a:

Small

Band of

Terrorist

Cidnappers.

And then it struck me.

We should be looking at a group of athletes working the European circus circuit. Who else could have possibly made it through that window without disturbing the spider web and glass fragment but a small, highly trained group of gymnasts, contortionists, and trapeze artists.

And by *small*, I don't mean that there were only *six* of them in the group of this "foreign faction." I am referring to their number being *small in stature*.

We ought to be looking for a troupe of highly skilled circus midgets - ones who are likely to carry attaché cases with them when they travel.

Truly another matter of speculation on my part, but I figured, what the hell! They were a group of foreigners who didn't know how to spell.

After all, when one takes all of the evidence into careful consideration, anything then becomes possible. Right?

E P I L O G U E

The decision to publish the details of my participation in the investigation of JonBenét's murder
has been extremely difficult. I have been a duly sworn law enforcement officer in the State of Colorado for over 35 years, which
accounts for the better part of my adult life. Granted the opportunity to serve the public in this capacity involves an incredible
amount of trust, not only on the part of the citizens whom I have
been sworn to protect, but for the agencies that have employed me
to work on their behalf.

I have worked many varied assignments over the course of my
career, and I am cognizant of the need for discretion when
protecting the rights of the innocent, as well as those of the
accused. By necessity, the very nature of many of the aspects of
police work involves the holding of a confidence, and I have strict-
ly held to that premise throughout my service.

An indiscreet comment could very well result in the compromise of a critical investigation, the death of an undercover officer,
or of an individual cooperating with authorities. Inappropriate
statements about a personnel matter could result in damaged
careers and costly lawsuits.

That being said, it is important to note that the management
of public safety is an extremely difficult business. It involves

a balancing act regarding the public's right to know, and government's need to protect the rights of everyone, while still addressing the need for transparency as we interact with our constituency.

Most people would probably describe me as a quiet, reserved person, and sometimes difficult to get to know. I would characterize myself as introspective and rather shy, and the nature of my personality has contributed to the internal struggle that has taken place in deciding whether the discoveries I made during my investigation of this child's death should be made a matter of public record.

The accumulation of months that gathered after my departure from the DA's office in the spring of 2006 served to distance me from the Ramsey investigation, and the immediacy of pursuing leads that I had developed in the case began to fade away. The passing of Patsy Ramsey in June of that year only seemed to underscore the tragedies that had been visited upon this family.

I began to question the necessity of pursuing evidence that pointed to a family's involvement in the death of their daughter, and debated whether it was really all that important for the mystery of this murder to be resolved. I had almost convinced myself to let it all go: to walk away, and let confusion reign. What harm could come from the decision to remain silent about the new discoveries that had been made in the investigation?

Then came John Mark Karr, and with that fiasco, came a clarification of purpose.

I was reminded of the demoralization and destruction that had been visited upon many of the people who were touched by the death of this innocent child. Law enforcement careers were ended by resignation, forced departure, and outright termination.

I had also given thought to the experiences of John and Patsy Ramsey as they tried to deal with the loss of their daughter. John had lost his oldest daughter from a previous marriage to a traffic accident in 1992, and he would ultimately lose his second wife to the ravages of a deadly disease. From my perspective, no husband, parent, or family, deserves to suffer this type of tragedy in their lives.

And yet, one must contemplate the social contract that we necessarily accept, and abide by, when we choose to live side-by-side in a civilized society. Personal accountability and responsibility are the cornerstones of that civil agreement, and unfortunately, history has repeatedly proven that many hold themselves *above* the fabric of that social dynamic.

I had originally put pen to paper with the intention of having something of a history prepared that could be released when this investigation was finally resolved. That was a dream that has gone unfulfilled.

For a variety of reasons, some of which are explained herein, I have chosen to part company with the Boulder County Law Enforcement community, and decided to go forward with the publication of this investigative treatise. I greatly admire the members, past and present, of the Boulder Police Department and the Twentieth Judicial District Attorney's Office, but after a lengthy period of silence, I felt the time had finally come to publically reveal the discoveries that had been made in the murder investigation of JonBenét Ramsey.

I proceeded with the understanding that the Boulder Police Department will *forever* be prohibited from fully commenting on the status of the open, yet unsolved murder investigation of JonBenét. The members of that department will never be in a position to defend themselves against the unwarranted allegations of incompetence and near-sightedness that were attributed to their efforts at solving this case.

It is equally important to recognize the position that Stan Garnett, the current district attorney of Boulder County, inherited when he took office in 2009. From my perspective, Garnett was dealt a hand that looked eerily similar to the first hours of Boulder P.D's response to the report of a *kidnapping* at the Ramsey household.

Boulder Police were confronted with an intensely chaotic scene on the morning of December 26, 1996, for which no one was prepared. A ransom note was shown that purported to evidence the kidnap of a little girl, and family friends were called to console the grieving family. In deference to the emotionally charged situation, officers granted the family their comfort while attempting to conduct a criminal investigation. Though they had their early suspicions about the circumstances being reported, officers responding to the scene never anticipated that the kidnap victim would eventually be found within the confines of her own home.

Boulder Police were quick to correct their initial mistakes, but District Attorney Alex Hunter's oversight and management of his portion of the case created a division between police investigators and his office that spanned the breadth of the Grand Canyon. Unfortunately, this philosophical division was more than a metaphor, and the gap that separated Boulder Police investigators from members of the prosecutor's office would never be bridged.

Political expediency, and the tendency of Hunter's office to craft defense pleas in advance of knowing the facts of a case, precluded a proper review of the true elements of this murder investigation. For many years, Boulder County law enforcement officials had voiced their concerns about the relationship that existed between the defense bar and prosecutors. It was not uncommon for the D.A.'s office to be having plea agreement discussions with a defense attorney *before* they had even received the full complement of investigative reports from a law enforcement agency.

More importantly, it appeared as though many in the D.A.'s office didn't want to consider *any of the evidence* that pointed to some type of family involvement, and totally discounted the opinions of the experts who counseled that all was not right with this "kidnapping" case.

Unfortunately, Stan Garnett inherited all of these problems when he took office in 2009. It was an active homicide investigation in which his predecessor had already publically exonerated the very people whom law enforcement authorities could never clear of involvement. The investigation had been so thoroughly compromised that it was unlikely the prosecution of anyone would ever take place.

Hope springs eternal, and I had always believed that the criminal justice system would eventually prevail. But like Steve Thomas, and many of the other un-named investigators who gave their heart and soul to the pursuit of justice in this case, I gradually lost my faith in the system that was supposed to protect the interests of an innocent and brutally murdered child.

For nearly six years, I have been pushing authorities to initiate another grand jury inquiry that would be able to pursue probative leads that I believed were key to discovering the truth of the matter regarding this child's death. This would be no fishing expedition, and the inquiry would be pursuing specific details that could lead to a definitive conclusion to this investigation.

Over a year has passed since I first sent the "Theory of Prosecution" to the offices of the District Attorney and Boulder Police Department. There had been no acknowledgement of the receipt of this correspondence, or any indication, that police and prosecutors were willing to consider the grand jury leads that were presented in the documents. It appeared that no one in Boulder wanted to ask the difficult questions, or pursue the sensitive information that could solve this murder case.

In all fairness, I can hardly say that I blame them. The investigative file consists of thousands of pages of documents and exhibits, and it would take months for a prosecutor to become fully conversant with all of the nuances and details of the case. Under the current set of legal circumstances, it may very well be that some of the leads I suggested in the case are beyond the reach of law enforcement authorities.

Additionally, the initiation of a grand jury inquiry would bring its attendant problems with the media, and the people of Boulder have truly had enough of that experience. Moreover, the ever-present threat of a Ramsey lawsuit further chills the investigative process.

And now, as outlined in closing chapters, it is readily apparent that the Statute of Limitations has expired, and for that and other reasons, no one will ever see the inside of a criminal court room for their involvement in the circumstances surrounding the murder of JonBenét. What prosecutor, or police chief, would want to expend additional public funds in pursuit of a murder investigation when they know that it will not result in the conviction of the person responsible for the crime?

When I returned to Boulder in 2004, I never envisioned myself stepping into the lead role of the JonBenét Ramsey murder investigation. Nor did I imagine, once I accepted that responsibility, I would discover the things that I have, or reach the beliefs that I now hold. This would not have been possible but for the efforts of the Boulder Police investigators who preceded me in this investigation.

Over the course of the first twelve years that Boulder Police had investigated the case, they conducted 590 interviews, collected handwriting and non-testimonial samples of evidence from 215 people, and had travelled to 17 states and 2 foreign countries in their pursuit of the perpetrator.

They thoroughly vetted well over 100 possible, viable suspects.

In addition, they received approximately 6500 telephone tips and over 5000 letters that purported to identify people involved in the murder.

Over 1500 pieces of physical evidence were collected, and 64 experts were consulted from a variety of fields.

The investigative file, which I came to describe as a *library*, exceeded 60,000 pages of reports and documents.

These were the details that emerged as I began to explore the steps that had been taken to investigate this murder.

This is hardly the picture the Ramsey camp has liked to paint about the Boulder Police Department's search for the murderer of JonBenét. The truth is, however, that a number of *other* potential suspects stood with the Ramseys beneath the *umbrella of suspicion* at one time or another.

The documentation of this case by Boulder Police investigators was nothing less than extraordinary, and allowed me to piece together the framework of an investigative theory that seems not only possible, but, in my opinion, probable when we attempt to understand and explain the circumstances that surround this child's death.

If it could be characterized that Hunter's office missed their opportunity, I would have to say that the investigation languished once it reached Mary Lacy's office. It is difficult for me to speak to this issue, because I worked in her office for nearly two years, and it was my personal observation that everyone there promoted a very positive "can-do" attitude when it came to carrying out their responsibilities as prosecutors.

And yet I could find no rational explanation for her singular view on the matter, and the ease with which she wrote off evidence that led experienced criminal investigators to the opinion that the Ramsey family had somehow been involved in the death of their daughter.

Evidence of this nature continued to be summarily dismissed out of hand, and Tom Bennett, as thorough and efficient an investigator as I observed him to be, was hamstrung when it came to pursuing leads of a probative nature.

Any lead that directed the investigation to an outside intruder was pursued with due diligence, and, regrettably, he spent a good deal of time logging inconsequential flotsam that continued to flood the office.

Following the arrest and release of John Mark Karr, when I was attempting to involve Governor Owen's office in pursuing another grand jury inquiry, it was suggested by certain individuals in the

DA's office that I was "obsessed" with the case. I have to presume that this also meant that I had lost my "objectivity" and couldn't see the *forest for the trees* when it came to evaluating the evidence gathered during the murder investigation.

I fully realize that some of the information provided herein is, at best, circumstantial, and there currently exists no *direct* evidence that could be used in a court of law to convict anyone who may have been involved in the death of this child. Regrettably, there are many murders committed in this country that present similar circumstances, and yet, in some fashion, many prosecutors have made the conscious decision to leave *no stone unturned* when pursuing the leads presented for the homicides committed in their jurisdictions.

I would, therefore, like to believe that, at some point in time, history will eventually resolve the question as to who exercised the better part of reasonable judgment in this particular matter.

It was a combination of all of these things that finally motivated me to move forward with the publication of this work.

Had there been *any* hope of prosecuting *anyone* for this child's murder, I might have felt otherwise. But that is no longer a viable option, and though I have had many second thoughts about this issue, it is my feeling that the truth should be revealed.

It has been extremely frustrating to tune into "investigative news programs" that purport to have "new" information about evidence in the case. Late in the spring of 2011, Aphrodite Jones, an investigative cable TV journalist, hosted a program during which a team of Ramsey defense investigators explored the *evidence* left behind by the *intruder* responsible for the crime.

A friend had alerted me to the upcoming program, and I actually went out and purchased a DVD video recorder so I could capture the show for later viewing. I was going to be traveling and would be unable to see the initial airing of the program.

I have to say that I was more than a little disgusted when I finally had the opportunity to see the program. From my personal perspective, the investigators showcased by the program were continuing to tout evidence that had been thoroughly discounted and no longer held any probative value. It was my opinion that none of the information presented in the program would help identify the actual perpetrators involved in the crime.

I believe the time has come to unveil the discoveries made in recent years and dispel the "BS" that intruder theorists have continued to peddle to an unsuspecting public.

Once my review of the investigation had, in my mind, thoroughly eliminated any significant possibility of involvement by an intruder, I set about examining the evidence, statements, and motives as to each of the surviving family members who were present in the home.

It was readily apparent to me that the parents were completely devastated by the death of their child, and I came to believe that their efforts to keep authorities at arm's length was to not only allow themselves the time to grieve, but to also insulate themselves from the prying questions that they might not be able to answer.

It is much harder to fashion a falsehood than it is to tell the truth, and I would submit that there were many examples of this hypothesis sprinkled throughout the investigation that proves this. Many of the statements provided by the Ramsey family pointed to *deception* and *collusion* rather than *cooperation*, and this was one of the very reasons police investigators continued to suspect their involvement in the crime.

We could enter into a continuous debate about how we think the parent of a murdered child should act, but the fact of the matter is that most parents who have experienced the horror of this type of situation have not sequestered themselves behind high-priced attorneys without justifiable cause. Innocent parents are typically the first people standing in line to be cleared of any suspected involvement by police so that investigators can get straight to the task of looking for the real perpetrators.

It is important to understand, however, that in our system of justice, the innocent frequently take advantage of legal counsel, and this is especially the case when they can afford to do so. But John Ramsey's explanation of the timing of attorney involvement didn't correspond to the facts when the details of witness statements came to light. Mike Bynum's attempt to explain the timing and the reasons behind attorney involvement betrayed his clients' ulterior motives in my view.

It appeared to me that the Ramseys were fortifying the ramparts within hours of the discovery of JonBenét's body, so that they could tactically manage not only the police inquiry, but the heat the media was soon bringing to bear to the investigation.

I watched with some degree of amusement, and anger, as the parents of 6-year-old Aronne Thompson took the same tack in Aurora, Colorado several years ago. Her parents reported that she had gone missing one day after a family argument in November 2005 and called police to seek their assistance in finding her.

The events described by the parents didn't quite ring true to investigators, however, and the parents soon were considered to be *persons of interest* in the investigation, something that I would describe as being similar to falling under the *umbrella of suspicion*. Lawyers coming to the defense appeared to be taking the same approach as Team Ramsey, and had at one point, sought a court order to obtain copies of police notes and reports while the case was still under active investigation. Prosecutors in this instance didn't cave to the defense bar, and successfully fought the motion to produce the records.

The disappearance of Aronne was a case that eventually was proven to involve real parental abuse. Interviews with the remaining siblings revealed that Aronne had mysteriously disappeared from the home well over a year previous, *not* on the afternoon that the parents called police to report her family tiff.

The body of Aronne was never found, but the parents were subsequently indicted by a grand jury on numerous counts of criminal conduct. The mother passed away just before the indictments were released, and Aronne's father was eventually sent to prison for her murder.

I considered this a prime example of where a police department and the prosecutor's office worked in partnership with one another to solve the disappearance and suspected murder of a small child. Unfortunately, this collaborative effort was virtually non-existent in the case involving JonBenét Ramsey, and it is my hope and desire that there is a lesson to be learned in all of this.

Some readers who are familiar with the details of this case may note that I never fully addressed the issue of Santa's *secret visit* in the body of this work. It had been reported by Barb Kostanik, the mother of one of JonBenét's friends, that she (JonBenét) was excited about a secret visit Santa had promised to make to her after Christmas day. When questioned about it by this mother, JonBenét had been explicit in her belief that Santa Claus was going to give her a special gift sometime after Christmas.

Intruder theorists believed this secret visit had been arranged by the pedophile who ultimately was responsible for kidnapping and murdering JonBenét. It was thought to have been someone close to the family, and who would have had easy access to her in order to speak to her about the secret visit.

I, after leaving the D.A.'s office, later became aware, that Mary Lacy and many others strongly believed that Bill McReynolds was the secret Santa who allegedly had made arrangements to meet with JonBenét after Christmas. Lacy was so convinced that McReynolds was the perpetrator, she resurrected him as a suspect on one or more occasions after police had already cleared him of involvement.

I proposed another theory in the correspondence that I sent to Mark Beckner in the fall of 2008. I suggested that the secret Santa referred to by JonBenét was not a *person*, but an *event*.

Patsy Ramsey, in her attempts to preserve and prolong the magical image of Christmas in the life of her young daughter, had to explain Santa's Christmas presents that were going to show up in Charlevoix for John Andrew, Melinda, and her fiancé, Stewart Long.

Additional presents were likely to be presented to JonBenét and Burke, so Patsy offered the explanation to her daughter that Santa was going to be making a secret appearance in Michigan after the immediate family had already celebrated the Christmas holiday in Boulder. The second Christmas experience in Charlevoix would be the opportunity for JonBenét to receive her special gift.

Evidence that tended to support this hypothesis was found in the family's holiday photographs and Boulder P.D.'s crime scene photos. A Christmas morning photograph of JonBenet and Burke depicted unwrapped gifts in the background as they posed by the tree with her new bicycle. Two presents bearing the same wrapping paper were later photographed in the Wine Cellar after JonBenet's body had been found.

I couldn't help but wonder if one of these presents, which remained hidden in the basement during the family's Christmas morning celebration, contained Santa's special gift for JonBenét.

It is unlikely that we'll ever know what secret gift Patsy may have intended to give her daughter. The content of the wrapped presents found in the basement was not revealed during the investigation. Moreover, investigators did not obtain a search warrant for the contents of John Ramsey's plane, which had been packed full of things on Christmas day in preparation for the flight to Michigan.

My alternate theory about the secret Santa was a matter of speculation, but I thought it a plausible explanation for the events that had been scheduled for the family's second holiday celebration in Michigan.

I have to report that I had also struggled with interpreting the facts surrounding John Ramsey's involvement. I was puzzled by his use of binoculars in Burke's room to scan the alley behind the

Barnhill residence, as well as his subsequent 1998 revelation that he had observed a suspicious van parked there, and another vehicle driving by the front of the house.

Crime scene photographs captured the image of a set of binoculars in the kitchen, so it seemed plausible that he actually *had* been scanning the neighborhood through the second floors of the home during the time that Linda Arndt lost track of his whereabouts.

But why not report the van and car driving by to officers when they were first observed that morning? Was he trying to cover his use of the binoculars for another reason?

I thought it possible that he had been checking the trash cans in the alley across the street behind the Barnhill residence because that is where the remnants of the duct tape, cord, and practice notes had been deposited. The alley was clearly visible from Burke's second floor bedroom windows. Was he scanning that alley to see if the evidence of the crime had yet been hauled away?

It wasn't until Steve Thomas reminded me that John Ramsey had stated he had found JonBenét at 11:00 a.m. that morning that I considered the possibility that he was not initially involved in any cover-up. This was a *spontaneous utterance* made to his daughter's fiancé upon their arrival at the Ramsey home that afternoon, and I considered this to be a truthful statement, spoken under emotionally charged circumstances.

There would have been no plausible reason for him to have fabricated the statement concerning the discovery of JonBenét's body at the time. It went against his penal interest and suggests that he was deliberately concealing information about the death from authorities.

Under those circumstances, I had to wonder whether John Ramsey was aware of the events surrounding the death of his daughter at the time he made this statement to Stewart Long. The changing story line revealed over the history of his statements led me to believe that it was only *later* that he became involved in the web of deception that became apparent after the discovery of his daughter's body.

I realize that the tongue-in-cheek nature of the "Last Lead" chapter may appear to some to be cruel and uncaring, but I want to make it clear that this chapter was crafted as an ultimate expression of the frustration that has constantly trailed my participation in the investigation of this murder. It speaks to the incredible lack of judgment that some people exercised when pursuing and interpreting leads in this case, and I carried an internal debate for many weeks before deciding to include this as a closing chapter of this book.

Make no mistake. The murder of this little girl was horrific and tragic, and there is nothing funny about that.

Nor is it funny when you consider the damage done by the Ramsey family when they intentionally chose to point the finger of suspicion at other people. It is with some degree of restraint that I don't expound on the travesty that this family has visited upon their *friends*, and other *innocent* bystanders, as they took steps to divert attention away from themselves, and their disingenuousness when it came to covering up the circumstances that surrounded the death of their daughter.

In retrospect, and I have to acknowledge that hindsight is always 20 - 20, Alex Hunter's office appears to have been outmaneuvered by defense attorneys when he agreed to permit the family their *island of privacy*. Unfortunately, this is not the first time that his office has provided this type of concession to the defense bar.

And despite having information that discounted the elements of the intruder theory, Mary Lacy's office chose not to seek credible information for the sole reason that she didn't want to 'harm her relationship' with the Ramsey family.

If I have interpreted this correctly, it would appear that the Ramsey family, and their cadre of defense attorneys, have successfully subverted the system of laws that purportedly were crafted to speak for, and protect the rights of, the innocent.

They embarked on a path to ridicule and defame the men and women of the Boulder Police Department when it finally became apparent that the grand jury would not be issuing an indictment or a formal report following their lengthy deliberations. Emboldened by the lack of criminal charges, the Ramseys were bent on destroying anyone who suggested that their family might have played a role in this murder.

They sued many people who dared to speak out, and, regrettably, these folks didn't know the weakness of the case against anyone outside the family.

John Ramsey continues to take disparaging shots at the Boulder Police Department to this day and recently expressed his anger at the members of the department for their mishandling of his daughter's murder investigation.

In his recently released book, *The Other Side of Suffering*[85], he indicates that "The police had made up its mind on day one and were not about to be swayed by facts or evidence. Police are supposed to investigate a crime and turn the results of the investigation over to the prosecuting attorney. They are not empowered to determine guilt or innocence."[86]

Ramsey refers to interviews that the family conducted with Barbara Walters and appearances made on *Larry King Live, CNN Early Primetime,* and other internationally broadcast programs as proof of their effort to see the case solved. He goes on to state: "We wanted to do whatever we could to find the killer of our daughter...We wanted to keep the pressure on the police to do the right thing and not just throw our daughter's murder in a cold case file."

Ramsey continues, "Our real priority was to get the case moved from the Boulder Police Department to another jurisdiction. Any other jurisdiction would be better. We believed that until a competent authority took over, the murder would never be solved. We learned the Boulder police rarely followed up on any of the hundreds of leads that came into their department. Even the district attorney asked our private investigators to follow up on a lead he had received perhaps because he knew the police would not."[87]

I can fully understand Ramsey's motivation for wishing to see the investigation assigned to another agency. As illustrated here, Boulder PD investigators were not so easily misled when it came to interpreting the *facts* and *evidence* that had been unearthed in the case. He and Patsy had to be very concerned that, at some point, the detective's inquiries would fully penetrate their carefully crafted smokescreen and eventually determine the underlying motive for a cover-up of JonBenét's death.

In their attempt to misdirect the course of the criminal investigation, the Ramsey family perpetuated a deception that cost the Boulder Police Department thousands of hours of manpower; resources that could have been assigned to the victims of other crimes were instead expended in pursuit of a phantom intruder. Ultimately, hundreds of thousands of taxpayer dollars were wasted in pursuit of this matter.

The real travesty, however, is that, as a law enforcement community, we failed in our duty to find justice for a murdered child. It seems to me that when we do that, we have somehow failed them all.

Undoubtedly, there may be some who will question why I chose to break silence after all of these years, and some will criticize the decision to publish this work. I have frequently asked myself the same questions and have had to clarify, for my own conscience, where my allegiance in this matter should stand.

In the final analysis, given the preponderance of the evidence that was presented in this matter, I felt that it was my responsibility to pursue, and eventually reveal, the untold truth about the circumstances surrounding the murder of a six-year-old child. Secondarily, my allegiance was due the agencies involved in the investigation.

Some may likely disagree with this position and argue that I should have continued to maintain my silence. I will leave it to the historians to eventually pass judgment on the matter.

An author must eventually bring his work to a close, and in so doing, I would like to state that my goal in preparing this manuscript was to provide a straight forward, factual accounting of as many of the pertinent details surrounding this case as was possible. I wanted to reveal to the reading audience the steps I took to investigate this murder, and to share the discoveries that had been made during my review of the documents that had been painstakingly prepared by the law enforcement personnel who worked this case.

Moreover, I felt compelled to explain the thought processes and reasoning used to reach the investigative theories that I had developed about the circumstances surrounding JonBenét's death.

My beliefs, conclusions and opinions, are stated fairly clearly and were based upon the information provided herein.

More importantly, I wish to stress that I undertook this work as a *private citizen,* who once played a lead role in this investigation. Nothing stated herein should be interpreted as being representative of the opinions of any other specific law enforcement agency, entity, or individual who may have played a part in this investigation.

With that said, I thought it appropriate to conclude this work by repeating Sherlock Holmes's investigative dictum:

"When you have eliminated the impossible, whatever remains, *however improbable,* must be the truth."

Expressed in another way, I would propose that we have a responsibility as criminal investigators to consider all of the *possibilities* that present themselves in a case, but we should carefully weigh the *probabilities* as we go about the task of investigating and eventually solving a crime.

I would, therefore, encourage you, the reader, to consider the same information that I pondered as I struggled to understand the circumstances surrounding the untimely death of a six- year-old girl. You are free to either accept, or reject, in whole, or in any part, the beliefs and opinions that I have presented in this work.

The discoveries made during my inquiry are now in your hands, and you are free to draw your own investigative conclusions.

Lastly, I feel it is necessary to point out that thousands of children continue to be victimized each year in this country by people, young and old, who by their actions perpetuate the violence associated with the abhorrent crimes of sexual abuse, exploitation, cruelty, and neglect. It is my feeling that prevention begins with education and foreknowledge, and it absolutely begins with parents and relatives who are willing to take steps to recognize the early warning signs of abuse and then do something about it.

As a police chief, I once had the opportunity to attend an executive training session sponsored by the National Center for Missing and Exploited Children, located in Alexandria, Virginia.[88] The mission of this private, non-profit organization is to help prevent child abduction and sexual exploitation, aid in the recovery of missing children, and assist other children who have been victimized by these types of crimes.

They are the frontrunners in addressing the issues of violence that directly affect the children of our communities, and a donation from the proceeds of the sale of this book is being directed to the NCMEC center to aid in their endeavor.

Ultimately, it is our children who represent the full embodiment of our future, and a positive change for tomorrow begins with what you decide to do today.

PERSONS OF
INTEREST & INDEX

There were a large number of people involved in this investigation, and the following is a listing of the investigators, witnesses, and other named individuals who are mentioned in this book. It is by no means an exhaustive accounting of every person who may have played a part in the on-going saga of this murder investigation.

For the sake of brevity, BPD refers to the Boulder Police Department; BCSO refers to the Boulder County Sheriff's Department; Boulder D.A. refers to the Boulder District Attorney's Office; BAU / CASKU refers to the Federal Bureau of Investigation Behavioral Analysis Unit / Child Abduction Serial Killer Unit.

Joe and Betty Barnhill – Ramsey neighbors in Boulder (p.44)

Mark Beckner – BPD Police Chief, successor to Tom Koby (p. x, 148, 153, 165, 169, 178-179, 185-186, 193, 201, 211, 291, 293, 297, 366, 381, 387, 393, 408, 425, 447, 480)

Tom Bennett – Retired Arvada PD investigator, hired by Mary Keenan (Lacy) to lead JonBenét's murder investigation for the DA's office (p. 216, 243, 285-286, 292-295, 304, 383, 499-500)

Suzanne Bernhard (Pinto) – Child Psychologist, second person to interview Burke Ramsey (p. 343, 346, 349-351, 353-354, 359, 372-373)

Dr. Francesco Beuf – JonBenét's pediatrician (p. 51, 69, 176)

Patrick Burke – Patsy Ramsey's attorney (p. 456)

Michael Bynum – Ramsey friend and attorney (p. 259)

Dan Caplis – BPD Dream Team organizer (p. 147)

Laurence "Trip" DeMuth – Boulder County Deputy D.A. (p. 173, 290-291, 494)

Jackie Dilson – Former girlfriend of Chris Wolf (p.459)

Michael Doberson – Arapahoe County Coroner, involved in stun gun investigation of Gerald Boggs (p. 107-108)

John Douglas – Retired FBI BAU profiler hired by Ramsey attorneys (p. 75-76, 176, 224, 306-309, 356, 365, 377, 502, 504)

John Eller – BPD Detective Division Commander (p. 43-45, 50, 318-320)

Jay Elowski "Pasta Jay" – Ramsey friend and owner of Pasta Jay's restaurant (p. 2-4, 73, 338, 384)

Mike Everett – BPD detective and crime scene investigator (p. 45, 47, 176)

Barbara and John Fernie – Ramsey friends, summoned to home on December 26th, 1996 (p. 27-28, 40-41, 50-51, 84, 86-88, 122, 177, 258, 266, 320, 325-327, 329, 338, 348, 400)

James R. Fitzgerald – FBI Supervisory Special Agent, Forensic Linguist (p. 364-367, 505)

Donald Foster – Vassar University professor and linguistic sleuth (p. xvi, xviii, 96-98, 364-365, 456, 466, 502)

Rick French – First BPD officer to arrive on the scene on December 26th, 1996 (p. x, 25-27, 29, 32-33, 37, 44, 72, 115, 122, 177, 346, 399-403, 505)

Stan Garnett – Boulder County District Attorney, succeeded Mary Keenan (Lacy) (p. 393, 419-422, 425, 428, 439-440, 457)

Ron Gosage – BPD investigator (p. x, 133, 135, 147, 177, 332-333, 338,)

Hal Haddon – Ramsey attorney (p. 175, 478, 486, 488-489)

A P P E N D I X

Floor plans of the Ramsey Home
755 15th Street
Boulder, Colorado

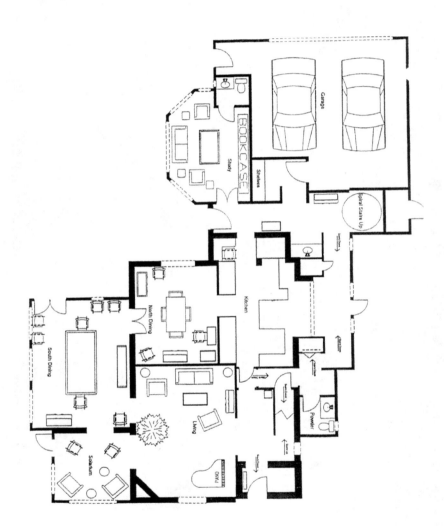

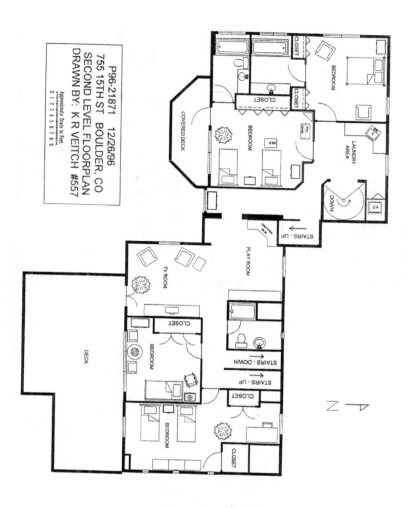

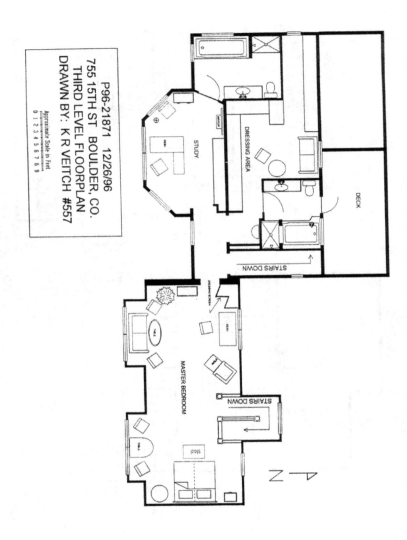

P96-21871　12/26/96
755 15TH ST　BOULDER, CO.
THIRD LEVEL FLOORPLAN
DRAWN BY: K R VEITCH #557

Approximate Scale in Feet
0 1 2 3 4 5 6 7 8 9

STUDY

DRESSING AREA

DECK

STAIRS DOWN

MASTER BEDROOM

STAIRS DOWN

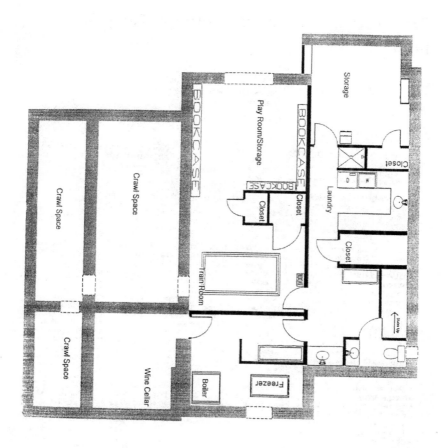

Professor Donald Foster's Letter to Patsy Ramsey June 18, 1997

VASSAR COLLEGE
POUGHKEEPSIE · NEW YORK 12604
Department of English

URGENT AND CONFIDENTIAL

Vassar College Box 388
18 June 1997

Donald W. Foster
Jean Webster Professor of Dramatic Literature

Mrs. Patricia Ramsey
112 Belvedere Ave
Charlevoix, MI 49720-1411

Dear Mrs. Ramsey,

This, first of all: I am terribly sorry for your irremediable loss. JonBenét was a remarkably charming and talented little girl, and I believe that you were an ideal mother, wise, protective, caring, truly devoted. I have no adequate words of consolation for your bereavement, or for its attendant horrors. I am sorry also to hear of your illness. I hope you that will overcome your cancer, not only for your own sake, but for Burke's. It must be hard to find the will to carry on, and the road ahead will be terribly difficult for you both. Your remark that you will soon be with JonBenét worries me--I urge you to find the strength, deep within your soul, to endure, not just for your sake and his, but for JonBenét's. If you succumb to your sorrow and illness, Burke may be lost at sea for the rest of his life, JonBenét may never receive justice, and the person who tortured and killed her will remain free to kill again.

I know that you are innocent--_know_ it, absolutely and unequivocally. I would stake my professional reputation on it-- indeed, my faith in humanity. But first, a word about my credentials (this comes from a sense of urgency, not immodesty): I have acquired some fame and prominence as an expert text analyst (true) and "computer expert" (not so true). I used to undertake such work only for myself or for fellow scholars; more recently, for attorneys (defense and prosecution alike) and investigative journalists. Most recently, I have been assisting the Prosecution in pretrial motions for the Ted Kaczynski/Unabom case (reference: Stephen Freccero, head prosecutor). I am the Vassar professor who identified Joe Klein as the author of the best-seller, Primary Colors ("by Anonymous") a few weeks after the book was first published (six months later, he finally confessed). I have also been effective in other, less high-profile, cases. I have correctly identified the author of documents as short as two pages, and I have been able been able to detect lies or misstatements or concealed information in more instances than I can count. In the 14 years that I have done scholarly text analysis, I have never made a substantive error; if I'm not sure, I bite my tongue or else offer multiple possibilities. In short, no one does what I do as well as I do it.

I try very hard to keep my name out the of the papers with respect to criminal trials and investigations--I do not enjoy the limelight, and I have a wife and two children to protect. Still, because of my notoriety, I have been asked almost daily--by friends, students, journalists, other scholars--to comment on the documents pertaining to the murder of your daughter. I have steadfastly refused comment. Until a month ago, I had not paid attention to the murder investigation, having been preoccupied with my regular obligations plus pretrial motions in the Unabom case; and until about two weeks ago, no one but my own wife was privy to my developing thoughts about this horrific murder. Lately, I have spoken more freely, but only to urge people not to make premature judgments concerning your presumed guilt. I cannot count, or even estimate, how many times I've been told or e-mailed something like this: "Hey, Don, just read those interview transcripts. See for yourself--the Ramseys are guilty, guilty, guilty." Well, I finally did read them, on May 20. I read them carefully, and I know that you are innocent. It has become obvious to me that you loved JonBenét very much, and that you always will, and that you would never harm her, even when angry. But those two interviews, and some of the advice given to you by your attorneys, certainly harmed you, damaging your reputation in ways you could not have anticipated. You can be vindicated. You will be vindicated.

I have also looked closely at police disclosures concerning the unpublished ransom note. My study of the incomplete transcript leads me to believe that you did not write it, and that police are wasting their time by trying to prove that you did. Unless police have misreported the note, it appears to have been written by a young adult with an adolescent imagination overheated by true crime literature and Hollywood thrillers, and by someone having prior issues with you and your husband. The near universal belief among ordinary Americans--a view encouraged by police behavior--is that you wrote the letter to protect the person who murdered your daughter. I find that impossible to believe.

As you may know--it pains me to say this--your reputation has been dragged through the mud on the World Wide Web, in thousands of posts on a half-dozen chatboards, and in household conversation from coast to coast. So has Burke's. One vocal minority has steadfastly accused Burke of killing JonBenét. It has been supposed--though wholly incredible--that Burke is a disturbed boy who killed his sister out of jealousy, and that you and John are covering for him; it has even been noted that the verb, to "burke," means "to strangle someone." Some of the things said about you are worse yet, too vile to repose. And it has been suggested in some chatboard discussion that the accusations will stick, that you will be blamed for the killing after you are gone. If the true killer is not revealed, Burke, too, will live his whole life under a cloud of suspicion. I'm sure you have already thought through these horrific problems. They will not go away by doing nothing.

last May I wrote to someone close to the investigation with
information that ought to have been investigated. I tried again.
Both offers were met with absolute indifference. I have since
come to think that there may be something quite rotten within the
investigative bureaucracy. Perhaps not. But be that as it may, I
have gathered a lot of information about this case on my own, from
a variety of sources, without being officially retained by anyone.
I do not wish to intrude where my counsel is not wanted, but I am
ready to assist you. At the very least, I think I can exonerate
you from a presumption of guilt with respect to the ransom note.
I may also be able to assist you in seeking justice for JonBenét.
I do not want money from you, now or ever. I just want to stop
this person from killing again, and to exonerate those who are
innocent.

I know a lot about what's been going on behind the scenes, on the
Internet and elsewhere, some of it deeply disturbing. While
pursuing these leads, I wish to protect my own wife and children.
I do not wish to be harassed by the FIA (a "phreakers" group
which I presume you know about, and from whom I have already
received a mocking but harmless threat). At this time I cannot
talk to police or attorneys, nor do I wish for it to be reported
that I have even taken an interest in the case.

I think it's quite important for me to speak with you--preferably
today, or ASAP. I do have some questions for you (which you may
choose not to answer), and some distressing but highly pertinent
information. I shall agree in advance to whatever restrictions
you may wish to place on our conversation. My only request is
that you keep our exchange absolutely private. I don't know whom I
can trust--but I do feel quite sure that you were sincere when you
said that you wish to expose the killer. In fact, I already have a
pretty well-formed opinion about who killed your daughter and
where he is hiding out.

If you are willing to talk to me, please call me ASAP. You may
call collect. I strongly prefer that you call me from your
minister's office; I urge you not to call from home on account of
doubtful telephone security. Don't worry about the hour--any
time, night or day, is okay. If I don't pick up, please leave a
message and I'll call back. If you do not wish to speak with me,
or are afraid to do so, or have reservations, please communicate
those concerns to me through your minister. I respect your
privacy. If you think I cannot help you, at least I tried. If
you cannot make this phone call with a good conscience, or without
fear, then don't. My number is 914/437-7074.

Sincerely and with deepest sympathy,

Donald Foster

Donald W. Foster / foster@vassar.edu

914/437-7074

"The truth shall make ye fr.
—John 8:32

Detective Steve Thomas' Letter of Resignation August 6, 1998

Chief Beckner,

On June 22, I submitted a letter to Chief Koby, requesting a leave of absence from the Boulder Police Department. In response to persistent speculation as to why I chose to leave the Ramsey investigation, this letter explains more fully those reasons. Although my concerns were well known for some time, I tried to be gracious in my departure, addressing only health concerns. However, after a month of soul searching and reflection, I feel I must now set the record straight.

The primary reason I chose to leave is my belief that the district attorney's office continues to mishandle the Ramsey case. I had been troubled for many months with many aspects of the investigation. Albeit an uphill battle for a case to begin with, it became a nearly impossible investigation because of political alliances, philosophical differences, and professional egos that blocked progress in more ways, and on more occasions, than I can detail in this memorandum. I and others voiced these concerns repeatedly. In the interest of hoping justice would be served, we tolerated it, except for those closed door sessions when detectives protested in frustration, where fists hit the table, and where detectives demanded that the right things be done. The wrong things were done, and made it a matter of simple principle that I could not continue to participate as it stood with the district attorney's office. As an organization, we remained silent, when we should have shouted.

The Boulder Police Department took a handful of detectives days after the murder, and handed us the case. As one of those five primary detectives, we tackled it for a year a half. We conducted an exhaustive investigation, followed the evidence where it led us, and were faithfully and professionally committed to this case although not perfect, cases rarely are. During eighteen months on the Ramsey investigation, my colleagues and I worked the case night and day, in spite of tied hands. On June 1 -2, 1998, we crunched thirty thousand pages of investigation to its essence, and put our cards on the table, delivering the case in a formal presentation to the district attorney's office. We stood confident in or work. Very shortly thereafter, though, the detectives who know the case better than anyone were advised by the district attorney's office that we would not be participating as grand jury advisory witnesses.

The very entity with whom we shared out investigative case file to see justice sought, I felt, was betraying this case. We were never afforded true prosecutorial support. There was never a consolidation of resources. All legal opportunities were not available. How were we expected to "solve" this case when the district attorney's office was crippling us with their positions? I believe they were, literally, facilitating the escape of justice. During this investigation, consider the following:

During the investigation detectives would discover, collect, and bring evidence to the district attorney's office, only to have it summarily dismissed or rationalized as insignificant. The most elementary of investigative efforts, such as obtaining telephone and credit card records, were met without support, search warrants denied The significant opinions of national experts were casually dismissed or ignored by the district attorney's office, even the experienced FBI were waived aside.

Those who chose not to cooperate were never compelled before a grand jury early in this case, as detectives suggested only weeks after the murder, while information and memories were fresh.

An informant, for reasons of his own, came to detectives about conduct occurring within the district attorney's office, including allegations of a plan to destroy a man's career. We carefully listened. With that knowledge, the department did nothing. Other than to alert the accused, and in the process burn the two detectives [who captured that exchange on an undercover wire, incidentally] who came forth with this information. One of the results of that internal whistleblowing was witnessing Detective Commander Eller, who also could not tolerate what was occurring, lose his career and reputation undeservedly; scapegoated in a manner which only heightened my concerns. It did not take much inferential reasoning to realize that any dissidents were readily silenced.

In a departure from protocol, police reports, physical evidence, and investigative information was shared with Ramsey defense attorneys, all of this in the district attorney's office "spirit of cooperation." I served a search warrant, only to find later defense attorneys were simply given copies of the evidence it yielded.

An FBI agent, whom I didn't even know, quietly tipped me off about what the DA's office was doing behind our back, conducting investigation the police department was wholly unaware of.

I was not advised not to speak to certain witnesses, and all but dissuaded from pursuing particular investigative efforts. Polygraphs were acceptable for some subjects, but others seemed immune from such requests.

Innocent people were not "cleared", publically or otherwise, even when it was unmistakably the right thing to do, as reputations and lives were destroyed.

Some in the district attorney's office, to this day, pursue weak, defenseless, and innocent people in shameless tactics that one couldn't believe more bizarre if it were made up.

I was told by one in the district attorney's office about being unable to "break" a particular police officer from his resolute account of events he had witnessed. In my opinion, this not trial preparation, this was an attempt to derail months of hard work.

I was repeatedly reminded by some in the district attorney's office just how powerful and talented and resourceful particular defense attorneys were. How could decisions be made this way?

There is evidence that was critical to the investigation, that to this day has never been collected, because neither search warrants or other means were supported to do so. Not to mention evidence which still sits today, untested in the laboratory, as differences continue about how to proceed.

While investigative efforts were rebuffed, my search warrant affidavits and attempts to gather evidence in the murder investigation of a six year old child were met with refusals and, instead, the suggestion that we "ask the permission of the Ramseys" before proceeding. And just before conducting the Ramsey interviews, I thought it inconceivable I was being lectured on "building trust."

These are but a few of the many examples of why I chose to leave. Having to convince, to plead at times, to a district attorney's office to assist us in the murder of a little girl, by way of the most basic investigative requests, was simply absurd.

When my detective partner and I had to literally hand search tens of thousands of receipts, because we didn't have a search warrant to assist us otherwise, we did so. But we lost tremendous opportunities to make progress, to seek justice, and to know the truth. Auspicious timing and strategy could have made a difference. When the might of the criminal justice system should have brought all it had to bear on this investigation, and didn't, we remained silent. We were trying to deliver a murder case with hands tied behind our backs. It was difficult, and our frustrations understandable. It was an assignment without a chance of success. Politics seemed to trump justice.

Even "outsiders" quickly assessed the situation, as the FBI politely noted early on: "the government isn't in charge of this investigation." As the nation watched, appropriately anticipating a fitting response to the murder of the most innocent of victims, I stood bothered as to what occurred behind the scenes. Those inside the case knew what was going on. Eighteen months gave us a unique perspective.

We learned to ignore the campaign of misinformation in which we were said to be bumbling along, or else just pursuing one or two suspects in ruthless vendetta. Much of what appeared in the press was orchestrated by particular sources wishing to discredit the Boulder Police Department. We watched the media spin, while we were prohibited from exercising First Amendment rights. As disappointment and frustration pervaded, detectives would remark to one another, "If it reaches a particular point, I'm walking away."

But we would always tolerate it "just one more time." Last year, when we discovered hidden cameras in the Ramsey house, only to realize the detectives had been unwittingly videotaped, this should have rocked the police department off its foundation. Instead, we allowed that too, to pass without challenge.

The detectives enthusiasm became simply resigned frustration, acquiescing to that which should never have been tolerated. In the media blitz, the pressure of the whole world watching, important decisions seemed to premised on "how it would play" publically.

Among at least a few of the detectives, "there's something wrong here" became a catch phrase. I witnessed others having to make decisions which impacted their lives and careers, watching the soul searching that occurred as the ultimate questions were pondered. As it goes, "evils that befall the world are not nearly so often caused by bad men, as they are by good men who are silent when an opinion must be voiced." Although several good men in the police department shouted loudly behind closed doors, the organization stood deafeningly silent at what continued to occur unchallenged.

Last Spring, you, too, seemed at a loss. I was taken aback when I was reminded of what happened to Commander Eller when he stuck his neck out. When reminded how politically powerful the DA was. When reminded of the hundreds of other cases the department had to file with the district attorney's office, and that this was but one case. And finally, when I was asked, "what do you want done? The system burned down?', it struck me dumb. But when you conceded that there were those inside the DA's office we had to simply accept as "defense witnesses," and when we were reduced to simply recording our objections for "documentation purposes" – I knew I was not going to participate in this much longer.

I believe the district attorney's office is thoroughly compromised. When we were told by one in the district attorney's office, months before we had ever completed our investigation, that this case "is not prosecutable," we shook our heads in disbelief. A lot could be forgiven, the lesser transgressions ignored, for the right things done. Instead, those in the district attorney's office encouraged us to allow them to "work their magic." (Which I never fully understood. Did that "magic" include sharing our case file information with the defense attorneys, dragging their feet in evidence collection, or believing that two decades of used-car-dealing-style-plea-bargaining was somehow going to solve this case?) Right and wrong is just that. Some of these issues were not shades of gray. Decisions should have been made as such. Whether a suspect is a penniless indigent with a public defender, or otherwise.

As contrasted by my experiences in Georgia, for example, where my warrant affidavits were met with a sense of support and obligation to the victim. Having worked with able prosecutors in other jurisdictions, having worked cases where justice was aggressively sought, I have familiarity with these prosecution professionals who hold a strong sense of justice. And then, from Georgia, the Great Lakes, the East Coast, the South, I would return to Boulder, to again be thoroughly demoralized.

We delayed and ignored, for far too long, that which was "right," in deference of maintaining this dysfunctional relationship with the district attorney's office. This wasn't a runaway train that couldn't be stopped. Some of us bit our tongues as the public was told of this "renewed cooperation" between the police department and district attorney's office —this at the very time the detectives and district attorney's office weren't even on speaking terms,, the same time you had to act as a liaison between the two agencies because the detectives couldn't tolerate it.. I was quite frankly surprised, as you remarked on this camaraderie, that there had not yet been a fistfight.

In Boulder, where the politics, policies, and pervasive thought has held for years, a criminal justice system designed to deal with such an event was not in place. Instead, we had an institution that when needed most, buckled. The system was paralyzed, as to this day one continues to get away with murder.

Will there be a real attempt at justice? I may be among the last to find out. The department assigned me some of the most sensitive and critical assignments in the Ramsey case, including search warrants and affidavits, the Atlanta projects, the interviews of the Ramseys, and many other sensitive assignments I won't mention I crisscrossed the country, conducting interviews and investigation, pursuing pedophiles and drifters, chasing and discarding leads. I submitted over 250 investigative reports for this case alone. I'd have been happy to assist the grand jury. But the detectives, who know this case better than anyone else, were told we would not be allowed as grand jury advisory witnesses, as is common place. If a grand.jury is convened, the records will be sealed, and we will not witness what goes on inside such a proceeding.

What part of the case gets presented, what doesn't?

District Attorney Hunters continued reference to a "runaway" grand jury is also puzzling. Is he afraid that he cannot control the outcome? Why would one not simply present evidence to jurors, and let the jury decide?

Perhaps the DA is hoping for a voluntary confession one day. What's needed, though, is an effective district attorney to conduct the inquiry, not a remorseful killer.

The district attorney's office should be the ethical and judicial compass for the community, ensuring justice is served – or at least, sought. Instead, our DA has become a spinning compass for the media. The perpetuating inference continues that justice is somehow just around the corner. I do not see that occurring, as the two year anniversary of this murder approaches.

It is my belief the district attorney's office has effectively crippled this case. The time for intervention is now. It is difficult to imagine a more compelling situation for the appointment of an entirely independent prosecution team to be introduced into this matter, who would oversee an attempt at righting the case.

Unmistakably and worst of all, we have a little girl named JonBenét. Six years old. Many good people, decent, innocent citizens, are forever bound by the murder of this child. There is a tremendous obligation to them. But an infinitely greater obligation to her, as she rests in a small cemetery far away from this anomaly of a place called Boulder.

A distant second stands the second tragedy – the failure of the system in Boulder. Ask the mistreated prosecution witnesses in this investigation, who cooperated for months, who now refuse to talk until a special prosecutor is established. As former detectives who have quietly tendered their shields in disheartenment. Ask all those innocent people personally affected by this case, who have had their lives upset because of the arbitrary label of "suspect" being attached. Ask the cops who cannot speak out because they still wear a badge. The list is long.

I know to speak out brings its own issues. But as you also know, there are those who are disheartened as I am, who are biting their tongues, searching their consciences. I what may occur – I may be portrayed as frustrated, disgruntled. Not so.

I have had an exemplary and decorated thirteen year career as a police officer and detective.

I didn't want to challenge the system. In no way do I wish to harm this case or subvert the long and arduous work that has been done. I only wish to speak up and ask for assistance in making a change. I want justice for a child who was killed in her home on Christmas night.

The case has defined many aspects of all our lives, and will continue to do so for all of our days. My colleagues put their hearts and souls into this case, and I will take some satisfaction that it was the detective team who showed tremendous efforts and loyalties to seeking justice for this victim. Many sacrifices were made. Families. Marriages. In the latter months of the investigation, I was diagnosed with a disease which will require a lifetime of medication. Although my health declined, I was resolved to see the case through to a satisfactory closure. I did that on June 1 – 2. And on June 22, I requested a leave of absence, without mention of what transpired in our department since Christmas 1996.

What I witnessed for two years of my life was so fundamentally flawed, it reduced me to tears. Everything the badge ever meant to me was so foundationally shaken, one should never have to sell one's soul as a prerequisite to wear it. On June 26, after leaving the investigation for the last time, and leaving the city of Boulder, I wept as I drove home, removing my detective shield and placing it on the seat beside me, later putting it in a desk drawer at home, knowing I could never put it back on.

There is some consolation that a greater justice awaits the person who committed these acts, independent of this system we call "justice." A great justice awaits. Of that, at least, we can be confident.

As a now infamous author, panicked in the night, once penned, "Use that good southern common sense of yours." I will do just that.

Originally from a small southern town where this would never have been tolerated, where respect for law and order and traditions were instilled in me, I will take that murderous author's out-of-context advice. And use my good southern common sense to put this case into perspective it necessitates – a precious child was murdered. There needs to be some consequence to that.

Regretfully, I tender this letter, and my police career, a calling which I loved. I do this because I cannot continue to sanction by my silence what has occurred in this case. It was never a fair playing field, the "game" was simply unacceptable anymore. And that's what makes this all so painful. The detectives never had a chance. If ever there was a case, and if ever there was a victim, who truly meant something to the detectives pursuing the truth, this is it. If not this case, what case? Until such time an independent prosecutor is appointed to oversee this case, I will not be a part of this. What went on is simply wrong.

I recalled a favorite passage recently, Atticus Finch speaking to his daughter: "Just remember that one thing does not abide my majority rule, Scout – it's your conscience."

At thirty six years old, I thought my life's passion as a police officer was carved in stone. I realize that although I may have to trade my badge for a carpenter's hammer, I will do so with a clear conscience. It is with a heavy heart that I offer my resignation from the Boulder Police Department, in protest of this continuing travesty.

Detective Steve Thomas #638
Detective Division
Boulder Police Department
August 6, 1998

LETTER FROM FLEET AND PRISCILLA WHITE
August 17, 1998

To the people of Colorado,

On August 12, 1998 Boulder District Attorney Alex Hunter announced that he would be presenting the JonBenét Ramsey murder case to a Boulder grand jury at the expense of the State of Colorado. Colorado grand jury law requires that both jurors and witnesses take an oath of secrecy regarding grand jury proceedings and testimony. In anticipation of receiving a subpoena to appear before that grand jury, we wish at this time to address matters concerning the investigation which we feel are of great importance to the people of Colorado and the Boulder community.

After JonBenét Ramsey was killed in Boulder nearly twenty months ago, her parents, John and Patsy Ramsey, immediately hired prominent Democratic criminal defense attorneys with the law firm of Haddon, Morgan and Foreman. This firm and its partners have close professional, political and personal ties to prosecutors, the Denver and Boulder legal and judicial communities, state legislators, and high-ranking members of Colorado government, including Governor Roy Romer. The investigation of her death has since been characterized by confusion and delays. The district attorney and Ramsey defense attorneys started early in the investigation to condition the public to believe that these delays and the lack of a prosecution have resulted almost entirely from initial police bungling of the case and the non-cooperation of witnesses. This has continued to this day. Advising the district attorney since the early days of the investigation have been Denver metropolitan district attorneys Bob Grant (Adams Count), Bill Ritter (Denver County), Jim Peters (18th Judicial District), and Dave Thomas (1st Judicial District).

Recently, Boulder police detective Steve Thomas, an investigator on the JonBenét Ramsey murder case, left the department in disgust. In his August 6 letter of resignation, he publically accused the district attorney of obstructing the police investigation and allowing politics to "trump" justice. He asked that a special prosecutor be brought in to handle the case.

We knew JonBenét and her parents very well and have been closely involved in the investigation as witnesses. During the past year, we have also come to know and respect Mr. Thomas and were saddened and discouraged by his departure from the investigation. We share Mr. Thomas' view regarding the district attorney and his contention that overwhelming pressure brought to bear on the district attorney and police leadership from various quarters has thwarted the investigation and delayed justice in the case. While it is unlikely that the district attorney has been corrupted by Ramsey defense attorneys, it certain that the district attorney and his prosecutors have been greatly influenced by their metro area district attorney advisers and by defense attorneys' chummy persuasiveness and threats of reprisals for anyone daring to jeopardize the civil rights of their victim clients. Indeed, the district attorney and the Ramsey attorneys have simultaneously rebuked the police for "focusing" their investigation on the Ramseys when in fact police were simply following evidence. During the course of the investigation, the district attorney has used inexplicable methods including the recruitment of magazine writers and tabloids to leak information concerning the case and to needle witnesses, "suspects", and police detectives. He has provided evidence to Ramsey defense attorneys at their request but denied reasonable requests by witnesses for their own statements to police. He has thoroughly alienated police detectives and key witnesses whose cooperation is vital to the investigation and prosecution. His public statements regarding the investigation have been erratic, evasive, and misleading. They have also been profoundly damaging to the case. Understandably, public confidence in the district attorney's handling of the investigation was low even before Mr. Thomas' letter.

Notwithstanding what the public has been led to believe, Boulder police leadership and detectives have been under the effective control of the district attorney and his advisors since the early days of the investigation. In December, 1997, we met with Governor Romer to request that the state intervene and appoint an independent special prosecutor *to take over the investigation and prosecution of the case. Citing the growing conflict between police and prosecutors and the delay of any progress in the investigation, we expressed our view that Boulder authorities were incapable of seeking justice. We also pointed out specific circumstances that we felt could inhibit or restrict Governor Romer's willingness to intervene. In early January, 1998, we were advised that he had decided against intervention on the advice of Boulder Police Chief Tom Koby. Chief Koby, who has since left the department, had told Governor Romer that the investigation was incomplete and therefore had not been given to the district attorney for prosecution. In short; there had been no failure to prosecute and thus no basis for the state's intervention. Upon learning of his decision, we wrote a letter published January 16, 1998, in the Boulder Daily Camera expressing our views and requesting Governor Romer reconsider his decision. Recently, Governor Romer publically stated that he did not recall the letter. We hope that this letter will make a stronger impression.*

Since our meeting with Governor Romer eight months ago, the public has been shown the forced reconciliation of demoralized police detectives with the district attorney and his prosecutors and a sequence of odd and highly publicized milestones in the case. In March, 1998, police Chief Koby and lead investigator Mark Beckner (later to be appointed police chief), made an unusual public appeal to the district attorney for a grand jury investigation on the pro bono advice of three prominent Denver attorneys. In response, the district attorney requested a complete presentation by police of evidence. The presentation occurred over two days in early June, 1998, and was witnessed by prosecutors, representatives of the State Attorney General's office, prominent forensic scientists, and advisors of the district attorney and the police department. The public was then told that the investigation had been finally transferred to the district attorney from the police department and that the district attorney would now require some indeterminate length of time to review the case prior to making a decision concerning the police request for a grand jury investigation. Upon leaving the presentation, both Alex Hunter and Mark Beckner made inappropriate but tantalizing comments designed to give the public hope that the case may yet be "solved". They warned, however, that there was still a lot of work to do and that additional evidence was needed. Then, in late June, 1998, the public was once again brought in on a major development in the case. The Ramseys were interviewed by the representatives of the district attorney in a carefully orchestrated demonstration of their willingness to cooperate in the investigation now that biased and incompetent police detectives were no longer involved.

Most developments in the case brought to the public's attention through 1997 should be regarded as well-publicized but clumsy attempts by the district attorney and police leadership to look busy, follow long "task lists," and clean up investigative files while the district attorney killed time and spread-out responsibility for the case. One the other hand, "advances" in the case since the early this year have been carefully planned to condition the public for a grand jury investigation. The district attorney's office past indecision and the need for the police to ask him for a grand jury investigation were deliberate attempts to mislead the public. If based on nothing other than the district attorney's repeated public statements and leaks characterizing the case as "not prosecutable," there can be little doubt, that absent a confession, the people running the investigation long ago had decided against filing charges in the case. Instead, they manipulated public opinion to favor the use of the grand jury. There is compelling evidence, however, that their motivation for presenting the case to the a grand jury has little or nothing to do with obtaining new evidence, grilling 'reluctant" witnesses, or returning an indictment and everything to do with sealing away the facts, circumstances and evidence gathered in the investigation in a grand jury transcript. It is our firm belief that the district attorney and others intend to use the grand jury and its secrecy in an attempt to protect their careers and also serve the conflicting interests of powerful, influential, and threatening people who something to hide or protect or who simply don't want to be publically linked to a dreadful murder investigation. Also weighing on the district attorney has been the matter of preserving and protecting the now "cooperative" and forthcoming Ramsey's rights as victims.

In direct response to Mt. Thomas's recent letter, Governor Romer met on August 12, 1998, with district attorneys Grant, Ritter, Peters, and Thomas. Later that day, Governor Romer announced at a press conference that Hunter had told him that the case was "on track for a grand jury." Romer said that "it would be improper to appoint a special prosecutor now" but that to improve public confidence in the case he would make available to Hunter additional prosecutorial expertise. Shortly after the press conference, Hunter's office announced that the case would be presented to a grand jury in "order to gain additional evidence in the case." On August 13, 1998, the Rocky Mountain News offered an editorial entitled "Calling in the Calvary" in which the editor generally supported Governor Romer's action but insightfully asked the obvious question: Why has it taken so long for Hunter's office to present the case to a grand jury? The editorial read:

"But if the Ramsey case is on track for a grand jury," as Romer insists, it seems to have been sitting on a siding for quite a long time awaiting clearance to proceed. This is all the more true given the fact the Ritter, Grant, Thomas, and Peters obviously believe that the grand jury must be used as an investigative tool in the Ramsey case, and not merely to reach a predetermined prosecutorial goal. If that is the case, why wasn't a grand jury used months ago? Indeed, why wasn't it used more than a year ago?"

Following Sid Wells murder in Boulder in August, 1983, a grand jury investigating the high-profile case met off- and – on for fifteen months without returning an indictment. Quoted in January 29, 1984, Denver Post, Boulder Assistant District Attorney Bill Wise revealed that the case had been originally referred to the grand jury "because of its power to further investigate the case. The district attorney didn't have subpoena power and we needed that tool." Hunter had waited less than three months before presenting the Wells murder case to a grand jury. Three months after the death of JonBenét Ramsey, police were still trying to interview John and Patsy Ramsey and obtain other evidence critical to the case.

There is a relatively simple but compelling answer to the question raised by the Rocky Mountain News editorial. Since very early in the case, there has been at least a tacit understanding in the district attorney, police leadership, those persons advising these agencies, and Ramsey defense attorneys that the case would be presented to a grand jury but not until the statutory Boulder grand jury was convened in April, 1998. This delay was deemed necessary by some or all of these parties in order to take advantage of a new statute (16-5-205.5, C.R.S.) concerning grand jury reporting procedures which was the result of legislation promoted by the Colorado District Attorney's Council and passed by the legislature in early March, 1997. By law, however, this change in procedure would only apply to reports issued by grand juries convened after October 1, 1997. In order to take advantage of the new statute, a Boulder grand jury would have to until April, 1998, the next convening of the statutory Boulder grand jury subsequent to October 1, 1997. In order to accomplish this, it was necessary for these people to stall and cynically rely on the public's relative ignorance of the statute and the purpose and general nature of grand juries. The district attorney and police leadership worked hard to create the fiction that the police investigation was not "complete" and therefore not ready to be transferred to the district attorney. As long as the district attorney didn't have the case it be difficult to fault him for not prosecuting or presenting the case to a grand jury. It was this fiction that was used by the district attorney to deflect mounting criticism including that contained in our letter in January, 1998. It also served as the basis for a Boulder court to throw out a suit brought against the district attorney by New York attorney Darnay Hoffman who had accused the district attorney of "constructively abandoning the case." The district attorney's publically expressed indecision in late 1997 regarding a grand jury investigation gave way to his progressively greater "leaning" toward such a decision as the date for convening the Boulder grand jury drew near.

House Bill 97-1009 was drafted by the Colorado District Attorney's Council in late 1996 and was introduced in the Colorado House of Representatives on January 8, 1997, two weeks after JonBenét was killed. HB 97-1009 was sponsored by Representative Bill Kaufman, a Republican, and Senator Ed Perlmutter, a Democrat.

The impetus for the bill was the desire of the Council to effect legislation changing an existing statute (16-5-204 (4), C.R.S.) regarding the issuance of grand jury reports in those cases where there is not an indictment. The matter was discussed by the district attorneys and legislators at a conference in the summer of 1996. The existing statute allowed the issuance of reports but was argued to be confusing and overly restrictive. As a result, grand jury reports were nonexistent. In a January 19, 1997 editorial supporting passage of the bill, the Denver Post pointed to the inconclusive grand jury investigations concerning DIA and police conduct in the high profile Ocrant case in Arapahoe County. Also mentioned was the recent Truax officer-involved shooting case in which Denver DA Bill Ritter chose not use a grand jury to investigate possible police officer misconduct because of his concern that the grand jury might not be able to report its findings to the public. Citing these cases, the Post"…urged that in the balance between the public's right to information and the statutory demand for grand jury secrecy, public disclosure should carry more weight than it does now." The Post editorial went on to say:

"The proposed law would instruct judges to determine whether the report should be released and allow for withholding any parts necessary to protect witnesses. It would also give witnesses an opportunity to see reports and file opposing motions if they object to their release."

Such reports could go a long way toward dispelling doubts like those that still linger over the DIA and Truax investigations, and by providing all witnesses with safeguards against disclosure that might damage or embarrass them, still preserve the confidentiality that is both the armor and the engine of the grand jury process.

The original draft of the bill presented to the House Judiciary Committee by Representative Kaufman at a hearing on January 21, 1997, long after the Ramsey case had exploded into the national news story amid growing suspicions of police mishandling of the case. Speaking in favor of the bill before the committee were district attorneys Ritter, Thomas, and Grant. All of these district attorneys, along with Jim Peters, would be named publically as advisers to Alex Hunter on the Ramsey case a few weeks later on February 14, 1997. It is clear from the draft bill and from their comments at this hearing that they intended reporting by grand juries to be on matters generally limited to allegations of non-criminal misconduct by public employees, official, and agencies but only when such information regarding those allegations was in the public interest. At the hearing, Mr. Ritter stated:

"...there are other matters where we bring...an issue to the grand jury for investigation and it grows legs and we find ourselves investigating the conduct of government officers, the conduct of public employees, the conduct of government programs where, because tax dollars are involved, the public does have a right to know something about the operation even if they fall short of the conduct being criminal and that, I think, is the real meaning behind a bill like this." Also speaking in favor of the bill were John Daily, Head of the Criminal Enforcement Unit of the Attorney General's office and Kim Morss of the Colorado Judicial Department appearing at the request of Chief Justice of the Colorado Supreme Court. Also speaking in favor of the bill was Marge Easton of the Colorado Press Association.

On March 5, 1997, Senator Perlmutter presented the bill to the Senate Judiciary Committee. Appearing once again to speak in favor of the bill were Bill Ritter, March Easton, and John Daily. Also speaking for the bill were Ray Slaughter and Stu Van Meveren of the Colorado District Attorneys' Council.

The final bill was passed on March 21, 1997. Included in the bill were specific criteria to be used by grand juries and prosecutors in determining what constitutes the "public interest" for the purpose of a grand jury report:

"(5) Release of a grand jury report pursuant to this section may be deemed to be in the public interest only if the report addresses one or more of the following:

Allegations of the misuse or misapplication of public funds;

Allegations of abuse of authority by a public servant, as defined in Section 18-1-903 (3)(o), C.R.S., or a peace officer, as defined in Section 18-1-901(3)(1) C.R.S.

Allegations of misfeasance or malfeasance with regard to govern-mental function, as defined in Section 18-1-901(3)(j), C.R.S.

Allegations of commission of a class 1, class 2, or class 3 felony.

The original intent of the Colorado District Attorney Council draft and that of Representative Kaufman was to make it easier for grand juries to issue reports in cases where there is not an indictment returned but where, in the public interest, the grand jury wishes to address allegations of misconduct by public employees falling short of criminal conduct. The final bill made it possible for a grand jury to address allegations of 1st and 2nd degree murder and the two classes of child abuse resulting in death. The new statute would enable a Boulder grand jury investigating the death of JonBenét to publically exonerate someone who has been alleged to have committed one of the crimes but only in the event an indictment was not returned. The bill was signed into law by Governor Romer on April 8, 1997. We strongly urge those wishing to investigate the intentions and motives of the Colorado District Attorneys Council, legislators, and those speaking on behalf of the bill to review the Senate and House Journals and listen to the tapes of the House and Senate Judiciary Hearings and floor debates on file at the Colorado State archives, 1313 Sherman Street, Room B20, Denver.

During the Senate Judiciary Hearing on March 5, 1997, and after the bill had been amended to include the criteria defining the public interest, Senator Perlmutter stated that he had "…contacted several defense attorneys I know in Denver and they were all supportive of the it (the bill). They thought it was a good idea." According to records at the Secretary of State's Office, Senator Perlmutter received a 1994 campaign contribution from Hal Haddon, defense attorney for John Ramsey. The Haddon firm is well known for its expertise in grand jury practice. Norman Mueller, a partner of the firm, once wrote in the April, 1998 issue of The Colorado Lawyer, "…defense counsel must creatively and vigorously scrutinize the grand jury process at the earliest possible stage of the case."

The May 6, 1998 issue of the Colorado Journal, a publication for the legal community, presented an article flattering to Alex Hunter entitled *"D.A. Winks At This One — With or Without a Grand Jury Indictment Boulder's Prosecutor Will Still Shine."* The article was written around comments received from Senator Perlmutter and district attorney Bill Ritter. It reads:

"If Hunter does take the matter to the grand jury and that panel manages to wrestle the evidence it needs to hand down an actual indictment, Hunter will appear the hero for going that route.

But if they fail to do so, Hunter could still come out smelling like a rose with the help of a little-known state law that went into effect last fall: That grand jury reports may be released to the public if no indictment results from its probe.

That way, a prosecutor facing pressure to file charges can say, "See even the grand jury couldn't find anything." Said Senator Ed Perlmutter, D-Golden, who co-sponsored the law in the 1997 Colorado Legislature.

The law, which only applies to Class 1, 2, and 3 felony cases, was intended to help ease the public's mind in certain investigations where a prosecutor fails to file charges, despite pressure from the police to do so as in the JonBenét case, he said."

In the article Senator Perlmutter indicated that he sponsored the bill because he "didn't want grand juries to be abused, especially in high-profile cases as this one (the Ramsey case)."

For his part, Mr. Ritter said:

"I don't think Alex Hunter would go to the grand jury for political cover, that's just not how Alex Hunter operates," said Denver District Attorney Bill Ritter.

"The reason you go to a grand jury is because, as DA you do not have the ability in the State of Colorado to compel testimony or compel the production of documents."

But then the article speculates:

"But no matter what the grand jury decides, its probe could help vindicate the impugned reputations of many members of the Boulder police and district attorney's office."

The article was misleading in that it stated that the new grand jury statute designed by Mr. Ritter and Senator Perlmutter to protect and *exonerate people and "vindicate" the reputations of public servants was "effective" and therefore available for use by a Boulder grand jury on October 1, 1997. It also inaccurately described what allegations the statute deemed of public interest.*

For the purpose of assisting them in the Ramsey investigation, the Boulder Police Department in July 1997 accepted the pro bono legal services of Daniel S. Hoffman with the firm of McKenna & Cueno, Robert N. Miller with the firm of LeBoeuf, Lamb, Green, and MacRae, and Richard N. Baer with the firm of Sherman & Howard. All are prominent Denver attorneys. Responding to our public information request, the Boulder city attorney's office supplied us with copies of the final agreement between the city and these attorneys dated July 30, 1997, and an earlier draft of that agreement dated July 28, 1997. In the draft, these attorneys jointly made the following disclosures to the city: "As we indicated to you, our respective firms have or had certain relationships that we feel obligated to disclose to you. Specifically:

Sherman & Howard L.L.C. ("S. & H.") represents Lockheed Martin in various matters. Lockheed Martin currently owns Access Graphics, the company that employs the father of the deceased. In addition, in 1994, S. & H. represented Access Graphics in a lawsuit brought by a terminated employee...

Mr. Hoffman is outside counsel for Lockheed Martin in a number of litigations, one of which is currently pending. It is reasonable to assume that during our representation of you, Mr. Hoffman may be retained by Lockheed Martin. Additionally, Mr. Haddon represents Mr. Hoffman personally, in a case against Mr. Hoffman, his former law firm, and a number of Mr. Hoffman's former partners at the firm.

Robert Miller is currently co-counsel with Mr. Haddon on litigation in which they obtained a significant verdict for their client and which will proceed on appeal.

John Ramsey was the president and chief executive officer of Access Graphics, a subsidiary of Lockheed Martin Corporation. In the fall of 1997 Access Graphics was sold by Lockheed Martin to GE Capital in a complicated transaction reported in the news media to be valued at $2.8 billion. The value attributed to Access Graphics was likely in excess of $200 million. Prior to the sale, John Ramsey left Access Graphics under adverse circumstances after attempting to purchase Access Graphics from Lockheed Martin. Mr. Hoffman was identified in the April 18, 1997 issue of the Colorado Journal to be the "lead attorney" for Lockheed Martin in an age discrimination case which days before had resulted in a $7.6 million settlement. The "Mr. Haddon" referred to in the disclosures is Harold Haddon, the criminal defense attorney currently representing John Ramsey. The final agreement that was executed by the city and these attorneys did not contain these disclosures. According to Mr. Baer, they were deleted at the request of the city attorney. The city attorney has recently indicated to us that he has no knowledge of the role these attorneys have played in the investigation.

On March 10, 1998, The Boulder Daily Camera reported that "DA hints Ramsey case headed for grand jury." Two days later, the Boulder police made their request for a grand jury on the advice of these attorneys and transferred the case to the district attorney.

On April 22, 1998, the Boulder grand jury was convened.

It is certain that Boulder County District Attorney Alex Hunter, the metro area district attorneys advising Mr. Hunter; the current leadership of the Boulder Police Department, the three attorneys advising the Boulder Police Department, and Ramsey defense attorneys have known since HB 97-1009 was signed by Governor Romer on April 8, 1997, that to take advantage of the new statute, it would be necessary to delay a grand jury investigation of the Ramsey case until April, 1998. In retrospect, it is clear that the case was delayed for that purpose. It is hard to imagine that Governor Romer and members of the office of the Attorney General and the Colorado Judiciary have not also long known this.

The Boulder County District Attorney and members of his office have delayed the investigation of the death of JonBenét Ramsey in order to take of a statute which will, if an indictment is not returned, enable him to persuade a grand jury to issue a report telling the public that the *case was delayed and that an indictment was not returned as a result of police misconduct and the noncooperation of witnesses. It will also enable him to publically exonerate anyone alleged to have murdered JonBenét Ramsey. If he wishes such a report to be made, and of course he does since it would contain precisely what he has been saying throughout the investigation, he must first cause the grand jury not to return an indictment.*

This, then, is how politics will have been allowed, finally, to trump justice.

Delaying the case in this manner simply to serve the selfish interests of a relatively small number of public servants and wealthy and powerful people has destroyed the case's infrastructure which consists of the confidence and trust of witnesses and the public in the criminal justice system and the hard work done in good faith by police detectives. That he has allowed this destruction is compelling evidence that Alex Hunter and those advising him have no intention of seeking an indictment from a grand jury. By their actions, these people have demonstrated cynical and callous disregard for the people of Colorado, the criminal justice system, and the well-being and safety of the Boulder community and its citizens.

What distinguishes the investigation of JonBenét's death from all others, and what has so seriously handicapped the investigation, is the extraordinary number of people that it has affected and influenced. The people of Colorado wish to see justice for JonBenét. They must not accept the "conclusion" to the case now being offered by the Boulder County District Attorney and Governor Romer. We will not.

After further assessing public opinion and reviewing contents of this letter and that of Mr. Thomas, we hope that it will occur to Governor Romer that evidence in this case must be reviewed by those who have no interest seeking anything other than justice for JonBenét. Any further involvement of the Boulder County District Attorney, his prosecutors, or anyone else responsible for the delay of the case is totally unacceptable. The people of Colorado must demand that Governor Romer resist the advice of interest parties, including the district attorneys advising Alex

Hunter, and immediately the Attorney General to take over the investigation and any future prosecution. He must then excuse himself from any further involvement. He is simply too close to people whose lives and careers may hinge on what becomes of the case.

Taking this action will be difficult for both Governor Romer and Attorney General Gale Norton who are serving the last months of their terms and are term limited from seeking re-election. They must nevertheless set politics and personal considerations aside and conscientiously deal with this problem now. It is unacceptable for them to further erode public confidence by passing that responsibility to their successors.

The people of Colorado are entitled to be frustrated and angry with those public officials and other persons who have brought this case to its current status. We must be mindful, however, of the first cause of the investigation's failure – the refusal of John and Patsy Ramsey to cooperate fully and genuinely with those officially charged with the responsibility of investigating the death of their daughter, JonBenét.

Fleet White, Jr. and Priscilla Brown White
August 17, 1998

Letter of Resignation by D.A. Investigator Lou Smit
September 28, 1998

Dear Alex,

It is with great reluctance and regret that I submit this letter of resignation. Even though I want to continue to participate in the official investigation and assist in finding the killer of JonBenét, I find that I cannot in good conscience be a part of the persecution of innocent people. It would be highly improper and unethical for me to stay when I so strongly believe this.

It has been almost 19 months since we talked that day in your office and you asked me to assist you in this investigation. It has turned out to be more of a challenge than either of us anticipated. When we first met I told you that my style of approaching an investigation is from the concept of not working a particular theory, but working the case. Detectives collect and record information from many sources, analyze it, couple that with their experience and training and let "the case" tell them where to go. This process may take days, weeks, or years, depending on the direction the case tells you to go. Sometimes you must investigate "many paths" in order to find the killer. It is not a political speed contest where expediency should outweigh justice, where "resolving" the case is solving the case.

Alex, even though I have been unable to actively investigate, I have been in a position to collect, record and analyze every piece of information given to your office in the course of this investigation. I believe that I know this case better than anyone does. I know what has been investigated and what hasn't, what evidence exists and what doesn't, what information has been leaked and what hasn't. I am a detective with a proven record of successful investigations. I have looked at the murder of JonBenét Ramsey through the eyes of age and experience and a thorough knowledge of the case.

At this point in the investigation, "the case" tells me that John and Patsy Ramsey did not kill their daughter, that a very dangerous killer is still out there and no one is actively looking for him. There are still many areas of investigation which must be explored before life and death decisions are made.

When I was hired I had no agenda one way or the other, my allegiance was to the case, not the Police Department nor John and Patsy Ramsey. My agenda has not changed. I only desire to be able to investigate the case and find the killer of JonBenét and will to do so as long as I am able. The chances of catching him working from the "outside looking in" are slim, but I have a great "Partner" who I'm sure will lead the way. There is no doubt that I will be facing a great deal of opposition and ridicule in the future, because I intend to stand with this family and somehow help them through this and find the killer of their daughter. Perhaps others who believe this will also help.

The Boulder Police Department has many fined and dedicated men and women who also want justice for JonBenét. They are just going in the wrong direction and have been since day one of the investigation. Instead of letting the case tell them where to go, they have elected to follow a theory and let their theory direct them rather that allowing the evidence to direct them. The case tells me there is substantial, credible, evidence of an intruder and lack of evidence that the parents are involved. If this is true, they too are tragic victims whose misery has been compounded by a misdirected and flawed investigation, unsubstantiated leaks, rumors and accusations.

I have worked in this profession for the past 32 years and have always been loyal to it, the men and women in it, and what it represents, because I believed that justice has always prevailed. In this case, however, I believe that justice is not being served, that innocent people are being targeted and could be charged with a murder they did not commit.

The law enforcement Code of Ethics states it very well. My fundamental duty is to "serve mankind; to safeguard lives and property; to protect the innocent against deception, the weak against oppression and intimidation, the peaceful against violence and disorder. To respect the constitutional rights of all men to liberty, equality and justice." This applies not only to JonBenét but to her mother and father as well.

I want to thank you and the others in the office for the wonderful support and treatment I have received. You have a great D.A.'s Office and the men and women who work with you are some of the most honest and dedicated people I have ever met. My life has been enriched because of this memorable time together. I have especially enjoyed working closely with Peter Hoffstrom and Trip Demuth, who also have dedicated so much of their lives to this case. I have never met two more fair, honest and dedicated defenders of our system.

Alex, you are in a difficult position. The media and peer pressure are incredible. You are inundated with conflicting facts and information, and "expert" opinions. And now you have an old detective telling you that the Ramseys did not do it and to wait and investigate this case more thoroughly before a very tragic mistake would be made. What a double travesty it could be; an innocent person indicted, and a vicious killer on the loose to prey on another innocent child and no one to stop him.

History will be the judge as to how we conducted ourselves and we how we handled our responsibilities.

Shoes, shoes, the victim's shoes, who will stand in the victim's shoes?

Good luck to you and your fine office and may God bless you in the awesome decisions you must soon make.

Sincerely,
Detective Lou Smit
September 28, 1998

Alex Hunter's Affidavit Clearing Burke Ramsey, completed at the request of L. Lin Wood.

L. LIN WOOD

ATTORNEY AT LAW

SUITE 2140, THE EQUITABLE BUILDING,
100 PEACHTREE STREET,
ATLANTA, GA, USA, 30303

PHONE: 404 522 1713
FAX: 404 522 1716

Confidential Facsimile Transmission

To: **Bill Wise**   From: L. Lin Wood

Fax: 303-441-1715
                              Pages Including Cover: 4

Date: October 11, 2000

Re: *Affidavit of Alexander M. Hunter*

Comments:

Bill:

Here is a revised Affidavit for review and consideration by you and Alex. If the Affidavit meets with Alex's approval and your approval, I would ask that Alex execute six (6) notorized originals of the Affidavit and return them to me via FedEx for Monday delivery. Please bill the FedEx delivery to my account. L. Lin Wood, P.C., 100 Peachtree Street, Suite 2140, Atlanta, Georgia 30303, Account Number   Of course, please feel free to call me if you have any questions. While there are no guarantees, hopefully this Affidavit will minimize or negate any future appearances by Alex or a representative of the D.A.'s office in the Burke Ramsey litigation. On behalf of Burke, I thank you for your time and consideration of this matter.

                              Lin Wood

AFFIDAVIT OF ALEXANDER M. HUNTER

STATE OF COLORADO,

COUNTY OF BOULDER.

Personally appeared before the undersigned officer duly authorized by law to administer oaths, ALEXANDER M. HUNTER, who being first duly sworn, deposes and says as follows:

1.

My name is Alexander M Hunter. I am over twenty-one (21) years of age and I am competent to make and give this Affidavit, and do so from personal knowledge.

2.

I am an attorney duly licensed in the State of Colorado. Since January 9, 1973, I have been the elected District Attorney for the Twentieth Judicial District, County of Boulder, State of Colorado.

3.

On or about December 26, 1996, JonBenét Ramsey, a six (6) year old minor child, was murdered in her home in Boulder, Colorado.

4.

Since the date of her death, I have been continuously involved in the investigation of JonBenét Ramsey's homicide.

5.

As part of the investigation into the murder of JonBenét Ramsey, questions about any possible involvement by her brother, Burke Ramsey, who was nine (9) years of age at the time of his sister's murder and who was one of the individuals present in the house at the time of her murder, were raised and investigated as part of standard investigative practices and procedures.

6.

All questions related to Burke Ramsey's possible involvement in the murder of JonBenét Ramsey were resolved to the satisfaction of the investigators and Burke Ramsey has never been viewed by investigators as a suspect in connection with the murder of his sister. No evidence has ever been developed in the investigation to justify elevating Burke Ramsey's status from that of witness to suspect.

7.

In May of 1999, I was made aware that tabloid newspapers had indicated that Burke Ramsey was a suspect in the murder of JonBenét Ramsey or was believed to be her killer. As a result of these articles, I was contacted by media representatives and I instructed my office to release a press statement which publicly and officially stated that Burke Ramsey was not a suspect in connection with the murder of his sister and that stated in part, "...almost a year ago (Boulder) Police Chief Mark Beckner stated during a news conference that Burke (Ramsey) was not a suspect and that we are not looking at him as a possible suspect. To this day Burke Ramsey is not a suspect." The information contained in the May 1999 press statement was true and correct.

OK

8.

From December 26, 1996 to the present date, I have never engaged in plea bargain negotiations, talks or discussions with anyone in connection with the investigation into the

-2-

murder of JonBenét Ramsey based in whole or in part on the premise that Burke Ramsey killed his sister. From December 26, 1996 to the present date, no member of my office has ever engaged in plea bargain negotiations, talks or discussions with anyone in connection with the investigation into the murder of JonBenét Ramsey based in whole or in part on the premise that Burke Ramsey killed his sister.

9.

From December 26, 1996 to the date of this Affidavit, Burke Ramsey has not been, and is not at present, a suspect in the investigation into the murder of his sister, JonBenét Ramsey.

9
10.

I am aware that this Affidavit may be used by counsel for Burke Ramsey in connection with libel litigation brought on his behalf in various jurisdictions.

FURTHER AFFIANT SAYETH NOT.

This 12th day of October, 2000.

ALEXANDER M. HUNTER
_____

Sworn to and subscribed before me
this 12th day of October, 2000.

_____
Notary Public
My commission expires _____

Redacted version of D.A. Mary Lacy's letter sent to author in January 2007

January 25, 2007

Chief James Kolar
Telluride Police Department
P.O. Box 372
Telluride, CO 81435

Dear Chief Kolar:

I have reviewed your presentation on the JonBenet Ramsey Murder Investigation. It has also been reviewed by First Assistant District Attorney Peter Maguire, Assistant District Attorney Bill Nagel and Chief Investigator Tom Bennett. We have spent substantial time examining your Investigative Report, Summary Report and PowerPoint Presentation. We have independently arrived at the same conclusions.

I hired you as my Chief Investigator in July 2005. At that time, we discussed your role regarding the Ramsey case. I was clear in my direction to you that we would follow-up leads from law enforcement and other credible sources that had indicia of reliability. That decision was based upon recent history that involved Chief Investigator Bennett having to spend an inordinate amount of time responding to leads that were marginal at best. We made a deliberate decision to put our investigatory priorities on recent cases. You obviously disregarded my direction. You proceeded without my approval and without consulting with me. You were clearly acting outside of your defined role.

When you departed from the employment of the Boulder District Attorney's Office in March of 2006, your role as an Investigator with this office terminated. The Ramsey case is still under my control. You have continued to proceed outside the limits of your jurisdiction. It appears that you have utilized confidential information that should legally have remained under the control of my office. This is quite concerning to me and to my management staff who placed their trust in your professionalism.

I am going to address your presentation although it galls me to respond to what I consider to be an abuse of authority. Chief Investigator Tom Bennett, First Assistant District Attorney Peter Maguire, Assistant Attorney Bill Nagel and myself are in agreement, reached independently, as to the value of your theory. We are in agreement that the first portion of your presentation is based on the Boulder Police Department's Case Summary and facts that have been previously documented and debated. There is nothing new in terms of evidence in this presentation. The last quarter of your PowerPoint Presentation which is the final seventy plus frames are not based on facts supported by evidence. You theory is based upon conjecture, which at times approaches pure flights of fantasy. Your conclusions are based upon suppositions and inferences with absolutely no support in evidence or in the record. Your presentation lacks the fundamental substantive factual basis from which reasonable minds cannot differ.

I must repeat, there is no substantive basis to your theory. It is almost pure speculation as to what could have happened rather than evidence as to what did happen.

You requested in your communication of January 5th that your presentation be shared with certain entities in Law Enforcement. It will not be shared with them. We will not be part of this mockery you are trying to market. We take our jobs and our role with regard to this case seriously. When and if we have a serious suspect based upon substantial evidence, we will work closely with all appropriate agencies. This is not that time.

I am requesting that you return forthwith any and all information you obtained while under the employment of the Boulder District Attorney's Office as it applies to the Ramsey investigation. You were not granted permission to remove any such information from this office. This includes all reports, documents, photographs, CD's or other materials and anything prepared using such documents.

Finally, I need to remind you that as of the date of your resignation from the Boulder District Attorney's Office, you are no longer protected by any immunity from civil litigation based on your conduct as an investigator. I recommend that you discuss your unauthorized activities with the City of Telluride's Risk Management Office to determine what if any liability you current employer might have as a result of your activities.

Mary T. Lacy
District Attorney
Twentieth Judicial District

cc: Attorney General John Suthers
     Deputy Attorney General Jeanne Smith

End Notes:

[1] The concept of "staging" is discussed at length in Chapter Twenty-Seven.

[2] *Boulder Daily Camera* staff writer Christopher Anderson reports that John Ramsey identified Fleet White as the person who "insisted" that the family do an interview with CNN during Ramsey's sworn deposition taken on October 20, 1998 in Stephen Miles' libel and slander law suit brought against Ramsey and the *National Enquirer.*

[3] *Rocky Mountain News* reporter Charlie Brennan quotes Marc Klaas from an AM Live program broadcast on WPVI, January 7, 1997.

[4] *The Cases That Haunt Us* John Douglas & Mark Olshaker. Scribner 2000. ISBN 0-684-84600-4. Page 295

[5] Ibid

[6] Over the course of the first 10 years of the murder investigation, the Ramsey family would interview with the media, and prepare a multitude of press releases and advertisements as they attempted to garner leads in the death of their daughter.

[7] A more detailed discussion of the kernel of glass and window frame is found in Chapter Twenty-one, "Revisiting Point of Entry".

[8] *Tribune* article written by Amanda Beeler, April 19, 1999

[9] Ibid

[10] Refer to Appendix for a copy of Foster's letter.

[11] Detective Steve Thomas's explanation of Professor Fosters presentation on the ransom note. *JonBenét: Inside the Ramsey Murder Investigation*. St. Martin's Press 2000. ISBN 0-312-25326-5

[12] The details of Archuleta's experiences are derived from an author interview conducted with her in December 2005.

[13] Details of this incident were personally related to the author by then-Detective Sergeant Tom Wickman, and is referenced in Steve Thomas' book, *JonBenét: Inside the Ramsey Murder Investigation*, St. Martin's Press , April 2000 ISBN 0-31225326-5

[14] Gary Oliva was a 38-year old convicted child sex offender from Oregon who lived in Boulder at the time of this crime

[15] Refer to the FBI's website for additional information on the development and use of DNA profiles in criminal and missing person investigations

[16] *Vanity Fair* "Missing Innocence: The JonBenét Ramsey Case" October 1997, by Ann Bardach

[17] Ibid

[18] People vs. James Thompson 97CR1233

[19] *Boulder Daily Camera* June 3, 1998

[20] See appendix for the full content of Steve Thomas' letter of resignation.

[21] See appendix for the full content of Fleet and Priscilla White's letter.

[22] See appendix for the full content of Lou Smit's letter of resignation

[23] BPD supplemental report and attachment completed by Steve Thomas, January 6, 1998

[24] BPD supplemental report and attachment. Steve Thomas, May 04, 1998

[25] Refer to the appendix for the full text of the Fleet and Priscilla White letter.

[26] *Denver Post,* Karen Auge, September 16, 1998

[27] Ibid

[28] *Rocky Mountain News,* "Grand Jurors Inspect Ramsey House." October 30, 1998

[29] Ibid

[30] *The Daily Camera,* Christopher Anderson. December 2, 1998

[31] *Rocky Mountain News,* Kevin McCullen. March 15, 2000

[32] Ibid

[33] Ibid

[34] *Rocky Mountain News,* Charlie Brennan, September 22, 1999

[35] Ibid

[36] *Denver Post,* Karen Auge, October 1, 1999

[37] *Rocky Mountain News,* Charlie Brennan. December 18, 2001

[38] Ibid

[39] *CNN.com.transcripts* August 30, 2000

[40] Ibid

[41] *Rocky Mountain News,* Charlie Brennan. December 18, 2001

[42] *The Death of Innocence,* Copyright by John and Patsy Ramsey, 2000. ISBN 0-7852-6816-2

[43] City of Boulder Ramsey Update #75. April 25, 2000

[44] Source: CNN transcript of live broadcast of Ramsey Press Conference May 24, 2000

[45] *New York Times* – National Briefing / Rockies: Colorado: "New Leader in Ramsey Case." Mindy Sink June 14, 2003

[46] Tricia Griffith, founder of the website *Forums for Justice,* www.forumsforjustice.com., provided a copy of this affidavit for the author. She acquired the document during her research into the investigation of the death of JonBenét Ramsey. Inquiries made by her at the time to the Boulder District Attorney's Office about the authenticity of the affidavit went unanswered.

⁴⁷ The kernel of glass on the top of the suitcase was about the size of a pea, and should not be confused with the rectangular shaped piece of glass located on the *outside* sill of the window. This piece of glass was not photographed with a scale, but looked to be approximately one and one half to three inches in length.

⁴⁸ For unknown reasons, Smit discounted the observations of prior vaginal trauma discovered during autopsy, and the opinions rendered by expert medical personnel on the matter.

⁴⁹ A copy of the letter is included in chapter fifteen.

⁵⁰ Ramsey described his positioning and examination of the ransom note during his April 1997, and June 1998 interviews.

⁵¹ Refer to Chapter Twenty-three, Stepping Off The Fence

⁵² *The Cases That Haunt Us,* by John Douglas and Mark Olshaker. Scribner 2000, ISBN 0-684-84600-4

⁵³ Boulder Police interview with Mary Ann Kaempfer, January 2, 1997

⁵⁴ *Primetime Live*, Diane Sawyer. September 10, 1997 transcript.

⁵⁵ Ibid

⁵⁶ Ibid

⁵⁷ *The Other Side of Suffering: The Father of JonBenét Ramsey Tells the Story of His Journey from Grief to Grace* . John Ramsey and Marie Chapian, Faith Words, ISBN 978-0-89296-385-0, January 2012

⁵⁸ Ibid. Page 24

⁵⁹ Ibid. Page 24

⁶⁰ Ibid. John Ramsey seemed to underscore my belief that he had not intended

to go golfing when he referred to his and Patsy's state of mind in his book, *The Other Side of Suffering,* pages 108 - 109. He indicates that in the days immediately following the murder of their daughter, it was difficult for either one of them to muster the will to eat, and that they could barely find the energy to get out of bed. He remarked that the emotional state of one suffering this type of tragedy didn't lend itself to resuming the daily activities of recreational exercise. This disclosure made it seem highly unlikely that Ramsey intended to play a round of golf, so I have to reiterate the question: Why was he asking that his bag of clubs be recovered from the home during the execution of the police search warrant?

⁶¹ CNN Interview with John and Patsy Ramsey, January 1, 1997

⁶² *JonBenét Ramsey, Inside the Ramsey Murder Investigation.* Pgs 55 - 56. St. Martin's Press April 2000 ISBN 0-312-25326-5

⁶³ *A Deadly Game – The Untold Story of the Scott Peterson Investigation.* Pg 50.

Crier Communications, Inc. 2005. ISBN 0-06-0766123

[64] BPD interview of Mary Kaempfer , January 2, 1997

[65] BPD Patterson – Burke Ramsey Interview 12/26/96

[66] BPD interview with Mary Ann Kaempfer and Anthony Pecchio, January 2, 1997

[67] *Boulder News Forum* July 14, 1997

[68] *Dateline NBC* Transcript of January 28, 1997 broadcast
Attorney Bryan Morgan during John Ramsey interview, June 25, 1998

[69] For more information about the cases that Fitzgerald has been involved with, please visit www.academy-group.com., or Google his name on the Internet.

[70] *Sexually Aggressive Children, Coming to Understand Them.* Sharon K. Araji, Sage Publications, Inc. Copyright 1997 Source material cited from the text *Sexually Aggressive Children*

[71] *Juveniles Who Have Sexually Offended – A Review of the Professional Literature.* U.S. Department of Justice, Office of Justice Programs. March 2001. Sue Righthand, Ph.D. and Carlann Welch, Psy.D.

[72] www.atsa.com

[73] U.S. Department of Justice – *Juveniles Who Have Sexually Offended,* page 15

[74] Ibid, page xii

[75] FBI Uniform Crime Reports 1996

[76] Refer to the Appendix for a copy of this correspondence CNN, *Larry King Live,* October 19, 1998

[77] Psychic Dorothy Allison had released a sketch of the person she believed responsible for JonBenét's kidnap and murder during a 1999 airing of the *Leeza Gibbons Show.* The sketch would subsequently be posted on the Ramsey's website as a potential lead for the public. The Press Photo I used of the Karr – Sketch comparison was obtained from *TheDenverChannel.com,* an Internet site affiliate of Denver Channel 7 News.

[78] The exact timing of French's and White's visit to the basement is difficult to pin down. French was attempting to control the movements of people arriving at the house, and he may not have inspected the basement until after Fleet White conducted his own first tour of the area.

[79] *Boulder Daily Camera* "Ramsey Decision May Scar DA's Legacy" July 12, 2008

[80] *Reporter News* "DA ties hands of successor in Ramsey Case" Paul Campos, July 17, 2008

[81] *Boulder Daily Camera* "Experts: Lacy's letter to Ramsey could have lasting implications" Zak Brown, July 9, 2008

[82] *Boulder Daily Camera* "Ramsey breakthrough comes via 'touch DNA' July 9, 2008

[83] Ibid

[84] See Chapter Fourteen, Mystery Man for a discussion of this evidence

[85] *The Other Side of Suffering: The Father of JonBenét Ramsey Tells the Story of His Journey from Grief to Grace* . John Ramsey and Marie Chapian, Faith Words, ISBN 978-0-89296-385-0, January 2012

[86] Ibid, page 37.

[87] Ibid, page 42, 46

[88] Visit the website, www.missingkids.com for additional information.

About the Author

J ames Kolar began his law enforcement career with the Boulder Police Department in 1976 as a reserve police officer. Ironically, he lived only blocks from what ultimately would become the home of the Ramsey family when they settled in Boulder in the early 1990s.

Over the course of his career, Kolar would serve as a patrol officer, detective, detective sergeant, supervisor of the department's narcotic and intelligence unit, and as a sergeant in the uniformed patrol division. He received an official commendation from the Denver U.S. Attorney's Office, Organized Crime Drug Enforcement Task Force, for his investigative work on several national, and international narcotic smuggling and distribution cases that involved organizations operating out of Boulder.

In collateral duties, he served as an assistant commander for the SWAT team, the coordinator for the department's gang unit, and as a supervisor for the recruit officer Field Training &

Evaluation Program. He instructed nationally on the topic of the FTEP program for over a decade.

As assistant commander of the SWAT team, Kolar was responsible for helping coordinate the 1990 manhunt for Colorado prison escapee, and serial murderer, Michael G. Bell. Following his escape from the Department of Corrections facility located in Florence, Colorado, Bell and a couple accomplices embarked on a 3 week robbery – killing spree that left three wounded, and four dead.

On the day of his capture, Bell had killed two out of five young men he had encountered target shooting in the foothills west of Boulder. Posing as a Park Ranger, he convinced the men to surrender their weapons and then had them kneel on the ground. He proceeded to execute two of them before a struggle ensued and he escaped.

A joint effort by the Boulder PD SWAT team, and the Boulder County Sheriff's Department STAR team, resulted in one of Boulder County's most intensive manhunts. Bell survived a gunshot wound he received during his capture, and is serving a term of life imprisonment in the Colorado Department of Corrections.

Kolar left the Boulder Police Department in 1993 to take the chief's position in the mountain resort community of Telluride, Colorado. He eventually returned to Denver's Front Range to fill an investigator's position with the Boulder County District Attorney's Office in 2004. He would subsequently be asked to take the lead role in the murder investigation of JonBenét Ramsey. Troubled by the conscious decision not to pursue probative leads that he had developed in the case, he ultimately resigned his position in the spring of 2006.

A thirty-five year veteran of law enforcement, Kolar currently serves as the chief of the Telluride Marshal's Department, situated in the mountains of southwestern Colorado.